SELF-GUIDED
Israel

SELF-GUIDED
Israel

With 72 illustrations and photographs;
49 maps in color and
black and white

LANGENSCHEIDT PUBLISHERS, NEW YORK

Publisher:	Langenscheidt Publishers, Inc.
Managing Editor:	Lisa Checchi Ross
U.S. Editorial Adaptation:	Stephen Brewer, Ann Whitman
U.S. Editorial Staff:	Dana Schwartz, Linda Eger
Cartography:	Franz Huber, Gert Oberländer; adaptations by Dan McAleese
Illustrations:	Vera Solymosi-Thurzó
Cover Design:	Diane Wagner
Cover Photograph:	Image Bank, Bavaria
Text Design:	Irving Perkins Associates
Production:	Ripinsky & Company
Photographs:	Prof. Dr. Hans A. Bloss, Nos. 1, 3, 5, 7, 8, 9, and 17; Hilde Schropp, Nos. 6, 10, 12, 13, 14, and 16; Eberhard Pirling, Nos. 2, 4, and 11; Gunter Wimmer, No. 15.
Original German Text:	Prof. Dr. Hans A. Bloss and Elisabeth Wolters-Alfs; Polyglott-Redaktion (editorial)
Translation:	James Hogarth
Letters:	We welcome your comments and suggestions.

Our address:
Langenscheidt Publishers, Inc.
46-35 54th Rd.
Maspeth, N.Y. 11378

Translated, adapted, and revised from *Der Grosse Polyglott Israel,*
© 1982 by Polyglott-Verlag Dr. Bolte KG, München.
Manufactured in the United States of America
10   9   8   7   6   5   4   3   2   1
ISBN: 0-88729-209-7

Contents

Foreword

Israel, a land sacred to Jews, Christians, and Muslims alike—a land rich with the relics of a historic past—has long been a magnet for pilgrims and travelers from both East and West. But it is not only a country for pilgrims and the historically minded: It has a host of other attractions to offer visitors—idyllic landscapes; vistas of breathtaking beauty and stark desolation; evidence of man's millennial struggle with nature and the vigorous developments of modern times; and luxurious facilities for shore vacations.

Langenscheidt's Self-Guided Israel puts all of this within reach of every independent traveler. Written especially for seasoned travelers by writers who specialize in the areas they cover, this unique guide includes extensive detailed tours of Jerusalem, as well as Israel's other major cities and the countryside. Travelers will find all the information they need to explore Israel at their own pace and follow their own interests.

Self-Guided Tours

The heart of this book is its self-guided tours. Walking tours of Jerusalem and other cities describe all the important sites and put them in historical perspective. Travel routes connect major cities and other areas of interest, covering many fascinating and beautiful areas of the countryside. Detailed maps outline every route.

We begin our tours with thirteen walks around Jerusalem, taking in the Old City with its Jewish, Christian, and Muslim shrines—but not forgetting the more modern districts of the New City. Then follow fourteen Travel Routes that take you to towns and areas of outstanding historical interest and charm throughout this vibrant country.

Using this Guide

This travel guide helps you plan, organize, and enjoy your trip to Israel. In "Getting Your Bearings," a brief rundown of Israel's geography, economy, population, and customs helps to introduce travelers to the land and its people. Essays on religion, culture, and art, as well as a chronology, provide helpful background and perspective on the sights you'll be seeing in this ancient and historic land.

Langenscheidt's writers also offer a subjective guide to the most appealing sights. Our unique three-star system appears throughout the guide:

   *** Worth a special trip—don't miss it!
    ** The most important sights on the tour
     * Highlights

Other sights along the way are also worth seeing, but are not necessarily as important as the starred sights.

Total distance is provided in kilometers and miles from the departure point of each tour.

Major towns and sights appear in boldface for easy reference, while other notable places appear in italics. Numbers and letters in parentheses correspond to locations on the maps.

The guide concludes with a Practical Information chapter, which is divided into two parts. The first is General Trip Planning, to help you gather information you'll need before you depart for Israel. The second part is specific information—such as local tourist information offices and hotels—listed town by town.

Notes and Observations

Travel information, like fruit, is perishable. We've made every effort to double-check information in this guide. But hotels do close and museums do shut down for renovation, so check ahead wherever possible.

We welcome your comments and updates of our information. Please write us at:

Langenscheidt Publishers, Inc.
46-35 54th Road
Maspeth, N.Y. 11378

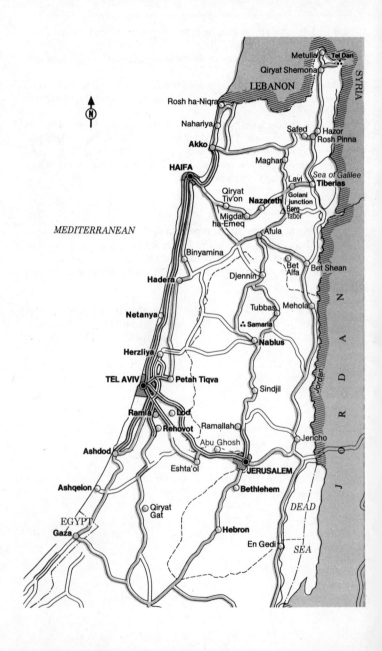

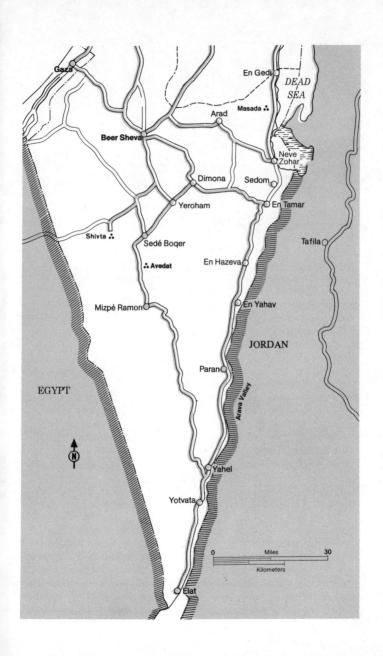

Getting Your Bearings

The territory of the present-day state of Israel has been a region of passage from time immemorial, but also a meeting place and a link between many different peoples from east, west, north, and south. Thanks to its location at the crossroads between Asia and Africa, Israel has been a busy trade route and an important bridge between the two continents throughout its history.

The Land

Israel lies at the extreme southwestern corner of the Asian continent, bordering Egypt in the southwest, Lebanon in the north, and Syria and Jordan in the east. Its diminutive area of just 20,700 square km. (7,990 square miles) supports a population of 4,033,000—that's 513 people per square mile!

Since its foundation in 1948, the young state of Israel has never had a permanent frontier. As a result of the Six-Day War in June 1967, the state of Israel increased its land area fourfold—from 20,000 square km. (8,000 square miles) to 89,359 square km. (34,500 square miles)—with territory taken from Egypt and Syria. However, Egypt and Syria regained territory in Sinai and the Golan Heights in the Yom Kippur War, launched on October 6, 1973. On the basis of the Camp David Accords, a peace treaty between Israel and Egypt was signed in March 1979 in Washington, D.C. Israel withdrew from the whole of Sinai except the Gaza Strip by April 1982.

Israel's is a widely varied terrain, with fertile areas that give way to the vast, empty stretches of the Negev Desert. The land is watered by three sizeable rivers, the Jordan, Yarkon, and Kishon, and contains within its boundaries two large inland seas: the Sea of Galilee and the Dead Sea.

Sea of Galilee

The pipes, aqueducts, and canals of Israel's Water Carrier Project convey water from this vast inland sea to every part of Israel. Also known as Lake Kinnere—a derivation of the Hebrew word for "harp," a reference to the sea's shape—it has an area of 170 square km. (66 square miles) and contains 4 billion cubic meters (about a trillion gallons) of water. The sea lies in a basin some 212 meters (696 feet) below sea level, and is fed by the River Jordan and by mineral springs that give its water a high saline content. It has been well fished since the days of Christ, and is still a source of the delicious St. Peter's fish. Steep slopes rise almost directly from the water's edge; those on its eastern shore lie in Syria.

Dead Sea

The Dead Sea, one of the saltiest bodies of water on earth (30 percent salinity, compared with four percent in the Mediterranean) supports no life, hence its name. However, the sea does yield many valuable mineral salts, and supports a thriving tourist industry. Swimmers find it virtually impossible to sink in these saline waters. Untold numbers of visitors have returned home from here with photographs of themselves sitting upright as if relaxing in an armchair in these buoyant saline waters. Israel's largest inland sea is 76 km. (47 miles) long and 4 km. (2.5 miles) wide, covering an area of about 1,000 square km. (390 square miles) on the Israel-Jordan border. Its surface is the lowest point on earth, lying 394 meters (1,293 feet) below sea level. Although the sea is fed by the River Jordan and several other streams, it has no outlet. It does, however, lose some water to evaporation. The ancient Biblical cities of Sodom and Gomorrah once stood on the southwestern shore of the Dead Sea.

Negev and Judean Deserts

Covering some 13,000 square km. (about 5,100 square miles) of southern Israel, the Negev comprises half the land area of the country. This arid landscape of deep craters and rugged peaks receives no more than 10 centimeters (4 inches) of rain a year. Even so, it is settled in parts with kibbutzim, and its mineral deposits encourage a lucrative mining industry, as they have since ancient times.

Israel's other vast desert, the Judean Desert, extends along the eastern portion of the country. The Dead Sea lies in its arid expanses, as does Jericho, the world's oldest inhabited plain.

Coastal Plain

Israel fronts 187 km. (116 miles) of the Mediterranean Sea. Most Israelis live on this coastal plain, and it is here that 80 percent of the industry—as well as most towns, cities, and ports, and the largest road networks—is located. The plain consists of three parts—the low-lying Shefela Plain (Judean Foothills) in the south, the Sharon Plain (which begins at Tel Aviv) in the middle, and the Zevulun Plain north of Haifa.

The Gaza Strip spans the southernmost portion of the coastline; it is 40 km. (25 miles) long and no more than 10 km. (6 miles) wide. Close to half a million Arabs live here under Israeli military administration.

Mountains

Several mountain ranges form a chain that runs the length of Israel for some 320 km. (200 miles). This mountain chain consists of the hills of

Upper and Lower Galilee, Mount Carmel, the hills of Samaria and Judea, and the Negev Hills. The peaks rise to an average height of 850 meters (about 2,800 feet) and, for the most part, form a bare, almost lunar landscape. The largest of these ranges is the Judean Hills. To the west of these rugged peaks—the highest, Mount Baal Hazor, rises 1,016 meters (3,333 feet)—lies the fertile coastal plain, and to the east the Judean Desert.

The River Jordan

This river, often referred to in the Bible and in whose waters Jesus Christ was baptized, runs almost the length of Israel. It forms the border with Jordan and connects Israel's great inland seas, the Sea of Galilee, and the Dead Sea. Although these two bodies of water are a mere 100 km. (62 miles) apart, the river's path curves some 320 km. (200 miles) in its journey to connect them. The life-giving waters of the river are valuable to this arid nation, and irrigate much of the country. The river's valley, known as the Jordan Rift, is part of the Great Rift, the huge depression that runs 5,600 km. (3,300 miles) south from Turkey to southeastern Africa.

Government

Israel is a parliamentary republic. It has no written constitution, but its four million citizens enjoy the privileges set down in the Declaration of Independence of May 14, 1948. The principles therein and laws subsequently enacted by the Israeli Parliament guarantee Israelis the following: complete equality in the eyes of the law for all citizens regardless of creed, race, or sex; freedom of opinion, speech, the press, assembly, and religious choice; and the right to education, cultural activity, free exercise of profession, demonstrate and strike, due process of the law, and the right to vote after age 18.

The parliament, known as the Knesset, is Israel's legislative body. This single-chamber, 120-member assembly sits in Jerusalem; debates are conducted in Hebrew with simultaneous translation into Arabic. Election is by representation, and each party draws up a list of candidates. Seats are allocated to the parties in proportion to the number of votes cast for each list and are assigned to candidates.

The Knesset elects the President, who serves a five-year term. The President, eligible for re-election only once, signs all legislation, appoints judges, ambassadors, and other state officials, and signs treaties after they have been ratified by the Knesset.

The Prime Minister heads the Cabinet, which serves as the governing arm of Israel. This body determines state policy and is responsible to the Knesset. Often, cabinet members are drawn from the Knesset, but they may come from outside the government, as well. The Cabinet remains in place for four years, unless it loses the confidence of the Knesset and is replaced.

Currently there are four major political groups in Israel that encompass some 15 parties: the Likud bloc (conservative); the Labor Alignment (socialist); the religious parties; and the Liberal parties.

Beneath the national level, there are several different strata of local government, including mayors, community officials, and the district commissioners who oversee six administrative regions of Israel: Jerusalem, the North, Haifa, the Central Region, Tel Aviv, and the South.

The judicial system operates on three levels: magistrate's court, district courts, and the Supreme Court in Jerusalem. Larger communities also have municipal courts.

Economy

In its short history, Israel has become a highly developed nation with a standard of living close to that of Europe. Its per capita income is now $4,400, almost ten times that of neighboring Egypt.

Much of Israel's phenomenal development is the work of its highly skilled immigrants—many of whom came from the United States and Europe. The capital that has fueled this development has come from the World Zionist Organization, reparation payments from West Germany, and loans from the United States, other nations, and the World Bank.

Agriculture

Agriculture has been one of the pillars of the Israeli economy since Biblical times. There are now 85,500 hectares (212,900 acres)—roughly 22 percent of Israel's territory—under cultivation. Israeli agricultural products account for 12.6 percent of total exports.

Israel's agricultural success certainly cannot be attributed to the fertility of the land. Few regions on earth are less hospitable to cultivation; yet, the persistence and determination of the Israelis has made the land a flourishing home for the Jewish people. Two organizations have been particularly ardent in their support for an agricultural Israel. Since the early days of this century, the Jewish National Fund (Keren Kayemeth LeIsrael, KKL) has purchased land for cultivation; it has promoted rural agricultural settlements in accordance with the Biblical injunction that land should be communally owned. The Jewish Organization promotes the immigration and settlement of Jews from all over the world, granting long-term loans for the purchase of farm equipment and seed.

Industry

Industrial production is now the leading sector of the Israeli economy in both output and employment. The largest single branch of industry—

accounting for 20 percent of production capacity—is the processing of agricultural produce to provide foodstuffs, drinks, and tobacco. The second-largest Israeli industrial sector is the textile, leather, and clothing industry. These are actually Israel's oldest industries—the word "gauze" probably derives from the town of Gaza and the word "blouse" from the ancient Palestinian city of Pelusium.

Other industries include cut diamonds—which account for a third of the value of all exports, as well as a third of world output—and the production of military equipment (a result of Israel's geopolitical position). Tourism, too, has become a major industry in Israel.

The trade union Histadru was founded in 1920 to represent the interests of the working class, create jobs, and help new immigrants find work. The organization now directly employs 20 percent of the nation's work force in its various enterprises, and includes some 95 percent of all Israeli workers in its membership.

Education

Israel's standard of education is high and its educational system caters to a wide range of needs. About a third of all Israelis usually attend school or training programs of some kind.

The Jewish educational system has three parts: the general state schools, the religious state schools, and the orthodox religious schools. There is a separate Arab school system. The literacy rate in Israel is 94 percent among Jews, and 83 percent among non-Jews.

Schooling is compulsory and free for children between the ages of 6 to 15. Children spend six years at a primary school, then three years at an intermediate school, followed by three years at a secondary school or a three-year training program at a vocational or agricultural college. Tuition is charged for secondary school, but fees are graduated according to the income of the parents. Those children who fail the final examination given when primary school ends must attend a vocational school until they are 18 years old.

Fourteen percent of all Israelis employed today have attended college—the highest percentage in the world. The country has seven major universities.

The People

The population of Israel is over four million, of whom three million are Jews. The non-Jewish population of Israel includes a half-million Muslims, 85,000 Christians, and 45,000 Druzes. More than a million people live under Israeli administration—650,000 on the West Bank and 400,000 in the Gaza Strip and northern Sinai.

Since the nation was established in 1948, Israel has attracted Jewish residents from all over the world. As many as 600,000 Jewish victims of Hitler's Europe emigrated to the new land in the late 1940s. More than half of the present-day Israelis were born in Israel, and a quarter of its Jewish population comes from the United States and Europe. Israel is a nation of young people—half of its population is under 25 years old. More than two-thirds of the Israelis live in the country's 36 urban communities, with a full quarter of the population living in Tel Aviv alone. In addition to cities, there are 128 villages, 864 smaller settlements, 230 kibbutzim, 350 moshavim, and 45 moshavim shitufim in Israel.

Language

Israel has two official languages, modern Hebrew and Arabic. Ninety percent of Israelis speak Hebrew, 45 percent speak Arabic, and many speak English, French, German, and Yiddish. Modern Hebrew and Arabic are used in government and appear together on all public signs.

English often appears on road signs, and the language is so widely spoken that English-speaking visitors should be able to make themselves understood anywhere in the country. There is much variation and confusion in transliterating Hebrew and Arabic into the Latin alphabet. For example, you may find the place name "Safed" in the alternative forms Saphet, Zephad, Tsefad, Zefat, Zfet, and Sfad.

Yiddish, developed by German Jews in the Middle Ages, is widely spoken throughout Israel, particularly among immigrants from Eastern and Central Europe. The language is written using the Hebrew alphabet, and incorporates many Hebrew words. Some ultra-orthodox Israeli Jews speak only Yiddish and will not use Hebrew. To them, Hebrew is a sacred language to be spoken in daily life only after the coming of the Messiah.

Scripts

Both the Hebrew and the Arabic script are derived from one that was used by the Phoenicians at least as early as the 13th century B.C. The Semitic scripts, reflecting the structure of their languages, represent only the consonants; the reader must decide, according to the context, what vowels must be added to make sense. Both the Hebrew and the Arabic scripts run from right to left. The Hebrew letters stand by themselves, but the Arabic characters are usually linked with one another, and have different forms according to whether they are joined on the left, on the right, or stand by themselves.

Hebrew still sometimes uses the letters of the alphabet as figures, but for the most part adopts the "Arabic" figures used in the West. The Arabs have special characters for figures, which, unlike the normal practice in Arabic, are read from left to right.

The Settlements

While the majority of Israelis reside in towns and cities, many live in the rural settlements that have grown up in some of the country's most remote regions. Most are devoted to agriculture, in many cases creating oases of cultivation in the most inhospitable landscapes.

Kibbutzim: There are some 230 kibbutzim, the best-known type of Israel's collective farms. About three percent of the population lives on kibbutzim, most of which are agricultural settlements that now also engage in light industry and, in some cases, even in tourism. Kibbutzim have played a vital role in the development of Israel, providing work and lodging for large numbers of immigrants and bringing large areas of the country under cultivation.

There is no private property on a kibbutz, and members live communally, usually in dormitories. Children are brought up by child-care workers rather than by their parents, and join their families only for leisure activities. The highest authority in a kibbutz is the General Assembly, the governing body in which all members of the commune have a vote. So ingrained are kibbutzim in the Israeli way of life that many are now inhabited by third-and fourth-generation members.

Moshavim: These are cooperative settlements in which settlers have their own homes and work their own lands, but matters relating to work—the purchase of seed or equipment, for example, and the sale of produce—are handled collectively. The moshav is run by a chairman and various committees responsible for economic, social, and cultural matters. About 4 percent of Israelis live on moshavim.

Social Conduct

Visitors enjoying the hospitality of a country should know the main rules governing the relationship between guest and host in order to avoid possible misunderstandings. This is particularly important in a country like Israel that has a mix of people of different cultures, religions, and ways of life living side by side, each with their own rules of conduct and social habits. The Jews living in Israel may be of European or Oriental origin; they may be open-minded or rigidly orthodox; they may be practical agricultural pioneers or unworldly urban intellectuals. The local Arabs may be either Christians or Muslims.

Be particularly careful to observe the rules on the Sabbath, lasting from sunset on Friday to sunset on Saturday. Smokers should avoid smoking in public, for religious Jews do not smoke on the Sabbath. Smoking is permitted in hotel lobbies, but not in restaurants.

Use discretion and sensitivity when taking photographs, particularly of holy sites such as synagogues and mosques, and on the Sabbath. Neither orthodox Jews nor Muslims appreciate being photographed as if they are curiosities. It is wise to ask permission before taking a picture, and respectfully comply if you are refused.

When visiting a synagogue or any holy place, men as well as women should wear some form of head covering and modest dress (no shorts or bare shoulders). Remove your shoes before entering a mosque.

Reserved, respectful, and polite behavior is appreciated throughout the country. If you are greeted by someone you meet along the way, you are expected to return the greeting—indeed, if he is older than you, you should greet him first. Among Jews, the word both of greeting and of response is "shalom" (peace). The Arab greeting is "Salam alaikum," to which the appropriate response is "Wa alaikum as-salam." You may also be greeted by the word "marhaba" (welcome), and should respond properly with "marhabitain" (doubly welcome).

Food and Drink

The most basic element shaping the cuisine of Israel is the commandment from the Book of Exodus, "Thou shalt not seethe a kid in his mother's milk." This is the ruling tenet of *kashru,* following a kosher diet. Only certain animals may be eaten and their flesh must be prepared and cooked according to kosher rules: Above all, the animals must be ritually slaughtered and drained of all blood. This means that the meat must lie for an hour in salt and half an hour in water before being cooked. Only animals that chew cud and are cloven-hoofed (thereby excluding the meat of pigs from the diet) and fishes with scales and fins (to the exclusion of all shellfish) may be eaten. It follows from the commandment that milk and meat products must never be eaten at the same time. Thus butter and cheese never appear on the table along with meat; only milk products are served for breakfast; and cheese can be accompanied only by fish or eggs, which are regarded as "neutral." A meat course cannot be followed by cheese or butter, and even milk in coffee is banned.

The rules also require the dishes and cutlery used with milk products to be kept separate from those used for meat products. This applies to washing dishes by hand and to using a dishwasher, as well. Most Israeli homes and most Israeli restaurants maintain kosher kitchens.

The second most striking feature of Israeli cuisine is its international character. Many of the dishes were brought to Israel from Europe and other parts of the world along with the floods of immigration. The favorite dishes, however, are still traditionally Middle Eastern: *falafel* (deep-fried chick peas served in pita); *humus* (a chick-pea purée); and *tahina* (a paste of ground sesame seeds, onions, and tomatoes). Some European specialties that have become Israeli staples are *latkes* (sweet potato fritters), *gefilte fish,* and *cholent* (a stew of rice, chick peas, barley, meat, eggs, and spices, often eaten for lunch on the Sabbath after simmering overnight). Markets throughout Israel overflow with the bounty of fruits and vegetables fresh from the kibbutzim.

Fruit beverages of many kinds and mineral water are popular keep-cool drinks in arid Israel. Ordinary water in good hotels and restaurants is also safe for drinking. Coffee is a favorite Israeli drink, and cafés and restaurants offer a range of choices—*kafe turko* (Turkish coffee), *kefe hafukh* (white coffee), espresso, cappuccino, among others. If you prefer tea, various kinds of black tea are available. Israel produces its own good beer, particularly in Netanya: Two popular brands are Gold Star and Maccabee. Israeli wines—white, red, and rosé—are very good, varied, and comparatively inexpensive. The best known wines come from the Mount Carmel area and around Ashqelon and Ashdod. Israeli sparkling wine (Jayim Hanassi) and brandy (Carmel Mizrachi) are also good. *Arak,* an aniseed brandy often drunk with food, is another popular drink.

Chronology

Prehistory and the First Biblical Accounts

Traces of human life from the Paleolithic era have been uncovered in Israel, such as the simple tools found in the caves on Mount Carmel, fashioned between 300,000 and 70,000 B.C. Later evidence of human existence are the remains of a hunter-gatherer culture in Galilee and around Lake Gennesaret. During the Mesolithic era (between 15,000 and 7,000 B.C.), farming was practiced in Upper Galilee. The first town dates from the Neolithic era. Excavations show that Jericho (settled by the Mesolithic era) was enclosed within a wall and protected by a tall stone tower during the early Neolithic era (around 7,000 B.C.).

Palestine first appears in historical records during the Bronze Age. To the Akkadians it was known as Anurru, and the Egyptians called it Rethenu.

The first events recorded in the Bible also date from this period. The Book of Genesis tells us how the patriarch Abraham migrated from Ur in Mesopotamia to Canaan, or Palestine, the land that God had promised to his people.

17th century B.C.: The Hyksos, a tribe of Semitic horsemen, move into Palestine and then into Egypt toward the end of the century; they rule for 50 years. At this time, Abraham's descendants wander into Egypt, where Joseph becomes the Pharaoh's viceroy. Joseph's father, Jacob, named Israel by God, is progenitor of the people later known as the Israelites.

The Israelites Occupy the Land

c. 1550 B.C.: The Hyksos are expelled from Egypt. Egypt establishes an empire whose influence extends to northeastern Africa, the eastern Mediterranean, and western Asia.

1480 B.C.: Pharaoh Tuthmosis III conquers the Canaanites, and Palestine becomes an Egyptian province.

c. 1250 B.C.: After 430 years of exile, the Israelites leave Egypt under the leadership of Moses. He reaffirms the importance of worshiping one God (Yahweh), and binds the Israelites by a covenant that promises them possession of the Promised Land, Canaan (Palestine). They wander throughout the desert for 40 years before Moses's successor, Joshua, conquers the Promised Land.

c. 1200 B.C.: The Israelites take possession of parts of Palestine.

During the next two centuries, the Israelites struggle with the Philistines and Canaanites, until they finally establish control over a unified territory. They give up their nomadic way of life and become farmers.

Israel Becomes a Kingdom

Constant battles against their enemies make it necessary to establish a central authority over the twelve tribes of Israel.

c. 1020 B.C.: Saul, of the tribe of Benjamin, is annointed king by Samuel, a judge.

1000–961 B.C.: Saul's successor David, who came from Bethlehem, unifies the twelve tribes of Israel. He captures Jerusalem from the Jebusites, a Canaanite tribe, and makes it his capital. He also establishes Jerusalem as the religious center of his kingdom by setting up the Ark of the Covenant, the Israelites' most sacred object, in the city. David wages successful wars against his neighbors, extends his territory across the Jordan, and even wins control over part of Syria, including Damascus.

c. 966–926 B.C.: The reign of David's son, Solomon, brings power and glory to Israel. He builds a magnificent Temple in Jerusalem. His kingdom extends from the Euphrates to the Red Sea and to the frontiers of Egypt. He is also successful commercially.

Division of the Kingdom

950–900 B.C.: Solomon's kingdom dissolves after his death. The northern tribes break away from the rule of his son, Rehoboam, who keeps the kingdom of Judah in the south, with Jerusalem as its capital. To the north is the kingdom of Israel, with its capital located first at Shechem, then later at Samaria. The north soon comes under pressure from Syria, while the army of Egyptian pharaoh Shoshenk I plunders Jerusalem in the south around the year 920 B.C.

The religious unity of the Israelites also begins to break up; some revert to pagan cults, rousing the anger of the pious. Jezebel, the wife of Ahab (king of Israel), builds a temple to the Canaanite god Baal. Her actions cause not only her own death at the hands of the worshipers of Yahweh, but also the overthrow of the royal family (c. 875 B.C.).

800–750 B.C.: Old Testament prophets Amos, Hosea, and Isaiah castigate the Israelites and their rulers for their moral decline and urge the renewal of religious ideals. They predict that a decline in religious values will lead to the fall of the kingdom of Israel.

732 B.C.: Tiglath-Pileser III (745–727 B.C.), founder of the Assyrian empire, devastates Israel and exacts tribute from Judah. Sargon II conquers Samaria and makes Israel an Assyrian province. The Assyrians carry the ruling classes off into exile.

605 B.C.: In the south, the kingdom of Judah survives the fall of Israel for 150 years, until the battle of Carchemish: The Babylonians destroy the Assyrian empire and take over its territory. Judah is now forced to pay the Babylonians tribute.

The Babylonian Captivity

597 B.C.: After uprisings by the Israelites, the Babylonian Nebuchadnezzar II advances on Jerusalem and takes it. Following a further uprising, he returns in 587, destroys the city (including the Temple), and carries off the upper classes to Mesopotamia.

539 B.C.: The period of exile "by the waters of Babylon" ends when the Persian king Cyrus the Great conquers Babylon. Yet, many of the exiles remain in their new home; it is only after the Temple is rebuilt (c. 520 B.C.) that large numbers of Jews return to Palestine. Under Persian rule, the Jews live in relative freedom in their own country.

The Babylonian Captivity has one positive benefit: It awakens the Jews to a consciousness of their own identity. After their return, the Jewish faith is consolidated.

The Jews in the Hellenistic Age

333 B.C.: Alexander the Great defeats the Persian empire.

323 B.C.: After Alexander's death, Palestine becomes part of Ptolemy's kingdom of Egypt. Under the Ptolemies, the Jews are not disturbed; however, as the Seleucid kings of Asia Minor and Syria gain control of Palestine, Greek culture becomes increasingly important.

167 B.C.: Antiochus IV bans the Jewish faith, and the Temple is dedicated to the cult of Olympian Zeus. In the Maccabean Revolt, the pious restore the worship of Yahweh, purify the Temple, and rededicate it.

c. 168 B.C.: The Book of Daniel is written around this time. In it, the prophet Daniel foresees the overthrowing of Israel's oppressors and the appearance of the "Son of Man," a Messiah who would establish an everlasting kingdom of all nations.

Under Roman Rule

63 B.C.: The Roman general Pompey conquers Jerusalem and makes Judah part of the Roman Empire.

40 B.C.: Pompey's son, Herod the Great, takes the title King of Judea. He embarks on lavish building programs, and makes Jerusalem a royal city.

4 B.C.: Herod dies: The people rejoice at his death. Jesus Christ is born around this time. He preaches his message of returning good for evil, humility, and righteousness as the way to attain entry to the Kingdom of God after death. He is regarded as a prophet by some and by others as the Messiah of whom the prophets foretold. After He is crucified (c. A.D. 30), His teachings are spread throughout the Mediterranean world by his disciples who believe in Christ's resurrection; His followers become known as Christians. The life and teachings of Jesus Christ and his Apostles and disciples form the content of the New Testament.

The Destruction of Jerusalem

A.D. 66–70: Uprisings by the Jews against the Romans.

A.D. 70: The Roman general Titus captures Jerusalem, and destroys it after a six-month siege. The last of the rebels retreat to the rock stronghold of Masada above the Dead Sea, where they put up a fierce resistance. Finally, to avoid falling into the hands of the Romans, they kill themselves in A.D. 73.

The Dispersal (Diaspora)

130–160: Once again, the Jews leave their land, migrating to all parts of the world. They wander throughout the Roman Empire, into Germany,

After the destruction of Jerusalem, the Temple furnishings are carried in
Titus' triumphal procession (relief on the Arch of Titus in Rome)

Gaul, the Iberian peninsula, and from Asia Minor to North Africa. (Much later, after experiencing brutal persecutions in the Middle Ages in what is now Germany, they move on to Poland and to Russia.)

Roman and Byzantine Palestine

From the second century, Palestine is a Roman province inhabited by Greeks and Romans, as well as by Samaritans and Nabateans. The religious and cultural centers of the Jews that remain are Bet Shearim and Tiberias.

313: Constantine recognizes Christianity; he is baptized on his death-bed in 337. Palestine becomes the Holy Land of the new Christian religion. One hundred years after Constantine's death, the majority of Palestine's population is Christian. Churches and chapels are built throughout the country, and pilgrims come from many lands to visit the holy sites.

386: The Roman Empire is divided into two. Palestine becomes part of the Eastern (Byzantine) Empire, with Constantinople as its capital.

c. 570: Mohammed is born in Mecca. He has his first revelation in 610, and teaches there is one God, Allah, and he, Mohammed, is his prophet. This and subsequent revelations form the text of the *Koran,* which emphasizes generosity, the goodness and power of Allah, and a final retribution on the Day of Judgment. The religion he founds becomes known as Islam, its followers as Muslims.

614: The Persian army reaches Jerusalem and takes the city.

622: The flight (Hegira) of the Prophet Mohammed from Mecca to Medina.

628: The Persians are forced to withdraw from Palestine, which once again comes under Byzantine Rule.

632: Death of Mohammed.

The Muslim Invasion

635: Muslim armies sweep into Palestine. Two years later they conquer Jerusalem and establish the Umayyad dynasty. Muslim conquests follow in Syria (638) and Egypt (642).

Arab rule in Palestine is unobtrusive: Both Christians and Jews are free to practice their faiths. Byzantine officials administer the country for its new masters, and Greeks work for them. Christian pilgrims continue to visit the Holy Land.

1071: Control of Palestine passes to the Seljuks, a tribe of Turkish horsemen. Life for both Jews and Christians becomes more difficult under their rule.

The Crusades

1000–1250: In these troubled times it becomes increasingly difficult for pilgrims to travel to Palestine, and the old trade routes between the West and the East are disrupted. In the West, Christians proclaim a crusade against the infidels. The Crusading armies are motivated in part by religious zeal, but also by the lure of rich booty.

1099: The armies of the First Crusade (1096–1099) take Jerusalem. They massacre the Muslim and Jewish inhabitants or sell them into slavery.

1174: The Kurdish leader Saladin (Salah ed Din) gains control of Syria and Egypt.

1187: Saladin defeats the Crusaders at the Horns of Hittim, and drives them from Palestine. The Crusaders remain on a small strip of land around Tyre.

1189–1191: In the Third Crusade, the West strikes back. Under Richard the Lion-Hearted, the Crusaders extend the coastal territory they control as far as Jaffa. Akko becomes the heavily fortified capital of their kingdom.

1244: Jerusalem falls to the Muslim Turks. By 1271, the Egyptian Mamelukes have taken all of Palestine except for Akko, which holds out until 1291.

Under the Mamelukes and the Turks

1516: Palestine is overrun by the Ottoman Turks; the Mameluke Empire falls a year later. Palestine remains under Turkish rule for almost four hundred years.

1520–1566: Under Sultan Suleiman the Magnificent, construction is promoted in Jerusalem, including city walls and gates. Many Spanish Jews (Sephardim) come to Palestine during this time, after their expulsion from Spain in 1492.

Under Suleiman's successors, order and prosperity give way to corruption, arbitrary rule, and impoverishment. All over the country, local feudal lords gain power and exact taxes from the Christian, Muslim, and Jewish populations.

European Influences

1798: Napoleon Bonaparte lands in Egypt, hoping to cut off Britain's communications with its possessions in India. The Turks, with British support, send an army against him. Napoleon takes Gaza and Jaffa, and he defeats the Turks on Mount Tabor. He is unable to take the strongly fortified town of Akko, and finally returns to France.

During the 19th century, Palestine remains an impoverished and neglected province of the Ottoman Empire. Technology is slowly introduced.

1868: The first road between Jaffa and Jerusalem is built. In 1892, the two towns are linked by a railroad.

Zionism and Arab Nationalism

1895: A manifesto is published by a Viennese journalist, Theodor Herzl, which sets down his belief that Jews can only lead normal lives if they live in their own state. The movement he launches takes the name of Zionism, after David's city of Zion.

1897: The first Zionist Congress is held in Basel. It lays out the movement's purpose: "To create a home for the Jewish people in Palestine secured by public law."

From the second half of the 19th century to the early 20th century, large waves of immigrants sweep into Palestine, particularly from Eastern Europe. Frequent pogroms lead tens of thousands of Jews to flee to America or Palestine where they can live without fear of persecution.

After the first Zionist Congress, Jews begin to negotiate with the Turkish authorities. They found organizations to acquire land in Palestine, and finance the work of construction in what is to become their new national home.

1909: The first Jewish town, Tel Aviv, is founded.

1914–1918: During World War I, Turkish and German troops advance from Palestine to the Suez Canal, but are repelled by British forces. In 1917, British General Allenby's army captures Palestine. After the collapse of the Ottoman Empire, Britain administers Palestine in accordance with the Balfour Declaration, which supports the idea of a Jewish state.

The Mandate

1919–1923: Britain receives the League of Nations mandate over Palestine in 1920. Immigrants stream into Palestine. The marshy Yizre'el

Plain is drained and turned into a fertile agricultural area, which is soon settled entirely by Jews. Kibbutz after kibbutz is founded, and, with immense idealism, the long-neglected land is cultivated. During these years, the ongoing conflict between the Jews and Arabs continues to escalate.

1929: An Arab riot erupts over religious rights at the Western Wall. The Mufti of Jerusalem, the spiritual head of the Muslim community, calls for a holy war against unbelievers—both the Jews and the British authorities. The Jews also begin to form armed units, and both sides conduct terrorist attacks. Zionists establish the Jewish Agency, headed by Chaim Weizmann (who later becomes Israel's first President). The Agency collects money from all over the world, buys land in Palestine for new immigrants, and creates a powerful trade union.

The State of Israel

1940s: The mass extermination of the Jews in Hitler's concentration camps forges a strong political consciousness among the survivors—to have a country of their own, free from persecution after thousands of years of suffering. The British ban further immigration into Palestine, yet Jews from Europe continue to enter the country illegally.

1947: The "insoluble" problem of Palestine is given to the United Nations, and on November 29, the General Assembly resolves to divide Palestine into separate Arab and Jewish states within an economic union. Although the Arabs reject this idea, the Jews begin to build their state.

1948: British forces give up the mandate and leave Palestine. The Zionist leader David Ben Gurion proclaims the independent state of Israel. The United States and the Soviet Union are among the first countries to recognize Israel.

Neither the Palestinian Arabs nor the neighboring Arab states accept Israel, and send their armies into the new country. In the fighting, thousands of Arabs flee Palestine for refugee camps in Lebanon, Jordan, and Egypt. In this War of Independence, the Israelis are victorious. Although Jordan occupies the West Bank of the River Jordan, the Israelis win access to Jerusalem.

1949: An armistice is signed: The Old City of Jerusalem remains in the hands of the Jordanians, while the New City to the west and an outlying area to the north are assigned to Israel. Terrorist attacks continue on both sides.

1956: After President Nasser of Egypt nationalizes the Suez Canal, Israel invades the Sinai peninsula. Israel, along with Britain and France (who held the majority of shares in the Canal) are compelled to withdraw under pressure from the United Nations, as well as the United States and the Soviet Union.

1964: Arabs housed in the refugee camps organize themselves and found the Palestine Liberation Organization (PLO). They form an army to fight Israel.

1967: U.N. troops, which had kept the two sides apart, withdraw from the Sinai in 1967. Following their departure, the Egyptians close the Gulf of Aqaba to Israeli shipping. Israel retaliates by launching an attack, which becomes known as the Six-Day War. Israel conquers all the Arab territory up to the Jordan, together with the Old City of Jerusalem, the Sinai peninsula, and the Golan Heights in Syria.

1973: Egypt and Syria attempt to recover their lost territories in a surprise attack known as the Yom Kippur War.

1974: A U.N. cease-fire and disengagement agreement is signed between Egypt and Syria and Israel.

1977: Egypt's President Anwar Sadat flies to Jerusalem to begin peace negotiations.

1979: With U.S. support, the Camp David Accords are signed in Washington on March 26, by President Sadat and Israel's Prime Minister Menachem Begin. Israel promises to return the whole of the Sinai peninsula to Egypt within three years and to begin negotiations on autonomy for the occupied West Bank. (President Sadat is assassinated in Egypt in 1981.)

1981: In December, Prime Minister Begin annexes the Golan Heights, leading to fresh tensions. Yet, on April 25, 1982, the Israelis evacuate the Sinai peninsula as agreed to in the Camp David Accords.

1982: In June, reacting to attacks on Israeli settlements in the Galilee, Israel invades Lebanon to eliminate the PLO. Although the PLO is driven out of the country, civil war continues. Unrest persists in the occupied territories.

1987: Palestinians in Israel begin a new series of protests and violent demonstrations in December.

1988: Intermittent rioting in Arab areas and suppression by Israeli forces continues, resulting in the death of many Palestinians and Israelis.

Culture, Art, and Literature

The land now known as Israel has been the home of some of the world's earliest cultures. A mix of many different peoples, religions, and races from prehistoric to modern times, it has been extraordinarily generous to archaeologists, who have discovered wonderful treasures. Finds from the land's earliest days are richly represented in Jerusalem at the Rockefeller and Israel Museums.

Prehistory

In this part of western Asia, urban cultures emerged as early as the Neolithic period. The oldest evidence of this is provided by the excavations at Jericho, dating from around 7000 B.C. Settlements that have been unearthed at Beer Sheva, Nahal Besor, and Hazor date to the Chalcolithic period (fifth and fourth millennia B.C.).

There is evidence of an independent Palestinian culture in the Bronze Age. In the Early Bronze Age (c. 3000–2100 B.C.), settlements were established here by the Canaanites, whose cities of Gezer, Megiddo, and Hazor had their heyday in the Middle Bronze Age. Hazor was then one of the largest cities in western Asia. For a time, the culture of the Canaanites was under Egyptian influence—an inevitable consequence of the political power centered in the Nile valley.

The Art of the Israelites

When the Israelites began to establish a foothold in Palestine around 1200 B.C., the Sea Peoples from the west appeared on the Mediterranean coast and began to carry on maritime trade from the coastal towns. The Philistines, as they were known to their neighbors, made pottery showing affinities with Late Mycenean work. They were also skilled in ironworking.

Little is known historically about the very early art of the Israelites, although there are fascinating hints of their talent: The Bible reports on the richness of Jerusalem's Temple, built during the period of the Kings. Its design was based upon North Syrian and Assyrian temples, and Phoenician builders helped construct it.

The fortifications of Megiddo, Ramath Rahel, and Hazor also date from the time of the Kings.

The Hellenistic and Roman Periods

Few remains have survived from the period between the conquest of Jerusalem by the Babylonians and Alexander's campaign against the

Persian Empire. Construction flourished during the reign of Herod the Great. He built a Third Temple in Jerusalem, the Antonia Fortress, and a theater. Likewise, he supported the building of temples and defensive walls outside of Jerusalem, and is credited with founding Caesarea on the Mediterranean coast.

The synagogue, the Jewish house of prayer, evolved in Jerusalem during the Babylonian Captivity. Synagogues were built in Palestine as well, particularly during Roman times. They followed the model of the Roman basilicas, which also served as market halls and courthouses. An example of these multi-purpose structures is the synagogue of Capernaum.

Early Christian and Byzantine Art

After Constantine the Great permitted the practice of Christianity in A.D. 313, it came to be accepted throughout the Roman world. Constantine and his mother Helena had splendid buildings constructed over the sacred sites, such as the Church of the Holy Sepulcher in Jerusalem, the Eleona or Pater Noster Church on the Mount of Olives, a church in Gethsemane, and the Church of the Nativity in Bethlehem. Fascinating fragments of churches erected during this period survive today, including beautiful mosaics.

During the Byzantine era, the Nabateans, who had become rich from the trade between southern Arabia and the Mediterranean, built flourishing cities in the Negev, such as Mamshit, Avedat, and Shivta. These communities included churches, monasteries, markets, fortifications, and irrigation systems. Mosaics dating from the Byzantine period have been found throughout Palestine; first-rate examples come from a church in Caesarea and from synagogues at Tabgha and Bet Alfa.

Decorative elements, including Solomon's seal,
from the synagogue in Capernaum

The Muslims, the Crusaders, and the Turks

Like preceding conquerors, the Arabs erected numerous grand buildings after they took control of Palestine. Most notable are the Dome of the Rock (687–691) and the el-Aqsa Mosque (705–715, altered around 1038), both in Jerusalem. Desert palaces sprang up under the Umayyad caliphs, among them Hisham's Palace at Khirbet el-Mafjar.

Churches and fortifications are the most visible survivors of the Crusades. It was at this time that the Church of the Holy Sepulcher was rebuilt in Jerusalem, as well as other important churches constructed by Constantine and Helena in the fourth century. St. Anne's and the Armenian Church of St. James were also restored during the period of the Crusades.

Some of the finest buildings of this period are in Akko, where the Crusaders held out for years before the fall of Jerusalem. One of the finest examples of Crusader fortifications is Castle Montfort, near Lebanon's frontier.

The White Tower at Ramla represents one of the best examples of Muslim architecture during the Mameluke period. And in the Muslim Quarter of Jerusalem's Old City, you can see Mameluke tombs, pilgrim hospices, and Koranic schools.

A tremendous amount of building took place under Turkish rule. Among the remaining treasures is the Damascus Gate, rebuilt by Suleiman the Magnificent. To see an example of late Ottoman-style architecture, visit the monumental el-Jazzar Mosque in Akko.

Many churches were built all over the country in the 19th and 20th

Hisham's Palace (Khirbet el-Mafjar), near Jericho

centuries, when Christianity was enjoying a fresh flowering in Palestine due to European pressure.

Modern Art and Architecture in Israel

Ancient Jewish art was of a predominantly religious nature, as was the art of the Jewish Diaspora. In all the countries in which Jews had sought refuge—going from Spain to Mesopotamia, and from Italy to Germany—they produced richly decorated Torah arks and Torah crowns, Hanukkah lamps, cups, and bookbindings. The book illumination of the Diaspora was also of exquisite quality.

In the 19th century, and even more so in the 20th, Jewish artists made a major contribution to the modern art of Europe and America. Great opportunities arose for architects during the years when immigration into Israel was at its height and the Jewish state was being built. Erich Mendelsohn, an immigrant from Germany (1934) who had studied at the Bauhaus, created many functional buildings between 1934 and 1941. Among the outstanding architectural achievements of later years are the Tel Aviv Museum, the Diaspora Museum in Tel Aviv, and the Shrine of the Book in Jerusalem.

The Bezalel School of Art in Jerusalem, founded in 1906, specializes in the field of applied art. In the years before World War II there were different trends among Jewish painters in Israel—some sought to create a distinctively Jewish art, while others looked toward contemporary European and American painting. In 1953, Marcel Janco (born in Bucharest in 1895), one of the co-initiators of Dadaism, founded the En Hod artists' colony on Mount Carmel.

Literature

In the course of more than three thousand years, many significant works of poetic, religious, and scholarly literature have been written in what is now the state of Israel and the surrounding areas. Some of them, like the Bible, have influenced the course of history; others belong to the heritage of world literature; and still others have contributed to the establishment of the spiritual identity of the peoples living in these areas.

These various writings that form the body of Jewish literature were written in many different languages and areas of the world. Poets and scholars wrote (and still write) in ancient or modern Hebrew, in Aramaic, Greek, Syriac, and Arabic. While the works written by Jewish authors of the Diaspora in Hebrew, Aramaic, Arabic, or various European languages technically do not belong to the literature of Israel, they are of great importance to the intellectual history of Jewry, and thus part of contemporary Israeli society.

One should not overlook the considerable contribution that Jewish writers have made to the literatures of Europe and America. Among them are the poet and philosopher Salomo ibn Gabirol (1020–1070), known in the West as Avencebrol; Yehuda ben Samuel ha-Levi (d. 1141), a physician in Spain who wrote his popular "Songs of Zion" on a pilgrimage from Granada to Palestine; Maimonides (Rabbi Mose ben Maimon), considered the greatest Jewish philospher and theologian of the Middle Ages, who wrote *Dalayat al Hayirin* in Arabic (Hebrew *Moreh Nevuchin*, "Guide for the Perplexed"), an attempt to reconcile the teachings of Judaism with medieval philosophy, and a *Commentary on the Mishnah,* a systematic compendium of Talmudic ethics; the modern Hebrew poet Immanuel Ha-Romi (1270–c. 1330); Israel Ben Mose, who wrote his mystical love songs, "Semoroth Israel" (Songs of Israel) in Palestine; Josef Karo (1488–1575), founder of a Cabbalistic and Talmudic center in Safed; the first great Yiddish novelist, Mendele Mocher Seforim (1835–1917); the great Yiddish writer and humorist Sholem Aleichem (Sholem Rabinowitz, 1859–1916); Chaim Nachman Bialic (1873–1924), who is regarded as the father of Hebrew as a modern literary language and as Israel's national poet; Samuel Josef Agnon, who won the Nobel Prize for literature in 1966 for his short stories and novels; the Jewish satirical writer Ephraim Kishon; and Isaac Bashevis Singer, the best known modern Yiddish writer and winner of the Nobel Prize for literature in 1978.

The Bible

For Jews, the Bible comprises most of the books of the Old Testament. For Christians, the Bible is the entire body of their canonical writings, consisting of both the Old and New Testaments. For both Jew and Christian, the Bible is sacred. The Old Testament consists of 39 books, mostly written in Hebrew. The 27 books of the New Testament were probably written in Greek, with the exception of St. Matthew's Gospel.

The Old Testament. The Old Testament has three sections. The first section of the Hebrew Old Testament is the Law, or Torah—the five books of Moses that are known as the Pentateuch in Greek. The first book, Genesis, tells of the creation of the world. The second, Exodus, relates the flight of the Israelites from Egypt. The third, Leviticus, sets down the rituals of the Jewish faith. The fourth book, Numbers, is probably named for the story of the census with which the book begins. The fifth book, Deuteronomy, consists of a speech given by Moses in which he sets down revised tenets of the Law.

The second section of the Bible (Prophets) contains the prophetic books. The book of Joshua tells of the Israelites' entry into the Promised

Land. Judges relates conflicts with the neighboring peoples and how Israel's leaders acted. The two books of Samuel deal with the time of the judge Samuel; Saul, the first king; and David, who followed him. The two books of Kings continue the history to the Babylonian Captivity.

Following are books relating information about the three major prophets, Isaiah, Jeremiah, and Ezekiel, and the twelve minor prophets.

The third section of the Old Testament consists of narrative books, the poetic books (Psalms, the Song of Solomon, and Jeremiah), and the Wisdom books (Proverbs, Ecclesiastes, and Job). Christians include Chronicles, Ezra, and Nehemiah among the historic books.

Today's version of the Hebrew Bible emerged between the sixth and tenth centuries A.D. The Dead Sea scrolls, dating from the third century B.C. to the first century A.D., have established that the Hebrew text is a faithful reproduction of the original scriptures.

The New Testament. The New Testament also has three parts. The first contains the historic books, the four Gospels, and the Acts of the Apostles. The Gospels relate Christ's life—his birth, his teachings, his death, and his resurrection. The Acts of the Apostles tell of Christ's disciples, and how they spread his teachings.

The second section of the New Testament contains the epistles of Peter, Paul, John, James, and Jude.

The final section is the prophetic revelation of St. John. In it, he relates a series of visions of the end of the world, including the Last Judgment.

Jewish Mystical Writing

For many centuries, Jewish literature consisted of learned studies of the sacred writings, brought together in the Torah. After the destruction of Jerusalem by Titus in A.D. 70, the soferim (scribes) lived in smaller towns in Palestine, like Jamnia, and in Babylonia. The tannaim (teachers of the Law) were concerned with the study and interpretation (Midrash) of the scriptures, expounded the laws handed down in oral or written tradition (Halachah), and wrote moral commentaries on them (Haggadah).

Around A.D. 200, Rabbi Yehuda Hanasi compiled all these writings the Mishnah (Oral Tradition), and they were recognized as binding. Together with the discussions on these writings in the Talmudic schools, they later formed the Talmud (Instruction).

There were two versions of this definitive code of Jewish religious, civil, and penal law: the fourth century Jerusalem Talmud, and the fifth century Babylonian Talmud. This compendium of the learning of the period is still useful as an aid toward understanding the prescriptions of Mosaic law.

Other Literatures in Palestine

Apart from the literature created by Jews writing either in the Holy Land or outside it, there are literatures in other languages that have close connections with Palestine.

The Greek ecclesiastical author Eusebius (c. 260–c. 340), who established a Christian library in Caesarea, wrote numerous works in defense of Christianity, as well as a history of the church, in which he depicted the sufferings of the Jewish people after Christ's death.

Parts of the Old Testament, as well as other works, were written in Aramaic, the official language of Palestine during the period of Persian rule (and, for a time, the everyday language of the Jews). The little Jewish religious community of Samaritans also spoke Aramaic, and produced theological and liturgical works in that language until it was displaced by Arabic. Palestinian Christians wrote various religious works, including hymns, sermons, and lives of the saints, in an Aramaic dialect known as the Christian Palestinian language.

After the coming of the Arabs, a rich Christian Arabic literature developed in Palestine and the surrounding areas. Notable among Muslim Arab writers was the Syrian knight Usama ibn Mundiq (1095–1188), who wrote of his experiences in the early Crusades in his *Book of Instruction*. Among modern Arab writers living in Israel are Moajad Hibrahim and Michael Haddad.

A special position among Jewish writers is occupied by the historian Flavius Josephus (born A.D. 37/38), who became a priest in Jerusalem. At the age of 19, he went to Rome to seek the release of Jewish priests held there in captivity. During the Jewish rising, in spite of his desire for peace, he became leader of a detachment of rebels. His *History of the Jewish War,* probably written in Aramaic, was published in Greek between 75 and 79. It gives an account of Jewish history from the time of the Maccabeans to the fall of Masada. Josephus also wrote *Jewish Antiquities,* an autobiography, and a work against anti-Semitism.

Religions

Eighty-three percent of Israelis are Jews. The rest of the population includes Muslims, Christians, Druzes, and adherents of the Baha'i faith. The country's Declaration of Independence guarantees its citizens religious freedom, and the Ministry of Religious Affairs ensures that all religious communities enjoy equal rights.

The Sabbath and the Jewish festivals are public holidays in Israel, but Israeli law grants all religious communities the right to observe their own weekly holiday.

Judaism

The country's highest religious authority is the Supreme Rabbinical Council, which is jointly headed by the Ashkenazi and Sephardi Chief Rabbis. The Council and its religious courts decide all matters concerning marriage and the family, including divorce and the religious education of children.

The cornerstone of the Jewish faith is a continual striving to carry out the will of God (Yahweh). This involves obeying laws contained in the Torah (the Law). Detailed provisions are set down in two collections, the Mishnah (compiled c. A.D. 200) and the Gemara (c. A.D. 500): Together they form the Talmud.

The Jews of Israel come from very different cultures. The two main communities are the Askenazim and the Sephardim. Both have maintained their own customs, way of life, cultural heritage, and language. There are also smaller communities of Oriental Jews, Karaites, and Samaritans.

The Ashkenazim and Sephardim

The Ashkenazim come from Central and Eastern Europe, particularly from Germany (*Ashkenaz* in Hebrew), Poland, and neighboring countries. Also grouped here are Jews from the United States, Australia, South Africa, and other countries, whose forefathers had emigrated from Europe. The language of the Ashkenazim is Yiddish, a dialect of Hebrew and medieval German that is still widely spoken among Jews throughout Israel and other parts of the world.

In the 16th century, the Ashkenazim began to emigrate to the Holy Land, then under Turkish rule, from Russia, Poland, Lithuania, and Hungary. They mostly settled in Jerusalem. Later on, immigrants continued coming from Russia, Poland, and Hungary. In 1948, when the state of Israel came into being, the Ashkenazim represented 85 percent of the Jewish population (now they account for half).

The Sephardim originally came from Spain (*Sefarad* in Hebrew) and spoke Ladino, a dialect of Hebrew and Castilian, which may still be heard among some Sephardi families in Israel. The Sephardim began to move into Palestine long before the Ashkenazim. The Hebrew poet of the Middle Ages, Rabbi Yehuda Halevi, settled here in 1140. The celebrated interpreter of the Torah, Rabbi Moshe Ben Nachman (Moses Nachmanides), reached the Holy Land in 1266 and founded the Jewish community in Jerusalem. After the expulsion of the Jews from Spain and Portugal in 1490, large numbers of Sephardim migrated to Palestine. They reinforced the Jewish community and absorbed the Arabic-speaking Byzantine Jews (Moriscos) who had remained in the country. Until the 19th century, the Sephardim formed the majority of the Jewish population.

Also included among the Sephardim are the Ma'aravim, Jewish groups from the North African countries of Morocco, Algeria, and Tunisia. During the 19th century, many Ma'aravim emigrated from these French colonies and settled mainly in the towns of Haifa and Jaffa. They speak the Arabic dialect of the Maghreb, and usually French, as well.

Oriental Jews

The Oriental Jews began coming to Palestine during the 16th century from the Arab countries of Yemen, Iraq, Persia, and Afghanistan. These Arabic-speaking Jewish communities form a small minority in Israel.

Karaites and Samaritans

The Karaites and Samaritans are smaller communities whose religions have close affinities with Judaism. The Karaites (numbering about 8,000 and living in Jerusalem) use the Jewish Torah, but do not accept the Talmud. The Samaritans, or Samarites, number about 500 and are the descendants of a very ancient Palestinian people from Samaria. They, too, use the Torah, but in an altered form.

Islam

Israel's Muslims, who are mainly Arabs, form the largest minority in Israel (446,000, excluding the occupied territories). Like Muslims in the surrounding Arab states, most belong to the Sunnite branch of Islam. Among the tenets of the Islamic faith are an absolute belief in Allah and his prophet Mohammed, the duty to pray five times a day, to give alms to the poor, to observe the Ramadan fast, and to make a pilgrimage to Mecca during one's lifetime.

Muslims living in Israel enjoy complete religious independence. In all

Arab towns and villages, there are state schools that teach Arabic, which is Israel's second national language.

Of the approximately 120 mosques in Israel, the largest is the Ahmed Mosque in Akko and the most important, the el-Aqsa Mosque in Jerusalem, which ranks as the third holiest place in Islam after Mecca and Medina.

The Islamic faith is also professed by Israel's Bedouin population, a separate group within the Muslim community who originally came from Arabia. They dwell in tent settlements in the desert oases or live a nomadic desert existence. Most of them center in the Negev, where they rear camels, sheep, and goats. The Bedouin are divided into tribes, each headed by a sheikh who represents their interests in dealings with the outside world.

The Circassians are another independent Muslim community. They came to Palestine from the Caucasus in 1880; now they mainly live in two villages in northern Israel. Some 1,200 in number, they speak their own language, Circassian. Unlike other Muslim Arabs, they cooperate with the Israeli state and serve in the Israel army. (A Circassian unit fought in the Israeli War of Independence.)

Finally, there is an Islamic sect, the Ahmadiya, that originally came from what is now Pakistan.

Christianity

By 1975, Israel had a Christian population of about 130,000. Most of these Christians are Arabs. More than 30 Christian denominations are represented in Israel, including the Greek Catholics, the Greek Orthodox, the Roman Catholics, the Protestants, and the Maronites. Smaller groups include Gregorian and Catholic Armenians, Syrian Catholics, Uniat Chaldeans, Greek Catholic Melchites, Syrian Orthodox, Copts, and Ethiopians. Most Christian communities are centered in Jerusalem.

The Druzes

The Druzes are a religious sect of Muslim origin whose faith is known in its entirety only to its religious leaders. They believe that Allah is the Almighty—a being with no beginning and no end, who is present in all things. They believe in the transmigration of souls in human incarnation, and that God himself has frequently revealed himself in the flesh. The last incarnation of God is believed to have been the Fatimid caliph el-Hakim, who was Sultan of Egypt from 996 to 1020. The Druzes live a strictly moral life; they are monogamous, and women have the same rights as men.

The 42,000 Druzes in Israel are Arabs. They live in villages in Galilee.

During the War of Independence in 1948, they fought in the Israeli army, and since then they have generally supported the Israeli state.

The Baha'i Faith

The Baha'i are a small religious sect with around 200 members in Israel. (The religion has more than five million believers worldwide.) They live in Haifa and Akko, where their holy places are located. The sect, which originated in Persia, preaches the equality of all men, universal brotherhood, world peace, and the solution of social ills.

Jewish Traditions and Festivals

Traditional ceremonies mark a number of important events in the personal life of a Jew. The first of these, circumcision, takes place when a boy is one week old and commemorates God's covenant with Abraham after his offer to sacrifice his son Isaac. At the age of 13, boys are regarded as capable of performing religious duties: This religious coming-of-age is marked by the bar mitzvah. Marriage ceremonies must be performed by a rabbi. Funerals must take place within 24 hours; the body is simply wrapped in a shroud and buried. According to the Jewish faith, "There is no cult of the dead: Judaism is a religion of life."

There are seven important Jewish festivals. Rosh Hashanah, Yom Kippur, Passah, Shavuot, and Sukkoth are of Biblical origin, while Purim and Hannukah developed during the rabbinical period.

Rosh Hashanah celebrates the Jewish New Year and is also the day of Creation.

Yom Kippur is a solemn holy day, the Day of Atonement. Pious Jews spend the day fasting and praying, begging God for forgiveness of sins committed during the year.

Sukkoth, the Festival of the Tabernacles, commemorates the exodus from Egypt, when the Jews built huts in the wilderness for their night's shelter. The festival lasts seven days and seven nights, during which each family builds a hut (outside if possible), where they take their meals and spend the night if the weather is good. Sukkoth ends with the day of the Rejoicing of the Law (Simchat Torah), when the annual cycles of readings from the Torah begins anew in the synagogue.

Purim commemorates the deliverance of the Jews from their Persian captivity. There are readings from the Book of Esther in the synagogues and joyous processions through the streets. At night, there are Purim dances.

Passover, or *Passah,* is a week-long festival marking the exodus and the end of Jewish slavery in Egypt. Jews eat unleavened bread as a reminder of the time when they were pursued by the Pharaoh's soldiers and could not wait for bread to rise. The festival begins with the Seder, an evening service in the home, where the head of the family leads the prayers and traditional foods are eaten.

Shavuot, the Festival of Weeks, commemorates the handing down of the Ten Commandments.

Hannukah, or the Festival of Lights, recalls Judas Maccabeus's victories over the Greek rulers of Palestine and the legend of the miracle of the oil. (When the Jews tried to light the candles in the plundered Temple, only a small flask of oil could be found; yet, it miraculously lasted long enough for the priests to prepare the consecrated oil.) On the first of the eight days, a single candle is lit; one more is added each successive day.

Independence Day (Yom Haatzmaut) is a new national festival marking the day Israel became a state in 1948.

Islamic Festivals

The Islamic weekly holyday is Friday, and the weekend begins at midday on Thursday. The most important religious event is the *Ramadan fast,* which lasts one month; the faithful must fast from dawn to dusk.

Id al Kabir or *Id al Adha,* the Festival of Sacrifice, is celebrated on the tenth day of the twelfth month. This is the time when great pilgrimages travel to Mecca. Each family slaughters an ox, a sheep, or a camel, and two-thirds of the meat is given to the poor. *Id al Fitr* or *Id as Sagir,* the Little Festival, marks the end of the great Ramadan fast. Each of these festivals lasts three days.

Maulid an Nabi, another important festival, celebrates the birth of the Prophet.

The starting point of the Islamic calendar, which is a lunar calendar, is July 16 in the year 622 of the Christian era. This is the day on which Mohammed and his followers left Mecca and settled in the Jewish town of Yasrib, later known as Medinet en Nabi (the City of the Prophet, now usually called Medina). The day of Mohammed's flight from Mecca (the Hegira) became the first day of the Muslim calendar from which subsequent years are counted; hence the Muslim year A.H. 3 *(anno Hegirae)* is equivalent to A.D. 623.

***Jerusalem

For spiritual and historical interest, there is no place in the world that quite compares to the ancient holy city of Jerusalem. Known in Hebrew as *Yerushalayim* (City of Peace), and in Arabic as *el-Kuds* (Holy City), Jerusalem is sacred to Muslims, Christians, and Jews alike. The capital of modern-day Israel has been the site of emerging kingdoms, impassioned uprisings, thriving commerce, bitter war, and pious religious life for more than 5,000 years. To the energetic traveler with an imaginative mind, Jerusalem offers a view of history that is unmatched in richness, variety, scope, and depth.

A Brief Overview

Jerusalem is surrounded on the west, north, and south by terraced hills typical of the upland region of central Israel. Most of the terrain in the city and the country to the west consists of a massive stratum of hard, gray dolomitic limestone, with a covering of brownish or reddish earth. Two or 3 km. (1.5– 2 miles) to the east, however, the countryside suddenly becomes an arid and almost totally barren wilderness. Here, soft white or whitish-yellow rocks are interspersed with bands of dark flint, covered here and there with a thin layer of gray earth. Through the center of the city runs the watershed between the Dead Sea and the Mediterranean.

Jerusalem is a city of dramatic hills reaching 600–830 meters (1,970–2,720 feet) high, but most of it lies at an altitude between 720–780 meters (2,360–2,560 feet). The walled Old City, in the center of the eastern part of modern Jerusalem, is built on the slopes of two hills rising from east to west. It is surrounded on the east and north by two higher hills, the Mount of Olives and Mount Scopus, from which there are fine views of the Old City. The steep-sided Kidron Valley, lying between the Old City and the Mount of Olives, is Jerusalem's lowest point; much of the valley is occupied by cemeteries. On the south the Old City is bounded by another steep escarpment, the Hinnom Valley (in Hebrew, *Gei-ben-Hinnom*), which runs into the Kidron Valley. The more modern areas of Jerusalem have been built on low-lying, rounded hills that rise above the arid valleys.

Until the mid-19th century, Jerusalem was a tiny city with an area of around one square kilometer (half a square mile); a population of 15,000 lived within the walls of the Old City. Recently, the city has grown enormously, particularly in the last 50 years. It now encompasses 40 square km. (15.5 square miles), and has a population of 400,000. Greater Jerusalem extends from Bethlehem in the south to Ramallah in the north, covering a developed area of over 108 square km. (42 square miles). The territory and its half-million inhabitants are administered by the municipality of Jerusalem.

Although Jerusalem has been unified since 1967, the city's population is distributed according to clear-cut geopolitical distinctions. West Jerusalem is home to the city's Jews, who make up about 70 percent of the population; while Muslims, Arab Christians, small minorities of Armenians, and Christians of various other nationalities dwell in East Jerusalem. The different groups mix fairly easily at the levels of commerce and trade, but the social gulf that separates them remains wide. Scarcely any part of the city has a mixed Arab-Jewish population.

Between 1948 and 1967, East Jerusalem (including the Old City) was under Jordanian rule, separated from the rest of the city by a strip of no man's land. The single crossing point, the Mandelbaum Gate, was carefully monitored, and only foreign diplomats and small numbers of non-Jewish tourists were allowed to pass through it.

Since the 1967 war, when the two parts of the city were brought together under Israeli rule, large new Jewish suburbs have grown up in the former Arab area of East Jerusalem, and the old north-south line of division has been considerably altered.

Today there is unrestricted, but not particularly close, communication between the two parts of the city. Each area has preserved its own distinctive character, its own shopping center and educational system, social services, and transportation structure. And despite the official unification of the city, many nations continue to regard East Jerusalem as part of the "Israeli-occupied territories" on the West Bank of the Jordan.

Jerusalem is the seat of the Israeli parliament (the Knesset), the government, almost all the ministries (with the exception of the Ministries of Defense and Agriculture), the highest judicial authorities, and most other national bodies and institutions. All of these are based in West Jerusalem, though recently some Israeli government agencies have been established in the eastern part of the city.

Many countries do not recognize Jerusalem as the capital of Israel; thus, all foreign embassies are located in Tel Aviv. There are many foreign consulates in Jerusalem with offices in both West and East Jerusalem.

Chronology

c. 3000 b.c.: The first known permanent settlement on the site of the Old City is established by Canaanite tribes. (Recent excavations have confirmed that this settlement, named for the god Shalem, lay in the southeastern corner of the present Old City, where remains of a wall and a gate were discovered.) A number of other fortified settlements are founded about the same time in other parts of the Judean hills.

c. 996 B.C.: King David establishes his capital in Jerusalem, bringing the Ark of the Covenant to the city. David enlarges and fortifies Jerusalem, which now becomes a center of political, administrative, and religious activity. David's successor, Solomon, extends the city to north and west and builds his temple (to house the Ark of the Covenant) and a royal palace on its south side, on what is now called the Temple Mount. Solomon also builds a new wall and some other public buildings (see 1 Kings 9:15 and 11:27). The first aqueduct bringing water from the Gihon Spring into the walled city is also believed to have been built in the reign of Solomon.

c. 922 B.C.: Solomon dies, and his son Rehoboam becomes king. Jeroboam, Solomon's other son, leads the secession of ten tribes of Israel and forms the Northern Kingdom of Israel with Shechem as its capital. Jerusalem becomes the capital of the Kingdom of Judah, led by Rehoboam.

Various kings of Judah, including Jehosophat (867–843 B.C.) and Uzziah (786–758 B.C.), continue to fortify and extend the city in order to bring outlying suburbs within the walls.

c. 715–686 B.C.: Hezekiah, the best-known of the kings of Judah, fortifies the city to withstand an Assyrian attack (see 2 Chron. 29–32). He constructs a secret tunnel that carries water from the Gihon Spring to the upper parts of the walled city, thus securing the inhabitants' water supply during the siege.

c. 586 B.C.: Jerusalem and its temple (the First Temple) are almost completely destroyed by Babylonian forces under Nebuchadnezzar; the inhabitants are driven out and banished. (Some remains of Jerusalem dating from the kingdom of Judah, including burial caves and the tombs of kings and other leading figures, have been excavated in recent years.) Tremendous religious crisis follows the devastation of the Temple.

c. 536 B.C.: Cyrus the Great of Persia conquers Jerusalem; the Israelites return from their Babylonian exile and rebuild the city and the Temple. (The construction of the Second Temple, which took some decades, is described in detail in the books of Ezra and Nehemiah.) It is a smaller and more modest urban center than the city destroyed by the Babylonians. (Excavations have shown that the walls erected by Nehemiah were partly rebuilt on older foundations.)

333 B.C.: Alexander the Great conquers Jerusalem. For the next 165 years, the city remains under Hellenistic rule, its boundaries expanding along the western hills of the Old City.

196–171 B.C.: Jerusalem witnesses frequent bloody fighting. Violent resistance to the process of Hellenization and the introduction of idol worship provokes the Syrian ruler Antiochus IV to devastate much of Jerusalem, killing many of its inhabitants and plundering the Temple.

165 B.C.: Led by Judas Maccabeus, the Israelites rebel, reclaiming and rededicating the Temple, and expelling the Greeks from most of Jerusalem.

162–143 B.C.: Jerusalem is divided; the Greeks occupy the new Hellenistic area of the city, and the Israelites hold the rest.

143 B.C.: The Israelites gain control of the whole city. For the next 80 years Jerusalem is again the capital of an Israelite kingdom, which grows and prospers in the reign of Alexander Jannaeus (102–76 B.C.). The city expands to the west and north, and new walls and defenses are built. (The walls and buildings of this period have been unearthed in a series of excavations over the past 120 years, and a number of fine cave burials from this period have been found to the east and north of the Old City.)

63 B.C.: Jerusalem falls to the Romans, led by Pompey, and becomes the capital of Judea. The city remains under Roman jurisdiction for the next four centuries.

37–4 B.C.: The reign of Herod the Great, known as the King of Judea, and a favorite of Mark Antony and Augustus. Herod undertakes an extensive building program, enlarging the Temple, improving the city's fortifications. He surrounds the Temple Mount with a high, massive, four-gated wall (part of which is the famous Western, or Wailing, Wall). Herod also improves the city's water supply. On the west side of the city (in the area now occupied by the Citadel, or David's Tower, the Jaffa Gate, and the Armenian Quarter), Herod builds a large, handsome, and highly fortified stronghold with three towers. (Some of the huge funerary monuments outside the city, such as Herod's Family Tomb near the King David Hotel and Absalom's Monument at the foot of the Mount of Olives, also date from this period.)

c. 4 B.C.–A.D. 39: Jerusalem is ruled by Herod's son, Herod Antipas, who is eventually banished by Caligula. The last ministry of Jesus of Nazareth occurs c. A.D. 29, followed by His arrest and Crucifixion.

A.D. 42–70: An additional wall is built on the north side of Jerusalem in order to protect the area most vulnerable to attack. (A section of this third wall can be seen near the Damascus Gate.)

70: The Israelites rise up against Roman rule. Roman troops, under the leadership of Titus, burn and devastate the city and the Second Temple. Only the towers of Herod's palace and the Western Wall escape destruction. Most of the population perish during the six-month siege by the Roman army, and those who do not die are enslaved.

130: The emperor Hadrian resolves to build a Roman city, with Roman temples and shrines, on the ruins of Jerusalem. In retaliation, Bar-Kochba leads a second Jewish uprising against the Romans. Jerusalem is taken by the Jews, who hold it for almost two years, but the Romans once more hold sway.

135: The Romans ruthlessly suppress the revolts, and Hadrian razes Jerusalem, erecting a new, considerably smaller city—Aelia Capitolina. The Jews are banned from the city, which lasts for over a hundred years. A Temple of Jupiter is built in the center of the temple precinct, on the ruins of the Jewish temple. (Remains of buildings and walls belonging to the Roman colony have been found in the northern and western parts of the Old City.)

c. 200–400: Jerusalem becomes increasingly Christianized, attracting pilgrims from the growing Christian communities in neighboring countries. Under the rule of Constantine the Great (288–337), Christians are granted the freedom to practice their religion in 313. Constantine declares Jerusalem a holy city in 324. Many churches are built under the direction of his mother, Helena; in particular, the Church of the Holy Sepulcher (on the traditional site of Jesus's tomb), a church built on the rock of Golgotha (Calvary, the traditional site of the Crucifixion), and the Eleona Church on the slopes of the Mount of Olives.

401–700: During the next three centuries, many churches, religious houses, and hospices for pilgrims are built in and around the city. Further enlarged and surrounded by new walls, Jerusalem is filled with Christian places of worship and other religious establishments, some associated with Biblical events, others dedicated to saints.

527–565: The development of Jerusalem under Byzantine rule reaches its peak during the reign of Justinian (527–565). Many of the present-day churches and religious houses in and around Jerusalem are built on the foundations or the remains of religious buildings of the Byzantine period. During this time, many sites of Biblical events are identified. (The famous Madaba mosaic map gives a good impression of the layout and size of Jerusalem during this period.)

614: The Persian army invades the Holy Land. The Persians raze many religious sites and occupy Jerusalem, holding it for 14 years.

628: The Persians are defeated, and Jerusalem is once more in Byzantine hands.

638: Byzantine Jerusalem falls to the invading armies of Persian caliph Omar. According to Islam, the Prophet Mohammed rested in the grounds of the Temple of Jerusalem on his Midnight Ride to heaven, where he received the word of Allah; Omar builds a mosque on this site.

691: Umayyad caliph Abd el-Malik completes the Dome of the Rock, constructed on the rock where the altar of the Jewish Second Temple is said to have stood (some Jewish scholars deny that this was the site of the altar). A palace and two caravanserais (inns) are built on the south side of the Temple Mount.

691–1099: A sequence of Muslim empires rule Jerusalem—the Persians, until c. 775; the Abbasids of Baghdad, c. 775–969; the Fatimids of Egypt, c. 969; and the Seljuk Turks, who take over in 1071. Many buildings in and around the Temple square and in other parts of the city date from this period. The Muslim rulers permit Jews to live and worship in Jerusalem, enabling the revival of a Jewish community, but there is increasing suppression of Christian religious activities. In the early 11th century, the Church of the Holy Sepulcher and other churches are destroyed on the orders of Caliph el-Hakim.

1099: After a five-week siege, Jerusalem is taken by the armies of the First Crusade, who are determined to reclaim Christian holy sites. The majority of the population—consisting chiefly of Muslims and Jews—is massacred; many of the survivors become slaves.

1100: The Latin Kingdom of Jerusalem is established and ruled by Baldwin I. The city draws a steady flow of pilgrims from Europe, and there is much new building by the kings, nobles, and religious leaders who had taken part in the Crusade; the Church of the Holy Sepulcher is largely rebuilt by the Crusaders. New walls are constructed to meet the requirements of the enlarged city, which now almost reaches the size and population of Herodian Jerusalem.

The city, now mainly populated by Christians from Europe, is divided into a number of districts for the different nationalities: the Germans, the Eastern Christians, and the French-speaking population.

The sites traditionally associated with various Biblical events originally identified during the Byzantine rule are confirmed.

1187: Saladin, Sultan of Egypt, routs the forces of the Crusaders at the Battle of the Horns of Hittim in Galilee. Jerusalem once more becomes a Muslim city, and most of the Christians are driven out. All the Islamic places of worship revert to their former importance, including the mosques and other religious buildings on the Temple Mount; new mosques, *madrasas* (theological schools), *zawityes* (small shrines), and *ribats* (hospices) are erected. Jews are once more permitted to settle in Jerusalem.

1229–1244: The Crusaders' attempts to recover Jerusalem are unsuccessful, but under an agreement between Frederick II, leader of the Holy Roman Empire, and the Egyptian rulers of Jerusalem, the Crusaders return to the city and recover partial possession. They are finally expelled in 1244. The last Crusader stronghold in the Holy Land, at Akko (Acre), falls in 1291.

1250: In Egypt, the belligerent Mamelukes, an elite corps of slaves, wrest control of the sultanate from the Ayyubids. The Mamelukes rule Jerusalem for two and a half centuries.

1516: The Ottoman Turks defeat the Mamelukes in Syria and take control of their empire. Jerusalem surrenders without a struggle to the Turkish sultan Selim I, whose dynasty rules the city for the next 401 years.

1520–1566: The reign of Sultan Suleiman the Magnificent spans nearly half a century. From 1537–1541, the sultan builds the walls that still surround the Old City today; he rebuilds and restores mosques, the Citadel, and the aqueduct that brings water into the city from Solomon's Pools to the south. Some of the city's fine public fountains are built in this period.

1567–c.1800: Jerusalem, no longer an important government or administrative center, falls into decay. Its importance within Palestine declines, while other towns, such as Akko, Safed, and Gaza, grow in importance. The population of the city begins to dwindle; by 1806, there are just 8,000 inhabitants, of whom more than half are Muslims and one-quarter Jews.

1832–1840: Mohammed (or Mehemet) Ali, the ruler of Egypt, rebels against the Ottoman Empire; his forces occupy Palestine and Syria. Jeru-

The Citadel and southwestern wall

salem again becomes a thriving administrative center. This brief period is a turning point in the city's history. The first European consulate (Britain's) opens in 1838, and a number of European Christian churches and other organizations reestablish themselves in Jerusalem.

c. 1840: With Britain's help, Mohammed Ali's army is expelled from Palestine. European nations gain more freedom to trade in the city, and all the other major European powers open consulates in Jerusalem. Churches and various religious institutions are built, at first within the Old City and later on its outskirts.

1847: A Catholic Patriarchate is instituted for the first time since the Crusades.

c. 1856–1900: The pace of development increases; following the Crimean War (1853–1856), the European powers gain great influence in the Turkish Empire and are granted special privileges in Jerusalem. Most of the churches and other Christian institutions in and around Jerusalem are built during the second half of the 19th century, with money and donations received from Christian organizations and churches in Europe, North America, and the Middle East.

The Jewish community also grows significantly, and new Jewish residential districts, synagogues, religious institutions, and public buildings are erected both within the walled Old City and outside it.

1917: The end of the Ottoman Empire. Jerusalem surrenders to British forces without a fight. The Balfour Declaration pledges British assistance in establishing a Jewish national home in Palestine.

1918–1948: Britain rules Palestine, its presence there confirmed (1922) by a mandate from the League of Nations. Once again the center of government, Jerusalem begins to develop and modernize, while retaining its distinctive character and holy sites. A number of well-conceived plans for the development and extension of the New City and for improvements in the Old City are partially carried out. Jerusalem acquires a modern water supply system and a power station that serve all parts of the city and the suburbs, as well as other municipal services. The population grows rapidly, particularly in the 1930s and 1940s, mainly as a result of Jewish immigration but also through the influx of Arabs from the country areas and small neighboring towns.

Political tensions between Arabs and Jews increase, resulting in a number of violent clashes. The two communities gradually develop their own residential and commercial areas. By the late 1930s, the city is divided into two parts, Arab and Jewish. The Christians, most of whom are Arabs, live mainly in the western districts of the New City.

1948: British forces pull out of Palestine, and violence erupts between Arabs and Jews. The Jordanian army moves into the Old City, the Arab suburbs of eastern and northern Jerusalem, and some of the surrounding villages, subjecting the Jewish part of the city to a heavy bombardment that lasts almost a month. The Egyptian army soon reaches the city's southern outskirts. After bitter street fighting, the Jewish quarter of the Old City falls into the hands of the Jordanian army and is burned down. For more than two months, Jewish Jerusalem is completely cut off from its supply sources, leaving the 100,000 inhabitants short of food and water.

In the middle of June, the Israeli army breaks through the Arab blockade and relieves the food shortage; the Israelis then establish a corridor between Jerusalem and the rest of Israel.

1949: Israel, Egypt, and Jordan sign an armistice that divides the city in two. East Jerusalem is now in Jordanian territory, and West Jerusalem becomes the capital of Israel. A narrow strip of no man's land separates the two parts of the city. They are linked by a single crossing point, the Mandelbaum Gate, controlled by the United Nations Armistice Commission.

1967: Outbreak of the Six-Day War, in which Israeli forces are pitted against the armies of Egypt, Syria, and Jordan. The Israeli army occupies East Jerusalem after three days of heavy fighting. Settlement of the Arab West Bank by Israelis begins, despite initial opposition from the Israeli government.

The City's Population

The Palestine war of 1948 and the political division of Jerusalem that followed it led to a complete separation between the Jews and Arabs. Only a very small number of non-Jews, most of them Christians, remained in the Israeli part of Jerusalem, while not a single Jew remained in Jordanian East Jerusalem. Many Christians left the city; some moved to neighboring towns, such as Bethlehem and Ramallah, others emigrated. While the Jewish and Muslim populations have grown to almost three times the size they were at the end of the British mandate, the number of Christians is well below the 1947 figure.

After the unification of the city following the 1967 war, Jerusalem had 268,000 inhabitants; nearly 75 percent were Jews, while Muslims accounted for about 20 percent, and Christians about four percent. By 1981, the city's population had grown to 400,000, with the three religious groups represented in approximately the same proportions since 1967.

Almost all Jerusalem's Muslims are Arabs and belong to the Sunni sect of Islam. Most are of Oriental origin, but a considerable number have arrived since 1920 from the towns and villages of Judea, mainly from Hebron and the surrounding area.

More than 80 percent of the Christians are Arabs; the rest are Armenians, Europeans, or come from neighboring Middle Eastern countries. Roughly one-third of Jerusalem's Christians belong to the Greek Orthodox church, but most are members of the Roman Catholic church or its associated churches, like the Maronite and Greek Catholic churches.

The majority of Jerusalem's Jewish population consists of Oriental Jews, many of whom are descendants of families that have lived in the city for more than 120 years. About 35 percent of the city's Jews have arrived since 1948. The Orthodox Jews, who live in the northern districts of the New City, come from Eastern Europe; many of these families settled in Jerusalem in the 19th century.

The New Suburbs

Jerusalem has grown rapidly in the last 20 years, and suburbs have been built on the hills around the city. To the south, halfway to Bethlehem, is the new suburb of Gillo, while to the north and northwest are Newe Yakow, Ramat Eshkol, and Ramot.

Over the last 30 years, there has also been much development along the main roads radiating from the city in all directions. The Arab suburbs lie mainly along the Ramallah road to the north, along the Jericho road to the east, and—on a smaller scale—along the Bethlehem road to the south.

Attractions

See color map and map on pages 44–45.

If you are lucky enough to have two weeks in Jerusalem, the 13 walking tours suggested here will enable you to see this majestic ancient city in its entirety. However, these tours are arranged to provide even the most casual visitor with a chance to explore the most important sights and holy places in this fabulous city. The sites sacred to Christians, Muslims, and Jews, as well as most of the city's landmarks, lie in East Jerusalem—particularly in the Old City (Walks 1–8) and to the east of the Old City (Walks 9–11).

After you choose a route, follow it at a leisurely pace. Keep your eyes and ears open and drink in the exotic atmosphere.

WALK 1: The Walls and the **Citadel

See map on pages 44–45.

Jerusalem was destroyed and rebuilt several times in the course of its long and eventful history. The city's extent and layout expanded and contracted through the centuries; its walls, towers, and gates were strengthened, pulled down, redesigned, and rebuilt. This walk seems to wind through the layers of time, showing you an historical portrait of the ever-changing city.

As can be seen from the plan below, the city of David [a] was originally a small settlement outside the present Old City. David's son Solomon, who reigned from 965–928 B.C., built the First Temple to house the Ark of the Covenant, involving an extension of the city along the hills to the north [b]. When Sennacherib's Assyrians were threatening Jerusalem in the seventh century B.C., the walled area was increased threefold in size to strengthen the city's defenses [c].

Some 50 years after the city was captured and destroyed by Nebuchadnezzar (586 B.C.), the inhabitants of Jerusalem returned from exile and rebuilt it [d], although much smaller than Solomon's. After the recovery of Jewish independence as a result of the Maccabean uprising in the

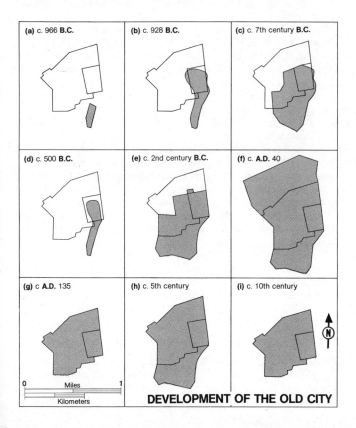

(a) c. 966 **B.C.**

(b) c. 928 **B.C.**

(c) c. 7th century **B.C.**

(d) c. 500 **B.C.**

(e) c. 2nd century **B.C.**

(f) c. **A.D.** 40

(g) c **A.D.** 135

(h) c. 5th century

(i) c. 10th century

0   Miles   1
Kilometers

DEVELOPMENT OF THE OLD CITY

second century B.C., the city began to grow again. Under the Hasmonean kings John Hyrcanus (134–104 B.C.) and Alexander Jannaeus (103–76 B.C.), it expanded to the west and north [e]. While Herod the Great (39–4 B.C.) built only outside the city, his great-nephew, Herod Agrippa I (A.D. 37–44), built the north wall, giving the walled city its greatest extent ever [f].

During the destruction of Jerusalem at the hands of the Romans in A.D. 70, Titus ordered the walls of the city to be slighted and that "only the highest towers, Phasael, Hippicus and Mariamne, together with the part of the walls that encloses the city on the left, should be left standing as a camp for the garrison; the towers being left to give posterity some idea of the strong fortifications which fell to Roman valour" (Flavius Josephus, *The Jewish War*, 7, 1–2).

The new city built by Hadrian in A.D. 135 was the Roman military colony of Aelia Capitolina [g], and the present street layout of the Old City derives from it.

The city began to grow again after Constantine the Great granted Christianity official recognition in 313. In the fifth century, Empress Eudocia enlarged the city again, bringing Mount Zion and the old city of David within the walls [h]. After Caliph el-Aziz abandoned this additional territory (975), and Suleiman made some minor changes during his reign (1520–1566), the Old City within the walls took on its present form [i]. The current walls were begun on the north side in 1537, construction continued down the east and west sides and was completed on the south side in 1541.

Suleiman built six gates and gave each an official name. These gates are now called by a variety of names, according to the language or religion of the inhabitants of the city. The L-shaped entrances were designed to foil hostile attempts to rush the gates. When goods entering the city increasingly began to be carried on carts rather than pack animals, the L-shaped entrances at Herod's Gate and Saint Stephen's Gate were redesigned to be straight. The Dung Gate was widened after the Second World War.

The walls of the Old City are now 4 km. (2 miles) long and enclose an area of almost 1 square km. (two-fifths of a square mile). They are almost rectangular in form, with the longest side (2,800 meters; 3,060 yards) on the north and the shortest (1,760 meters; 1,925 yards) on the east. The walls are 10–12 meters (33–40 feet) high and 4–6 meters (13–20 feet) thick. The 34 towers increase the height of the walls by another few meters.

Around the Old City Walls

The walls are open daily from
10:00 A.M.–4:00 P.M.

You can get your best first impression of the Old City from the top of the walls. From here, you can make a nearly complete circuit of the city, with superb views of the bustle and activity in its streets. There are good steps up to the wall walk at all the gates except Saint Stephen's.

Nowadays, you may enter the city by any one of seven gates. In the time of Suleiman the Magnificent, there were only six gates, all in Ottoman style; of these, only three survive in their original form—the Jaffa Gate, the Damascus Gate, and the Zion Gate.

The Jaffa and Damascus gates are the most frequently used entrances to the two main streets and the bazaars in the center of the city. Automobiles can enter the Old City only by the Jaffa Gate, the New Gate, or Saint Stephen's Gate.

The best starting point for a tour of the Old City is the main entrance, the ****Jaffa Gate** [1]. This entryway is still known to the Arabs by its original name, *Bab el-Halil* (Friend's Gate), after an inscription over the entrance, "There is no God but Allah, and Abraham is his friend."

The 12-meter- (40-foot-) wide Jaffa Gate is the principal means of access from the New City to the Old, with an entranceway wide enough to accommodate automobiles without difficulty. (There is a special reason for this: When Kaiser Wilhelm II of Germany visited Jerusalem in 1898, the Turkish sultan Abdul Hamid had the wall between the Jaffa Gate and the Citadel pulled down and the moat filled in to allow passage for the carriages of the kaiser and his retinue.) Legend has it that the

two *tombs* behind the wrought-iron railings just at the entrance belong to the architects of the wall. According to one story, Suleiman had these men executed because they had failed to include Mount Zion, with the Tomb of King David, within the walls. Another legend holds that the sultan, greatly pleased with their work, had them killed to ensure they could never build anything more beautiful for anyone else. Immediately to the right of the gate is the *Citadel* (see page 47).

The century-old ***New Gate** [2] was opened in 1887 by Sultan Abdul Hamid to facilitate communications between the Old City and the new suburbs outside the walls—particularly between the Christian Quarter within and the Christian residential districts outside. The New Gate, like the Jaffa Gate and the Zion Gate, was closed from 1948–1967.

The ****Damascus Gate** [3], known in Hebrew as *Shaar Shechem* and as *Bab el-Amud* (Gate of the Column) in Arabic, is the most elaborate of the city's entrances and its finest example of Ottoman architecture. It marks the starting point of the Nablus Road, which once led to Damascus, and stands on the remains of two earlier entrances to the Old City, dating from the time of Herod Agrippa I (A.D. 37–44) and from Hadrian's Aelia Capitolina (around A.D. 135). It now serves as the main thoroughfare between the Arab areas in East Jerusalem and the Old City. Hadrian is believed to have erected a column in an an-

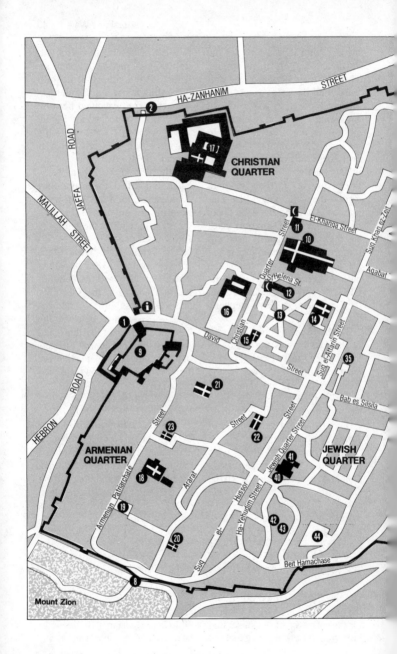

HA-ZANHANIM STREET

CHRISTIAN QUARTER

El-Khanqa Street

St Helena St.

Suq Khan ez Zeit

Aqabat

Suq el-Attarin Street

Bab es Silsila

JEWISH QUARTER

Christian Quarter Street

David Street

Jewish Quarter Street

ARMENIAN QUARTER

Armenian Patriarchate

Ararat Street

Hussor Street

Suq el-

Ha-Yehudim Street

Beit Hamachase

Mount Zion

JAFFA ROAD

MALILLAH STREET

HEBRON ROAD

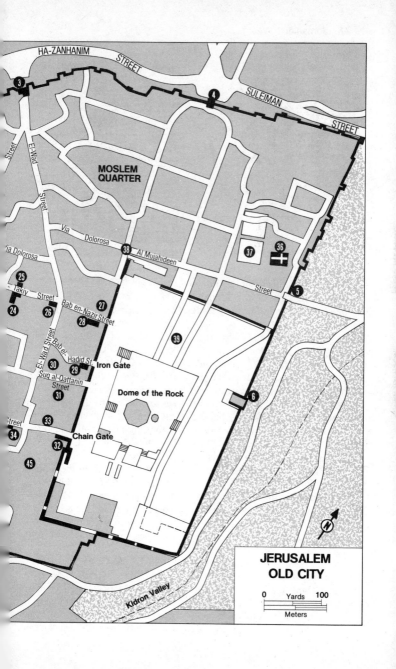

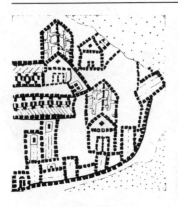

The Madaba mosaic map

St. Stephen's Gate

cient plaza at this point, as shown here in a copy of the Madaba mosaic map of sixth-century Jerusalem.

*Herod's Gate [4] was originally called *Bab ez-Zahra* (Blooming Gate). Christian pilgrims came to believe that the house of Herod Antipas, who condemned Jesus, stood nearby; most scholars today, however, believe that Herod's house was on Mount Zion. It was at Herod's Gate that the armies of the First Crusade broke through the walls of Jerusalem on July 15, 1099.

*Saint Stephen's Gate [5] is also known as the Lion's Gate (in Hebrew, *Shaar Haarajot*) for the carvings of lions on its arch. The carvings are said to represent the legend that Suleiman would have been torn apart by lions if he had not built a wall around Jerusalem. The first Christian martyr, Saint Stephen, was taken through the gate to his place of execution.

The Arabs call the gate *Bab Sittna Miriam* (Gate of the Lady Mary) because it leads to the tomb of the Virgin (see Walk 11).

The ***Golden Gate** [6] (in Arabic, *Bab el-Tobe,* Gate of Repentance; in Hebrew, *Shaar Harakhamim*) on the Temple Mount has been walled up since the time of the Crusaders. This gate, opposite the Mount of Olives, was probably closed by the Muslims to bar unbelievers from the Temple Mount. During the Middle Ages, it was opened only on Palm Sunday and on Good Friday. According to Jewish tradition, the door will open again when the Messiah comes.

The ***Dung Gate** [7] was originally known as *Bab el-Maghar-ibeh* (the Moors' Gate), because immigrants from North Africa lived in a nearby district. The small Ottoman *arch* over the undecorated modern lintel indicates that the original gate was much smaller. The entryway has a long history of useful—if unappealing—service: from the second century onward the city's rubbish and offal were taken out through it. It is the gate nearest the Temple Mount and the Western (Wailing) Wall.

The ***Zion Gate** [8] leads to Mount Zion. The Arabs call it *Bab en-Nabi Daoud* (Gate of the Prophet David) because it gives access to King David's tomb. The damaged exterior of the gate bears witness to the fierce fighting for the Jewish Quarter in 1948.

From the Zion Gate, continue to the southwest corner of the walls and from there turn north to reach the *Citadel* [9].

****The Citadel**

See plan on page 48.

Open daily from 8:30 A.M.–4:00 P.M.; closed Saturdays and public holidays.

The Citadel, with its minaret and towers, dominates the west side of the Old City at the Jaffa Gate. In 24 B.C., King Herod the Great built a luxurious palace here, surrounded by walls and protected on the north side by three towers; he named them after his friend Hippicus, his brother Phasael, and his wife Mariamne. After the Roman conquest of Palestine in A.D. 6, the procurator, whose headquarters were in Caesarea, used the palace as his Jerusalem residence. Thus, this was the praetorium in which Pilate sat in judgment on Jesus (John 18:28–19:16).

After his victory over the Jewish uprising in A.D. 70, the Roman emperor Titus left the three towers standing as a memorial to the strength and valor of his forces, and stationed his Tenth Legion in the palace. In A.D. 135, Hadrian damaged the citadel walls, but part of Phasael's tower, also known as David's Tower, was left standing. The masonry and the massive stone blocks in the foundations, characteristic of Herodian architecture, can still be seen.

The Citadel was erected in its present general form in 1312 by the Mameluke sultan Malik en Nasir, who constructed it on the foundations of a Crusader palace dating from 1128. Suleiman the Magnificent completed the structure, adding the outer approach road, the stone bridge, and the western terrace between 1531 and 1538. The minaret on David's Tower was erected in 1655.

It was here, on the platform before the Citadel entrance, that Britain's General Allenby proclaimed the liberation of Jerusalem from Turkish rule in 1917. From 1948–1967, the Citadel was occupied by the Jordanian army.

The Citadel now houses a *Municipal Museum*, with regularly changing displays, and it is the setting for a sound and light show, "A Stone in David's Tower," that reviews Jerusalem's 4,000 years of history.

From the *platform* [A], you pass through the *Outer Gate* and over the *Stone Bridge* spanning the moat to reach the Mameluke *Main Gate* [B]. Continuing through a hexagonal *courtyard* [C] dating from the 14th century, you then climb an exterior staircase to enter the *Phasael Tower*. From its *platform* [D], there is a splendid view of Jerusalem, and a closer view of the excavations. The walls in the *Moat* [E] were built to retain the rubble that was deposited here to provide a platform for the construction of Herod's palace. On one side it is supported by a wall on which there were two towers. The position of one *tower* [F] was changed in the Middle Ages; the remains of the other *tower* [G] are original.

Adjoining the Mameluke-period *Mosque* [H], stood a *gate* [I] built by the Crusaders, from which a wall ran to the *Northwest Tower* [J]. Suleiman the Magnificent built the *Outer Ward* [K] and

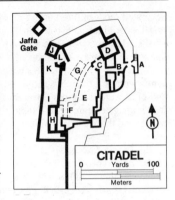

the *Gateway* [L], giving access to the Northwest Tower. When you go through the gate, you will come to the road that runs down outside the walls to the southwest corner of the Citadel. At this point, the walls are exposed right down to the foundations, making it easy to identify the various stages of construction. Look particularly for the 16th-century Ottoman walls, built on the foundations of the Hasmonean walls of the second century B.C.

WALK 2: The Christian Quarter

See map on pages 44–45.

Distinguished by its large numbers of churches, religious houses, and other Christian establishments, the Christian Quarter is dominated by the Church of the Holy Sepulcher with its great, dark-colored dome. This walk starts at the Church of the Holy Sepulcher, and leads you through some of the chief sights in the quarter.

In this part of the city, the little streets and lanes are broader and better paved than in other areas, and the buildings are higher, reaching three or four stories. Much of the architecture is relatively new, dating from the end of the 19th century onward. The Roman Catholic, Greek Catholic, and Greek Orthodox Patriarchs have their seats in this quarter, and the religious affairs of the great majority of the Christians in Israel and Jordan are administered from this district.

The main entrances to the Christian Quarter are the Jaffa Gate [1] and the New Gate [2]. The principal shopping area is Christian Quarter Street, and you'll also find many hotels and hospices in the Christian Quarter.

The starting-point of this walk is the ***Church of the Holy Sepulcher* [10] (for a description see Walk 3). On the north and south sides of the church are two small mosques, whose minarets add a colorful note to the spires of the churches, cathedrals, and religious houses.

At the corner of *Christian Quarter Street* and *el-Khanqa Street* is the **el-Khanqa Mosque** [11], built by Saladin between 1187–1189 on the site of the palace of the Patriarchs of the Latin Kingdom of Jerusalem. When the mosque was restored in 1418, a minaret was built on its roof, apparently to match the minaret of the **Mosque of Omar** [12], south of the Church of the Holy Sepulcher in *Saint Helena Street*. The half-way point of a line between the two minarets roughly coincides with the entrance to Christ's tomb in the adjoining Church of the Holy Sepulcher. The mosque, erected to commemorate the occasion when Caliph Omar prayed in the courtyard of the Church of the Holy Sepulcher in 638, was built in 1193 and restored in the mid-13th century; the minaret in its courtyard dates from 1458–1465.

South of the Mosque of Omar is a square area bounded by four streets, the **Muristan** [13], with the Lutheran Church of the Redeemer and the Church of Saint John the Baptist at diagonally opposite corners. The name Muristan (Arabic, meaning "hospice") is a reminder that this area once contained many hospices and hostelries for pilgrims. The hospices were under the control of the order of Knights of Saint John of the Hospital, which later became the military order of the Knights Hospitallers (Johannites). The Knights' hospice fell into disrepair after the collapse of the Latin Kingdom of Jerusalem at the end of the 13th century; nonetheless, it was able to accommodate up to 400 pilgrims until the 15th century. The Hospitaller's edifice was destroyed in the 16th century, when Suleiman the Magnificent used the massive stones of the hospice to build the walls of Jerusalem. In 1869, the Turks divided the area of the Muristan between Russian monks of the Orthodox church, who built a handsome arched entrance and the decorated *Muristan Fountain,* and the Prussian Protestants, who constructed the Church of the Redeemer.

Built in 1898, the ****Church of**

the Redeemer [14] is the young-est church in the Old City. (*Open daily 9:00 A.M.–1:00 P.M., 2:00–5:00 P.M.; Friday 9:00 A.M.–1:00 P.M.*) It stands on the foundations of the monastic Church of Saint Mary of the Latins, which dates from the period of harsh suppres-sion of Christian worship. De-stroyed in 1009 during the reign of Caliph el-Hakim, the church was rebuilt in 1063 by merchants from Amalfi, Italy, with an associated hospice. The Church of the Re-deemer was inaugurated by Kaiser Wilhelm II of Germany during his state visit to Jerusalem in 1898. The north doorway, decorated with signs of the zodiac and repre-sentations of the months, dates from the period of the Crusades.

On the south side of the Church of the Redeemer is an excellently preserved medieval monastery with a two-story cloister, parts of which date from the 11th–13th centuries. A massive wall was found during recent excavations under the center of the Church of the Redeemer, assumed to be the south retaining wall supporting the forum of Hadrian's Aelia Cap-itolina (A.D. 135).

From the gallery of the *church tower* there are stunning views of the Old City, the Temple Mount, the Mount of Olives, the Kidron Valley, the New City, and Mount Zion.

The ***Church of Saint John the Baptist** [15] lies hidden in the Muristan. It is the oldest pre-served church in Jerusalem. The entrance in Christian Quarter Street leads into the courtyard of a monastery, where a priest will ad-mit you into this Greek Ortho-dox church. The façade, with its two small bell towers, is a mod-ern addition; the church itself was built by merchants from Am-alfi in the 11th century. The cradle of the order of Saint John, the structure was erected over a much earlier *crypt*—well worth see-ing—dating from the mid-fifth century and rebuilt after its de-struction by the Persians in 614.

To the east of the Muristan, on the far side of Christian Quarter Street, is **Hezekiah's Pool** (or *Pool of the Patriarch's Baths*) [16]. This ancient reservoir has been so enclosed by later building that it can be reached only by way of the *Coptic Khan,* an old caravanserai now occupied by a variety of workshops. Although the local people will be glad to let you look into the pool, you may be dis-mayed to find that it is now used as a refuse dump. Popularly attrib-uted to the Old Testament king Hezekiah, the pool is now be-lieved to date from the Herodian period, when it was supplied with water by an aqueduct (still pre-served) from the Mamilla Pool. Flavius Josephus called it the Amygdalon, a name that presum-ably referred to the nearby towers of Herod's palace (*migdal* is the Hebrew word for "tower"). The present name alludes to the fact that the pool supplied water to the baths of the Patriarchate, which adjoined the Church of the Holy Sepulcher.

Near the *New Gate,* in the Latin district of the Christian Quarter, is the **Convent of Saint Saviour** [17], built in 1551 by Franciscans who had been expelled from their convent on Mount Zion by Sala-din. The *church* was rebuilt in 1885; the upper part of the widely visible *bell tower* was given its final form in 1931. The convent has a bakery, an oil press, a wine cellar, a library, and a printing house.

WALK 3: The ***Church of the Holy Sepulcher

See plans on pages 52 and 55.

Open from 4:00 A.M.–7:00 P.M.; there is no charge for admission. Remember to dress appropriately: shorts and sleeveless blouses are banned.

The holiest place in Christendom dominates the Christian Quarter of the Old City. The Church of the Holy Sepulcher is held by Christian tradition to mark the location not only of Jesus Christ's tomb but also of the Crucifixion on Golgotha (Calvary). The Christian community of Jerusalem held liturgical ceremonies at the sepulcher as early as A.D. 66; recently, archaeological excavations have largely confirmed that Christ died and was buried at this place.

The present-day Church of the Holy Sepulcher complex is made up of numerous individual buildings. The different architectural styles and the complicated rights of possession of these edifices are best understood in the light of the church's historical development.

History

The oldest parts of the Church of the Holy Sepulcher are the remains of a large basilica built in the early fourth century by Constantine, in accordance with the wishes of his mother, Helena, who had visited Jerusalem in 325. This basilica occupied the site of the Roman emperor Hadrian's Temple to Aphrodite, erected in A.D. 135 on the leveled site of Jesus' Crucifixion and burial. Constantine resolved to build a basilica dedicated to the Resurrection. Jerusalem's Christian community evidently had preserved a clear recollection of the site, for excavations of the foundation of the temple of Aphrodite revealed many vestiges of the sepulcher and indications that this was indeed Golgotha.

Work began on the Byzantine basilica in 326, and it was consecrated in 335. The church was not completed, however, until 348.

The first Church of the Holy Sepulcher consisted of four elements (see plan on page 52). The *Atrium* [A] at the top of the steps, rising up from the main street, led into a roofed *Basilica* with an *Apse* [B]. Beyond this,

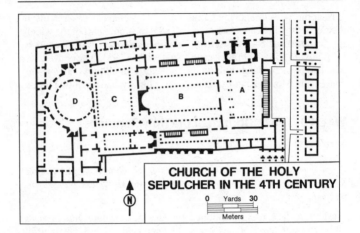

CHURCH OF THE HOLY
SEPULCHER IN THE 4TH CENTURY

0   Yards   30

Meters

an *Inner Courtyard* [C], with the rock of Golgotha in the southeast corner, opened to the *Sepulcher* [D]. In spite of all the later rebuilding and new construction, the original layout can still be discerned.

A mighty rotunda, 38 meters (125 feet) in diameter, was built over the sepulcher, following the model of Roman mausolea. This impressive domed space, also known as the Anastasis or Resurrection, has survived almost completely unchanged. The inner courtyard, with the site of the Crucifixion in its southeast corner, is now radically different from the original structure, as is the five-aisled basilica, in whose crypt was built the Chapel of the Finding of the Cross.

The Byzantine basilica was destroyed by the Persians in 614. The Greek Orthodox Abbot Modestus began to rebuild it in almost exactly the same fashion only 15 years later. This second Church of the Holy Sepulcher was decimated in 1009 by the Fatimid caliph el-Hakim. The destruction was so thorough that even the block of stone containing Christ's tomb was smashed.

The small Christian community in Jerusalem could not afford to rebuild the church. It was only after the accession of Byzantine emperor Constantine Monomachus (1042) that a start was made toward construction. The imperial treasury in Constantinople lacked the necessary funds to restore the church to its original dimensions; thus, the basilica was not rebuilt. However, the rotunda was given an upper gallery and an apse on the east side, and the open courtyard was preserved.

The Crusaders found the church in this dilapidated condition when they took Jerusalem on July 15, 1099. They at once set about rebuilding and beautifying in a manner worthy of such a sacred site—a process that

The Dome of the Rock on the Temple Mount, an extraordinary mosque of mosaics and marble, is among the holiest places in Islam.

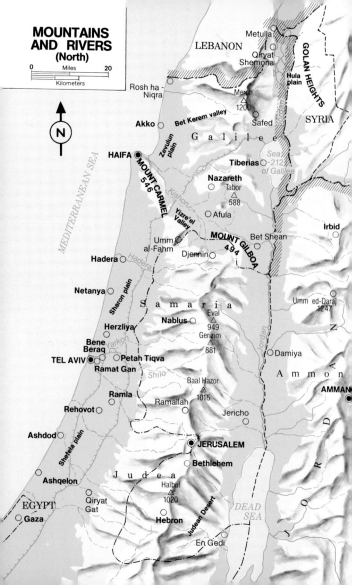

MOUNTAINS
AND RIVERS
(North)

0   Miles   20

Kilometers

N

MEDITERRANEAN SEA

LEBANON

Metulla

Qiryat
Shemona

Hula
plain

GOLAN
HEIGHTS

SYRIA

Rosh ha-
Niqra

Meron
1200

Safed

Akko

Bet Kerem valley

Galilee

Sea
-212
of Galilee

HAIFA

MOUNT CARMEL
546

Zevulun
plain

Tiberias

Nazareth

Tabor
588

Kishon

Yizre'el
Valley

Afula

MOUNT GILBOA
484

Bet Shean

Irbid

Umm
al-Fahm

Djennin

Hadera

Hadera

Netanya

Sharon plain

S a m a r i a

Eval
949

Gerizim
881

Umm ed-Daraj
1247

Herzliya

Nablus

Z

Bene
Beraq

Yarkon

TEL AVIV

Petah Tiqva

Ramat Gan

Shilo

Damiya

A m m o n

Baal Hazor
1016

Ramla

Rehovot

Ramallah

AMMAN

Ashdod

Shefela plain

Jericho

J u d e a

JERUSALEM

Bethlehem

R

Ashqelon

Halhul
1020

Qiryat
Gat

Judean Desert

DEAD
SEA

O

EGYPT

Gaza

Hebron

En Gedi

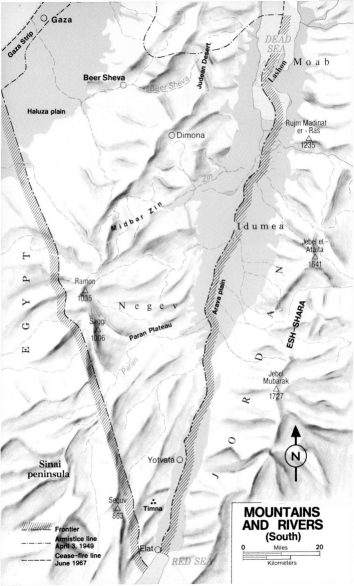

Gaza

Gaza Strip

DEAD SEA

Moab

Beer Sheva

Judean Desert

Lashon

Haluza plain

Rujm Madinat er - Ras
△ 1235

Dimona

Zin

Midbar Zin

Idumea

Jebel el - Ataita
△ 1641

E G Y P T

Ramon
△ 1035

Negev

Arava plain

J O R D A N

Saggi
△ 1006

Paran Plateau

Paran

Jebel Mubarak
△ 1727

ESH-SHARA

Sinai peninsula

Yotvata

Seguv
△ 863

Timna

Elat

RED SEA

N

MOUNTAINS AND RIVERS (South)

0   Miles   20
Kilometers

Frontier
Armistice line April 3, 1949
Cease-fire line June 1967

The Damascus Gate, with its imposing battlements, is one of seven gates that give access to the walled Old City of Jerusalem.

The golden domes of Mary Magdalene Church glitter beyond the Church of All Nations and the nearby Garden of Gethsemane on the Mount of Olives.

An array of leather goods, clothing, and souvenirs tempt shoppers along the streets of Jerusalem's Old City.

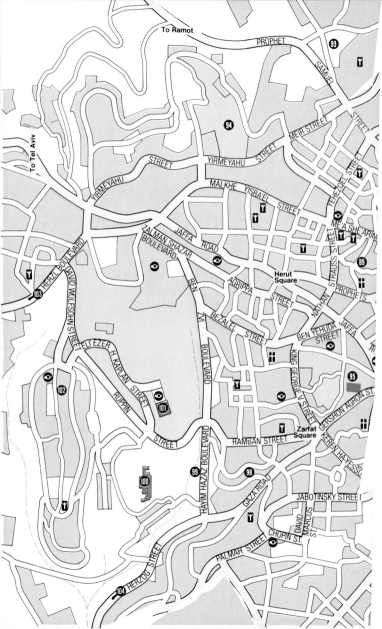

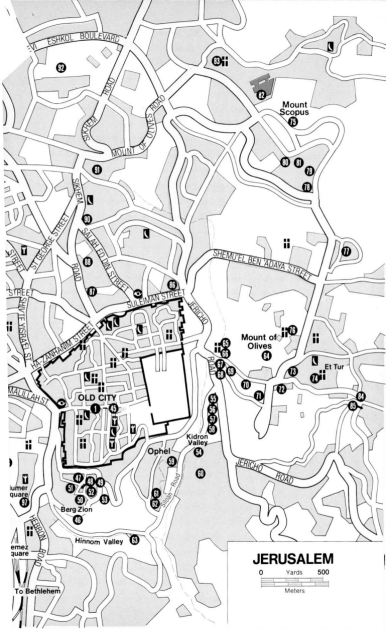

LEVI ESHKOL BOULEVARD

92

83

82

Mount
Scopus
75

80 81 79

78

91

90

ST GEORGE STREET

SALAH ED DIN STREET

SHEMU'EL BEN 'ADAYA STREET

88

87

SIKHEM ROAD

MOUNT OF OLIVES ROAD

SIKHEM ROAD

HA-ZANHANIM STREET

SHE VTE YISRAEL ST

STREET

emez
quare

SULEIMAN STREET

86

77

76

Mount of
Olives
64

65
66

67
68 69

73

Et Tur
72

70
71 72

74

84
85

JERICHO ROAD

OLD CITY

MALILAH ST

1 45

55
56
57
58

Ophel

Kidron
Valley

54

59

60

JERICHO ROAD

47

48 49

51 52
50 53

46

Berg Zion

61
62

Siloah Road

63

Hinnom Valley

lumer
quare
97

HEBRON ROAD

emez
quare

To Bethlehem

JERUSALEM

0   Yards   500

Meters

Israel's best preserved Roman ampitheater, located on the outskirts of Bet Shean, dates from the third century and could accommodate 5,000 spectators.

The el-Jazzar Mosque in Akko, easily distinguished by its dome and minaret, has a beautiful courtyard with marble columns and fountains.

took 50 years. Although they preserved the rotunda without alteration, they erected a Romanesque church over the open courtyard of Constantine's basilica. This new church was based on a plan similar to the present Greek Orthodox Katholikon. The chapels that had been built in the reign of Constantine Monomachus were incorporated in the ambulatory around the choir. The new church was consecrated in 1149.

The Church of the Holy Sepulcher that we see today broadly corresponds to this Crusader church. A fire in 1808 and an earthquake in 1927 caused great damage, and it was not until 1959 that agreement was reached on plans for a comprehensive restoration of the church. Throughout this long improvement project, the underlying principle has been to preserve the structure of the church and to restore it in the original styles.

Rights to the Church

Many different Christian denominations historically have had an interest in the Church of the Holy Sepulcher. The Patriarchate of Jerusalem, established in A.D. 451, was originally under the authority of the Pope in Rome. The Latin (Roman Catholic) protectorate of the Church of the Holy Sepulcher began in 806 when the Pope gave Charlemagne the keys to the church—and lasted until 1009, when Caliph el-Hakim destroyed the building. Its construction by Emperor Constantine Monomachus in 1042 marked the beginning of the Greek Orthodox protectorate, for Christendom was now divided into the Roman Catholic church in the west and the Greek Orthodox church, centered in Constantinople.

The Roman Catholics gained possession of the Church of the Holy Sepulcher for a brief period (1099–1187) during the Crusaders' occupation of Jerusalem. In 1291, when the Crusaders finally left the Holy Land, only the Roman Catholic order of Minorites (Franciscans) remained in the city. Their rights of possession of the Holy Places were confirmed in a treaty between the sultan and the king of Naples in 1333. In subsequent centuries, the rights and privileges of the different denominations, particularly in relation to Calvary (Golgotha) and the rotunda containing Christ's sepulcher, varied with political circumstances.

The dilemma incurred by religious politics was broadly settled in 1852 on the basis of the status quo, taking account of certain rights acquired by the Greeks in 1757. There are now six different religious communities represented in the Church of the Holy Sepulcher: the Greek Orthodox church, the Roman Catholic church (often called the "Latins"), the Armenian Orthodox church, the Coptic Orthodox church, the Syrian Orthodox church (called the "Jacobites") and the Ethiopian Coptic church. Of these, however, only the first three have rights of possession of major importance.

One more curious feature of this already complicated situation is that the entrance to the Church of the Holy Sepulcher is formally controlled by a Muslim family. Many centuries ago, the Turkish sultan entrusted this family with the keys to the holiest of Christian sites.

The ownership rights of the various churches are as follows (see plan on page 55):

Common to all churches: Christ's Sepulcher [L], with the vestibule and the tomb chamber within the Rotunda [K]; the Stone of Unction [C], where Jesus' body was prepared for burial.

Greek Orthodox church: the northern half of Mount Calvary, with the Altar of the Crucifixion [H]; Adam's Chapel [D], below this; the Katholikon [I]; "Christ's Prison" [S]; two chapels in the ambulatory [T, X]; and a number of smaller areas in the Rotunda.

Roman Catholic church: the southern half of Mount Calvary, with the Altar of the Nailing to the Cross [E]; the "Latin Choir" [Y] in the Rotunda; the Altar of Mary Magdalene [P]; the Franciscan church [Q], with the adjoining Franciscan convent and the Chapel of the Finding of the Cross [W].

Armenian Orthodox church: Saint Helen's Chapel [V]; the Stela of the Three Marys [J]; the Chapel of the Division of the Raiment [U]; and an area in the Rotunda.

Coptic Orthodox church: a chapel [M] behind Christ's Sepulcher [L] and two other small areas.

Syrian Orthodox church (Jacobites): a chapel [N] in the Rotunda.

Ethiopian Coptic church: the Tomb of Joseph of Arimathea [O].

Tour of the Church

See plan on page 55.

The Church of the Holy Sepulcher is usually very full during important Christian festivals, so you should try to do your sightseeing at other times. Every day at 4:00 P.M., the Franciscans lead a procession that takes in the principal holy places within the church.

The tour starts from the **Forecourt** [A], along the sides of which are a number of chapels belonging to the Greeks, the Armenians, and the Copts. Immediately on the right is the Greek Orthodox *Monastery of Abraham*. The stumps of columns in the forecourt are Roman.

The façade of the Church of the Holy Sepulcher dates from the period of Crusader occupation (12th century). The renovation of the stonework that was damaged in the 1927 earthquake is now almost complete.

In front of the entrance to the church, to the right, is a *stone slab* marking the tomb of the English Crusader Philippe d'Aubigny. Here, too, are steps and an aedicula (small building) marking the Crusaders' entrance to the rock of Golgotha. The entrance has been closed since 1197; the building is now the *Chapel of the Franks* or *Chapel of the Sorrows* [F]. You can get a glimpse of the interior only from the Calvary Chapel.

Immediately beyond the entrance, on the left, is the *Place of the Muslim Guards* [B], thus named because a Muslim family of Jerusalem has a centuries-old right to open and close the Church of the Holy Sepulcher. Straight ahead of the entrance is the *Stone of Unction* [C]. According to Roman Catholic tradition, Christ's body was embalmed here before the Entombment (John 19:39); the Greek Orthodox believe that this was the spot where Christ was taken down from the Cross. The slab of reddish sandstone was placed here in 1810.

To the right of the Stone of Unction is **Adam's Chapel** [D], which owes its name to the legend that Adam's skull was found here after Christ's death on the Cross. Through a pane of glass in the chapel you can see the *Cleft in the Rock,* which opened up after Christ's death (Matthew 27:52). The Crusaders Godfrey de Bouillon and Baldwin were buried near the entrance inside this chapel; their tombs were replaced by wooden benches when the Greeks took possession of Adam's Chapel in 1810.

On both sides of Adam's Chapel, steep staircases ascend 5 meters (16 feet) to *Calvary.* The chapel, with its three *altars* [E, G, H], and the two flights of steps belong to the Greeks and Roman Catholics. Here are Stations X to XIII of the Via Dolorosa (see Walk 6). Calvary (Latin, *calvariae*

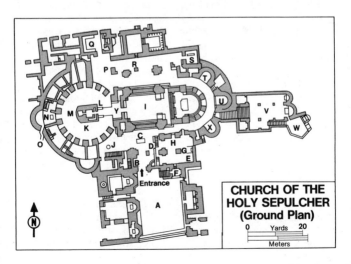

CHURCH OF THE HOLY SEPULCHER (Ground Plan)

0   Yards   20

Meters

locus, Place of the Skull) originally stood outside the city walls,
because of the Jewish belief that
graves are impure.

Going up one of the flights of
steps onto Calvary, you will see
two large altars flanking a smaller
one. To the right, at the far end of
the chapel, is the *Altar of the Nailing to the Cross* [E], with fine copper reliefs from 1588; it belongs to
the Roman Catholic church. Medieval mosaics decorate the ceiling of the altar, and through the
small window to its right, you can
look into the Chapel of the Franks
or Chapel of the Sorrows [F] (see
page 55). To the left of the Altar
of the Nailing to the Cross is the
smaller *Stabat Mater Altar* [G],
which also belongs to the Roman
Catholics. Christians believe that
this is where Mary stood during
the death of her Son. From this
spot you can see part of the original block of stone from the ancient
quarry.

Farther left is the *Altar of the
Crucifixion* [H], belonging to the
Greek Orthodox church, with life-
size icons of Christ, Mary, and
John the Baptist, surrounded by
numerous lamps. Below the altar
is a hole in which Christ's cross is
believed to have been set, and behind this, on either side, are
sockets for the crosses of the two
thieves who were crucified along
with Him.

Straight ahead as you come
down from Calvary, you see the
Katholikon [I], the principal
Greek Orthodox church, also
known as the *Greek Cathedral.*

The Katholikon, roofed with a
large dome, occupies the site of
the nave of the Crusaders' church.
Situated exactly in the center under the dome is a basin containing
a marble hemisphere. According
to Christian tradition, this hemisphere represents the "navel of the
world"—a feature depicted on
many medieval maps. (Jewish tradition, on the other hand, holds
that the center of the world is the
Sacred Rock on the Temple
Mount.)

From the Katholikon, walk past
the *Stela of Three Marys* [J], which
belongs to the Armenian church,
to the domed **Rotunda** [K],
which houses the *Sepulcher of
Christ.* In spite of all later alterations, the Rotunda—which the
Greeks call the *Anastasis* (Resurrection)—has survived mostly as
it was in the time of Constantine.
The outer walls date from the
fourth century. The dome, 21 meters (69 feet) in diameter, rises
21.5 meters (70.5 feet) above the
ground. The 11th-century pillars
and columns, which were badly
damaged in the fire of 1808, have
been restored to their original
form. The tall, fourth-century
columns that support the dome
were split in half during the rebuilding that took place in the 11th
century under Constantine Monomachus; the other halves were
used to support the upper gallery.

The *Latin Choir* [Y] leads into a
small vestibule known as the *Angel's Chapel* because it contains
part of the stone on which the angel sat at the Resurrection. A low

entrance (keep your head well down!) gives access to the *Chapel of the Holy Sepulcher* [L], the 14th and final Station on the Via Dolorosa. This tiny, marble-clad chapel has room for only two or three people at a time. Forty-three precious lamps hang from the ceiling in precisely calculated positions. They belong to four different religious communities (13 each to the Roman Catholics, Greeks, and Armenians, and four to the Copts). On the right is a 2-meter- (6.5-foot-) long *marble slab* over the Sepulcher of Christ.

Like all the other tombs of this period in Palestine, this was a family tomb. According to Christian tradition Jesus was the first to be buried here: "And when Joseph had taken the body, he wrapped it in a clean linen cloth, and laid it in his own new tomb, which he had hewn out in the rock: and he rolled a great stone to the door of the sepulcher, and departed" (Matthew 27:59–60). The inscription on a metal plaque reads: "He is risen; He is not here: behold the place where they laid Him" (Mark 16:6). Beneath a figure of the Virgin, are remains of the original rock tomb.

On Greek Orthodox Easter, an impressive ceremony takes place at the Sepulcher. While a great concourse of believers wait silently in the Rotunda, the Patriarch lays aside his vestments and crown and enters the Angel's Chapel, where he lights the Holy Fire. The smoke from this fire finds its way out to the Rotunda through two holes in the side walls of the chapel and is greeted with triumphant cries of the faithful.

On the rear wall of the Chapel of the Sepulcher is the *Coptic Chapel* [M], in which a fragment of the original rock tomb can be seen in the base of the altar. Immediately opposite is the *Chapel of the Jacobites* [N], with a fourth-century wall and apse. Next to it, through a dark hole in the wall, is the *Tomb of Joseph of Arimathea* [O], part of a family tomb with grave shafts in the walls and bone shafts in the floor.

The Roman Catholic part of the Church of the Holy Sepulcher lies on the north side of the Rotunda. The first feature you'll encounter is the *Altar of Mary Magdalene* [P], where Jesus is believed to have appeared to Mary Magdalene after his resurrection (John 20:14–18). Beside this altar is the only organ in the Church of the Holy Sepulcher.

Beyond the altar is the *Franciscan Church* [Q], also known as the *Church of the Apparition,* originally a Byzantine oratory of 1048. To the right of the entrance is the stump of a column known as the *Column of the Flagellation,* but nothing is known of its origin.

Continuing along the side of the Katholikon from the Altar of Mary Magdalene, you come to the *Seven Arches of the Virgin* [R], where Jesus is believed to have appeared to Mary, his mother, after the Resurrection. Some of the columns, which have been restored, date from the Byzantine period.

Beyond the arches, in the northeast corner of the Church of the Holy Sepulcher, is *Christ's Prison* [S], in which Jesus and the two thieves are said to have been confined before the Crucifixion.

Farther east, you pass the *Chapel of Longinus* [T] and the *Chapel of the Division of the Raiment* [U]. At the east end of the Church of the Holy Sepulcher, **Saint Helen's Chapel** [V] sits at the foot of a long flight of steps. This impressive crypt chapel, which belongs to the Armenian church, is one of the jewels of the Church of the Holy Sepulcher. It is dedicated to Helena, Constantine's mother, who was divinely guided to the site of the True Cross upon which Christ was crucified. Although the chapel was constructed in the 12th century on the site of an earlier cistern, its north and south walls (to right and left when facing the altar) are the foundations of the nave of Constantine's fourth-century basilica. The dome, built by the Crusaders, rests on four columns partly dating from the seventh century. To the right of the altar is the niche from which Helena is said to have watched the excavations in which the True Cross was brought to light.

In the right-hand corner of Saint Helen's Chapel, a flight of stairs descends to the Roman Catholic *Chapel of the Finding of the Cross* [W], where Helena discovered the cross that was recognized as the True Cross. The altar and the statue of Saint Helen were presented in the 19th century by Archduke Maximilian of Austria, briefly emperor of Mexico.

On the way back from Saint Helen's Chapel you come to the last chapel in the ambulatory, the *Chapel of the Mocking* [X], which has another Column of the Flagellation.

WALK 4: The Armenian Quarter

See map on pages 44–45 and plan on page 59.

Located in the southwest corner of the Old City and separated from it by a wall, the Armenian Quarter is a little city in itself. The area takes its name from the Armenian Monastery; nearby are its residential districts, schools, workshops, library, theological seminary, and the seat of the Armenian Patriarchate. The central feature of this complex is the Cathedral of Saint James, around which all the other buildings are grouped. The Armenian Quarter is noted for its Library, which contains numerous old manuscripts and works of art, and its Printing House, the largest Armenian printing house outside Armenia.

The houses in this quarter, mostly of two or three stories, are almost exclusively occupied by Armenians, although the Armenian population in Jerusalem has declined considerably over the past 30 years.

The Armenians officially adopted Christianity at the beginning of the fourth century, and were the first nation to do so. When the kingdom of Armenia fell a century later, persecutions and expulsions followed; the Armenian community in exile maintained its identity only through its deep attachment to the church.

A good place to start your walking tour of the Armenian Quarter is **Saint James's Cathedral** [18]. This colorful, domed church, with its rich treasures of art, is very different from the dark Church of the Holy Sepulcher. The Cathedral, often simply called *Saint James's Church,* was built in the 11th century on the site of an earlier chapel dedicated to the Egyptian martyr, Saint Menas. Much altered and enlarged since then, it commemorates the apostle Saint James the Great, said to have been executed on this spot in A.D. 44 by Herod Agrippa (Acts 12:1).

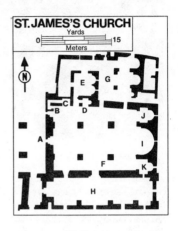

It is easiest to see the church during the afternoon service when it is open to visitors *(weekdays at 3:00 P.M.; Saturdays and Sundays at 2:30 P.M.).* If you want to visit the church and its precincts outside these times you can make an appointment by calling the Patriarchate.

You enter the church through a small *Forecourt* [A], which was added in the 17th century. Immediately to the right of the main entrance are two old *symandra*—gonglike contrivances that were used during the 9th century, when Christians were forbidden to ring bells. One of the symandra is wood, the other bronze.

A small door in the northwest corner [B] leads to a flight of steps up to the *Chapel of Saint Macarius*

[C], who was bishop of Jerusalem during the reign of Constantine.

Opposite is *Saint James's Chapel* [D], and just before this is the entrance to the fifth-century *Saint Menas's Chapel* [E]. These two chapels, the oldest parts of the church, house the church treasury and are not open to the public.

On the other side in the south wall, there's a panel between the painted tiles. It conceals a finely carved door that opens to a small, once-secret passage leading to *chapels* [F] over the two lateral apses.

The former *Saint Stephen's Chapel* [G], which dates from the 10th and 11th centuries, is now the sacristy and contains a baptistery.

There is also a font in the *Etchmiadzin Chapel* [H], which

Armenian priests

was the narthex of the medieval church. The chapel takes its name from Etchmiadzin, near Erevan (Armenian Soviet Socialist Republic), the residence of the Katholikos (leader) of all Armenian Christians. A shrine on the altar holds stones from Mount Sinai, Mount Tabor, the Jordan, and the Holy Sepulcher. The tiles by the altar and the entrance to the chapel are particularly fine.

In the choir is *Saint James's Throne,* on which James is said to have been beheaded. The *high altar* [I], carved from cedarwood from Lebanon, dates from 1721. The *altars* on each side of the high altar are dedicated to the *Virgin* [J] and *John the Baptist* [K].

From Saint James's Cathedral, the route continues past the *Gulbenkian Library* [19], which has a large collection of documents, manuscripts, and books. Continue down the steps to a narrow lane, Ararat Street, and through a wide gateway in the wall

to the interesting chapel traditionally known as the ***House of the High Priest Annas** [20]. This little chapel, built sometime around 1300, marks the site of the house in which Annas, father-in-law of Caiaphas (John 18:13), is traditionally said to have lived. (Modern scholars believe it is more probable, however, that Annas lived in Caiaphas's house on Mount Zion.)

The chapel is a fine example of Armenian architecture, and has an unusually large vestibule. A passage to the right of the apse leads into a small oratory with a carved wooden door dating from 1649. Since the 15th century, the *olive tree* at the northeast corner of the chapel has been revered as the tree to which Jesus was tied during the Flagellation; the chapel is accordingly known as *Deir ez Zeitouneh* (Chapel of the Olive Tree). A stone is built into the outside wall of the chapel. When the Pharisees called on Christ to silence his disciples, he replied that "if these should hold their peace, the stones would immediately cry out" (Luke 19:37–40). Tradition holds that this stone is one of the stones referred to by Christ.

There are three more small, single-apsed medieval churches in the Armenian Quarter: *Saint James* [21], now a small mosque; the ruined *Church of Saint Thomas* [22], which is claimed both by Armenians and Muslims; and the *Church of Saint Mark,* the center of the Syrian Orthodox community, the smallest Christian community in Jerusalem.

WALK 5: The Muslim Quarter

See map on pages 44–45.

Bounded by the Damascus Gate, Herod's Gate, and Saint Stephen's Gate, the densely populated Muslim Quarter occupies an area of 22.5 hectares (55 acres) in the northeast of the Old City. It is a maze of narrow lanes, busy bazaars, and numbers of small workshops. Most of the closely packed and rather dilapidated houses are of one or two stories, with small inner courtyards.

There are still many interesting old buildings of the Mameluke period (1250–1516) in the Muslim Quarter to the west and north of the Temple Mount; only the most important are mentioned here. If you take time for a leisurely look around this area, you will discover a corner of Old Jerusalem that offers many surprises.

This walk starts in Aqabat et Takiya Street and takes in most of the high points, including Suq el-Qattanin (the Cotton Dealers' Market) and several elegant pilgrims' hospices, as well as Saint Anne's Church.

The Mamelukes were members of an imperial guard of Turkish slaves, who rose to high offices under the Ayyubid dynasty founded by Saladin. After the death of the last sultan in 1250, the Mamelukes seized power in Egypt, which then controlled Syria and Palestine. Heraldic emblems appear on many buildings from this period—perhaps a handkerchief, or a pair of polo mallets, or a goblet—indicating the profession of the Mameluke dignitary who built the house.

Most of the buildings from the Mameluke period are now private dwellings. It does not matter that the interiors are inaccessible since Mameluke buildings are mainly notable for the magnificence of their façades and entrances.

The walk begins in *Aqabat et Takiya Street,* which runs east from the Church of the Holy Sepulcher through Old Jerusalem toward the Dome of the Rock. In this street is an old palace, the **Serai es Sitt Tunshuq** [24], built between 1379–1382 as the residence of the Tatar princess Tunshuq. Under the Turks the palace became a Dervish convent; it is now an orphanage for Muslim boys. Its three fine doorways are all different; the delicate ornament on the lintels

and central pillars is particularly striking.

Directly across the street is the *Turba es Sitt Tunshuq* [25], the princess's vaulted tomb. Note the mosaic door panels and the black, white, and red stones in the vaulting.

The **Ribat Bayram Jawish** [26], an old pilgrim hospice built by Emir Bayram in 1540, stands at the intersection at the end of the street. Another fine example of Mameluke architecture, its most striking feature is its elaborate entrance doorway of pink marble, black basalt, and white limestone. It is now occupied by a school.

The route continues along *Bab en Nazir Street,* one of the main access roads to the Temple Mount. Like all the other streets to the Temple Mount, this one is named for the gate from which it leads—in this case, the Gate of the Inspector. (Since that entrance is also known as the Prison Gate, the street has an alternative name, *Bab el-Habs Street.*)

Near the gate at the end of the street stand two interesting buildings. On the left is a former pilgrim hospice, the **Ribat Ala ed Din el-Basir** [27], built in 1267 by the Mameluke emir el-Basir. In spite of his blindness, the emir was known as el-Basir, the "Clear-Sighted," for his wisdom and piety. The Turks used the building as a prison—hence the grating on the door and the little cells in the courtyard. This is an early Mameluke building, and no colored stones were used in its construction. The door pillar and the pointed arch are particularly fine.

Across the street is the **Ribat Mansuri** [28], built in the reign of Sultan el-Mansur Qalawun. The building originally served as a hospice, and was later used as a Turkish barracks, then as a prison. The forecourt has stone paving similar to that of the Antonia Fortress. The entrance, built of colored stone, resembles that of the Ribat el-Basir but is even more elegant.

When you return to the intersection, turn left onto *el-Wad Street,* one of the main arteries of the Old City, and then left again almost at once into narrow, curving *Bab el-Hadid Street,* which runs through a tunnel to the *Iron Gate,* an entrance to the Temple Mount. The tunnel, which is very short, runs into a quiet, wider street with many fine Mameluke buildings of different periods. On the right stands the most impressive of these, the **Madrasa Muzhiriya** [29], a religious college built in 1480 by Abu Bakr Mohammed ibn Muzhir, head of the Egyptian Chancellory. The entrance has a setback cloverleaf arch with eight rows of irregular stalactite vaulting, and the windows are finely decorated. The second story was built over the adjoining building to provide direct access to the Temple Mount.

Now return to el-Wad Street and continue south to the ***Suq el-Qattanin,** (the Cotton Dealers' Market) [30]. This vaulted market (littered for many years with rubbish and refuse but now restored) is a particularly interesting example of Mameluke architecture. If you look closely, you can see that it was built in two phases. The front entrance facing el-Wad Street has plain arches, while the arches at the end nearest the Temple Mount have heavy lintels. There are a number of inscriptions mentioning the name of Emir Tankiz, who served for 28 years (1312–1340) as governor of Damascus and viceroy of Syria; he made a major

A market in Jerusalem's Old City

contribution to the building of the market in its present form.

It seems likely that this square with the market buildings dates back to around the year 1000; the cotton market held here was of great importance in trade between East and West until Ottoman times. The "Cotton Gate" is best seen from the Temple Mount.

In the center of the market stands an old Turkish bath, the **Hammam esh Shifa** [31], formerly known as the Bath of Ala ed Din, which was supplied with water by channels from the underground cisterns on the Temple Mount.

Farther south, el-Wad Street runs into *Bab es Silsila Street,* (Street of the Chain Gate), one of the Old City's main traffic arteries. (The Bab es Silsila, or Chain Gate, is the only two-lane gateway giving access to the Temple Mount.)

The twin columns on each side date from the period of the Crusades.

Around the open space in front of the Bab es Silsila are a number of interesting buildings, including *Suleiman's Fountain,* constructed in the 16th century to store water from Solomon's Pools at Bethlehem. Many fountains in the Muslim Quarter incorporate decorative fragments from earlier buildings. This foundation is a late Roman sarcophagus, and some of the ornamentation dates from the time of the Crusades.

To the right of the gate is another religious college, the **Madrasa Tankiziyya** [32]. It was built in 1328 by Emir Tankiz, whose name is vigorously emblazoned in the Cotton Dealers' Market. Be sure to look at the fine entrance doorway, with its large inscription and three goblets as heraldic emblems (the Mameluke coat of arms), and the stalactite vaulting and modeling of the half-dome. For centuries the Madrasa Tankiziyya was the seat of the Is-

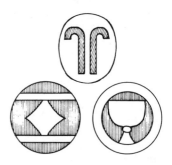

Mameluke heraldic emblems

lamic religious court; it is now occupied by various offices, including a section of the supreme religious court.

As you return toward el-Wad Street, you will cross over the old arch that spanned the Tyropoeon Valley 2,000 years ago, linking Herod's Temple with the upper part of Jerusalem. The only vestige of it is the Wilson Arch (named for its discoverer) below the Madrasa Tankiziyya, which can be seen from the Western Wall.

Halfway along this section of the street, on the right, is the **Tomb of Turkan Khatun** [33], a Mongol princess who died here while making her pilgrimage to Mecca. The inscription includes the name of her grandfather, a Mameluke in the service of Mohammed Uzbek, ruler of the Golden Horde (Tatars) from 1312–1340. The main feature of the tomb is its façade, with delicately carved arabesques in gray stone depicting leaves, palms, and geometric patterns.

Just after crossing el-Wad Street, you will see the **Turba Barakat Khan** [34] on the left, the 13th-century tomb of Emir Barakat Khan and his two sons. In 1900, the tomb was converted into the *Khalidi Library,* which contains over 12,000 valuable books and manuscripts. Among the building's especially interesting architectural features are the double lintel of the central window and the finely executed central portion of the facing, inscribed

with the word "Allah." The heraldic emblems on each side of the inscription are assumed to be those of Barakat Khan.

Farther along Bab es Silsila Street, you will encounter a narrow street on the right that runs under a vaulted entrance and into the large courtyard of the **Khan es Sultan** [35]. An old caravanserai built by Sultan Barquq in 1386, it had stables on the ground floor and rooms for travelers above. The inn is now occupied by workshops.

In the part of the Muslim Quarter north of the Temple Mount, tucked just inside and to the right of Saint Stephen's Gate, is ****Saint Anne's Church** [36] (*open daily from 8:00 A.M. to noon, 2:00– 6:00 P.M.*). This Romanesque building is one of Jerusalem's oldest and finest churches, a classic example of sacred architecture from the time of the Crusades. Saint Anne's was built in 1142 by Queen Arda, the widow of Baldwin I, the first ruler of the Latin Kingdom of Jerusalem. According to a Byzantine tradition, the *crypt* contains the birthplace of the Virgin Mary and her parents Anne and Joachim. A fifth-century Byzantine chapel dedicated to Saint Anne that stood on this site was completely destroyed by Caliph el-Hakim in 1009. On the ruins of that structure, the Crusaders built first a chapel, and then a church, to serve a convent of nuns. The facility soon proved to be too small for the growing community, and it was enlarged by moving the façade 7 meters (23 feet) forward. In 1192, Saladin converted the church and convent to a Koranic school, as attested by the Arabic inscription over the main doorway. Thereafter, the building fell into disrepair until the 19th century, when the sultan presented it and the adjoining area to the French in gratitude for their help in the Crimean War. Administration of the facility was taken over by the White Fathers.

Next door is the little *Biblical Museum,* with interesting excavations. You may see the museum only by special arrangement.

West of Saint Anne's Church is a large excavation area on the site of the Biblical **Pool of Bethesda** or *Sheep Pool (Piscina Probatica)* [37]. John wrote (5:2): "Now there is at Jerusalem by the sheep market a pool, which is called in the Hebrew tongue Bethesda [Place of mercy], having five porches." Many of the lame and ill came here, hoping to be made well again by the curative waters. Excavations by the White Fathers in 1871 brought to light the remains of two water basins and five porches. Here Christ cured a man who had been crippled for 38 years, saying to him "Rise, take up thy bed, and walk" (John 5:5–13). According to the historian Eusebius, one of the pools was used in early times for washing sheep— hence the name Sheep Pool.

From Saint Anne's Church, *el-Mujahideen Street* continues up into the Old City and comes to the site of the **Antonia Fortress** [38], which is known from its detailed description by Flavius Josephus (*The Jewish War,* 5, 238– 247). Unfortunately, little survives today. The fortress was built by Herod the Great between 37– 35 B.C., and named in honor of his friend Mark Antony (Marcus Antonius).

The huge, square fortress had massive towers at its four corners. The western third was paved with stone and used by the Roman forces for parades, training, and games. Because it was a good place from which to observe the Temple area—where riots and uprisings against Roman rule usually began—the fortress later housed a garrison. It was demolished by Titus during his destruction of Jerusalem in A.D. 70. It is traditionally held that it was here that Pontius Pilate, the Roman procurator, condemned Christ to death. (Many scholars now hold that the first Station on the Via Dolorosa at Al Omariya School was almost certainly not the spot where Jesus was condemned to death. According to John 19:13, the condemnation took place at the site known as Gabbatha, "the Pavement," on the highest point in the city—which is at the Citadel. In fact, the Citadel was the site of Herod's Palace, and Pilate usually resided there when he came from Caesarea to Jerusalem.)

Josephus reported that the fortress was built northwest of the Temple, "on a rock 50 cubits high;" its location may have been on the present-day site of the *Al*

Omariya Koranic School, which is reached from the street by a flight of steps. Certainly there is a very fine view of the Temple Mount from the top floor of Al Omariya.

Here the Roman soldiers mocked Jesus and set a crown of thorns on His head; thus began His Via Dolorosa (see Walk 6).

WALK 6: The ***Via Dolorosa (Way of the Cross)

See map on page 67 and plan on page 55.

The Way of the Cross follows the painful route that Jesus took from the Antonia Fortress, where He is believed to have been condemned to death by Pilate, to Calvary in the Church of the Holy Sepulcher. The route is around 700 meters (765 yards) long, its course is marked by the 14 Stations of the Cross, the last five of which are in the Church of the Holy Sepulcher.

Station I: Jesus is condemned to death, the first stop, sits atop what was probably the highest point in the *Antonia Fortress* (see page 65), now occupied by the *Al Omariya Koranic School.* Here—on the platform of the steps leading up to the school—is where Pontius Pilate is traditionally believed to have condemned Jesus to death. Christ's condemnation is commemorated every Friday afternoon by a procession of Italian Franciscans,

who leave here at 3:00 P.M. and follow the Via Dolorosa to the Church of the Holy Sepulcher.

Station II: Jesus takes up the Cross, is on the opposite side of the street from the Al Omariya School, at the foot of the steps up to the Franciscan convent. It is marked by a Roman numeral *II* on the wall to the left of the entrance.

The **Franciscan convent** has two chapels worth visiting: to the right is the Chapel of the Flagellation, and to the left the Chapel of the Judgment. The convent also houses an important *Bible school,* a library, and a museum with interesting excavations and displays on the flora and fauna of the Holy Land.

The *Chapel of the Flagellation* [A], which dates from medieval times, was renovated in 1927. The three stained-glass windows by Cambelotti depict the Flagellation, Pilate washing his hands, and

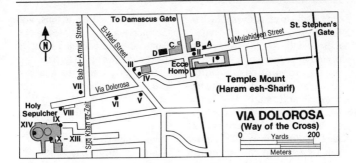

the triumph of Barabbas. The Crown of Thorns over the altar is a masterpiece of craftsmanship, as is the entire decoration of the interior.

The *Chapel of the Judgment* [B] is said to mark the spot where Pilate pronounced judgment on Jesus. The chapel, on a square plan, is in Byzantine style. Figures of tortured angels decorate the windows in the dome. Paintings depict the Judgment and Jesus's meeting with his mother (Station IV).

In the floor of the chapel are remains of the *Lithostrotos* (Pavement), in the courtyard of the Antonia Fortress, on which it is believed that Jesus was handed over to Pilate. The paving extends to the *Convent of the Sisters of Zion* [C], on the other side of the street.

The nuns at the convent are happy to show visitors the extensive ruins of the Antonia Fortress (*open 8:00 A.M. to noon, 2:30– 6:00 P.M.; closed on Sunday*). The ruins, along with models and graphic displays, give an excellent impression of the massive stone paving. The designs scratched on the stones were used by Roman soldiers, who played board games to while away the time in the fortress; it is said that the idea of giving Jesus a crown of thorns came to the soldiers during one such game. (John 19:1–2: "Then Pilate therefore took Jesus, and scourged Him. And the soldiers platted a crown of thorns, and put it on His head.")

The cisterns below the Lithostrotos are also worth a look. The cisterns collected rainwater, which flowed into them through small channels cut in the stones. You can see the cisterns through a small grating at the entrance to the Lithostrotos—but to get the full effect, you should go down the adjoining steps into the cisterns themselves.

The convent was founded by a Jewish convert, Father Alfons Ratisbone of Strasbourg, and construction began in 1857. The entranceway to the convent church—the *Ecce Homo Basilica*—incorporates an old arch that rose over the Via Dolorosa; the arch is said to mark the spot where Pilate exclaimed "Ecce homo!" ("Behold the man!"), as Jesus appeared after the scourging, wearing the crown of thorns and the purple robe given Him by the Roman soldiers (John 19:5). In actual fact, however, the Ecce Homo Arch was erected a century after the Crucifixion in A.D. 135; it was part of a three-arched triumphal gateway that formed the eastern entrance to Hadrian's pagan city, the Aelia Capitolina.

Beyond the *Ecce Homo Arch,* the Via Dolorosa slopes gently downhill. On the right, adjoining the entrance to the Convent of the Sisters of Zion, is a *Greek Orthodox monastery* [D]. It contains more ruins of the paving of the Antonia Fortress, as well as small recesses where the cavalry of the Roman legions probably tied up their horses. The caves or grottoes in the basement of the convent

On the Via Dolorosa

may have served as prisons, and the monks claim that Jesus and Barabbas were confined here, in the *Praetorium* of the fortress.

Soon afterwards, the Via Dolorosa takes a sharp bend to the left. To the right, along el-Wad Street, you will see the Damascus Gate.

Just around the corner to the left is **Station III: Jesus falls with the Cross.** A small Polish Catholic chapel was built here in 1941. The relief over the entrance depicts Jesus collapsing under the weight of the Cross. There is a small *museum.*

Beyond this, also on the left, is **Station IV: Jesus meets his Mother.** The relief over the doorway of a small chapel depicts the meeting. In the crypt of the adjoining *Armenian Church* is a sixth-century mosaic pavement marking the spot where Mary is believed to have stood when she met her Son.

Soon after this the Via Dolorosa turns to the right and continues up a narrow, stepped lane. On the corner, to the left, is a small 19th-century Franciscan chapel marking **Station V: Simon of Cyrene helps Jesus.**

Simon, who had come from Libya for the feast of the Passover, was compelled by the Roman soldiers to help Jesus carry the Cross. (Luke 23:26: "And as they led Him away, they laid hold upon one Simon, a Cyrenian, coming out of the country, and on him they laid the cross, that he might bear it after Jesus.")

Halfway up the little bazaar

street, on the left, is **Station VI: Veronica gives Jesus her handkerchief.** Like Station III, this Station is not mentioned in the Bible but, is based on a Christian legend. In an act of compassion, Veronica gave Jesus her handkerchief to wipe his brow. After He wiped his face, He returned it to Veronica; the handerchief retained the image of His face on it. The "handkerchief of Saint Veronica" has been preserved in Saint Peter's Basilica in Rome since A.D. 707.

On this spot is the *House of Saint Veronica,* with a *Greek Catholic church,* built in 1895 on the ruins of a sixth-century religious house. It was renovated in 1953 by Antonio Barluzzi.

The Via Dolorosa now runs into the main bazaar street, the covered *Suq Khan ez Zeit* (Oil Pressers' Street); to the right, it leads to the Damascus Gate, and to the left, to the Church of the Holy Sepulcher. After crossing this street you will see, just beyond the intersection on the right, **Station VII: Jesus falls for the second time.**

There are two *Franciscan chapels* at this station. In one of them is a monolithic column of reddish stone, a relic of Hadrian's Aelia Capitolina. Jesus is believed to have left the walled city here by the Porta Judiciaria (Gate of Judgment), so called because sentences of death were posted here. You are now on *el-Khanqa Street;* farther along, on the left, is **Station VIII: Jesus speaks to the women of Jerusalem.**

This Station marks the spot where Jesus foretold the destruction of Jerusalem (Luke 23:27–30); a cross is set into the outer wall of the *Greek Orthodox Monastery of Saint Charalambus.*

Since the direct road to the site of Calvary was covered over by buildings in the Middle Ages, the Via Dolorosa now runs back to the intersection of Suq Khan ez Zeit, the bazaar street, and turns right. A few yards along it, a flight of steps on the right ascends to **Station IX: Jesus falls for the third time.**

Here you will see the shaft of a *Roman column* built into the entrance to a *Coptic church.* The round dome visible above it is the roof of Saint Helen's Chapel in the Church of the Holy Sepulcher.

The *Coptic monastery,* built over the remains of a Crusader church, contains a huge underground cistern.

From here, you must return to Suq Khan ez Zeit since you are not allowed to pass through the Abyssinian Monastery. Continue past the *Church of the Redeemer* (see page 50), on the left, to reach a small doorway into the *Church of the Holy Sepulcher.* Stations X to XIV are on *Calvary* and at the *tomb* in the Church of the Holy Sepulcher (see Walk 3, and plan on page 55).

At the entrance to the *Calvary Chapel,* **Station X: Jesus is stripped of his garments and given vinegar to drink** is indicated by a mark on the floor. If you look up, you will see a mosaic of Abraham preparing to sacrifice his son, Isaac.

At the *Altar of the Nailing to the Cross* [E] is the next site, **Station XI: Jesus is nailed to the Cross.** A mosaic dating from Crusader times depicts the torturing and Crucifixion of Christ and the two thieves. The fine copper reliefs date from 1588.

Jesus's death is marked by **Station XII: Jesus dies on the Cross** at the *Altar of the Crucifixion* [H]. This Greek Orthodox altar has life-size icons of Christ, Mary, and John surrounded by many lamps.

The *Stabat Mater Altar* [G], between the other two altars, marks **Station XIII: Jesus is taken down from the Cross.**

You now reach the last Station of the Cross, **Station XIV: Jesus is laid in the tomb.** The *Holy Sepulcher* [L] is located in the domed *Rotunda* of the church.

WALK 7: The ***Temple Mount

See map on pages 44–45.

The mosques are open daily from 8:00 A.M.–4:00 P.M. except on Friday and during the midday prayers.

The Temple Mount is a sacred site, so dress accordingly. Admission is free, but there is a small charge for entry to the Dome of the Rock and the el-Aqsa Mosque (you may purchase tickets at the gates). Bags, cameras, and shoes must be left at the entrance. All visitors may leave the Temple Mount by any of the gates, but non-Muslims may enter only by certain gates: Bab el-Hadid (Iron Gate) or Bab el-Magharibeh (Moors' Gate).

This vast religious enclosure, crowned by the magnificent Dome of the Rock, is one of Jerusalem's most fabulous attractions. Known to the Arabs as Haram es Sharif (the Noble Sanctuary) and also called Mount Moriah for the rock on the summit, the Temple Mount is a place of enormous significance to the three great religions that claim Jerusalem as a holy city. For Jews, the Temple Mount is one of the holiest places in Israel: Abraham built an altar here; and Solomon later built the First Temple on this site, to house the Ark of the Covenant. The Temple Mount is also closely connected with the life and death of Christ, who taught in the Temple. The Temple Mount is the third holiest place in Islam after Mecca and Medina; the Muslim faith holds that Mohammed, on his horse Burak (Lightning), rode here from Medina (in Saudi Arabia) in a single night and then ascended into heaven. According to tradition, the Prophet would have taken the whole hill with him, had not the Archangel Gabriel held it back with his hand. Pious Muslims claim to see the marks left on the rock by Gabriel's fingers and the horse's hooves.

The Temple Mount covers a more or less rectangular area of about 14.5 hectares (36 acres) on the east side of the Old City—roughly one-sixth of its total area. The precincts are surrounded by a high, ten-gated wall, which also forms the wall of the Old City on the east and southeast sides.

The summit of the Temple Mount is nearly flat. A lower area, which takes up the greater part of the Mount, is largely undeveloped, with a scanty growth of trees; excavations are in progress around the edges.

Dominating it all, on the slightly higher central area, is the golden Dome of the Rock (sometimes erroneously referred to as the Mosque of Omar). With its spacious and peaceful forecourt, it is indeed a "noble sanctuary," and is a striking contrast to the narrow, crowded streets of the Old City.

History

A rich combination of ancient legend and fact makes up the history of the Temple Mount. In the time of the earliest Canaanite settlements of the Bronze Age, Mount Moriah sheltered the population from the wind. There is evidence that it was also used as a threshing floor, which David purchased from Araunah the Jebusite. David established an altar, where he made offerings to the Lord to check the course of the plague that had killed 70,000 people (2 Samuel 24:18–25). David's son Solomon built a temple on the rock (c. 960 B.C.) to house the Ark of the Covenant, and the rocky summit of the hill was levelled to provide a platform for it. This First Temple was destroyed in 587 B.C. when the Babylonian king Nebuchadnezzar took Jerusalem and condemned the Jews to their Babylonian Captivity. After their return from exile, the Temple was rebuilt (from 520 B.C.); this Second Temple stood for almost 500 years. The Western (Wailing) Wall contains stones from the temple enclosure wall of this period.

In the time of Nehemiah (c. 450–432 B.C.), Mount Moriah was again altered and the tower of Hananeel was built on its vulnerable north side. In Hellenistic times (333–63 B.C.), the Hasmoneans surrounded the Temple with walls and towers, making the whole precinct a well-fortified stronghold.

Herod the Great (37–4 B.C.) may have made the most stunning architectural contributions to the Temple Mount. In 20 B.C., he erected the Third (and last) Temple on the site of the Second Temple, which far surpassed its predecessors in size and beauty. Although not a trace survives today, Flavius Josephus rendered a detailed description of the building in his *Jewish Antiquities* (15, 380– 425).

In order to create a large enough base for his magnificent building, Herod leveled the irregular surface of the hill and surrounded the crest of the ridge on the east, south, and west sides by massive retaining walls. This mighty platform has survived all the vicissitudes of history, and the esplanade on the summit of the Mount remains as Herod left it.

Around all four sides of Herod's Temple *(see the plan on page 73)* ran covered galleries [A]; the one on the south side, called the Stoa of Herod [B], was twice the breadth of the others. At each end of the Stoa were monumental staircases [C]. An enclosing wall [D] 2 meters (6 feet) high surrounded the central precinct, which non-Jews were forbidden to enter on pain of death. Paul, in his epistle to the Ephesians (Ephesians 2:14), refers to this as the "wall of partition"—a symbol of the separation between Gentile and Jew. The Temple itself was at the west end of the precinct, with the altar of sacrifice [E] in the Court of the Priests. Beyond the Beautiful Gate was the Court of the Women [F]. The rock that is now preserved in the Dome of the Rock stood in the Holy of Holies, the innermost part of the Temple. The Antonia Fortress [G] was built against the north wall of the Temple precinct.

Titus burned the Temple when he destroyed Jerusalem in A.D. 70; in 136, Hadrian built a Temple of Jupiter on its ruins. Jews were admitted one day in the year to ritually anoint the Rock. Two hundred years later, the pagan temple of the Romans was destroyed by Constantine the Great.

In the later years of Byzantine rule, this spot within the Temple precincts fell into decay. When Caliph Omar entered Jerusalem in 638, he visited the rock—from which Mohammed is believed to have ridden up into heaven—and resolved to build a mosque here. Omar's mosque was a modest building, but later caliphs of the Umayyad dynasty would replace it with grander structures. In fact, fifty years later, the Caliph Abd el-Malik sought to surpass the magnificence and splendor of the mosque in Mecca, which was ruled by his rival Abdullah ibn Zobeir: The caliph built the fabulous Dome of the Rock in Jerusalem, on the spot where Mohammed departed for heaven to receive the commandments of the Lord. It was completed in 691.

In 1099, the Dome of the Rock was taken by the Crusaders and converted into a church they called Templum Domini. Saladin took over the site in 1187 when he ousted the Crusaders, and since then the basic structure of this imposing shrine has remained unchanged.

The present layout of the Temple Mount took shape during the Mameluke period, when further restoration and redecoration also enhanced the Dome. Suleiman the Magnificent rebuilt the walls in the 16th century, and refurbished the mosque with new windows, as well as fine mosaic and tile work.

The most important sights (see plan on page 75) on the Temple Mount [39] are the *Dome of the Rock* [A], the *Dome of the Chain* [B], the *Chapel of the Ascent into Heaven* [C], the *Qaytbay Fountain*

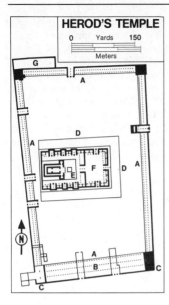

The Dome of the Rock and Mount
of Olives

[D], the *Pulpit* [E], the *el-Kas Fountain* with the *Olive Tree* [F], the *el-Aqsa Mosque* [G], the *Museum of Islamic Art* [H], *Solomon's Stables* [I], the *Golden Gate* [J] and *Solomon's Throne* [K].

The best place to start your tour of the Temple Mount is the *****Dome of the Rock** (*Qubbates Sakhra* in Arabic) [A], whose glittering golden dome is Jerusalem's landmark and emblem. This is the third most important Islamic holy place, after the Kaaba in Mecca and the mosque at Medina containing the tombs of Mohammed and his daughter Fatima. This harmoniously proportioned building is decorated externally with marble and Persian tiles. The octagonally de-

signed interior has a diameter of 53 meters (174 feet), and is articulated by two circles of columns.

The *inner colonnade,* which encloses the Sacred Rock and supports the dome, consists of eight marble pillars and 16 columns, some topped by Byzantine and Greek capitals. The columns in both the inner and outer colonnades are of different sizes; those bearing crosses were taken from churches. The wrought-iron grille linking the columns in the inner ring was handcrafted by the French in the 12th century; it was set up here when the Crusaders converted the mosque into a church.

Faced externally with gilded aluminum sheets, the massive *dome* has a diameter of 20.3 meters (66 feet) and rises to a height of 20.5 meters (67 feet). Most of its 16 stained-glass windows date from the 18th and 19th centuries; however, a few date to the 15th century. Beneath the dome lies the *Sacred Rock*, a monolith almost 18 meters (58 feet) long, 13.5 meters (44 feet) across, and 1.5–2 meters (5–6 feet) high. In Jewish tradition, the Sacred Rock marks the site where Abraham prepared to sacrifice Isaac; pious Muslims claim to see the hoofprints of Mohammed's horse, Burak, on the rock, as well as the fingerprints of the Archangel Gabriel.

The *reliquary* beside the rock contains a hair from Mohammed's beard. Muslims call the cave under the rock *Bir el-Arwah* (Well of the Souls), believing that the voices of the dead rise in prayer here and mingle with the waterfalls on the rivers of paradise as they enter into eternity.

The floor of the Dome of the Rock is paved with marble slabs, and the walls above the windowsills are faced with Persian tiles presented by Suleiman the Magnificent in 1561. Their matte blue coloring contrasts strikingly with the white and green of the square panels along the edge of the tiled area. The arcades have beautiful mosaics in geometric and floral designs, and are further enhanced by ornate Arabic script. (Islamic law forbids the representation of humans and animals in art.)

Although the fine inscription on both sides of the inner octagon ascribes the building of the Dome to the Abbasid caliph el-Mamun,

tradition has it that he substituted his own name for that of Abd el-Malik, who actually had it built; Mamun's deception was discovered because he neglected to change the date of construction. Texts from the Koran in decorative script run around the outer walls like a frieze. The carved ceilings on both sides of the octagon display the Mameluke star as their principal motif. These ceilings were not part of the original structure, but were added in the 13th century and then restored several times thereafter.

Of the mosque's four doorways, the finest is the one on the south side, facing Mecca and the el-Aqsa Mosque. You reach the doorway by passing through an ornate portico with eight linked columns.

*

Leaving the Dome of the Rock, on the east side—exactly in the center of the Temple Mount—you will see the ****Dome of the Chain** (in Arabic, *Qubbat es Silsila*) [B]. This mosque, dating from the same period as the Dome of the Rock, looks like a small-scale replica of it. Like the larger mosques, it has two rings of columns, six in the inner ring and eleven in the outer; all 17—which are mostly of Byzantine origin—can be seen from any point in the interior.

Various legends are associated with the Dome of the Chain. It is said that David's courthouse stood here, and Solomon hung a chain

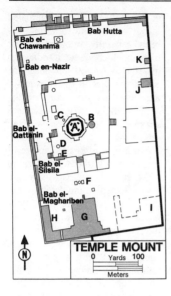

Bab el-Chawanima
Bab Hutta
Bab en-Nazir
K
J
C
B
A
Bab el-Qattanin
D
E
Bab el-Silsila
F
Bab el-Maghariben
H   G
I

TEMPLE MOUNT
0   Yards   100

Meters

N

from the roof of the building: Anyone taking an oath was required to hold the chain, and would be struck by lightning if he lied. One popular but improbable tale tells us that this mosque predates the Dome of the Rock, and it so impressed Caliph Abd el-Malik that he modeled his mosque on its smaller predecessor. Another legend asserts that the Dome of the Chain housed the caliph's state treasury—a likely but unproven hypothesis.

On the northwest side of the Dome of the Rock is the small **Chapel of the Ascent into Heaven** (*Qubbat el-Mirraj*), built to commemorate Mohammed's nocturnal ride. According to an inscription, the chapel was renovated in 1200. It is very similar to

the Chapel of the Ascension on the Mount of Olives, which dates from the period of the Crusades.

A number of smaller domed buildings lend a picturesque touch to the northwest side of the large plaza. Notable among them are the 16th-century *Mihrab en Nebi* (Prayer Niche of the Prophet, 1538), the 19th-century *Qubbat el-Khalil* (Dome of Hebron), the *Qubbat el-Khadr* (Dome of Saint George), and the 15th-century *Qubbat el-Arwaah* (Dome of the Winds).

Another attraction of the Temple Mount is the ****Sabil Qaytbay** [D], a public fountain built by Sultan Qaytbay in 1482. Located at the southwest corner of the plaza, the fountain is often overlooked by visitors, who tend to be entirely caught up in the Dome of the Rock. A classic example of Mameluke architecture, the Sabil Qaytbay evidently owes its lavish style to the extensive experience of its builder, who specialized in ornate funerary monuments. A richly decorative inscription runs around all four sides of the fountain; in addition to texts from the Koran, it includes references to an earlier fountain as well as to restoration work carried out in 1883.

The lintels of the fountain house windows are in Ottoman style, while the ribbon work of the interior, with its star motifs, reflects Mameluke influence. Troughs originally stood under the window, and water flowed into them from the fountain inside.

Before you go through the arcading *(mawazin)* and down the steps to the southern part of the platform, it is worth taking a look at the elegant **minbar** (pulpit) [E], built by Burhan ed Din in 1456. If you stand with your back to the Dome of the Rock, you will see the minbar off on the right.

When you come to the foot of the steps, you will see the **el-Kas Fountain** [F], in which Muslims wash their feet before entering the mosque. Built in 709, it is surrounded by a large number of underground cisterns for storing water. To the right of the fountain is an *olive tree* that is said to date from the time of Mohammed's nocturnal ride.

**El-Aqsa Mosque

Next you will move on to **el-Aqsa Mosque** [G], whose name in Arabic, *Jami el-Aqsa*, means the "Distant" or "Farther Mosque"—a reference to Mohammed's night ride from the beginning of the 17th sura (chapter) of the Koran: "Glory be to Him who carried His servant by night from the Holy Mosque to the Farther Mosque."

The first el-Aqsa Mosque was built between 705–715 in the reign of Caliph el-Walid, a son of Abd el-Malik. Nothing remains of this first structure, which was destroyed by earthquake within 60 years of its completion, but its original proportions are known. The most important rebuilding of the mosque was carried out by Caliph ez Zahir after an earthquake in 1033. The seven-aisled layout of the new building has been generally retained in the form in which we see it today. An inscription from 1035 dates the oldest mosaics in the mosque—appearing on the drum of the dome and the front of the arch spanning the central aisle—from this period.

For a time after the capture of Jerusalem by the Crusaders in 1099, the mosque was used as a royal residence and later as the headquarters of the Knights Templar. In 1187, Saladin returned the building to its original function, embellishing it with mosaics and equipping it with a sumptuous mihrab (prayer niche) and an elaborately carved cedarwood pulpit. (In a tragic act of vandalism, the pulpit—considered the finest in the whole of the East—was burned in 1969 by a deranged Christian visitor who wanted to rid the Temple Mount of "heathen" buildings.)

Suleiman the Magnificent restored the mosque and installed glass windows in the 16th century. The last major rebuilding and restoration was carried out in 1927 and 1938–1942, after earthquakes had caused heavy damage. The columns of Carrara marble were presented by Mussolini, and the painting of the vaulted ceilings was financed by King Farouk of Egypt.

King Abdullah of Transjordan, grandfather of King Hussein, was assassinated shortly after entering the mosque in 1951, in the presence of his grandson. The marks of the bullets can still be seen on one of the columns.

Able to accommodate 5,000 worshipers, the el-Aqsa Mosque is 80 meters (260 feet) long by 55 meters (180 feet) wide. The imposing 13th-century *porch* has seven arches, corresponding to the seven aisles of the mosque. From the porch, after passing a *cistern,* you come into the impressive *prayer hall,* with its forest of 81 columns and 33 pillars. The *mihrab,* indicating the direction of Mecca, is on the south side of the mosque, opposite the main entrance. The *dome,* in front of the mihrab, is smaller than the Dome of the Rock, rising to a height of 18 meters (59 feet) above the floor and borne on eight piers. The dome is surfaced with sheets of lead, which creates its bright silvery gleam. The striking contrast between this dome and the golden Dome of the Rock is especially breathtaking when both domes glow in the evening light.

Immediately inside the *main entrance* is a flight of steps leading down to a basement. Normally this interesting area is closed-off by a green door, but it is sometimes possible to win permission to enter from the Supreme Islamic Council, located near the Bab el-Chawanima. In the interior, a long, vaulted passage leads to a vestibule in front of a walled-up double doorway—the *Hulda Gate,* referred to in the Talmud, which was also known as the *Mole's Gate* because it gave access

to a long, low tunnel leading into the heart of the Temple Mount. In the time of Herod, this gate was one of the main entrances to the Temple.

*

When you leave el-Aqsa, you may still feel fresh enough to visit the **Museum of Islamic Art** [H], in the southwest corner of the Temple Mount (to the right when facing the el-Aqsa Mosque). The museum has a rich collection of material recovered by excavations, and works of Islamic art of many different periods.

On the other side of the el-Aqsa Mosque, in the southeast corner of the Temple Mount, is a vaulted underground area known as **Solomon's Stables** [I]. The area can be seen only with special permission from the Supreme Islamic Council. In reality, these stables have no connection with Solomon: The outer walls date from the time of Herod the Great, and the Knights Templar used the stables for their war horses. Ten rows of pillars support the roof; holes in the pillars show where the horses were tethered.

In the extreme southeast corner of the plaza, near Solomon's Stables, are two features with traditional Christian associations. In the crypt of a basilica dating from the time of Justinian is "Christ's Cradle," represented by a Roman niche laid down horizontally. In the angle of the platform walls is the spot in the Temple where Satan tried to tempt Jesus.

In the east wall of the Temple Mount (also the wall of the Old City), is the ***Golden Gate** [J], now closed. There are many legends associated with this gate, but little is known of its real history. The Mishnah (Middoth 1:3) tells us that in the time of Herod, the Temple Mount had an east gate facing the Mount of Olives. Some Herodian elements have indeed been identified in the Golden Gate. It is probable, however, that the gate was constructed in the mid-fifth century during the reign of Empress Eudocia, to commemorate Peter's healing of a lame man at the Beautiful Gate (Acts 3:1–10), as it was then called. The present name resulted from a confusion between the Greek word *horaia* (beautiful), and the Latin *aurea* (golden).

The gate was closed when Jerusalem came under Islamic rule, to deny unbelievers access to the Temple Mount. In the Middle Ages, it was opened only twice a year—on Palm Sunday to commemorate the day on which Jesus rode through this gate into the city seated on an ass, and on Good Friday, the day of His Crucifixion. Presumably, there were also practical grounds (safety considerations, no doubt) for closing the gate. There is a legend that the gate will reopen only when Christ returns for the Last Judgment. The Muslims call one part of the gate the "Gate of Grace" and the other the "Gate of Atonement," for they believe that through this gate the righteous will one day enter along with their Judge.

Along the wall from the Golden Gate is the so-called **Throne of Solomon** [K], from which Solomon is said to have watched the building of the Temple. It is now a mosque.

WALK 8: The Jewish Quarter and the Western (Wailing) Wall

See map on pages 44–45.

This walking tour takes you from Jewish Quarter Street through the principal areas of the quarter, and ends at the Western (Wailing) Wall, which is the holiest site in Jerusalem for Jews.

The Jewish Quarter lies in the southeastern part of the Old City. Excavations have shown that this area was settled during the time of the First Temple (seventh century B.C.). Its precincts were enlarged considerably during the Hasmonean and Herodian periods (in the time of the Second Temple); with its palaces and fine houses, it became known as the "Upper City." This development reached its peak in the reign of Herod the Great (37–4 B.C.), whose patronage made the area the center of life for the community. After the destruction of Jerusalem by the Romans in A.D. 70 under Titus, and then in 135 at the hands of Hadrian, little was left of the Old City. For centuries, it was closed to all Jews, and the few remaining Jewish families were driven out by the Crusaders.

During the period of Mameluke rule—when the first synagogue was built (1267)—and under Turkish rule, there was a slow, gradual process of resettlement, which continued more actively under the British mandate (1917–1948). In 1948, the Jewish Quarter was occupied by Arab troops and destroyed once again; the Jewish population sought refuge in the New City. In the Six-Day War of 1967, the Israelis reclaimed the quarter along with the rest of the Old City; since that time it has undergone a continuing process of reconstruction and development.

The process of restoration has led to many exciting archaeological discoveries. Amid the rubble of the old Jewish Quarter, archaeologists found an opportunity to retrieve and reconstruct much of the area's ancient history. During redevelopment of the quarter, every effort has been made toward sensible and harmonious planning so that the new and the old blend charmingly together. Today the Jewish Quarter is a picturesque and fascinating area—arguably the most delightful part of the Old City.

The walking tour starts in *Jewish Quarter Street* (Rehov ha-Yehudim), at the **Ramban Synagogue** [40], the first synagogue built in Jerusalem in the years after Christ's birth. The synagogue was founded by Rabbi Moses Nachmanides, a well-known medieval Jewish scholar. Upon settling in Jerusalem in 1267, he was appalled to find only two Jewish families left in the city; a copy of a letter by the Rabbi lamenting this situation is displayed in the synagogue. The building was erected on the ruins of the Crusader Church of Saint Martin, as evidenced by the massive pillars in the interior.

The persecutions of Jews, particularly in Spain (1492) and in other parts of Europe, brought more Jews to Jerusalem. The Sephardim (Spanish Jews) and Ashkenazim (Eastern European Jews) worshiped together in the Ramban Synagogue until 1585, when the Mufti of Jerusalem turned the building into a mosque. After destruction and rebuilding, the synagogue reopened in 1967 on the same site as its 13th-century predecessor.

The **Hurva Synagogue** [41] was also built on the ruins of the Church of Saint Martin. In 1700, the first organized group of Ashkenazi immigrants, a party of 1,000 Polish Jews, bought land in Jerusalem and began to build a synagogue. It remained when the Jewish community was split and the Muslims hindered the building of the synagogue: hence its name (the Hebrew word *hurva* means "ruin"). The building was finally completed in 1864, but was destroyed in the 1948 fighting, and has remained in a state of ruin ever since.

In Jewish Quarter Street, you'll find some recently excavated vestiges of the Roman *cardo maximus,* the main street of Jeru-

In the Old City

salem in Roman and Byzantine times. This handsome 8-meter- (26-foot-) wide avenue, lined by columns and now flanked by elegant shops, ran through the whole of the Old City from the Damascus Gate to the Zion Gate.

A little way south is ***Jerusalem Square** [42], from which there is one of the finest prospects in the Old City, extending over the Old City itself, Siloam, and the Kidron Valley to the Judean Hills and the Dead Sea. Here, too, is the large *Rabbinical Center,* with training schools and seminaries for Sephardic Jews.

Beyond the Rabbinical Center, a short flight of steps leads down to the **Yochanan Ben Zakkai Synagogue** [43], in the *Four Synagogue Complex (open 9:00 A.M.– 4:00 P.M.; Friday to 2:00 P.M.; Saturday during services).* This synagogue was built in 1586 to compensate for the loss of the Ramban Synagogue and to pro-

vide a place of worship for Jews who settled here after their expulsion from Spain in 1492. It became the religious and spiritual center of Sephardic Jews in Jerusalem, under the vigorous leadership of the Chief Rabbi, Rishon LeZion.

The synagogue complex consists of four adjoining prayer halls that were destroyed in 1948 but have been rebuilt since. The largest of the four is the Yochanan Ben Zakkai, named for the great Talmudic scholar who is said to have preached here at the time of the Roman conquest of Jerusalem. The Jewish faith holds that the prophet Elijah will announce the coming of the Messiah on the site of the adjoining 400-year-old *Elijah the Prophet Synagogue.* The carved wooden ark containing the Torah scrolls dates from the same period as the synagogue. The ark came from an Italian synagogue destroyed in Word War II.

From here *Beit Hamachase Street* leads to **German Square** [44], which was settled in the mid-19th century by Jewish immigrants from Germany and Holland. Destroyed in 1948, the houses have since been rebuilt.

***Western (Wailing Wall)

Continuing along Beit Hamachase Street, you come to the square facing the *****Western (Wailing) Wall** [45], considered to be the holiest place in Israel by the Jews. The Western Wall (in Hebrew, *Hakotel ha-Maaravi*) is a fragment of the western section of a retaining wall built around the Temple esplanade by Herod in 20 B.C. After the destruction of the Temple by the Romans in A.D. 70, Jews were routinely denied access to their most sacred site; after Bar-Kochba's uprising (A.D. 132–135), the Romans banned the Jews from this area on pain of death. The Western Wall was as close as Jews could get to the Temple—and thus, it was here that they chose to pray.

The original length of this western wall was 485 meters (530 yards); the surviving part at its southern end is 170 meters (186 yards). Until 1967, there were buildings near the wall, but these were demolished, leaving a wide and impressive space in front of the holy wall.

The Western Wall is built of 26 courses of massive stone blocks dating from Herodian times, of which only seven are exposed to view above ground level. Only a few of the other 19 courses have

At the Western Wall

been excavated: They can be seen outside the Temple Mount at the southwest corner. Above the seven courses of the Herodian period are 17 courses of smaller stones; the first four of these, which use larger stones than the rest, are Roman, while the others date from later centuries. The topmost courses of the 18-meter- (60-foot-) high wall were added during the British mandate (1917–1948).

Jews believe that the Shechinah (the "Indwelling" of God), which once hovered over the Second Temple in the mystical form of a dove, has been confined to the Western Wall since the destruction of the Temple. Muslims say that Mohammed, on his wondrous ride from Mecca to Jerusalem, left his horse Burak here when he went up to the Temple Mount to pray.

At the ends of the Western Wall, excavations have revealed two distinctive archaeological features. At the north end is *Wilson's Arch* (excavated by Sir Charles Wilson in 1868), through which the road from the Tyropoeon Valley reached the Temple in Herod's time. At the southern end is a huge door lintel, 7 meters (23 feet) long, from one of the original entrances to the Temple; its placement in the wall indicates how much the level of the ground has risen since Roman times.

Prayers are said at the Western Wall from morning until late at night; men and women are segregated, as they would be in an Orthodox synagogue. Some worshipers follow the old custom of writing their supplications on small pieces of paper and placing them in cracks in the wall. Particularly large numbers of people come to the Wall on the Sabbath and on Jewish festivals, and the yeshiva students (seminarians) often sing there. At these times photography is prohibited, as is smoking. Remember, too, that this is a sacred place—your clothing and behavior should be in accordance with the contemplative spiritual tone here.

WALK 9: Mount Zion

See color map.

Located just outside the present boundaries of the Old City, Mount Zion is a holy place to Jews, Christians, and Muslims. It was here that Jesus celebrated the Last Supper with His disciples. Mount Zion is also believed to be where the Virgin Mary died. For Jews and Muslims, Mount Zion is sacred because it is traditionally regarded as the location of the tomb of David, who is revered by both faiths.

Mount Zion extends onto the part of the western hill that lies outside the south wall of the Old City at the Zion Gate. It is surrounded by two valleys, the Hinnom Valley on the west and south and the Tyropoeon Valley on the east.

History

In the time of the First Temple, during the reign of David (tenth century B.C.), Mount Zion lay outside the city walls. It was brought within the walls for the first time under the Hasmoneans (Maccabees) in the second century B.C., who made use of the natural fortifications that the mount afforded to help their defense of Jerusalem against the Syrians.

When Titus took Jerusalem in A.D. 70, the walls bounding the Old City were destroyed again. Sixty-five years later, Hadrian laid out the new plan for his Aelia Capitolina, once more excluding Mount Zion from its precincts. However, the walls built by Empress Eudocia between A.D. 444–460 encompassed Mount Zion.

The sixth-century mosaic map in the paving of a church in Madaba, Jordan, of which a copy can be seen at the Damascus Gate (see page 43), gives an astonishingly exact picture of Mount Zion as it was in Byzantine times. From the city gate (in front, left) the wall runs south past David's Tower (beyond the gate), taking in the church on Mount Zion (to the right) and the Siloam Church (right, to the rear). The colonnaded street ends at a gate (in the center) in the old walls of the Aelia Capitolina.

The walls built by Empress Eudocia stood until 975, when they were razed by Caliph el-Aziz because the area they enclosed was too vast to be defended effectively. This change reduced Jerusalem to the size of the present Old City, the area that Suleiman the Magnificent included when he rebuilt the walls (1537–1540). One legend holds that Suleiman ordered the builders of the walls executed because they had failed to include Mount Zion.

The principal sights on Mount Zion [46] are the *House of Caiaphas* [47], the *Franciscan Convent* [48], the *Cenacle* (the "Upper Room" referred to in the Gospels as the scene of the Last Supper) [49], the *Tomb of David* [50], the *Church of the Dormition* [51], the *Chamber of the Holocaust* [52] and the *Church of Saint Peter in Gallicantu* [53].

Leave the Old City by the Zion Gate and take the street that runs up opposite it. On the right is the supposed site of the **House of Caiaphas** [47], high priest of Jerusalem and member of the Sanhedrin, who judged Christ. Its location, which includes an excellent view of the Temple precinct, makes it quite probable that Caiaphas did live here (also see the Church of Saint Peter in Gallicantu, on page 84). The earliest reference to this as the site of his residence dates from the fourth century. The ruins of a 15th-century Armenian church now occupy the spot. Nearby are the ruins of a Byzantine church and a Crusader chapel, as well as the tombs of the Armenian Patriarchs of Jerusalem.

From the gate leading to the House of Caiaphas, turn right, and and then make another right at the next road junction. This route will bring you to the **Franciscan Convent** [48]. In 1551, the Mamelukes expelled the Franciscans and turned their Gothic church into a mosque; for almost five centuries thereafter, both Jews and Christians were prohibited from returning to the holy church of Zion. Archaeological evidence has shown that a church burned down on this site in 614 and again in 965; it has not been determined whether it was always a Christian church or if it was originally a synagogue that had been taken over by the Christian community. When the Crusaders arrived in 1099, the church, which lay outside the city walls, already had been destroyed. The building that now stands here was erected in 1936, when the Franciscans were permitted to return to Mount Zion.

A domed *mosque* stands near the convent, its minaret offering a fine view of Jerusalem.

A flight of steps and a narrow terrace lead to the ****Cenacle** [49], believed to have been the scene of the Last Supper. Opposite the Islamic *mihrab* (prayer niche), you can see the place where Jesus broke the bread and poured the wine for His disciples—initiating the sacrament of the Eucharist in Christian tradition.

The Cenacle was once part of the *Church of Zion,* built by the Franciscans on the remains of a Crusader chapel. The massive piers and ribbed vaulting date to the time of the Crusades. According to the Acts of the Apostles, the Holy Ghost descended on the Apostles at Pentecost in an "upper room," later identified with the Cenacle.

Under the Cenacle is the *Hall of the Washing of the Feet,* now a synagogue. In front of a niche in the adjoining room, is the ****Tomb of David** [50]. This stone sarcophagus is covered by an embroidered velvet cloth that features a series of silver crowns—one for each year of Israel's independence. The walls are decorated with Armenian tiles. Although the tomb is one of the most important Jewish shrines in Jerusalem, it is doubtful that David is actually buried here. Because of the niche in the north wall, archaeologists believe that this room is an ancient synagogue; it is more likely that David was buried on Mount Ophel, to the south of the Temple Mount.

From here you must retrace your steps to the road junction and turn right to reach the ****Church of the Dormition** [51]. With its squat bell tower topped by a conical dome, this Roman Catholic church is one of the most striking buildings in Jerusalem and a prominent landmark. Designed by a German architect, the neo-Romanesque style church was built at the turn of the 19th century on the supposed site of the Virgin

Mary's death. Consecrated in 1910, it is dedicated to the Dormition (the Falling Asleep) of the Virgin, a feast traditionally celebrated by the Greek Orthodox church. The church suffered some damage in the wars of 1948 and 1967 but has since been completely restored; it is now held by the Benedictines. Its most notable features are the *Crypt of the Dormition,* with a mosaic dome over a figure of the Virgin on her deathbed, and the *mosaic pavement,* with symbolic designs.

Close by is the **Chamber of the Holocaust** [52], dedicated to the six million Jews who died during World War II. It contains much documentation on the period and a memorial room.

On the eastern slopes of Mount Zion stands the **Church of Saint Peter in Gallicantu** [53], built in 1931, which belongs to the Roman Catholic Order of Assumptionist Fathers. The church marks the spot where Peter is believed to have denied Jesus three times before the cock crowed twice (Mark 14:72); "in Gallicantu" means "at the crowing of the cock." Assumptionists claim that the house of Caiaphas stood here. It seems more likely, however, that the high priest's house was on higher ground (also see the House of Caiaphas, page 83).

The church has a colorful mosaic façade and contains rock-cut cellars, cisterns, and stables dating from the period between the reign of Herod and the destruction of the Temple by Titus (27 B.C.–

A.D. 70). Guides will be glad to show you the so-called "Prison of Christ," which gives a good hint as to what a dungeon of the period was like.

Excavations brought to light an ancient stepped path here, leading from Mount Zion to the Pool of Siloam, which Jesus probably used on his way from the Last Supper to Gethsemane. There are fine views of Jerusalem and its three valleys from the path that winds around the church.

WALK 10: **The Kidron Valley, the City of David and the Pool of Siloam

See color map.

This walk takes you through the Kidron Valley—the Valley of the Kings—in the east and the Tyropoeon (Cheese Makers') Valley in the west, along roads that meet at Mount Ophel.

The highlights of the tour include the tunnel of the Gihon Spring—a miracle of engineering, even by modern standards. Although the sights described here can be reached by car or bus, you will absorb more of the rich historical flavor of the area if you go on foot.

Starting from *Jericho Road* on the east side of the Old City, take *Siloam (Siloah) Road,* which branches off to the right soon after the *Church of All Nations* (Gethsemane) and runs into the *Kidron Valley.* After passing four *tombs* on the left, you come to *Mount Ophel,* below the Temple Mount, where David founded his city of Jerusalem. Continue to the site of the *Pool of Siloam,* now occupied by the Arab village of *Silwan.*

The **Kidron Valley** [54], called the "Valley of Jehosophat" in the Old Testament and the "brook Cedron" in the New Testament, is also known as the *Valley of the Kings* because it is said that David, Solomon, and other Jewish kings are buried here. The valley historically marks the scene of the Last Judgment when the trumpets shall announce the coming of the Lord (Joel 3:12); thus, it served as a traditional Jewish burial place for centuries.

On the left-hand side of Siloah Road you will see the ***Tomb of Absalom** [55], or *Absalom's Monument,* the largest and most imposing of the four tombs. Despite its name, there is no doubt that the monument was erected 700 years after Absalom's day, in the time of the Second Temple (first century A.D.). The square lower structure of the tomb was hewn from the native rock. The upper section, which resembles the top of a bottle, was built in masonry. The position of the entrance to the burial chamber shows that it was hewn from the rock before the outer structure was formed. The attribution of the tomb to Ab-

Tomb of Absalom

salom, the beloved son of David, is probably based on the second book of Samuel, which tells us that before Absalom's death, he had "reared up for himself a pillar . . . in the king's dale" (2 Samuel 18:18).

Beyond this, on the left, is the **Tomb of Jehosophat** [56], carved from the same rock. This also seems to date from the first century A.D.; the decorations on the pediment are in the same style as those on the Tomb of Absalom.

Farther along on the right is the **Tomb of the Bene Hezir** [57]. The oldest of the four tombs, it dates from the second century B.C. A skeleton found here in the fourth century A.D. was believed

to be that of James the Less, one of the Twelve Apostles; in subsequent centuries the tomb was ascribed to Saint James. It is clear from the inscription on the architrave above the two Doric columns, however, that this was the tomb of a priestly family, the Bene Hezir.

Moving on, you will see the **Tomb of Zacharias** [58] on the right, carved entirely from the rock and surmounted by a pyramidal tip. This tomb is the latest and best preserved of the four, dating from the first century A.D. Christians believe it to be the tomb of the prophet Zacharias, husband of Elizabeth and father of John the Baptist. A tunnel running through the rock connects this chamber to the tomb of the Bene Hezir.

Farther south, in a bank on the left of the road, are a number of other interesting burial spots. One of the oldest is the *Tomb of the Pharaoh's Daughter,* which dates from between the ninth and seventh centuries B.C.

Continuing along the Kidron Valley, you will come to a flight of stairs on the right that lead to the ****Gihon Spring** [59]. Also known as the *Spring of the Virgin Mary,* because she is said to have drawn water here to wash Jesus's clothes, it is the area's only abundant year-round source of water. It played an important part in the history and development of ancient Jerusalem. Before David's arrival in 997 B.C., the inhabitants of the little town of Jebus on Mount Ophel had driven a tunnel through the rock to obtain water for their beleaguered city. David captured the town by sending his men in through the tunnel, and established his capital here. He then brought the Ark of the Covenant to his new city, thus making Jerusalem the hub of his kingdom. Fragments of the old wall built by the Jebusites to defend their town can still be seen.

The name Gihon is first mentioned in the account of the time when Solomon was anointed as king (1 Kings 1). The name means "gusher;" indeed, the spring justifies its name by spewing great quantities of water for half an hour or so and then remaining quiescent for anywhere from four to ten hours. Its output is sufficient to supply water to a population of 2,500.

In order to ensure an adequate water supply for his growing city, Solomon (965–928 B.C.) built the **Gihon Tunnel** [61] along the foot of the hill. Sluices, placed at intervals along the tunnel, enabled water to be stored and channeled to the fields in the Kidron Valley. The tunnel, a cross section of which still can be seen at the tip of Mount Ophel, ended in a large pool at the end of the *Tyropoeon Valley*. This area, now known as *Birket el-Hamra,* is planted with fig trees.

The Gihon Spring lay outside the city walls, however, and the pool and the tunnel were vulnerable to enemy attack; therefore, King Hezekiah (727–698 B.C.) resolved to conceal the spring. He made a new pool, the Pool of Si-

loam (Siloah), and constructed a conduit to bring water into the city (2 Kings 20:20). "This same Hezekiah also stopped the upper watercourse of Gihon, and brought it straight down to the west side of the city of David" (2 Chronicles 32:30). Hezekiah's tunnel channeled the water to the *Pool of Siloam,* which now lay within the walls and provided a secure water supply in the event of attack.

In 1880, a Hebrew inscription was found in the tunnel near the pool. It describes how the tunnelers worked from both ends: "Behold the tunnel. This is the history of its building. When the men swung their picks, one towards the other, and when only three cubits remained to be cut, then they heard the voice of one calling to his comrade, for there was an echo in the rock from the north and from the south. So smote the workmen on the day they broke through, one towards the other, stroke upon stroke; and the water streamed from the spring into the pool, 1200 cubits long. The height of the rock over their heads was 100 cubits." A copy of the inscription can be seen in the Israel Museum (see page 101); the original is in Turkey's Istanbul Museum.

The tunnel was a great engineering achievement for its time. Five hundred twelve meters (560 yards) long, it follows a winding course to the pool. If you are not afraid of getting your feet wet, you can walk through the tunnel from the Gihon Spring to the Pool of Siloam; and if you give a small tip to the custodian, he will supply candles and open the iron gate at the spring. The tunnel is narrow and very low at some points, so you will have to keep your head down, but there is no danger. Even if the water begins to rise (the "gusher" effect described earlier) you need not worry, for its depth only ranges between 30–50 centimeters (12–20 inches).

No trace remains of the original form of the **Pool of Siloam** (Siloah) [62], which was the scene of Christ's miraculous healing of the blind man (John 9:11). The decimation of Jerusalem by the Romans in A.D. 70 was so thorough that they "destroyed the whole city as far as Siloah" (Flavius Josephus, *The Jewish War*, 6, 363). There is archaeological evidence that the pool was reconstructed during the reign of Hadrian (A.D. 135). The first church on the site was built by the Byzantine empress Eudocia about A.D. 450. The pool was given its present form in the 19th century; its fate in the intervening centuries is unknown. The *mosque* nearby was built in 1890.

If you continue along the valley bottom you finally come to the cemetery of **Haceldama** (*Aceldama*) [63], the "Field of Blood." This potter's field "to bury strangers in" (Matthew 27:5–10) was purchased with the thirty pieces of silver Judas received when he betrayed Christ. Another reference is found in Acts 1:18–19, which states that Judas, who had bought the field, died there. For many centuries Haceldama was the burial place for pilgrims who died in Jerusalem. The Greek *Monastery of Saint Onuphrius* stands here now; if you visit the monastery you can see the cave where the Apostles are said to have hidden during the trial and condemnation of Jesus.

WALK 11: Around the **Mount of Olives

See color map.

Rising to a height of about 100 meters (330 feet) above the city, the Mount of Olives is a spectacular place from which to view the Old City, the Judean Desert, the Jordan Valley, the Dead Sea, and the hills of Moab. The Garden of Gethsemane here was the scene of Judas's betrayal of Christ. Judas knew this place well, for "Jesus ofttimes resorted thither with His disciples" (John 18:1–2).

This walk takes you through the chief sights on the Mount, including the Garden of Gethsemane and the Church of All Nations. You conclude your tour in Bethphage (from which Jesus set out for Jerusalem on Palm Sunday) and Bethany, where Jesus often stayed and where He raised Lazarus from the dead.

Unless you want to walk uphill and down dale through rolling country, there is really only one possible route for this walk. From Bethany, follow the ridge to Bethphage and continue from there along another ridge to Et Tur (roughly on the line of the modern road) before turning down toward Gethsemane.

The first place of interest on this walk around the ****Mount of Olives** [64] is the ****Tomb of the Virgin** [65] (see plan below). It can be reached by taking *Jericho Road,* to the east of the Temple Mount, or alternatively by leaving from the *Lion Gate.* The *façade* of the church and the monumental *staircase* within that leads down into the *crypt* date from the period of the Crusades (early 12th century). Halfway down the steps, on the right, is the *Tomb of the Crusader Queen Melisande* [A]; on the left is a tomb niche belonging to the family of *Baldwin II* [B]. The *crypt* [C] was originally Byzantine, though most of it was destroyed by Caliph el-Hakim in

1009. Opposite the foot of the stairs is a medieval entrance to a number of underground *tombs* [D]. Looking to the right in the dimly lit room, you can just distinguish an *altar,* behind which is the rock-cut *Tomb of the Virgin* [E]. (Whether this tomb really marks the grave of the Virgin is still open to argument; many people believe she is buried at Ephesus in Turkey.) To the left, higher up, is a *grating* [F] covering part of a tomb that dates to the first century A.D.

Because Mohammed saw a light here on his nocturnal journey to Jerusalem, the vaulted *mihrab* [G] on the other side of the Tomb of the Virgin is a holy place for Muslims. To the left of the stairs is a *cistern* [H], whose water is credited with the power to cure all diseases. The eastern part of the chapel is dedicated to the Virgin's parents, Anne and Joachim, and the western part to Joseph, her husband.

Leaving the chapel and going past a narrow passage, you will see the **Grotto of Gethsemane** on the left, in part of the *Garden of Gethsemane.* After the Last Supper on Mount Zion, Jesus came here with his disciples "as He was wont" (Luke 22:39). He then withdrew from the disciples "about a stone's cast" (Luke 22:41) to pray

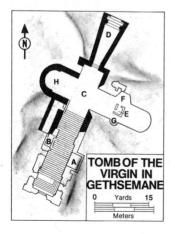

TOMB OF THE VIRGIN IN GETHSEMANE

0   Yards   15

Meters

on the spot now occupied by the Church of All Nations. The Grotto (*open 8:30 A.M. to noon and 2:00–5:00 P.M.*) has been restored several times. Immediately to the right of the entrance are two layers of *mosaic pavement* dating from Byzantine times. A *grating* covers a floor on a lower level, with a channel in the stone running down to it. It is thought that olive oil was produced in this basement (in Hebrew, *Gat-shemen* means "oil press").

Now return to Jericho Road and turn left to reach the ****Church of All Nations** [67], also called the *Church of the Agony.* This is the spot where, shortly before being arrested, Jesus prayed that "if it were possible, the hour might pass from him" (Mark 14:35).

It is not known exactly where Jesus knelt in prayer, but it must have been very near the road running up the Mount of Olives. The church cannot, therefore, be far from the actual spot.

The present Church of All Nations occupies the site of earlier

The Church of All Nations

churches discovered in excavations in 1891. The first of these churches was erected between A.D. 379 and 384; smaller than the present church, it was destroyed by an earthquake around 750. In 1170, the Crusaders built another church on the site, slightly off a true east-west orientation. How long this church stood is not known; the last mention of it dates from 1345. The Church of All Nations, which is served by Franciscans, was rebuilt between 1919–1924 with money contributed by many different countries. Designed by Antonio Barluzzi, it is an imposing and beautiful building with twelve domes, a sumptuous interior, and beautiful mosaics over the entrance.

In the interior of the church, you can see part of the rock on which Jesus knelt in prayer in front of the *altar*. The positions of the walls and pillars of the fourth-century church are marked by black lines. The Byzantine *mosaic pavement* is protected by sheets of glass. Part of the present south wall is built of massive blocks of stone, marking the site of the nave of the Crusader church.

Adjoining the church is the ***Garden of Gethsemane** [68], where Judas betrayed Jesus. To reach the entrance to the Garden from the Church of All Nations, walk along the fence and turn right into a narrow street (now asphalted) that runs up onto the Mount of Olives, bearing right behind the church. Eight ancient olive trees stand here, believed to be

Gethsemane: an ancient olive tree

direct descendants of the trees that grew here in the time of Jesus.

A short, steep climb will take you to the entrance to the Russian Orthodox ***Church of Saint Mary Magdalene** [69], built in 1888 by Czar Alexander III of Russia in memory of his mother, Empress Maria Alexandrovna. This church, a fine example of old Russian architecture with seven golden domes, fits perfectly into the townscape of Jerusalem. The church contains the *tomb of Grand Princess Elizabeth Fyodorovna*, who was assassinated in 1918, as well as old *icons* and beautiful *ceiling and wall paintings.* (*Open Sundays 10:00 A.M. to noon; Thursdays and Saturdays 9:00 A.M. to noon, 2:00–5:00 P.M.*).

Continuing uphill, you come to a church on the left with a tear-shaped dome—the **Church of Dominus Flevit** (The Lord Wept) [70]. A chapel stood just below here in the fifth century, on the spot where Jesus wept, foreseeing the destruction of Jerusalem (Luke 19:41). The present church, which belongs to the Franciscans, was built in 1955 on the foundations of a Byzantine chapel. The position of the Byzantine altar can still be identified, and parts of the old mosaic pavement have been preserved.

The slopes of the Mount of Olives below the church have served as a vast cemetery area since ancient times. This originates from the Jewish belief that the nearby Kidron Valley is the future scene of the Messiah's appearance, where he will raise the dead and lead them into Jerusalem through the Golden Gate (the Gate of Mercy). In 1954, archaeologists discovered a cemetery that had been in use from 1600–1300 B.C.; it was used again from 100 B.C.– A.D. 135, and from A.D. 200–400. The excavations yielded much information about different types of burial.

Still farther up the Mount of Olives, on the right, are the **Tombs of the Prophets** [71]. The placard on the iron gate at the entrance to these catacombs claims that they contain the tombs of the prophets Haggai, Zechariah, and Malachi, who lived in the sixth and fifth centuries B.C. This assertion is most likely false, however, because the graves are typical *kokhim* (shaft graves) of a kind found only from the first century A.D. and later. The layout of the catacombs is quite interesting, as it has two concentric passages containing 36 tomb niches.

When you reach the summit of the Mount of Olives, you will be treated to a stunning view of Jerusalem. Now turn left and head toward the village of *Et Tur.* Just before the turn off, on the right, is the **Pater Noster Church** [72], built on the site of the grotto where Jesus taught the Apostles to say the Lord's Prayer (Luke 11:2–4) and spoke of His second coming (Matthew 24–25). In 333, the empress Helena, mother of Constantine the Great, built the Eleona Church here, traces of which were discovered during excavations in 1910. The present buildings were erected in 1868 by Princesse de La Tour d'Auvergne; she bought the site, with its ruins dating from the time of the Crusades, and built a church and convent for Carmelite nuns here. Features of particular interest are the *faience tiles* in the convent, with the Lord's Prayer in 44 different languages and, behind the convent, the original *grotto* over which the Byzantine church was built. Half of Empress Helena's basilica has been rebuilt; it gives a good idea of what the Eleona Church was like, with its sanctuary on a higher level over the grotto.

From here, continue straight ahead into the village of *Et Tur.* The ***Chapel of the Ascension** [73], on the right, marks the spot where Jesus ascended into heaven. An account of the Ascension is given by Luke: "And He led them

out as far as to Bethany, and He lifted up his hands, and He blessed them. And it came to pass, while He blessed them, He was parted from them, and carried up into heaven" (Luke 24:50–51).

Nothing remains of the first Byzantine building, a rotunda, that once stood here. The present octagonal chapel dates from the Crusader period; the Muslims, to whom the building has belonged since 1198, added the dome. The chapel contains the *Sacred Rock,* which bears a mark believed to be the imprint of Christ's foot. If you ask, the custodian will allow you to go up into the gallery over the chapel, where you will have one of the finest views of the Old City, the Jordan Valley, and the Dead Sea.

Farther along the main road you'll find a narrow side road on the right that leads to the **Russian Church** [74], whose bell tower is the highest point in Jerusalem. The Orthodox believe that the church, built in 1880, marks the true site of Christ's Ascension. From the top of the 60-meter- (200-foot-) high bell tower, there is a breathtaking panorama of the city and the surrounding area.

Side trip to Mount Scopus

If you return to the main road (Mount of Olives Road), you can take a side trip to **Mount Scopus** [75], to the north of the Mount of Olives. The name Scopus (from the Hebrew *Zofim,* meaning "watchman") is well chosen, considering its history. It was from here that Alexander the Great is said to have looked down on the city in 333 B.C. The Roman emperor Titus launched his attack on Jerusalem from here in A.D. 70; the Crusaders also used the spot as a staging area. Between 1948–1967, Mount Scopus was an Israeli enclave within Arab territory.

The first buildings of note make up the complex known as **Viri Galilaei** [76], which belongs to the Greek Orthodox church. It stands on the site where the witnesses of the Ascension saw "two men . . . in white apparel" (Acts 1:10–11).

At the crossroads where the Mount of Olives Road meets *Mount Scopus Road,* turn right along Mount Scopus Road. On the right, you will see the *Augusta Victoria Hospital* [77], which opened in 1910. Beyond you'll find the *Truman Research Center* [78], which has gained an international reputation as a meeting place for scientists, and the ancient *Amphitheater* [79], from which there is a superb view of the Judean Desert.

Farther on are the striking buildings occupied by the *Jewish National Library* [80], the *Hebrew University* [81] with its various institutes and its 13,000 students, and the *Hadassah Hospital* [82], whose synagogue has stained-glass windows by Marc Chagall. Finally, at the north end of Mount Scopus, there is the *British Military Cemetery* [83] from the First World War.

To **Bethphage and **Bethany

From the *Pater Noster Church* (see page 92) take the road that goes off to the left and runs east. A 20-minute walk will bring you to **Bethphage** [84], traditionally considered the point from which Jesus set out for his triumphal entry into Jerusalem from Jericho. This is the starting point of the Palm Sunday procession that ends in Saint Anne's Church at the Lion Gate.

A medieval chapel once stood on the site of the present 19th-century *church;* it contained a stone that the Crusaders believed was used by Jesus to mount the ass that he rode into Jerusalem. In 1883, the Franciscans built a small church on the ruins of the medieval chapel. The stone has medieval carvings depicting the raising of Lazarus, the taking of the ass, and the Palm Sunday procession. Behind the church are cisterns, tombs, and a wine press decorated with mosaic tiles, all dating to the time of Christ.

To reach **Bethany** [85], the last place on this walk, turn left when you leave the church at Bethphage and follow the road along the high monastery walls. In 50 meters (55 yards) or so, take the stony track to the left where the road forks and you will soon see Bethany. (If you wish to travel by car or bus, take the Jericho Road, which runs around the Mount of

Olives and passes the terraced village of Bethany on the left.)

Jesus stayed in Bethany with his friends Martha, Mary, and Lazarus during His visits to Jerusalem. (The Arabic name of Bethany, *el-Azariya,* preserves the old Greek name Lazarion, the "place of Lazarus.") Here, He raised Lazarus from the dead (John 11), and it was also here that Mary anointed His feet (John 12:3). Excavations have shown that many churches have occupied this site; the first was recorded in the fourth century, and the second was built in the sixth century. A Benedictine abbey was built here by Queen Melisande in 1138, during the Crusades.

The present *Church of Lazarus* was built by the Franciscans in 1953. Its modern mosaics depict the events of Christ's last days on earth; fragments of ancient mosaics in the floor, together with an old mill and an oil press, bear witness to the eventful history of the little town.

Adjoining the Church of Lazarus is the 15th-century *el-Ozir Mosque,* from which visitors used to find their way to the *Tomb of Lazarus.* You now enter the tomb directly from the road by going down a flight of steps.

Continuing up the road, you pass a new *Greek Orthodox church* and come to a junction. To the left are the ruins of a watchtower from the Crusader period; to the right is a path that winds its way up to Bethphage.

WALK 12: The New City—North

See color map.

Once you have explored what the Old City has to offer, be sure to venture beyond Suleiman's walls for a sampling of the flavor of the New City. This walk will take you to the chief sights lying north of the Old City: the Rockefeller Museum; Garden Tomb; Saint Stephen's Church; Mea Shearim; Tombs of the Kings; and the Tomb of Simon the Just. An optional side trip, best taken by car or bus, includes three other interesting spots in the northern part of the New City: Ammunition Hill; Tombs of the Sanhedrin; and the Biblical Zoo.

The starting point of this walk is the *Damascus Gate* [3] in the north wall of the Old City. From here, turn right up the broad *Suleiman Street;* opposite the northeast corner of the walls, you will see the ****Rockefeller Museum** [86]. Built in 1927, with the help of John D. Rockefeller, the museum is devoted to archaeology (*open Sunday–Thursday, 10:00 A.M.–6:00 P.M.; Fridays and Saturdays 10:00 A.M.–2:00 P.M.*). It contains a wide range of antiquities of high artistic and historical value from Palestine and neighboring regions.

The *entrance lobby* [A] leads

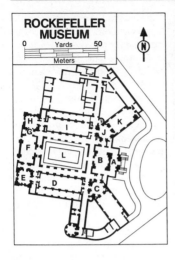

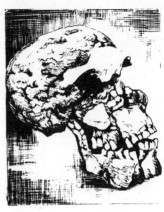

The skull of Carmel Man

into the *Tower Room* [B], with casts of reliefs from the Nineveh palace of the Assyrian king Sennacherib, whose attempt to take Jerusalem in 701 B.C. failed. To the left is the *South Octagon* [C], with interesting finds from Egypt and Mesopotamia. Particularly notable is a stela of the Egyptian king Seti I (1319– 1304 B.C.).

Beyond this is the *South Gallery* [D], which contains objects covering the time span from about 200,000 B.C. to A.D. 1200. The most interesting exhibits are the Galilee Skull, which is about 200,000 years old; the skull of Carmel Man (about 100,000 years old); and various symbolic figures and weapons of bronze and copper ranging in date between 3000– 1500 B.C. Moving on again, you will come to the *South Room* [E], with wood carvings from the eighth-century el-Aqsa Mosque.

In the *West Gallery* [F] are sculptures from the Khirbet el-Mafjar palace in Jericho, which was built by the Umayyad Caliph Hisham in 724 and destroyed by an earthquake in 747. The *Jewel Room* [G] displays a range of fine ancient jewelry, including enormous gold earrings from the Roman period.

Next you will go through the *North Room* [H] into the *North Gallery* [I], where a variety of material, dating from 1200 B.C. to A.D 1700, is displayed. Be sure to note the terra-cotta sarcophagus with a human face (c. 1100 B.C.); the "Lachish letters"—painted clay shards with Hebrew characters—from 588 B.C.; ivories from the palace of King Ahab in Samaria, from about 850 B.C.; a Greek oil flask (c. 450 B.C.); and a Hellenistic bronze statuette of Heracles (second century B.C.). From here, the *North Octagon* [J] leads into the *Northeast Gallery* [K], with Phoenician coins from Tyre and wood and leather objects (c. 3500 B.C.).

The last stop in the museum is the *Courtyard* [L], which has a small pool in the center. Around the walls are ten reliefs representing the various countries that have influenced the culture and history of Palestine.

Now return to the Damascus Gate and take *Nablus Road* (Derech Shechem), going north; turn into the first road on the right, and in a few yards you will come to the ***Garden Tomb** [87] (*open daily, except Sundays, 8:00 A.M.–1:00 P.M., 3:00–5:30 P.M.*).

This rock-hewn tomb was discovered in 1882 by the British general Charles George Gordon, who was struck by the resemblance of a nearby rock to a skull. Gordon believed that Christ's tomb lay outside the present city walls, which he thought followed the same course as at the time of the Crucifixion. He felt that the skull-like rock must be Golgotha (Place of the Skull), and he became convinced that this spot was the true tomb of Christ.

Recent excavations have proved, however, that the site now occupied by the Church of the Holy Sepulcher was brought within the city after Christ's death by the construction of a new wall. Gordon's theory still has many supporters, particularly in England, and the custodians of the site are an Anglican organization. If you walk from the Damascus

Gate toward Herod's Gate you will see what Gordon saw: Above the bus station are two holes in the rock, the result of weathering, which look like the eye sockets of a skull.

Defenders of Gordon's theory also point to the fact that the layout of this two-chambered tomb broadly matches the description of the one Christ was laid in according to the Gospels: For example, there is a window through which light fell on the empty tomb when the women went there on Easter Sunday.

Most authorities now agree that the Garden Tomb dates from Byzantine (not Roman) times; yet, its general structure, with the groove in which a stone could be rolled in front of the entrance, is representative of tombs in the time of Christ—much more so than what remains of the tomb in the Church of the Holy Sepulcher.

Now return to the Nablus Road and continue north. A short distance along the road, on the right, is a *Dominican monastery* founded by French monks, with ***Saint Stephen's Church** [88]. The church and monastery occupy the site of a basilica built by Empress Eudocia in A.D. 460 to house the relics of Saint Stephen, the first Christian martyr. (His life story is told in Acts 6:8–7:60). The basilica was burned down by the Persians in 614, rebuilt by the Crusaders, and finally destroyed by Saladin in 1187 when he took Jerusalem. In 1881, French Dominicans acquired the site, carried out excavations, and built a new church on the ruins of the Byzantine basilica. The *French Institute of Biblical Archaeology* is housed in the complex of buildings associated with the church.

From Saint Stephen's Church, you can take a side trip into ****Mea Shearim,** the quarter occupied by Orthodox Jews, by going west along *Shiftei Yisrael Street* and *Mea Shearim Street.* This is one of the oldest and most exotic quarters of Jerusalem outside the Old City. It was established in 1875 by Orthodox Jews from Europe as a Jewish ghetto in an Arab environment, and has preserved its strict Orthodox flavor to the present day.

The name Mea Shearim means "a hundredfold"—a reference to Genesis 26:12: "Then Isaac sowed in that land, and received in the same year an hundredfold; and the Lord blessed him." This passage from the Torah was part of the reading for the week of November 1873, when this bastion of Orthodox Judaism was established— hence the name.

The Mea Shearim quarter is inhabited almost exclusively by those who maintain the strictest adherence to Orthodoxy; most wear the Hasidic garb of 18th- and 19th-century Europe. Here, particularly during preparations for *Shabbos* (the Sabbath) on Friday afternoons, as well as on holy days, you can see the *bachurei yeshiva* (seminarians) with their *peiyot* (side curls), *streimel* (felt hats), and caftan. These ultraorthodox Jews reject Zionism and

In Mea Shearim

the Supreme Rabbinical Council, and elect their own rabbis and religious courts. Since they believe that only the Messiah can lead Jews into the Promised Land, they do not recognize the political leaders of Israel. Accordingly, they pay no taxes, do no military service, and recognize no secular jurisdiction.

The market, the hub of Mea Shearim's life, is at its busiest on Friday afternoons before the beginning of the Sabbath at sundown. A visit to the market at this time is an experience you won't forget. All business, down to the purchase of a simple loaf of bread, is suspended just before sundown, so there is tremendous hustle and bustle to make all ready. To avoid offending the local people, married women and *all* men should wear some form of head covering; all women should dress with modesty in mind—no shorts, trousers, short skirts, short sleeves, or off-the-shoulder dresses or tops. It is forbidden to drive in Mea Shearim on the Sabbath and on holy days. Cameras are likewise unwelcome.

Mea Shearim has numerous Jewish religious institutions—schools, theological seminaries, synagogues—and almost all the male inhabitants are rabbis, teachers, students, or writers of religious works.

If you continue north on the Nablus Road and turn right into *Saladin Street,* you will come to the entrance to the ***Tombs of the Kings** [90] on the right. This monumental complex—containing perhaps the most impressive rock-cut tombs in the whole of Israel—was originally believed to have been the burial place of the kings of Judah. Although the name has stuck, we now know that these tombs were constructed by Helen, the widowed queen of Adiabene in Mesopotamia. She converted to Judaism and came to Jerusalem as a pilgrim between A.D. 46 and 48. There was a great famine in the city at that time, and Helen brought in supplies of food from Egypt and Cyprus. She continued to live in Jerusalem for 20 years, and when her son died, she built this complex of tombs; soon afterwards, she and some of her other descendants were buried here, as well.

You enter the tombs via a broad flight of steps hewn from the rock, down which rainwater flows into two ancient cisterns. Water from these cisterns once supplied the basin in the vestibule, which served for the washing of the dead. A narrow entrance to the left of the vestibule, which could be closed by rolling a stone in front of it, leads into a central courtyard, where there are the entrances to four tomb chambers containing double *kokhim,* or shaft graves. A secret staircase led to the chamber containing the queen's sarcophagus; fortunately, the staircase escaped the notice of tomb robbers (the sarcophagus now rests in the Louvre in Paris).

Now return to the Nablus Road and continue north. This route will bring you to the ***Tomb of Simon the Just** [91], on the right. Jewish tradition ascribes this tomb to Simon, a high priest in the time of the Second Temple (335–270 B.C.), who said, "The world rests on three columns: law, service in the Temple, and brotherly love." This is an important place of pilgrimage for Oriental Jews. Archaeological evidence has shown that the tomb is not really Simon's, however, but that of a Roman woman named Julia Sabina.

Side trip by car or bus

The last three sights in this group are probably a little too far away to be reached comfortably on foot; they are included here, however, because of their proximity to the other sights featured in Walk 12.

To reach **Ammunition Hill** [92], continue north through the *Sheikh Jarrah Quarter,* with its small mosque, and turn left just before the end of the Nablus Road into a narrow side street running up the hill. From 1948–1967, the hill was in Jordanian hands, and during the Six-Day War, it was the decisive strategic point in the Jewish conquest of East Jerusalem. The five hours of bitter hand-to-hand fighting that ended in the taking of the hill are documented in the museum on Ammunition Hill.

From here follow *Levi Eshkol Street* into *Shmuel Hanavi Street,* continue north, and then turn right into *Sanhedrin Street.* In the gardens at the far end of this street are the **Tombs of the Sanhedrin** [93]. The most notable feature of these tombs is the pediment, dating from the first century A.D. It is decorated with pomegranates and other fruits between stylized acanthus leaves—one of the finest pieces of carving in Jerusalem. The large tomb chamber imme-diately inside the entrance contains two rows of shaft tombs, one over the other, with arcosolia (arched tomb recesses) linking the upper tombs in pairs. There are several smaller chambers on different levels. The tombs are believed to have housed members of the Sanhedrin, the supreme Jewish religious and civic council of which the priest Caiaphas was a member.

Now return south on Shmuel Hanavi Street and turn right into *Bar Ilan Street* and *Yirmiyahu Street,* and then right again into *Shamgar Street,* which leads to the **Biblical Zoo** [94]. Established in 1939, the zoo was founded, as you might suspect, with the object of bringing together all the animals, birds, and reptiles mentioned in the Bible. The zoo suffered damage during the war of 1948 and was removed to Mount Scopus, where it remained between 1948 and 1967; the Six-Day War did further damage to it. As a result, the zoo lost much of its stock, but it has now been built up again to include more than 500 animals.

WALK 13: The New City—West

See color map.

This last walk in Jerusalem fittingly brings you into the heart of 20th-century Israel. West Jerusalem is modern in every sense—hardly anyone lived in its districts before 1860—although there are several old sights worth visiting. The main features of the walk include Mamilla Independence Park, Herod's Family Tomb, the Montefiore Windmill, Jason's Tomb, the Monastery of the Cross, the Israel Museum, the Knesset, the Hebrew University, Mount Herzl, Yad Vashem, and the Holyland Hotel, with the model of Herodian Jerusalem.

From the *Jaffa Gate,* [1] take *Mamilla Street* and then *Gershon Agron Street,* where you will see the main entrance to **Mamilla Independence Park** [95]. It occupies part of a Muslim cemetery that has not been used for burials. At its eastern end is an interesting square-domed building, the *Tomb of Emir Aidughdi Kubaki,* who was interred here in 1289; the architectural features date from the time of the Crusades. Born a slave in Syria, Aidughdi Kubaki rose to become governor of Safed and Aleppo; but he fell into disfavor and was exiled to Jerusalem, where he died. In the center of the park is the enormous *Mamilla Pool* (5,400 square meters; 6,452 square yards). A canal (probably constructed in Herod's time) linked it to the Patriarchs' Pool in the Christian Quarter, and the system supplied water to the Old City. Its other name, the Lion's Den, stems from a legend that a lion guarded the remains of Christian martyrs here.

Now turn back on Agron Street to the junction with *Mamilla Street* and turn right into *King David Street.* On the left, beyond the King David Hotel, is a cul-de-sac, *Abu Sikhra Street.* At the end of the street is a large round stone marking the entrance to the **Family Tomb of Herod the Great** [96] (*open Sunday–Thursday, 9:00 A.M.–5:00 P.M.; Fridays 9:00 A.M.–2:00 P.M.; Saturdays 10:00 A.M.–5:00 P.M.*). Traversing the forecourt, you will come to a narrow passage that leads to four tomb chambers walled with dressed stone; three of the chambers are square and the fourth is rectangular. The tombs probably had been raided by tomb robbers before archaeologists made their way here in 1892. While Herod himself was buried in the Herodion (see page 218), we know from Flavius Josephus that various members of his family were buried here, including his wife Mariamne, her mother Alexandra, his father Antipas, and others.

After taking a look around, return to King David Street and continue along it to *Plumer Square,* to the left of which is the **Montefiore Windmill** [97], a striking, relatively modern addition to Jerusalem's skyline. The windmill was built in 1857 by Sir Moses Montefiore, an English philanthropist, to mark the construction

The Montefiore Windmill

of the first new district outside the Old City. This part of the city, originally called *Yemin Moshe,* is now an artists' quarter. The windmill houses a museum commemorating Sir Moses' contribution to the development of Jerusalem.

From here you can either walk or ride (on a No. 5 bus) along *Keren Hayessod Street* and over the junction in *Zarfat Square* into *Azza Street,* then to the right along *Radak Street* and to the left along *Alfasi Street.* Here, in *Rehavya Square,* the center of a quiet residential district, is **Jason's Tomb** [98] (*open daily 10:00 A.M.–5:00 P.M.; Fridays 10:00 A.M.– 2:00 P.M.*). Also known as the *Alfasi Cave,* the tomb, which dates from the Roman era, is inscribed with the name Jason, accompanied by representations of a warship and a merchant ship. A vaulted entrance leads into three forecourts and then into a vestibule containing the inscriptions, surmounted by a pyramid. The tomb chamber contains eight *kokhim* shaft tombs.

A little to the west, on the right-hand side of *Ben Zvi Boulevard,* is the **Monastery of the Cross** [99]. Legend has it that the tree from which Christ's cross was made grew here. The monastery was founded by King Bagrat of Georgia (Russia) in 1039–1056 on the ruins of a fifth-century church. In later centuries the monastery was partly destroyed and then rebuilt several times. When the number of Georgian monks shrank, the monastery was sold to the Greek Orthodox church. The

monastery's high medieval walls conceal an extensive complex of buildings, with arcades, staircases, and terraces—all planted with ancient cypresses. The *church,* with its gleaming silver dome, dates largely from the Crusader period and contains old frescoes and mosaics. (*Open daily except Saturday 8:00 A.M. to noon; in the afternoon by appointment, tel. 28 49 17*).

Nearby is the ****Israel Museum** [100], an eclectic collection housed in four separate museums (described below). The museum complex, which opened in 1965, has some of the finest exhibits of their kind of any museum in the world. (*Open Sunday, Monday, Wednesday, and Thursday 10:00 A.M.–5:00 P.M.; Tuesday 4:00– 10:00 P.M.; Friday and Saturday 10:00 A.M.–2:00 P.M. A single ticket covers admission to all four museums.*)

The *Bezalel Museum of Folk Art and Traditions* contains a large collection of Jewish folk art of the 17th to 19th centuries, and a particularly fine collection of Judaica. There is also a worthy assemblage of classic and modern art, including works by Rembrandt, Chagall, and Picasso.

The *Bronfmann Archaeological Museum,* housed in a number of separate pavilions, has artifacts dating from the Stone Age to the Middle Ages. Among the most notable items are a Nabatean bronze leopard from Avedat (first century), and sacrificial altars from Arad and Hazor. There is also an interesting section devoted to the Bar-Kochba uprising in the second century.

The *Billy Rose Sculpture Garden,* designed by the late landscape architect Isamu Noguchi, is laid out on artificially-constructed, semicircular rock terraces. Rose's collection, which he bequeathed to the museum, includes works by Rodin, Daumier, Epstein, and Lipchitz.

The most fascinating of the four museums, however, is undoubtedly the *Shrine of the Book,* where the Dead Sea Scrolls are housed. The discovery of these scrolls—which were written (or perhaps copied) between the first century B.C. and A.D. 68—constituted one of the most stunning archaeological finds of all time. The first scrolls were unearthed by a goatherd in 1947, who found them in a cave above the Dead Sea at Qumran. Included in this spectacular treasure trove are two copies of the Book of

In the Shrine of the Book

Isaiah, both predating any previously known Hebrew texts by 1,000 years. The *Manual of Discipline* from the ascetic Essene settlement at Qumran (see page 229) was also in the find, along with letters written by Bar-Kochba and fragments of scrolls from Masada. The Shrine of the Book is designed to recreate the feeling of one of the caves in which the scrolls were found: a tunnel-like entrance slopes down to the main chamber on a lower level.

From the Israel Museum, you can walk or ride (buses 5, 9, and 16) a short distance to the modern building occupied by the Israeli Parliament, the ***Knesset** [101], on the other side of *Ruppin Street.* In front of the rectangular Knesset

The Shrine of the Book

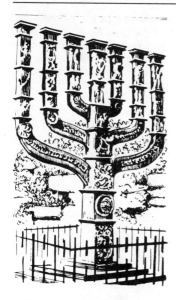

Menorah in front of the Knesset

Building is an enormous *Menorah,* the candelabrum that is Israel's national emblem, as well as the symbol of Hannukah. This huge bronze sculpture, fashioned by the British artist Benno Elkan, was a gift from the British Labour Party, led at the time by Clement Attlee. The Menorah is decorated with themes from Jewish history. The Parliament Building itself, financed by the British Rothschild dynasty, has been the seat of the Israeli Parliament since 1966 (from 1949–1966, the Knesset met in a building in King George Street).

In the Knesset chamber, the 120 members are seated in a semicircle. Visitors are admitted to the gallery—after strict identity and security checks—when the Knesset is in session. (*Monday and Tuesday 4:00–9:00 P.M.; Wednesday 11:00 A.M.–1:00 P.M. There are conducted tours of the building daily.*)

Farther along Ruppin Street, is the **New Hebrew University** [102], set in extensive gardens. (You can walk or ride the 5, 19, 16, 24, or 28 bus there.) This new campus in the *Givat Ram* district was laid out in 1954, when it became evident that the university on Mount Scopus—situated in an enclave within what was then Jordanian territory—could not function effectively. The principal buildings serving the University's 17,000 students are the *Jewish National Library* (the largest library in the whole of the Near East), the *Auditorium,* the *Student Center,* the *College of Social Work,* the *Sports Stadium,* the *Swimming Pool,* the *Amphitheater,* and the futuristic *Synagogue.* After the Six-Day War in 1967, the original Hebrew University on Mount Scopus was extended and incorporated in the new university complex. (*There are conducted tours of the campus daily at 9:00 and 11:00 A.M., starting from the Auditorium.*)

From the university, Ruppin Street continues north, where it runs into *Herzl Boulevard.* ***Mount Herzl** stretches along to the left of the boulevard. Buses 12, 18, 20, 21, and 26 will also bring you to this lovely park honoring Dr. Theodor Herzl, the

Theodor Herzl

founder of the political Zionist movement and spiritual father of the new state of Israel. (*Mount Herzl is open daily 8:00 A.M.– 6:00 P.M. See the park plan below.*)

The *Herzl Museum* [A] has a collection of pictures, letters, documents, and other mementoes; the Herzl Room shows how he lived and worked during his last years in Vienna (1898–1904).

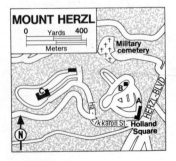

Near the museum, *Herzl's Tomb* [B], a large black granite structure, rests atop the highest point on the hill. Herzl's remains, and those of his family, were brought here from Vienna in 1949. Other national leaders of Israel, including Zeev Jabotinsky, Levi Eshkol, the third prime minister of Israel, and Golda Meir, are also buried on Mount Herzl.

On the north side of Mount Herzl is the *Military Cemetery,* with the graves of Israeli soldiers who fell in the War of Independence, the Sinai campaign, and the Six-Day War.

From Mount Herzl, *Zicharon Street* runs in a wide curve to the *Mount of Remembrance* (also reached by bus no. 33), with the national memorial ****Yad Vashem** [C]. (*Open Sunday– Thursday, 9:00 A.M.–6:00 P.M.; Fridays, 9:00 A.M.–2:00 P.M.*) This somber site, a place of pilgrimage for many who visit Israel, is dedicated to the memory of the six million Jews killed in the Holocaust. The *Avenue of the Righteous* is framed by a path lined with carob trees that bear plaques inscribed with the names of Gentiles who risked their lives helping Jews. This pathway leads to the *Yad Vashem* (Remembrance and Name) monument, a simple memorial erected in 1957. An eternal flame burns at the monument in remembrance of those who died, and the names of the various Nazi death camps are carved into the paving. Attached to the memorial is a documentation and research center in which the horrors of the Nazi period are preserved; much of the documentation was recorded by the Nazis themselves. The *Hall of Names* contains information concerning about half of the Jews who lost their lives.

From Mount Herzl, it is 2.5 km. (1.5 miles) south on *Harav Uziel Street* to the *Holyland Hotel,* where you can see the ***model of Herodian Jerusalem** [104] in its gardens (also accessible by buses 12, 18, 20, 21, and 26). The remarkable scale model, masterminded by Professor Avi Yona of the Hebrew University, covers several hundred square yards. It gives a fascinating picture of the city of Herod the Great, with its palaces, streets, houses, and Temple, just before the first Jewish uprising against the Romans in A.D. 66.

*Tel Aviv-Yafo (Jaffa)

New York with a Mediterranean flair—that describes Tel Aviv. Bustling by day and lively by night, Israel's largest city has its share of enthusiastic boosters as well as solemn detractors—who tend to take a dim view of the city's fast-paced, boisterous style.

Tel Aviv was founded by Zionist immigrants in 1909 as a garden suburb of Jaffa, or Yafo, an ancient town that is now regarded as part of Tel Aviv. (In fact, the city's official name is Tel Aviv-Yafo.) Sprawling, modern, and not too attractive, Tel Aviv nonetheless has attracted one-quarter of Israel's population; it is the center of the country's communications, commerce, and cultural life. The city's charms may not be readily apparent—but in a few days, Tel Aviv will work its magic on you.

Tel Aviv has a population of 340,000, 98 percent of whom are Jews. About half of its Jewish population was born in Israel, while the other half are immigrants who came here after 1948. Tel Aviv is surrounded by suburbs and satellite towns, making it the densest population center in Israel. Its university was founded in 1956. The city is also the home of the Israel Philharmonic Orchestra (the only orchestra of its caliber in the Near East) and boasts nine of Israel's 12 theaters, including the Habimah National Theater and the Cameri Theater (the most popular in Israel).

Tel Aviv extends for 13.5 km. (8 miles) along the Mediterranean coast, and encompasses a total area of almost 50 square km. (19 square miles).

The former city of Jaffa lies on the only promontory on the otherwise straight coastline. The promontory, rising to 30 meters (100 feet) above sea level, is bounded on the west and north by cliffs, while sand dunes and marshland hinder access on the south and southeast. A line of reefs runs parallel to the coast on the north side of the promontory, forming a natural breakwater for the small harbor. This advantageous location made Jaffa the best port between the Nile delta and Akko (Acre) Bay.

Modern Tel Aviv is built on three chains of low sandstone hills that run north-south parallel to the coastline. As a result, the city's main traffic arteries run either at an angle to the hills or along the shallow depressions between them; thus, once you stray from the main roads, you may be completely bewildered by the wrangle of streets within the city limits.

The coast is edged by a wide, level, sandy beach. Tel Aviv's large, modern hotels stand at the tip of the first line of hills. Running between the first and second chains of hills are the two main north-south arteries, Ben Yehuda Street and Dizengoff Street.

A number of suburban areas surround Tel Aviv—Ramat Gan and Givatayim to the east, Bat Yam and Holon to the south, and Herzliya and Ramat ha-Sharon to the north. To the east of Ramat Gan, the developed areas include the towns of Bene Beraq, Petah Tiqva, Qiryat Ono, and Or Yehuda. The largest industrial complex in the urban region extends along

Tel Aviv: Marina on the Mediterranean coast

the main road, running northeast from Tel Aviv within the towns of Ramat Gan, Bene Beraq, and Petah Tiqva.

Old Jaffa has become an appealing tourist center, with a variety of galleries, souvenir shops, cafés, and night spots. The liveliest area, however, lies northwest of Tel Aviv along the western section of Allenby Street and part of Dizengoff Street. Most of the government buildings are located in the Hakiria district (once the German village of Sarona). The poorer areas in the southeast of the city are occupied mainly by Jewish immigrants from Arabic-speaking countries.

Israel's economic life revolves around Tel Aviv. One-quarter of all employed persons in the country work within the city limits. Tel Aviv is the headquarters for all of Israel's major commercial and financial interests: banking and insurance companies; savings and investment organizations; large commercial companies; construction and transportation concerns; and large travel agencies—altogether there are about 1,400 firms of this kind in the city. Israel's stock exchange is situated in Tel Aviv's bustling business and commercial district. Tel Aviv also serves as the principal center of Israel's tourist industry, as implied by its approximately 72 hotels (several of them in the luxury class).

History

Jaffa. The origins of Jaffa (*Yafo* in Hebrew) are indisputably ancient, but historians and archaeologists do not always agree on whom to credit for establishing this charming port. Some say it was founded by Noah's son Japhet; but the Roman writer Pliny tells us its founder was Joppa, daughter of the wind god Aeolus, who built her city here 40 years after the Flood. In Greek legend Jaffa was the place where Joppa's daughter, Andromeda, was chained to a rock by the villagers to appease a sea monster; fortunately, Perseus killed the monster, saved Andromeda, and made her his wife. Visitors can still see the rock to which Andromeda is said to have been bound. Sea monster or no, the sailors of old found it perilous to navigate the line of jagged, wave-swept rocks that guard the entrance to Jaffa's harbor.

Fascinating fragments of information survive from Jaffa's early history. The Old Testament provides the first reference to the town as one of the cities assigned to the tribe of Dan, under the name of Japho (the Beautiful). A stone doorway, inscribed in 1270 B.C. with the name of Ramesses, suggests that Jaffa must have been part of the Pharaoh's holdings at that time. When the Egyptians withdrew, Jaffa was held by the Philistines—as finds of potsherds have shown. Around 1000 B.C., King David took Jaffa from the Philistines, and his son Solomon used the harbor (and a river harbor on the Yarkon at Tel Qasila) to bring in cedarwood and other building materials from Lebanon for the construction of the Temple in Jerusalem (2 Chronicles 2:16).

According to the Bible, during the reign of Jereboam II in the eighth century B.C., the prophet Jonah received the Lord's command to go to Ninevah, the great Assyrian city on the upper Tigris, to spread the word of God. Jonah, afraid of the mighty and godless Assyrians, defied the Lord. Arriving in Joppa, he set out on a boat for distant Tarshish (probably Tartessus in Spain). But the Lord was angry and sent a huge tempest that threatened to capsize the boat. To calm the storm, the sailors threw Jonah into the sea, where he was swallowed by a great fish; when he repented, the whale disgorged him onto dry land. Tradition has it that Jonah came ashore after his adventure at Tel Yona, 8 km. (5 miles) south of Jaffa.

After Jonah's time, Jaffa was held by the Assyrians, the Phoenicians, and the Greeks until the time of the Maccabees (around 142 B.C.), when the port came into Jewish hands. It then developed into an important trading and seafaring town until it was displaced by Caesarea, which Herod made his principal port in A.D. 50.

In Christian tradition, Jaffa first made history when the Apostle Peter performed a miracle there. Peter was called from nearby Lydda (Lod) upon the death of Tabitha, a Christian woman (c. A.D. 50) who lived in Jaffa. Peter brought Tabitha back to life; afterwards, he remained here for some time as the guest of Simon, a tanner, who lived by the sea (Acts 9:36–43).

The Roman general Vespasian took Jaffa during his march on Jerusalem in A.D. 60; only the few Jews who submitted to him were permitted to stay in the town.

Jaffa came under Muslim rule in 636, and its new masters showed tolerance to both Jews and Christians. But when the Crusaders captured Jerusalem in 1099 they also overwhelmed and destroyed Jaffa; many of its inhabitants fled. In later centuries, the town sank into virtual insignificance, although its strategic possibilities were not lost on Napoleon. In 1798, he captured Jaffa during his attempt to conquer Egypt, and the Armenian monastery on the coast became a military hospital.

By the end of the 19th century, Jaffa was again a busy and densely populated town. In the early days of the Jewish national movement, it was a favorite port of arrival for the increasing numbers of Jewish immigrants. Jaffa's crowded Jewish quarters spawned the foundation of Tel Aviv.

Tel Aviv. Whereas Jaffa has been an important port and urban center since the year 2000 B.C., Tel Aviv is very much a 20th-century city. It was originally conceived as a spacious modern suburb of the Arab town of Jaffa, where the narrow-laned Jewish quarters had become very overcrowded.

In 1909, the Zionist founders of Tel Aviv, headed by Meir Dizengoff, set out to create a garden suburb in the European style (Tel Aviv means "Hill of Spring")—complete with straight, wide streets, parks and gardens, and modern urban amenities. The new city was run by an elected, self-governing municipal council, chaired by Dizengoff, who eventually became the town's first mayor (1921–1936). Although nominally part of Jaffa, Tel Aviv had spread over an area of 99 hectares (245 acres) and had a population of 1,500 by the end of 1914. In the 1930s, the oldest part of Tel Aviv became the nucleus of the city's commerical and shopping district.

In its early days, Tel Aviv was a residential district centered on the Herzliya School, around which the town's cultural and economic life revolved. The Shalom Tower, the city's tallest skyscraper, now occupies this area.

Tel Aviv's development virtually ground to a halt during World War I. In 1917, Turkish military authorities evacuated the whole population of Tel Aviv plus the Jewish population of Jaffa; they suspected them of sympathy with the advancing British army. While the Jews were kept to the north for almost a year, Tel Aviv was completely abandoned. It was not until some months after Jaffa and Tel Aviv were occupied by British forces (November 10, 1917) that the city's residents began to return to their homes.

The second stage of development began in 1920 with the wave of Jewish immigration that followed the Balfour Declaration and the establishment of the British Mandate. In May 1921, violent Arab disturbances rocked Jaffa: Many Jews were killed and property was destroyed. As a result, the British authorities decided to combine Tel Aviv and the neighboring Jewish quarters of Jaffa into a separate town. The central area of Tel Aviv—the section built before the First World War—evolved into a busy traffic and commercial center. The developed area was extended mainly to the north along a narrow strip of dunes running parallel to the coast. Agricultural settlements were established during this period that eventually became the outer suburbs and satellite towns.

Tel Aviv witnessed a further population influx in the early 1930s, following Hitler's rise to power in Germany. Most of the immigrants who came to Israel at this time settled in and around Tel Aviv, which had become the largest city in Palestine; by 1940, the city had a population of 165,000—99 percent of which was Jewish. The city's boundaries continued to expand farther, mainly northwards, to the banks of the River Yarkon.

The foundation of the state of Israel touched off the fourth and most dynamic stage in Tel Aviv's development: It was here that the independence of the new state was proclaimed on May 14, 1948. Tel Aviv became Israel's first capital, and retained that position until December 1949, when Jerusalem prevailed as the official center of government.

When Jaffa surrendered to the Jewish army on May 13, 1948 after weeks of violent fighting, nearly all its 65,000 Arab residents departed. The empty town was reoccupied by Jewish immigrants. In 1950, Jaffa was incorporated in the city of Tel Aviv, which became officially known as Tel Aviv-Yafo.

In the course of its expansion, Tel Aviv has absorbed six villages, five of them Arab (Jarisha, Jamussin, Salame, Sumeil, and Sheikh Nuwanis) and one German (Sarona). The Arab villages were abandoned during the 1948 war. Inhabitants of the German village (founded in 1871 by members of a small Protestant sect) were deported by the British authorities during World War II, and its site has been taken over by the government district of Tel Aviv.

The population of Tel Aviv reached its peak in 1963, when it had 394,000 inhabitants. But people gradually began to move away to the suburban districts outside the city area; this decline was most keenly felt in the residential districts near the industrial and commercial quarters. On the other hand, the population of the urban region of Tel Aviv has been steadily increasing by an average of 20,000 people a year. It is estimated that 30 percent of new immigrants settle in the region of Tel Aviv.

In 1980, the non-Jewish population of Tel Aviv-Yafo was around 8,000, most of whom were Arabs. Today, most Arabs live in central Jaffa, south of the old town and the former harbor district. More than half of Tel Aviv's Arabs are Muslim; the rest are Christians—mainly Greek Orthodox and Catholic. The other non-Jewish residents include small numbers of Druzes, Armenians, and European Christians.

Attractions

One of the best ways to see Tel Aviv is on foot, mainly because the city's streets are often a confusing jumble for the uninitiated. The four walks described below will take you through the most interesting parts of the city and introduce you to its principal sights. Three of them guide you around modern Tel Aviv; the fourth is devoted to the old town of Jaffa.

WALK 1: The City Center—North

See color map.

This walk takes in some of the city's principal cultural attractions. Among these sites are the Cultural Center complex, with the renowned Habimah Theater, and the Tel Aviv Museum.

Your starting point is the ***Dizen-goff Circle** (Kikar Dizengoff) [1], also known as *Kikar Zina*, after the popular wife of Tel Aviv's first mayor, Meir Dizengoff. In the heart of Tel Aviv's elegant shopping and commercial district, Dizengoff Circle is a beautifully laid out, palm-shaded square. It lies at the hub of Tel Aviv's northern and southern districts, and is a focal point of the city's life. On public holidays, the illuminated fountain in the circle adds its complex light effects to the festive scene.

Dizengoff Street, a wide boulevard, curves gently from north to

Dizengoff Circle

southeast and runs into Kaplan Street in the center of the city. Shortly before you reach this point, after you cross *King George Street,* your eye will be caught by the ****Cultural Center** [2]—composed of the *Helena Rubinstein Museum of Modern Art,* the *Mann Auditorium,* and the *Habimah Theater.* The works of modern artists are exhibited on two floors in the pavilion containing the Helena Rubinstein Museum (open Sunday–Thursday, 10:00 A.M.–1:00 P.M., 4:00–7:00 P.M.; Friday 10:00 A.M.–1:00 P.M.). Behind the museum is *Jacob's Garden* (Gan Yaakov), a beautiful little park with shady trees. In earlier times, the settlers met here on the Sabbath and watered their camels at a nearby fountain.

The *Frederic Mann Auditorium* (Heikhal Hatarbut) adjoining the garden is the home of the Israel Philharmonic Orchestra. This modern building has excellent acoustics and an unusual seating arrangement.

In *Habimah Square,* on the south side of Jacob's Garden near *Rothschild Boulevard,* stands the *Habimah Theater.* This circular structure, built in the Bauhaus style in 1935, was designed by the Berlin theater architect Oskar Kaufmann. The Habimah (Stage), Israel's world-famed national theater, was founded in Moscow in 1918 as a Jewish theater. It moved to Tel Aviv in 1928. If you do not understand Hebrew, you can rent headphones that relay a simultaneous English translation.

Return to Dizengoff Street and turn left into *Ibn Gevirol Street*. On the right-hand side is **ZOA House** [3], home of the Zionist Organization of America. "Sabbath Evenings" are held here on Fridays; the program may include Bible readings, folk dancing, or other folk events.

Turn right from here along *King Saul Avenue* (Sderot Shaul ha-Melekh), which leads to the **Tel Aviv Museum** [4], housed in one of the world's finest museum buildings (open Sunday–Friday, 10:00 A.M.–1:00 P.M.). The museum formerly occupied the Dizengoff House on Rothschild Boulevard. Founded in 1931 by Meir Dizengoff, the museum has a sizable collection of classical and modern painting and sculpture, with many works by Jewish artists. There are special exhibitions from time to time, as well as frequent concerts, film shows, and lectures in Kaufmann Hall and Rekani Auditorium.

WALK 2: The City Center—South

See color map.

The development of Tel Aviv lies before you on this walk. You can see the city's history in a nutshell at the Museum of the History of Tel Aviv, or witness various stages by visiting the colorful Carmel Market, the old-world Yemenite Quarter, and the site where Israel was declared an independent state in 1948.

This walk begins at **Shield of David Square** (Kikar Magen David) [5], where the junction of six streets resembles the six-pointed Star of David. Shield of David Square divides Tel Aviv's second largest traffic artery, *Allenby Street*, into a southeastern and a northwestern part. The Allenby, as it is commonly known in Tel Aviv, honors General Allenby, commander of the British forces that captured Palestine from the Turks in 1917–1918. When the

street was first named in 1918, it ran through an almost uninhabited area: It is now one of the busiest thoroughfares in the city.

Going northwest along Allenby Street from Shield of David Square, turn right onto *Bialik Street*. No. 22 is the *Bialik Museum* (Bet Bialik), established in the house where the poet Chaim Nachman Bialik lived from 1924 to 1934. The museum contains his library and mementoes.

Continue up Bialik Street to its

terminus in *Bialik Square* (Kikar Bialik), where you will see the ***Museum of the History of Tel Aviv**, housed in the former City Hall. Its collections document Tel Aviv's past from its foundation on the sand dunes in 1909 to the present time. Meir Dizengoff's former office is also located here.

Continue northwest along Allenby Street to *November 2 Square* (Kikar Bet Be-November), at the intersection with Ben Yehuda Street. The name of the square commemorates the signing of the Balfour Declaration in 1917. The document expressed the British government's support for the establishment of a national homeland for the Jews in Palestine.

From *Shield of David Square* [5], *Carmel Street* (Rehov ha-Karmel) runs southwest to the ****Carmel Market** (Shuq ha-Karmel), Tel Aviv's largest and most colorful market. In a setting that looks as if it came straight out of a Hollywood adventure tale, hundreds of vocal merchants will be glad to sell you just about anything you can think of—antiques, clocks, watches, clothing, textiles, pottery, and, above all, fruit and vegetables. The bustling scene, at its peak in the morning or on Thursday afternoons, offers a fascinating picture of local trading styles and business skills. By all means, feel free to negotiate prices!

To the northwest of the Carmel Market extends the ***Yemenite Quarter** (Kerem ha-Temanim). This area is occupied by the Yemeni Jews who came to Israel during the 1920s and 1930s, and who have largely preserved their Oriental way of life and customs. The narrow streets and lanes of this quarter have their own special charm. The Kerem, or "Vineyard," is noted for its numerous specialty restaurants.

From Allenby Street or *Naholet Binyamin Street,* which runs parallel to it, turn right into *Ahad Haam Street,* which leads to the ***Shalom Tower** (Migdal Shalom) [6] or Shalom Mayer Tower. Standing 132 meters (433 feet) high, it is the tallest building in Israel. Shalom Tower's 34 floors contain many shops, offices, and restaurants. An elevator will whisk you up to the observation deck, where you can enjoy stunning views of Tel Aviv, the coastline, and the surrounding countryside. In clear weather, particularly in the morning, you can see Mount Carmel and Haifa on the Mediterranean coast, and as far east as the Judean Hills and Jerusalem.

In downtown Tel Aviv

The Shalom Tower also features the only *Wax Museum* in Israel and a ceramic-panelled wall that depicts the old Herzliya Secondary School of 1910.

Now return to Ahad Haam Street and follow it southeast to the junction with Allenby Street. At the corner, on the right, is the **Great Synagogue** (Bet ha-Knesset ha-Gadol) [7], Tel Aviv's principal synagogue; it was built between 1923 and 1926, and renovated in 1970.

At the junction of Allenby Street and *Rothschild Boulevard,* turn right and follow Rothschild along to *Bet Tanach* (Bible House) [8]. The building, once the residence of Meir Dizengoff and then occupied by the Tel Aviv Museum (now in King Saul Street; see Walk 1), now belongs to the city. On May 14, 1948, the independent state of Israel was proclaimed here by a group of Jewish politicians under the leadership of David Ben Gurion. The house now contains a collection of rare editions and translations of the Bible, with such exotic versions as those in Amharic (the language of Ethiopia) and Eskimo.

WALK 3: The Northern Districts

See color map.

This walk takes you into the northern areas of Tel Aviv, marked by expanses of parklands, memorials, and gardens. The Haaretz Museum complex is the highlight of this tour, where you can spend hours exploring its different departments.

The main road leading to the northern districts of Tel Aviv is *Ibn Gevirol Street,* which passes through *Kings of Israel Square* (Kikar Malkhe Yisrael), a large public garden. It is a gathering place for thousands of gaily clad children during the Purim festival, and Independence Day (May 14) is celebrated with music and fireworks in the square. On the north side of the park is Tel Aviv's *City Hall. Ben Gurion Boulevard,* lined with elegant boutiques, bookshops, and cafés, runs from the square down to the harbor.

Proceed north along Ibn Gevirol Street to its junction with *Arlozoroff Street,* and turn right. At No. 93 is the **Histadrut Building** [9], headquarters of the massive union Histadrut, the General Federation of Labor. A special section of the organization, Tiyur Vetiyul, provides information for visitors and conducts trips to the various Histadrut establishments.

Going west along Arlozoroff Street toward the sea, you come to the coast road, *Hayarkon Street.* Farther north is **Independence Park** (Gan ha-Azmaut) [10], which was laid out in 1948. The War of Independence is commemorated by a monument with the figure of an airman.

It is a short distance from here to the *Yarkon River* (Nahal Yarkon), which marked the northern boundary of Tel Aviv until the 1950s. Various residential districts occupy this area, along with *Yarkon Park* (the city's largest), the *university* campus, and the *Haaretz museum* complex. (This part of Tel Aviv can also be reached from the city center on buses 1, 4, 5, 24, and 25.)

After you cross the bridge over the Yarkon on the road into the *Ramat Aviv* district, you will come to the hill of **Tel Qasila.** Excavations that began here in 1948 unearthed the ruins of a Philistine port dating from 1200-1000 B.C., including houses, warehouses, workshops, and a temple. The town was laid out on a regular plan, with streets crossing at right angles. Twelve different settlement levels have been found that bear evidence of active trading relations with many Mediterranean peoples. The finds made here are displayed in a *museum* on the excavation site. Tel Qasila and two neighboring hills, *Tel Gerisa* (2 km./1 mile north) and *Tel Qudadi* (2 km./1 mile west), were the scene of fighting between British and Turkish forces in December 1917.

The ****Haaretz Museum** (Museum of the Land) sits on Tel Qasila. This is actually a complex of museums consisting of the *Glass Museum,* the *Museum of Ceramics,* the *Kadman Numismatic Museum,* the *Lasky Planetarium,* the *Museum of Science and Technology,* the *Museum of Ethnography and Folklore,* the *Labor Museum,* the *Alphabet*

Roman glass (Glass Museum)

Museum, and the *Nechushtan Pavilion.*

The *Glass Museum* has an interesting collection of glassworks—mainly from Mediterranean countries—spanning the

Oil jar (Museum of Ceramics)

ages from Biblical times to the modern glass industry. The *Museum of Ceramics* displays pottery vessels and other objects ranging in time from the Neolithic period to the present day.

The *Kadman Numismatic Museum,* named for its founder Leo Kadman, has one of the world's finest collections of ancient coins, found mainly in Israel. The building also has a display of agricultural implements and tools ranging from ancient times to the beginning of the 20th century, and models of old Arab peasant houses and irrigation systems.

The domed *Lasky Planetarium* is the first of the *Museum of Science and Technology* buildings, which also includes departments of astronautics, mathematics, transportation, and energy.

The *Museum of Ethnography and Folklore* illustrates the Jewish heritage through displays of Judaica and folk art. Exhibits feature Torah scrolls and dioramas representing the ceremonies and rituals of Jewish life. The folk traditions of the Ashkenazim, the Sephardim, and the Oriental Jews are included in the scope of the museum's artifacts.

The *Alphabet Museum* documents the history and development of the local language, from the first inscriptions on stone by way of the various Semitic alphabets to the modern Hebrew alphabet.

The *Nechushtan Pavilion* displays finds from the excavations at Timna, near Elat—the site of Solomon's copper mines. The exhibition illustrates the history and significance of copper mining from the Chalcolithic period to Roman times.

It is a short distance from the Haaretz Museum to the ***University of Tel Aviv,** situated on a hill in the Ramat Aviv district. The university campus, whose first buildings were constructed in 1964, covers a large area, with plenty of open space. Nine faculties are housed here, together with various research institutes, libraries, and scientific collections. The University has approximately 16,000 students.

In the center of the university complex stands the boat-shaped *Central Library,* notable for its award-winning architecture. The *Wiener Library*, in the same building, was brought here from London in 1980. It contains one of the world's largest collections on the history of Central Europe over the last hundred years, with a unique collection of documents, journals, and other publications.

Also located here is the ****Nahum Goldmann Museum of the Jewish Diaspora** (Bet ha-Tefutsot), which documents the history of the Jewish people and their dispersal throughout history, as well as their way of life, traditions, and cultural achievements.

On the east side of the campus is a *Botanic Garden* featuring almost every type of wild plant that grows in Israel and a collection of tropical and subtropical plants.

You should not leave this part of the city without a visit to the **Yarkon Park,** the largest in Tel Aviv. The park is an oasis for the citizens of Tel Aviv, with great expanses of grass and carefully tended trees. Within the confines of the park are the *Exhibition Grounds,* which house the Levant Trade Fair, and an *amusement park* that attracts large numbers of visitors, particularly on the weekends.

WALK 4: **Jaffa (Yafo)

See color map.

Jaffa is the most ancient and interesting part of the metropolis. Far from the bustle and noise of the modern city, this ancient, narrow-laned Oriental port lies on a low hill from which there is a magnificent view of the sea. The area has become an artists' haunt, with numerous galleries and studios. The walk ends at a pretty beach, so you may want to be prepared to linger by the shore.

From the center of Tel Aviv it is a 10- to 15-minute ride by automobile or bus (No. 10, 18, 24, 25, 42, or 46) to Jaffa. Ride the bus as far as the old *Main Square* (Kikar ha-Hagana) at the entrance to the town, where you will see a three-story *Clock Tower* built by Sultan Abdul Hamid II in 1906 to mark the 30th anniversary of his accession.

Going left from the square along *Bet Eshkol Street,* you will come to the *Flea Market* (Shuq ha-Pishpishim), a noisy and colorful emporium. Be wary of items whose "antiquity" is too sincerely vouched for by their sellers.

Turn right on *Mifraz Shlomo Street,* and you will come to the **Mahmudiye Mosque** [11], built in 1810 by Pasha Mahmud Abu Nabut. It has a beautiful inner courtyard with stumps of columns from Ashqelon. The mosque's or-namental *wall fountain* is the finest in Jaffa.

From here the route continues up Mifraz Shlomo Street, past many kiosks and open-air cafés. On the hillside to the left is the ***Archaeological Museum** [12]. Below the museum, on the north edge of the hill at the northern entrance to the harbor, is the **Armenian Monastery** [13], with *Saint Nicholas's Church.* The Armenians believe that this was the site of the house of Simon the Tanner, in which Saint Peter stayed. (Some believe that Simon's house stood near the Jama Budrus, Peter's Mosque, see page 118). The monastery was built in the 17th century on the remains of an earlier Armenian monastery and served as a pilgrim hospice and then as a military hospital for Napoleon's soldiers. It is said that when Napoleon decided to withdraw from Jaffa in 1799, he ordered the poisoning of all his soldiers suffering from plague and cholera or who were unfit to march.

As you continue up Mifraz Shlomo Street, you have a superb panoramic view of the Mediterranean coast and the skyline of Tel Aviv. Down by the harbor, you can see the dark shape of *Andromeda's Rock* [14], where, in Greek mythology, Andromeda was chained as a sacrifice to a sea monster.

Still farther up Mifraz Shlomo Street stands the ***Franciscan Church of Saint Peter** [15], a prominent landmark. Built in 1654 on the ruins of Jaffa's medieval fortress, it originally served as a monastery and pilgrim hospice. Remains of the medieval fortifications can be seen in the cellars of the monastery. Most of the present church and monastic buildings date from the 19th century.

The finest feature of the church is the beautiful carved woodwork in its interior. A statue of the French king Louis IX (Saint Louis) stands in the courtyard, honoring his arrival in the Holy Land; as leader of a Crusade, Louis captured Jaffa and stayed for a long time in the town. A flight of steps next to the church leads down to the old harbor, which is now used only by a few fishing boats.

From the forecourt of the church, another flight of steps leads up to *Kikar Kedumim*, Jaffa's spacious square. It is surrounded by cafés, shops, studios, and night spots. The different levels of a small *excavation site* in the center of the square trace the history of the occupation of Jaffa dating from Egyptian, Greek, and Roman times.

From here, you can walk a short distance to the little *public garden* set on the highest point in Jaffa. Locals and visitors alike enjoy the magnificent view of Tel Aviv and the Mediterranean coast.

From the left-hand side of Kikar Kedumim, steps lead into *Simtat Masal Dagim* (Fishermen's Lane). This is your entrée to the narrow streets and lanes of the artists' quarter of Old Jaffa, which has been partly reconstructed. You will find an irresistible succession of shops here selling antiques, jewelry, and arts and crafts, as well as fine art galleries.

When you return to the central square, go down a stepped lane on the right called *Rehov Shimon Haburski* (Simon the Tanner Street), until you see a house with a huge wooden door near the lighthouse. This site is traditionally known as the ***House of Simon the Tanner,** where Saint Peter reputedly stayed after bringing Tabitha back to life. The adjoining little mosque, the *Jama Budrus* (Peter's Mosque), was built on the remains of a Crusader church.

From here, continue east over the hill into *Yehuda Hayamit Street,* which runs into *Yafet Street.* **Saint Anthony's Church** [15] stands on the far side of the junction. Like Saint Peter's, this church also belongs to the Franciscans; they were the only representatives of the Roman Catholic church in the Holy Land after the Crusades.

From Saint Anthony's Church the street continues south to the *Giv' at Aliya* district and the *Bat Yam* (Daughter of the Sea) area with its resort and fine beach.

*Haifa

Haifa, whose name is a contraction of the Hebrew *Hof Yaffe* (Beautiful Shore) is one of Israel's most attractive cities, with carefully tended parks and lovely gardens. It is the country's largest port and third-largest city, and has a population of 260,000—most of whom pride themselves on their dedication to hard work.

Haifa seems to climb up on the slopes of Mount Carmel, with three main areas, or stages, of development. Its promontories offer expansive views over Haifa Bay, extending as far as Akko and Nahariya. The panorama is at its most breathtaking in the evening, when a sea of light bathes the city above the harbor.

History

Although the Bible mentions only Mount Carmel—and not Haifa—by name, excavations on Tel Shiqmona have revealed the existence of a number of small settlements here by about 520 B.C. In Byzantine times, these settlements became known collectively as Haifa. Under Byzantine rule, the city was notorious for its persecution of Jews—culminating in a massacre in 628 A.D. when the Persians were expelled. When the Arabs returned to Haifa, the city emerged once more as a place of some consequence; however, it suffered again at the hands of the Crusaders. In 1156, the Carmelite Order was founded here by hermits who lived on Mount Carmel. The Mamelukes destroyed Haifa when they invaded the Holy Land in the 13th century, and the city was finally abandoned as the century drew to a close.

Haifa remained fairly obscure until the end of the 19th century, when a railroad linking Constantinople and Medina was constructed; a spur line was built between Damascus and Haifa, ushering in a new period of growth. The harbor was deepened in 1929–1931, which eventually led to the city's development into one of the leading commercial centers in the Middle East.

The first waves of European Jewish immigrants came to Haifa in the late 19th and early 20th centuries; many settled on the slopes of Mount Carmel. From the early 1940s until after World War II, Haifa was a center of Jewish immigration—which had been rendered illegal by the terms of the notorious White Paper (a policy statement of the British government) of 1939. In spite of the British ruling, thousands of Jews fleeing Hitler's Europe sought refuge in Palestine. Many boatloads of refugees were caught by British forces when they attempted to land at Haifa; most were forced to return to Europe or sent to Cyprus. The effects of those tragic years still linger in the hearts of Haifa's citizens. During the War of Independence in 1948, the city served as the military headquarters of the Haganah (Jewish militia).

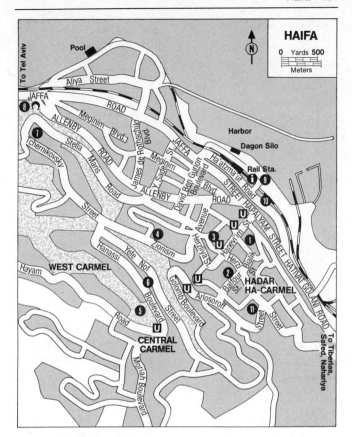

Modern Haifa is a busy port with a bustling industrial and commerical center. Its lovely setting, enhanced by the mountains and the sea, make it an ideal city for visitors and locals alike.

Attractions

See plan above.

The steep slopes of Mount Carmel can make a walking tour of Haifa rather exhausting. We suggest you take advantage of the city's good bus system or its plentiful taxi service.

This tour of the city begins in the central business district, *Hadar ha-Karmel*. Haifa's shopping and commercial district lies mainly along *Independence Street* (Rehov ha-Atzmaut), where you will find **Remembrance Park** [1]. Laid out on the site of a Turkish fort, the park features a memorial commemorating those who fell during the War of Independence in 1948.

A short distance away lies the **Old Technion** (Qiryat ha-Technion) [2], a college of technology founded in 1912 by Zionists from Germany. Most of its departments have moved to the new campus, known as Technion City.

From here, *Shabtai Levi Herzl Street* leads to the **Haifa Museum** [3], whose collection includes ancient coins and pottery from the north of the country, Byzantine mosaics, and finds from Caesarea.

On higher ground in the *Persian Gardens* stands the spectacular ***Baha'i Shrine of the Bab** [4], easily the most splendid building in Haifa. Preaching the unity of all mankind, the Baha'i faith is an outgrowth of a Persian sect of Shiite Islam, and regards Mohammed, Jesus Christ, Buddha, Zoroaster, and Moses as God's messengers. It derived from the prophecies of Mirza Ali Mohammed of Shiraz, who, in 1844, proclaimed himself the forerunner—literally, the Bab (Gate)—of the Promised One. The Bab was martyred in Tabriz, Persia in 1850, and his remains were moved here in 1909. This sumptuous

The Baha'i Shrine

building, with its golden dome and Corinthian-style columns, was erected over his tomb in 1953.

In 1863, Mirza Husayn Ali Nuri, a follower of Babism (as it had come to be known), proclaimed himself Baha Ullah (the Promised One). Already exiled from Persia for proselytizing the Bab, Baha Ullah was subsequently banished from Turkey; he finally established himself in Akko, across the bay from Haifa, where he is now buried. Today, Baha'i has millions of adherents; the Shrine of the Bab is the most sacred place for followers of Baha'i, and Haifa is the religion's world capital.

The interior of the shrine is furnished with valuable carpets and crystal chandeliers. (Please remember to remove your shoes before you enter.) In the gardens you will find the *Baha'i Archives* and a *museum* designed in the style of the Parthenon.

Located in the district of *Central Carmel,* Haifa's most beautiful park, the **Gan Ha'em** [5], boasts a year-round show of blooming plants and many exotic trees. A short step away is the *Japanese Museum* [6], established in 1958 by a foundation that presented several thousand works of Far Eastern art to the city of Haifa. The fine collection is housed in the Japanese-style building.

From here, *Hanassi Street* and *Tchernikovsky Street* lead to **Stella Maris** [7], the Carmelite Monastery. (There is also a cable car that runs between the monastery and the seaside town of Bat Gallim.) The Carmelite order was founded here in 1156 by a group of Crusaders seeking a secluded refuge for prayer; it takes its name from Mount Carmel, the "Vineyard of the Lord." The original monastery on the site was destroyed by Pasha Abdullah of Akko in 1821; the present structure was built in 1828.

The pyramid in front of the monastery marks the graves of French soldiers. The French troops beat a hasty retreat following Napoleon's unsuccessful siege of Akko in 1799; the wounded, who were abandoned, were killed by Ahmed el-Jazzar. The church is dedicated to the prophet Elijah, a major figure in both the Old Testament and the Koran, who struggled against the forces of idolatry. Elijah's emblem over the entrance bears the words "Zelo zelatus sum pro Domino Deo exercituum" (I have been zealous for the Lord God of Hosts). Inside, the church is adorned with scenes from Elijah's life; there is a figure of the prophet on the altar. A cedarwood statue of the Virgin with a porcelain head dates from 1820. Below the high altar is the cave in which Elijah is said to have lived (c. 875 B.C.).

A footpath opposite the monastery runs over *Cape Carmel* and into the valley. After passing the ruins of an old Carmelite hermitage, you come to the *School of the Prophets* [8], a 40-meter- (130-foot-) long cave in the midst of a garden where Elijah is said to have gathered his disciples around him. Joseph and Mary were also reputed to have stayed in the cave after their return from Egypt. Until 1948, the cave was occupied by the El-Chidr Mosque; El-Chidr, meaning "the Green One," is the name under which Muslims revere Elijah.

From here, you may want to wander down toward the *Old City*. In sharp contrast to the neat residential districts on Mount Carmel, this busy quarter features the narrow streets, lanes, and colorful mix of people that so often characterize a Mediterranean port. Your route brings you to the entrance to the **Harbor** [9], but you must receive special permission to gain access; even then, photography is forbidden. However, it is possible to get a good view by taking a boat trip around the harbor.

A huge grain elevator, the

Dagon Silo (*dagon* means "harvest"), dominates the harbor. A museum in the office block has an interesting exhibition on the cultivation of grain and a surprisingly absorbing story of the history of bread. The façade of the building depicts the process of growing grain in ancient Israel. The museum was founded by Reuben Hecht, a member of a Swiss shipping family.

Nearby at 198 Allenby Street stands the **National Maritime Museum** [10]. It presents an exceptional overview of the 5,000-year history of seafaring and the ports of Israel, and illustrates the contribution seafarers have made to the history of human settlement and civilization. Founded in 1955 by a former naval officer named Ariyeh Ben Eli, it is one of the finest maritime museums in the Mediterranean area. Among the exhibits are models of historic ships, maps, charts, renderings of old ships, and an American vessel that was successfully pressed into service to transport Jewish refugees from Europe to safety in the 1940s.

Bus No. 10 or 12 will take you from the harbor entrance to *Arlozoroff Street,* where you will find the **Museum of Ethnology** [11]. Its displays include material from different periods in Israel's history. Special presentations provide visitors with information about Jewish music, folk art, customs, and legends.

From here, bus No. 19 will take you to the *New Technion* (College of Technology) in *Newe Shaanan.* In nearby *Bat Gallim,* you'll find fine beaches and many good restaurants specializing in—what else?—seafood.

14 Travel Routes Through Israel

Israel's compactness makes it handy to traverse by car: its roads are reasonably good, and the distances between cities or attractions tend to be short. This convenient arrangement gives you plenty of time to savor the countryside and to make as many stops as you please.

We have designed the 14 travel routes in this section to allow you to make the most of your visit. The routes cover Israel's principal sights, shrines and holy places, historic sites and monuments, artistic treasures, and areas of scenic beauty.

The first two routes take you around the coastal regions and northern Israel; the next ten routes concentrate on the central regions; and the last two routes cover southern Israel as far as the Red Sea.

TRAVEL ROUTE 1: *Tel Aviv–*Haifa (93/98 km.; 58/61 miles)

See map on page 126.

The journey from Tel Aviv to Haifa is reasonably short, yet it is packed with interesting sights both ancient and modern. Although the highlight for most visitors is the ancient port of Caesarea, now a luxurious resort town, the trip along the coastal plain also illuminates the country's modern history, for here lie many of the *moshavim* (cooperative farms) and kibbutzim (collective farms) that have become intrinsic to modern-day Israel.

You have a choice of two routes you can travel from Tel Aviv to Haifa. The cities are linked by the fairly modern Highway 2. Construction began on its southern section soon after the foundation of the state of Israel, and its northern section, between Atlit and Haifa, was completed in the 1960s. If you use the highway, however, you will by-pass some of the interesting sights along the way. The old road, Route 4 via Petah Tiqva and Hadera, runs parallel to the highway a little way inland, and lengthens the trip only by about 5 km. (3 miles). Both options are described below, and if you are driving round trip, we suggest you take one option going out and the other on the return trip.

A: By Highway 2

Follow the route marked "A" on the map on page 126.

Begin your journey in *Tel Aviv* (see description beginning on page 106) on Highway 2, near the bridge over the dry bed of the *River Ayalon* (on the right). Beyond the bridge you can see the two tower blocks of the Diamond Exchange in the town of Ramat Gan.

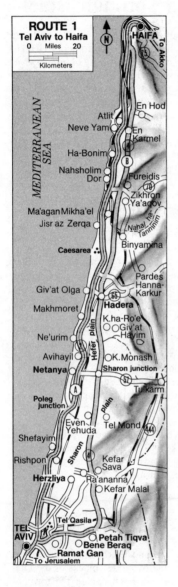

ROUTE 1
Tel Aviv to Haifa
0   Miles   20
Kilometers

MEDITERRANEAN SEA

HAIFA
To Akko
En Hod
Atlit
Neve Yam
En Karmel
Ha-Bonim
Nahsholim
Dor
Fureidis
Zikhron Ya'aqov
Ma'agan Mikha'el
Jisr az Zerqa
Nahal Tanninim
Caesarea
Binyamina
Pardes Hanna-Karkur
Giv'at Olga
Makhmoret
Hadera
K.ha-Ro'e
Giv'at Hayim
Ne'urim
Avihayil
K. Monash
Netanya
Sharon junction
Tulkarm
Poleg junction
Even Yehuda
Tel Mond
Shefayim
Kefar Sava
Rishpon
Herzliya
Ra'ananna
Kefar Malal
Tel Qasila
TEL AVIV
Petah Tiqva
Bene Beraq
Ramat Gan
To Jerusalem

After you cross the *River Yarkon* (5 km.; 3 miles from Tel Aviv), the highway enters the southern Sharon Plain. To the right lies the archaeological site of **Tel Qasila* (see page 115). Excavations by Hebrew University have established that Tel Qasila was a large, fortified port and trading city during the time of Solomon; Jaffa, which was probably held by the Philistines, lay opposite. Some historians think that it may have been here that the ships of Hiram, king of Tyre, discharged their cargoes of cedarwood that was used for building the Temple in Jerusalem. The foundations of embrasures and various public and private buildings were brought to light, and some of the finds are displayed in a small museum nearby.

On the far side of the hill, you can see the ***Haaretz Museum* complex (see page 115). The road that branches off to the right leads to Tel Aviv's modern suburbs and garden cities, and to the campus of *Tel Aviv University*. To the left is the *Reading Power Station,* its chimneys a prominent landmark.

The developed area extends to the right of Highway 2 almost without a break from Tel Aviv to Herzliya, but areas of open country and stretches of sand dunes lie to the left. About 10 km. (6 miles) outside the city, you will see Tel Aviv's *Country Club* on the left, a large recreation and entertainment park. The road that cuts in on the right here leads to the Ben Gurion Airport and Jerusalem.

Farther on, you pass Herzliya's

industrial zone to the left of the highway; beyond this you can see a string of hotels built along the seafront (the Accadia, Sharon, Daniel Tower, Apollonia, and others).

The road to the right runs up to *Kefar Shemaryahu* (13 km.; 8 miles from Tel Aviv), a garden suburb founded in 1936 by settlers from Germany, many of whom had left professional and academic fields to become farmers. The settlement, named for the Zionist leader Shemaryahu Levin (1870–1924), was originally a moshav that specialized in intensive poultry production and orange-growing. Although some agricultural cultivation continues, Kefar Shemaryahu has developed into a residential district and vacation center. Its population is approximately 15,000.

At the northern end of Tel Aviv lies **Herzliya** (15 km.; 9 miles from Tel Aviv). Named for Theodor Herzl, it was originally a village founded with help from the Zion Commonwealth Corporation (an organization formed by American Jews). Herzliya soon developed into a major center of citrus fruit production. The interruption of orange exports during World War II created an economic crisis that was soon overcome by the development of industry and vacation holiday trade.

The town is composed of three distinct parts. To the east, beyond green fields and fruit orchards, is the original settlement, which is now mainly residential; an industrial zone (metalworking, electronics, dyestuffs, foodstuffs, and textiles) spreads southwest; and to the west and northwest are Herzliya Gimel ("Herzliya C") and the adjoining neighborhood of *Nof Yam*—both pleasant suburbs where many of Tel Aviv's foreign diplomats live. Several first-class hotels and a series of public beaches are located on the seafront. Herzliya is the seat of Israel's principal hotel school, the center of the film industry, and also home of the country's most important television studio.

North of Herzliya is the Muslim ****tomb of Sidna Ali**, near the site of ancient *Apollonia* (also called Arsuf or Arsur). The site was originally occupied by the Canaanite town of Rishpon, or Rishpona, and named after a divinity called Reshef. The Seleucid rulers established the port town of Apollonia here in the second century B.C. After that, it was captured by the Hasmoneans and then recovered by Pompey in the first century A.D. Gabinius eventually rebuilt Apollonia as a Hellenistic city. The Arabs, whose influence extended here in the seventh century, called the town Arsuf, a derivation of its original Canaanite name; the Crusaders, who arrived some centuries later, called it Arsur. The town fell to Saladin in 1187, but was recaptured by Richard I (Richard the Lion-Hearted) four years later. The Crusaders were finally expelled in the 13th century by the Mameluke ruler Baibars; his general, Ali, son of Ulim, was killed in battle and is believed to be buried in the tomb on the seashore. A section of the town walls has collapsed down the steep-sided sandstone hill, which is constantly lashed and eroded by the surf.

As you continue north, you'll pass the moshav of *Rishpon* (18 km.; 11 miles from Tel Aviv) on the right, which perpetuates the name of the original Canaanite settlement, and the kibbutz of *Shefayim* on the left, which has beautiful gardens, a beach, and a well-known guest house. Established in 1935, Shefayim practices intensive agriculture, producing chiefly citrus fruits; it also has some industry. The members of the kibbutz rescued a group of illegal immigrants—refugees from persecution in Europe—who had made their way to Israel in an unseaworthy vessel; as a result, the kibbutzniks were subjected to interrogation and frequent searches by British troops.

Farther north, Highway 2 is lined by orange groves for much of the way. To the right, you will see a broad gash in the sandstone ridge. It originally was thought to date to Roman times as a means of providing the Poleg brook with an outlet to the sea, and of draining the marshland to the southeast. Recent archaeological investigation, however, has shown it to be the defensive moat surrounding an old Israelite stronghold. The marshes were finally drained by Jewish settlers in the 1930s and 1940s.

To the left, on the high dunes opposite the highway, is the *Win-gate Institute of Physical Education,* a top-level training center for athletes and sports instructors. It is named in honor of the British colonel Orde Wingate, a keen advocate of fitness training who was stationed in Palestine during the British mandate. A devout Christian, Wingate was a strong supporter of Jewish nationalism nonetheless, and he secretly trained the Jewish militia in anti-terrorist techniques. His covert aid to the Jews during the disturbances in 1936–1939 eventually came to light, and he was banished from Palestine by the British authorities.

At the *Poleg Junction* (26 km.; 16 miles from Tel Aviv), the road to the left leads to the southern entrance of Netanya; the one on the right goes to eastern Sharon. Take the Netanya road: You will pass Israel's largest brewery—easily recognizable by the giant bottle on its roof—on the right; and, on the left, some of Netanya's southern suburbs. When you come to another crossroads, the main road into Netanya branches off to the left; the road to the right runs east to the Sharon Junction (see page 136) and on to Tulkarm.

Netanya (32 km.; 20 miles from Tel Aviv) is the largest town in central Sharon, with a population of 105,000. It began as a moshav, founded in 1929 by the sons of veterans of the first moshavim, in an inhospitable area of dunes and malaria-ridden marshland. The settlement soon developed into an important center of citrus fruit production. After the purchase and settlement of the Hefer Plain to the north, Netanya became a market town for the area. It was named for the Jewish-American merchant and philanthropist Nathan Straus, owner of Macy's department store, who was a Zionist leader as well as an outstanding contributor to programs for the needy and the sick, particularly children.

During the Second World War, the town received an influx of refugees from Belgium and Holland, many of whom descended from generations of diamond-cutters.

As a result, Netanya became the center of the Israeli diamond industry. Eventually, it developed into one of the leading industrial centers in the country.

Netanya's hotel trade had begun to develop even before World War II. The city Netanya now has more than 80 hotels, ranging from luxury resorts to good, middle-range hostelries. The city has a long, well-maintained *beach* and an extensive, attractive seafront promenade on the steep-sided sandstone ridge overlooking the sea.

The highway continues north

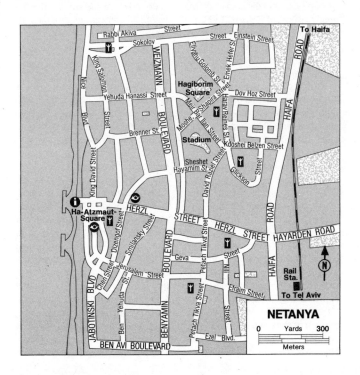

over the *Hefer Plain*. After its acquisition by the Jewish National Fund in 1930, this area was transformed from a barren, mosquito-infested tract of dunes into a showpiece of modern development. Now more than 30 settlements practice highly intensive agriculture in this area. The kibbutzim also have some industry, and in many places there are tourist and vacation facilities.

You will pass a rapid succession of moshavim as you continue north: like *Avihayil* (founded by veterans of World War I); *Bet Yannai; Kefar Vitkin* (founded by the early pioneers in the area); and the youth village of *Ne' urim* (39 km.; 24 miles from Tel Aviv), where children of the Youth Aliyah—the immigration movement—are brought up.

Running close to the shore now, Highway 2 crosses a broad bridge that spans the *River Alexander* near its mouth. The river probably takes its name from the Hasmonean king Alexander Jannaeus, who incorporated this area in his kingdom. A road to the left heads northwest to the beach of *Mikhmoret,* whose beautiful bay provides the setting for the Mevo'ot Yam nautical school.

Beyond this point, more orange groves flank the highway, followed by grass-covered sandstone hills scattered with carob trees. You come next to *Giv' at Olga* (47 km.; 29 miles from Tel Aviv), a western outpost of the town of Hadera (see page 137). In the 1930s and 1940s, Hadera served as a lookout post,

where the British kept watch for illegal immigrants landing by boat.

From Highway 2, which runs close to the luminous sea at this point, a road branches left (west) to the kibbutz of *Sedot Yam* and the site of Caesarea.

**CAESAREA

See plan on page 132.

This ancient city—one of Israel's "younger" antiquities—lies in a charming vacation area that boasts a number of hotels and Israel's only 18-hole golf course. The site is bounded on the east by the developing immigrant settlement of *Or Aqiva,* founded in 1952.

History

The first settlement on this site was probably established in the fourth century B.C. by Strato, or Straton, of the Phoenician port of Sidon; it became known as "Strato's Tower." In 104 B.C., it was occupied by the Hasmonean king Alexander Jannaeus, and Herod the Great began building a magnificent city here in 13 B.C. He called the new city Caesarea in honor of Augustus Caesar, his patron. In *The Jewish War,* Flavius Joseph gives an account of the construction of a fine harbor; his description is confirmed by the ruins that survive. At this point, the low-lying coast runs in a straight line; thus, a deep harbor basin had to be dredged and protected by a massive breakwater. The quays within the harbor were built of large ashlar blocks. The town itself was equipped with spacious market squares, splendid temples, and colossal statues; the townspeople were entertained at the large amphitheater—with seating for 20,000 and a hippodrome. Most of the people who came to live in the new town were Hellenic.

In A.D. 63, a conflict arose here between Jews and pagans, touched off by a pagan display next to the synagogue; these sparks kindled a revolt against the Romans three years later. At about the same time, the Apostle Paul was imprisoned here by the Romans before being sent on to Rome.

After Titus destroyed Jerusalem in A.D. 70, Caesarea became the capital of the Roman colony. During the Bar-Kochba rebellion (113–136), it served as the headquarters of the Roman legions.

In the fourth century, Caesarea was one of the leading cities of the Roman Empire and a center of Christianity. It was the home of the great theologian Origen and of Eusebius (380–420), bishop and church historian, whose "Onomastikon"—a list of places in Palestine—provided the basis for the famous mosaic map of Madaba. The two large aqueducts that brought water to the city from the Crocodile River to the north and Mount Carmel to the northeast also date from this period.

During the Arab conquest of Palestine, Caesarea held out against the invaders longer than any other city—it was not taken

until 640. The Arabs first made Lod, and then Ramla, the provincial capital; Caesarea began to decline.

When the Crusaders took Caesarea in 1101, they found an ancient glass cup there that they believed to be the Holy Grail—the chalice in which Christ's blood was collected at the Crucifixion. (The cup is now in Italy at the cathedral of San Lorenzo in Genoa.) The Crusaders rebuilt the harbor on a smaller scale than the ancient one. The town was captured by Saladin in 1187 but Christian forces recovered it in 1218. Louis IX (Saint Louis), who lived in the Holy Land for several years in the mid-13th century, rebuilt Caesarea. As part of his program to strengthen Christian defenses, Louis added stout walls and a deep moat to the town's fortifications.

In 1265, the Mameluke ruler Baibars captured Caesarea. To prevent any landings by European forces, he destroyed the city, along with all the other port towns in Palestine.

Attractions

When you enter the site through the remains of the *Herodian wall* [1], you will see the *Hippodrome* [2] on the left, a race track 230 meters (250 yards) long surrounded by seating for 20,000 spectators. Beyond this, also to the left of the road, are the remains of the Roman *Forum* [3], with two statues dating from the second century A.D. Within the medieval town

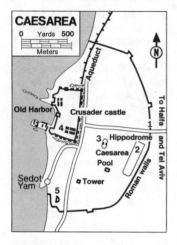

CAESAREA
0 Yards 500
Meters

Aqueduct

N

Old Harbor

Crusader castle

To Haifa and Tel Aviv

4

3 Hippodrome

Caesarea Pool

2

Roman walls

Sedot Yam

Tower

5

walls are the remains of a Herodian temple dedicated to Augustus; immediately south of this lie the ruins of the *Crusader cathedral* [4], where the Holy Grail is said to have been preserved. At the southern end of the site stands the restored *Theater* [5], where the Israel Music Festival is held every summer. The old city has found new life as a tourist center, with cafés, restaurants, and galleries.

*

As you continue north from Caesarea on Highway 2 toward Haifa, you will pass the large village of *Jisr az Zerqa*, situated on a ridge of sandstone hills on the left. The settlement is populated by Bedouin who have given up their nomadic life. The remains of ancient quarries scar the slopes of the hills. Next you will pass *Ma'agan Mikha'el* (59 km.; 37 miles from

Tel Aviv), one of Israel's largest kibbutzim. Founded in 1949, the kibbutz has large fish ponds and practices intensive agriculture; there is some industry as well. At the mouth of the *Crocodile River* (Nahal ha-Tanninim)— where there were crocodiles until about 80 years ago—lies a nature reserve. You can see large flocks of marsh and water birds here in winter, such as herons, cormorants, sea gulls, and storks. Tiny *Pigeon Island* (I ha-Yonim) floats offshore.

The road now leaves northern Sharon and continues along the narrow coastal strip known as the Carmel Coast. To the west are the moshav of *Dor* and the kibbutz of **Nahsholim Dor** (64 km.; 40 miles from Tel Aviv). This area, which is mentioned as Dor in the book of Joshua (11:2), was first a Phoenician and later a Hellenistic port. The ruins of an ancient boat-building yard were discovered here. In its heyday, Dor was famous for its purple dyes derived from a locally abundant sea snail. Toward the end of the 19th century, Baron Edmond de Rothschild purchased land here with the intention of setting up a glass factory; however, his plan was aborted when the sand proved to be unsuitable for glass manufacture. The kibbutz was founded in 1948 as a fishing settlement; the moshav was established in 1949 by immigrants from Greece. Together they run the seaside resort of *Hof Dor,* situated on shallow bays protected from the breakers by a number of small islands. The resort offers full board as well as self-service cottages for families.

Farther north to the left of Highway 2 is *Ha-Bonim* (68 km.; 42 miles from Tel Aviv). This settlement—whose name means "builders"—is a moshav shitufi, a kind of hybrid between kibbutz and moshav, with communal production but individually owned homes.

Six km. (4 miles) beyond this is **Atlit** (74 km.; 46 miles from Tel Aviv). Little is known of the history of the town, though Paleolithic and Mesolithic tools and hut sites have been found in the nearby Nahal Oren Gorge. Even the source of its name has not been traced.

Between 1217 and 1222, the Knights Templar, with the help of Austrian and Hungarian pilgrims, built a massive castle with a large refectory and a tall tower here on the shore. This Castellum Peregrinorum, or Château des Pèlerins, had a church, a cemetery, a bathhouse, and a harbor; it provided lodging and food for pilgrims arriving from Europe. Christian forces held this powerful stronghold until the end of the Crusades. It was finally taken by the Mamelukes some months after the fall of Akko in 1291. The majestic ruins of the tower can still be admired from a distance, but access to the grounds is prohibited.

At the turn of the 19th century, most of this area was bought by Baron Edmond de Rothschild, who initiated the establishment of the Jewish settlement of Atlit. In 1947 and 1949, the kibbutzim of *En Karmel* and *Neve Yam* were established near Atlit. The British authorities maintained a detention camp here for illegal immigrants; the site is now a closed military area.

The highway continues north, running parallel to the railroad along the narrowing coastal strip. About 10 km. (6 miles) south of Haifa, Highway 2 is joined by the old road (Route 4) that runs to the east (see page 138). The intensively cultivated cotton fields, vineyards, and banana plantations gradually give way to urban development; industrial installations stand on the seaward side, and housing areas on the slopes of the Carmel range to the right. The road, lined by palm trees and divided into two by a central reservation planted with oleanders, runs around Cape Carmel. On a hill to the left, beside the *Oceanographical Institute,* is the site of ancient *Shiqmona,* currently undergoing excavation.

The road continues through the districts of *Bat Gallim* and *Qiryat Eliyahu* before it enters the city of ***Haifa** (93 km.; 58 miles from Tel Aviv): see the description beginning on page 120.

B: Via Petah Tiqva and Hadera on Route 4

Follow the route marked "B" on the map on page 126.

The old road—Route 4—really begins in the center of Tel Aviv. Crossing the River Ayalon (see page 125) to the east, the road enters the town of Ramat Gan, running along Jabotinsky Street.

Ramat Gan (population 150,000), the sixth-largest city in Israel, was founded in December 1921 as a garden suburb of Jaffa. The settlement, whose name means "Garden Hill," was the creation of a group who wanted to combine the amenities of town and country life; they built their houses with their own hands, and banned industry from their settlement. Due to its close proximity to Jaffa and Tel Aviv, however, the site soon grew bigger, and the low cost of land attracted industrial development.

The town now has a large industrial zone, as well as pleasant residential districts and numerous municipal parks and gardens. The largest of these is a 200-hectare (500-acre) *National Park,* featuring a tropical garden, a rose garden, a boating pond, a safari park, and a zoo. Ramat Gan also has the country's largest sports stadium, and the associated *Makkabia Village,* which provides accommodation for athletes and international congresses. At the south end of the town is the *Bar Ilan University,* which specializes in Jewish studies.

Ramat Gan merges imperceptibly into **Bene Beraq** (population 87,000). Founded in 1924 by Orthodox Jews from Poland, the town was named for a settlement belonging to the Biblical tribe of Dan. In the time of the Second Temple, the area was famed for its fertile land. Bene Beraq is known to Jews throughout the world; on the Seder evening of the Passover, a passage read from the Haggadah refers to the four sages who spent an entire night here telling the story of the Exodus until their disciples called them to the morning prayer. The celebrated Rabbi Akiva also lived in Bene Beraq. In much later times, the Crusaders built a castle here, which they called Bombrac.

Like its western neighbor Ramat Gan, Bene Beraq rapidly increased in size—it now covers an area of more than 700 hectares (1,700 acres). In spite of its growth, it has preserved its Orthodox Jewish character, and on the Sabbath, most of its streets are closed to traffic. It has many yeshivot (Talmudic colleges), the best known of which is the *Ponevezh Yeshiva.* Bene Beraq is also an important industrial center, and has almost 200 factories.

Continue north along the road. About 8 km. (5 miles) past the intersection with the Geha Expressway, you will pass the large *Beilinson Hospital;* a few kilometers farther, the road enters **Petah Tiqva** (population 120,000).

In 1878, a number of Jews living in the Old City of Jerusalem resolved to become farmers and bought land on the River Yarkon from a Greek landowner. In spite of the warnings of their friends, the settlers moved in and named their new home Petah Tiqva (Gateway of Hope). But they soon became victims of malaria and were forced to contend with the hostility of their Bedouin neighbors. The pioneers were compelled to move their settlement farther south out of the marshland. In 1883, along with the first immigrants of the Lovers of Zion movement, they resettled on the present site. Thereafter, Petah Tiqva prospered, and, as the first of the moshavim to be established, it became known as the "mother of the moshavim."

During World War I, Petah Tiqva lay between the Turkish and Germans on the one hand and the Allies on the other; in 1920, the inhabitants had to repel a violent attack by Arabs. The town recovered rapidly, however, and strengthened by the growth of agriculture (chiefly fruits), it began to attract industry. By the late 1930s, Petah Tiqva's population had increased to more than 20,000, and it was granted its municipal charter in 1939. Today the settlement is a typical satellite town of Tel Aviv, with its own strong economic base.

The *Yad la Banim* (Memorial to the Sons), a museum and cultural center, commemorates members of the local population who fell in the War of Independence and other wars.

Route 4 continues north from Petah Tiqva, crosses the River Yarkon (which is only a small stream overgrown by reeds at this point), and enters the Sharon Plain. The soil takes on the brilliant orange-red color characteristic of this area, and the landscape is dominated by orange groves. The road passes through the *Hod ha-Sharon* district, which encompasses a number of villages and

has a total population of 175,000. The road continues along a shady avenue of Casuarina trees and passes *Kefar Malal*, one of the first moshavim in Israel, founded in 1922. Beyond the intersection with the Geha Expressway, you will pass between the towns of Kefar Sava and Ra'ananna.

To the right of the road is **Kefar Sava** (23 km./14 miles from Tel Aviv; population 36,800), a town that has been twice reborn since it was founded. Originally established as a moshav in 1903, it was completely destroyed during fighting between Turkish and Allied forces during World War I. Rebuilding had scarcely begun when Arabs attacked the village in 1920. The settlers returned a few weeks later, and Kefar Sava began to grow and prosper—at first due to intensive agriculture, then later because of industry. There is a good view of the *Meir Hospital* from the road.

To the left of Route 4 is *Ra'ananna* (population 27,300). Founded in 1921 as an orange-growing village, it is now one of the outer ring of satellite towns of Tel Aviv. Ra'ananna spreads over a considerable area. The population still lives mainly by farming, but industry also plays a part in its survival.

For the next 20 km. (12 miles), Route 4 runs through the fresh, green countryside of southern Sharon, a region of intensive agriculture as illustrated by the many plantations, orchards, and fields of vegetables and flowers. One settlement follows another in rapid succession, most of them moshavim. To the left of the road lie *Bazera, Bene,* and the kibbutz of *Yizhaq.* To the right of Route 4 you will pass *Tel Mond,* named after the British Zionist Sir Alfred Mond, later Lord Melchett. Beyond this, on the left, is the large settlement of *Even Yehuda,* named after Eliezer Ben Yehuda, who revived Hebrew as a spoken language; nearby are *Hadassim* and *Neve Hadassa,* two youth villages and colleges of agriculture. On the right, near the road, stands Tel Mond prison. The vast plain of Sharon was once a magnificent forest, but 2,000 years of settlements, warfare, and agriculture have rendered it nearly treeless. The *Ilanot Forestry Research Institute,* to the right of the road, has done valuable work in reforestation.

About 30 km. (18 miles) from Tel Aviv, you come to the *Sharon Junction* (Bet Lid). The road to the left leads to Netanya (see page 128), 4 km. (2 miles) away on the coast. Fourteen km. (9 miles) to the east lies the little Arab town of *Tulkarm,* the "wasp waist" of Israel within the country's pre-1967 frontiers.

For the next 10 km. (6 miles) the road crosses the *Hefer Plain* (see page 130), with its many flourishing settlements. To the left are *Yedidya* and *Bet Yizhaq,* founded in 1935 and 1940 respectively by middle-class immigrants from Germany. To the right is the agricultural college of *Midreshet Ruppin,* with the Havvat Noy

nursery of ornamental trees, a natural history museum, and facilities for the acclimatization of rare plants.

Beyond this, on the right of Route 4, are the following settlements: the moshav of *Kefar Monash,* founded by World War II veterans and named after a Jewish-Australian general of World War I; the moshav of *Bet ha-Levi,* established by Jews from Bulgaria and named for Yehuda ha-Levi, the greatest Hebrew poet of the Middle Ages; the kibbutz of *Ha-Ogen,* and others. To the left are the kibbutzim of *Mishmar ha-Sharon* (mainly engaged in growing flowers) and *Ma'abarot.* After the bridge over the River Alexander (which is only a small stream at this point, and usually dry in summer), the road runs past the moshav of *Elyashiv* (42 km.; 25 miles from Tel Aviv), founded by Yemeni Jews, and the religious moshav of *Kefar ha-Ro'e,* with a domed yeshiva that offers instruction in agricultural science as well as in the Talmud.

Also to the right, a road branches some distance to the two kibbutzim that make up the **Giv'at Hayyim**. The original kibbutz, founded in 1932, was divided in two to settle a political dispute. One of Israel's first canning plants was established here, as well as a barrel-making shop, a stud farm for horse breeding, a research institute, and a well-known puppet theater.

*Theresienstadt House, situated in Giv'at Hayyim, commem-

orates the Jews who died in the Theresienstadt concentration camp in Czechoslovakia. Opened in 1975, it also serves as the cultural center of the kibbutz, with reading rooms and a library. Its memorial room contains an index of all the 150,000 Jews transported to Theresienstadt from Czechoslovakia, Germany, Austria, Denmark, Holland, and other countries. The design of the room evokes the concentration camp, and a mosaic in the center of the floor depicts a ghetto.

Forty-seven km. (29 miles) from Tel Aviv, you will come to **Hadera** (population 37,200), the chief town in northern Sharon. Hadera is typical of a town whose residents have not completely given up farming, and its history bears witness to the self-sacrificing spirit of the early settlers. It was originally a moshav on the little River Khudeira, founded in 1890 by members of the Lovers of Zion movement, most of whom hailed from the Baltic countries. Named Hadera (the Green Place), in deference to the surrounding marshland and the promise of agricultural prosperity that the pioneers ascribed to it, the settlement turned out to be a deathtrap. Well over half the settlers, including most of their children, died of malaria within the first 20 years. In 1895, Baron Edmond de Rothschild began to buy up large tracts of land and plant them with eucalyptus trees, whose heavy absorption of water accelerated the drainage of the marshes. Malaria

was not completely eradicated until the 1920s, and the last areas of marshland disappeared only in 1945, when a large canal was cut through to the sea.

Since World War II, various industries have been established in Hadera, primarily in the dune country on the north side of the town. The population, which totaled 152 in 1898, swelled to 11,819 by 1948. Hadera is also a highway junction where the north-south artery (Route 4) intersects Route 65, which runs east to Megiddo and the Yizre'el Valley (see Travel Route 6).

About 5 km. (3 miles) from Hadera, a road branches to the right and runs 5 km. (3 miles) east through the dunes to the little country town of *Pardes Hanna-Karkur.* About 8 km. (5 miles) north of Hadera is a turn off to the left that will take you to Caesarea (see page 130).

If you stay on Route 4 instead of turning toward Caesarea, you will soon pass the moshav of *Binyamina,* tucked away in the greenery to the right of the road. Founded in 1922, it was given the Hebrew name for Baron Edmond de Rothschild. This charming spot has managed to preserve its appealing rural character.

As you continue, Route 4 crosses the railroad and, flanked on the right by the rocky southern spur of the Carmel range, runs along the narrow coastal strip. A side road on the right leads to **Zikhron Ya'aqov** (65 km./40 miles from Tel Aviv; population

5,000), one of the earliest Zionist settlements, which was established in 1882 by Rumanian immigrants. A year later, Baron Edmond de Rothschild took the place under his patronage, naming it for his father James (Jacob). The baron built the large Carmel winery here in 1886; it became one of the first industrial establishments in the country and remains an important commercial enterprise today. Zikhron Ya'aqov developed into a prominent center of the Zionist movement, and the Hebrew Teachers' Union was founded here in 1903. Thanks to its pleasant climate, Zikhron Ya'aqov has become a favorite summer resort.

The *Rothschild Mausoleum* is set in a beautiful botanic garden. The remains of Baron Edmond de Rothschild were transferred here in 1954. You can also visit the *winery* and the *Aaronson Museum*, home of the botanist Aaron Aaronson (1876–1919), who discovered wild wheat growing in Galilee and on Mount Hermon.

Route 4 now runs close to the steep slopes of Mount Carmel. With its fertile black soil and abundance of water, Mount Carmel shelters the coast from rough winds and ensures successful agriculture here; bananas are an important crop.

Just beyond the turn off for Zikhron Ya'aqov, Route 4 comes to the large Arab village of **Fureidis** (population 5000). The name derives from the Greek word *paradeisos,* which, like the Hebrew *pardes,* means "fruit garden." This particular garden chiefly grows citrus fruits.

Beyond Fureidis, you will see a number of moshavim to the left of the road. In the flanks of the Carmel range are large *limestone caves,* where evidence of habitation by prehistoric man some 50,000 years ago was discovered in 1929. Just beyond the Carmel Caves, a road to the right leads to the idyllic village of *En Hod.* Residents of this artists' colony include painters, sculptors, and other craftsmen. Following the lead of Dadaist painter Marcel Janco who settled here in 1950, they have created a colony that fosters artistic expression.

The road continues to the youth village of *Yemin Orde,* named after Colonel Orde Wingate (see page 128), and the kibbutz of *Nir Ezyon,* established here in 1950 after the destruction of Kefar Ezyon in the Hebron hills during the War of Independence. Beyond this, the road draws closer to Highway 2 and soon merges with it. The 10-km.- (6-mile-) drive on Highway 2 from this point to *Haifa* (see page 120) is described on page 133.

TRAVEL ROUTE 2: *Haifa–**Akko (Acre)–Nahariya– *Rosh ha-Niqra (42 km.; 26 miles)

See map on page 140.

This travel route brings you north as far as the Lebanese border. Although the distance is short, there is a tremendous amount to see. Akko (Acre) has a venerable 4,000-year history that includes service as the second capital for Christian forces during the Crusades. The area possesses great natural beauty; at the end of this travel route (Rosh ha-Niqra), you will have a chance to explore the magnificent grottoes formed on the coast by the protracted power of the Mediterranean.

Leave *Haifa* (described on pages 120–124) on the road that dips southeast toward Nazareth and the Yizre'el Valley and runs for 3 km. (2 miles) under the forbidding shadow of the Carmel range. When you reach the *Mifraz Junction*, turn left (north) on Highway 4, and you will find yourself in the country's most important industrial center. Immediately after crossing the little *River Kishon*, 5 km. (3 miles) from Haifa, you'll see a large oil refinery surrounded by a water-filled moat to your right. The refinery was built in the 1930s as the terminus of the pipeline that carries crude oil from Iraq; this refinery and the new one at Ashdod (see page 260) enables Israel to meet its needs for petroleum products. Beyond the refinery are petrochemical and fertilizer plants.

The highway passes from the industrial zone into residential districts, which are separated from one another by a green belt of eucalyptus trees. To the right are the *Central Tree Nursery* and the offices of the Reclamation Department of the Jewish National Fund.

The road now runs through the residential areas of *Qiryat Hayyim*, still within the suburban reaches of Haifa, and *Qiryat Motzkin* (population 22,600), founded in 1934. On the shores of the bay farther west lies *Qiryat Yam*. These settlements began as garden districts of single-story houses, but such structures have mostly given way to multi-story blocks.

Qiryat Bialik, named for the great modern Hebrew poet, was originally settled by immigrants from Germany. The children's village of *Ahava* (Love) lies within its parameters, and on its eastern edge is the moshav of *Kefar Bialik*, also established by German settlers.

As Route 4 continues north, factories alternate with housing developments, with occasional tracts of undeveloped land lying between them. Farther on, you'll see a long row of fish ponds on the right, while a belt of white sand dunes fringes the bay to the left. You'll pass "Steel City"—once the domain of blast furnaces but now mainly mills—which lies 17

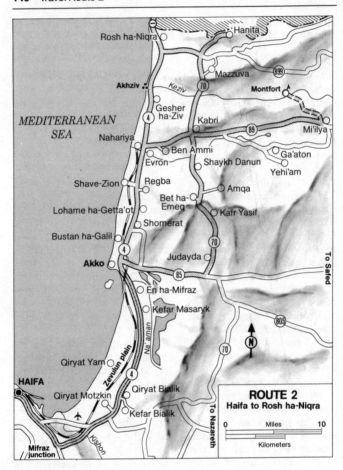

Rosh ha-Niqra
Hanita
Mazzuva
899
Akhziv
Keziv
70
Montfort
MEDITERRANEAN
SEA
Gesher
ha-Ziv
4
Kabri
89
Mi'ilya
Nahariya
Ben Ammi
Ga'aton
Evron
Shaykh Danun
Yehi'am
Shave-Zion
Regba
Amqa
Bet ha-
Emeq
Lohame ha-Getta'ot
Kafr Yasif
Shomerat
Bustan ha-Galil
4
Judayda
70
Akko
85
To Safed
En ha-Mifraz
Kefar Masaryk
805
N
Qiryat Yam
70
HAIFA
4
Qiryat Motzkin
Qiryat Bialik
Kefar Bialik
To Nazareth
Mifraz
junction
Kishon

ROUTE 2
Haifa to Rosh ha-Niqra

0   Miles   10

Kilometers

km. (11 miles) from Haifa to the left.

Opposite "Steel City" is *Kefar Masaryk*, a kibbutz founded in 1938 by immigrants from Czechoslovakia. They named it for Thomas Masaryk, the first president of Czechoslovakia. Kefar Masaryk and *En ha-Mifraz*, another kibbutz located immediately north of it, work jointly with private companies to run a number of industrial enterprises, including a dyeworks and a ceramics factory.

Twenty km. (12.5 miles) from Haifa, you will cross the *River*

Na' aman near its mouth. This area consisted of brackish marshland until the 1930s. According to local lore, Phoenician seafarers discovered the secret of making glass here from the fine-grained sand of the dunes. (Israel's modern Phoenician glass factory is situated farther down the bay to the south.) At the end of Haifa Bay to the left, the romantic vistas of ancient Akko (23 km.; 14 miles from Haifa) come into view.

**AKKO (Acre)

See map on page 143.

Akko, known as Acre in English, is one of the world's oldest ports—although the present form of the ancient-looking walls and caravanserais in the town date from the 18th and 19th centuries.

History

Akko boasts a very long history. Although it was a strategic and commercially vital port for the Phoenicians, Akko's name also appears on Egyptian potsherds from the 19th century B.C.; however, it may well have been in existence long before that. The original town stood on a hill 2 km. (1 mile) to the east of its present location, and was surrounded by a colossal rampart of earth. At a later stage, the port town was built on a narrow promontory reaching south into the bay. In ancient times, the town had two anchorages; the eastern side enjoyed shelter from the breakers, while the western side suffered more exposure from the sea. A short wall at the north end of town provided adequate protection against attack. The inhabitants not only thrived as fishermen and seafarers, but also extracted a precious purple dye from a local seagoing snail (the murex), and discovered how to make glass at an early stage.

The city changed hands several times. In the 12th century B.C., the Israelites were unable to conquer the Phoenician city, but the tribe of Asher settled in the surrounding area; by the time of King David's reign (10th century B.C.), the town belonged to the Israelites. Around 650 B.C., Akko rebelled against the conquering Assyrians.

Akko grew in importance after Alexander the Great conquered it. It became a Hellenistic city during the 2nd century B.C., and was renamed Ptolemais by King Ptolemy II of Egypt. In 143 B.C., Jonathan, a member of the family of Maccabees, was lured into the city by Tryphon and slain. Akko remained the only unvanquished city in Palestine, despite efforts by the Hasmonean ruler Alexander Jannaeus to take it. During the Jewish War, it served as Vespasian's headquarters at the time of his campaign in Galilee.

Akko was taken in 1104 by the Crusaders under King Baldwin I. In 1187, after the sweeping defeat of the Crusaders at the Horns of Hittim, the city unequivocally surrendered to Saladin. However, four years later, the Crusaders— led by Philippe-Auguste II of France and Richard the Lion-Hearted of England—recaptured it and made it the capital of their kingdom in place of Jerusalem, which they had lost. Akko was also the scene of the confrontation between Richard and Duke Leopold of Austria that eventually led to grave consequences, which included Richard's capture and imprisonment in Austria.

Although the Crusaders erected many buildings in the city and fortified it, the Muslims—from whom it had been wrested— considered it a vile and unclean place. The Knights Templar, the Hospitallers (Johannites), the Genoese, the Pisans, and the Venetians each established separate communities within the town and squabbled with one another. In 1291, Akko fell once again—this time to the Mamelukes under their third Sultan, el-Ashraf Khalil. The Mamelukes utterly destroyed the town and slaughtered every Crusader; this decisive defeat dealt one of the death blows that ended the Crusader period. Akko did not recover from its devastation and regain some importance as a port until after the Ottoman conquest in 1516.

In the 18th century, the Turkish governors who rebelled against the Sultan's authority made Akko a stronghold of their power. Ahmed el-Jazzar, also known as "the Butcher," refortified the town with stout walls and deep moats, and built caravansaries and markets with stones from ancient Caesarea.

During his failed Egyptian campaign, Napoleon set siege to Akko in 1799. But thanks to the combination of Akko's excellent fortifications and assistance from the British fleet, the Turkish garrison repelled all attacks; Napoleon abandoned his attempt after 60 days and headed home to France.

In the early 20th century, Akko again fell into a decline as more modern ports emerged to keep pace with the technological advances. Its harbor slowly silted up and Haifa displaced Akko as the country's leading port.

There has been a Jewish community in Akko since the Middle Ages; the town produced great teachers, such as Moses Nachmanides. Until the disturbances of 1936–1939, Jews and Muslims

In Akko harbor

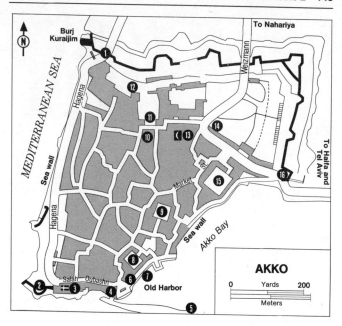

lived peaceably alongside one another here. During the War of Independence, Akko was originally
an Arab base; but it was taken by
Jewish units on the eve of the proc-
lamation of the Jewish state in May
1948. Many Arab residents remained in the old part of the city,
while Jewish immigrants settled in
the New City to the north and established a new district of the
town.

Attractions

Following the road west through
the New City, turn left into *Haha-
gana Street,* which runs along the
seafront. On the right, you will

see the Turkish fortress of *Burj
Kuraijim.*

Passing over the deep moat and
through a wide *breach in the walls*
[1], you enter the Old City. A can-
non, supplied to Ahmed el-Jazzar
by the British during Napoleon's
stands on the sea wall. The Citadel
can be seen to the right.

Some remains of the western
harbor are visible on the shore farther south. The old *lighthouse* [2]
stands at the tip of the promontory,
with remains of Templar buildings
from the Crusader period. The
walls that once stood here collapsed in a great earthquake in
1837. At this point, you may want
to park your car and continue on

foot, because the flavor of the Old City is best sampled at a leisurely pace. Turning left (east), you pass *Saint John's Church* [3], built in 1737 on the ruins of a Crusader church. You then come to the *Sea Gate* [4] and the old *East Harbor,* with fishing boats at its eastern end and the remains of the ancient *breakwater.* At the east end of the breakwater stands the *Tower of Flies* [5], a former lighthouse. In front of the tall *bell tower* [6], built by the Turks at the end of the 19th century, is the *fishing harbor* [7], where you can watch the Arab fishermen mending their nets. Turn left toward the **Khan el-Umdan* (Inn of the Pillars) [8], a two-story caravanserai built around a courtyard containing a drinking trough for camels and columns of granite, porphyry, and marble brought from Caesarea by Ahmed el-Jazzar.

From here, the route continues through the narrow streets of the *Bazaar.* It passes the *Khan el-Afranj* (Caravanserai of the Franks) [9], built on the ruins of a Clarissine convent. Beyond this is the *Municipal Museum* [10], housed in an old Turkish bathhouse. It contains a large collection of Arab and Druze folk art, including clothing and jewelry.

A number of nearby ****Crusader buildings** [11] have undergone extensive excavation. On the south side of el-Jazzar Street is the *Crypt of the Hospitallers* (or the *Crypt of the Johannites*), and opposite it is the buttressed **Knights' Hall,* one of the oldest

Akko: the Knights' Hall

Gothic buildings in the world. From here, you go through a number of underground structures to the *Royal Palace* and the **Citadel** [12]. This fortress, built by Ahmed el-Jazzar in the 18th century over ruins of a Crusader structure and later enlarged, was used both by the Turks and the British as a prison. Among those confined here was Baha Ullah, founder of the Baha'i religion; in a later period, Jewish freedom fighters were detained and executed here.

The Citadel now houses the *Heroes' Museum,* which contains documents about the freedom fighters and the great escape of prisoners in 1947. It also includes the room in which some of the prisoners were hanged.

From the Citadel, el-Jazzar Street leads to the ***Ahmed el-Jazzar Mosque** [13], one of the grandest mosques in Israel. Its beautiful garden forecourt contains a number of small fountains—one of which is used for the ritual washing of feet—and columns. The mosque, built in 1781–1782, stands on the ruins of the Crusaders' Cathedral of the Holy Cross (Santa Croce). The mosque contains the tombs of Ahmed el-Jazzar and his adopted son Suleiman (unrelated to Suleiman the Magnificent), as well as a shrine that holds a single hair from Mohammed's beard. Low buildings around the courtyard are occupied by religious who hold various offices.

A little farther east is the domed *White Market* (Suq el-Abyad) [14], built in the 18th century by Zaher el-Amr, a Turkish governor. From here, Saladin Street leads to an ancient caravanserai, the *Khan ash Shawarda* [15]. Nearby is an old *Crusader arsenal.*

From the southeast corner of the walled town, the *Land Gate* [16] leads out to the *Argaman* (Purple Strand), a beach of fine sand.

*

After you have sampled the historic charms of Akko, you can resume your trip on Route 4. The highway continues north toward Nahariya, passing an agricultural experimental station on the right, concealed behind tall eucalyptus trees in a fresh green setting. Beyond this, a side road branches off on the right to the **Tomb of Baha Ullah,** one of the holiest places of the Baha'i religion. Together with the Baha'i Shrine in Haifa (page 122), these holy sites comprise the two western centers of the Baha'i faith. The tomb, set in a carefully tended Persian garden, contains relics of the first three leaders of the faith, together with books and documents relating to them.

Just off the road to the left lies the moshav of *Bustan ha-Galil,* founded in 1948 by immigrants from Central Europe; to the right is the kibbutz of *Shomerat,* also founded in 1948. Not far beyond these settlements, about 26 km. (16 miles) from Haifa, you can see sections of an aqueduct against the backdrop of the Galilean hills to the right. This picturesque structure was built in the late 18th and early 19th centuries to bring water to Akko from the Kabri springs on the edge of the Upper Galilean uplands. The aqueduct, which may have been built on Roman foundations, was designed in imitation of the antique style.

A museum belonging to the kibbutz of *Lohame ha-Geta'ot* (the Ghetto Fighters) perches on a hill overlooking the aqueduct. The kibbutz was established in 1949 by a handful of survivors from the ghettos of Warsaw and Bialystok, where the Nazis slaughtered the Jews. A museum and research center dedicated to Lithuanian and Polish Jews was established here in 1951.

Twenty seven km. (17 miles) from Haifa, take the road that turns off to the right, which leads to the unusual community of *Nes Ammim* (Banner of the Peoples). The members of this ecumenical Christian settlement established in 1964 have dedicated their lives to transforming the relations between Christians and Jews. Their philosophy eschews the missionary approach. The goal of Nes Ammim is to demonstrate the wisdom of peaceable coexistence.

Continuing along Route 4, another road to the right leads to *Regba*, a moshav shitufi founded in 1946 by Jews from Central Europe. The moshav practices intensive agriculture, and there is also a factory here that produces furniture and kitchen equipment. To the left of the road is *Shave Zion* (Return to Zion), a moshav shitufi founded in 1938 by settlers from a village in Germany's Black Forest. In addition to productive agricultural lands, the moshav also has a hotel. The remains of a third-century Byzantine church with a fine mosaic floor were discovered here in 1955, near the beach.

After a short distance, you will pass the kibbutz of *Evron* (30 km.; 18 miles from Haifa) on the right, founded in 1945 by Polish immigrants. As you continue past Evron, you'll soon see the road to Nahariya that goes off on the left.

Nahariya (31 km./19 miles from Haifa; population 30,000) was founded in 1934 by refugees from Germany who gave up their professional and commercial careers for a simpler agrarian life. However, farming proved more arduous than the settlers had

dreamed; to supplement their income, they turned Nahariya's beautiful beach to their advantage. Within a few years, the town was transformed into a popular spot for honeymooners and vacationers. In the 1940s, its secluded location made it a prime landing stage for desperate Jewish refugees from Europe attempting to slip past the British authorities who guarded the coast.

Nahariya was once the only Jewish outpost in the Akkota Plain, and it was almost completely cut off from the rest of Palestine during the War of Independence. Despite its tremendous growth in the years that followed the war, the town still retains its distinctive European charm. There are now about 40 hotels in this appealing resort town.

Lined by mighty eucalyptus trees, Nahariya's main street, *Ha-Ga'aton Boulevard,* runs down to the sea on both sides of the little *River Ga'aton.* In 1947, a *Ca-*

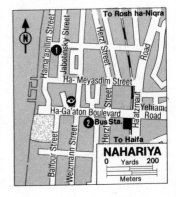

naanite (or *Phoenician*) *temple* [1] from the Middle Bronze Age (17th–18th centuries B.C.) was discovered on the beach. The temple, dedicated to Astarte, the sea goddess of fertility and love, includes a large hall, a colonnade, and an inner sanctuary. Among the finds were gold and silver statuettes of the goddess, their casting molds, and a number of seven-branched pottery lamps that probably served some ritual purpose. The *City Hall* [2] houses the *Municipal Museum,* with archaeological material from the surrounding area.

Side trip to Castle Montfort

If you're in the mood for a picnic in a magnificent setting, pack up your lunch and head for Castle Montfort, 12 km. (7 miles) from Nahariya. The direct route to the ruins of this medieval fortress runs from the main road into Nahariya, passing through the town's eastern districts. You will travel through a tract of fertile, low-lying land, past the moshav of *Ben Ammi,* and then cut across the north-south road from *Shelomi* to *Kafr Yasif* (see page 149).

On the left, you pass the kibbutz of *Kabri,* founded in 1949 by pioneers who had previously settled on the River Hordanein near the Dead Sea. Its abundant natural springs fed the aqueduct to Akko (see page 145). The landscape changes dramatically beyond this point, and the road begins a steep climb to the Upper Galilean hills.

Deep gorges slash the limestone rock, and the red soil of the hillsides hosts an abundance of olive trees interplanted with tobacco crops. In 8 km. (5 miles), a road branches off to the right and runs southeast through beautiful hill country to the kibbutzim of *Ga'aton* and *Yehi'am,* built around the imposing ruins of the Crusader castle of *Jiddin.*

From the junction, the road to Montfort continues climbing to the village of **Mi'ilya** (16 km.; 10 miles from Nahariya), which is occupied by Eastern Orthodox Arabs. There was a settlement here at least as early as 2000 B.C., but the only significant remains of the past date from the period of the Crusades. Most notable is the *Chastiau du Roi,* or *Castrum Regium,* now surrounded by a huddle of houses in the center of the village.

From Mi'ilya, a road (treacherous in places) winds down to the romantic, deeply slashed gorge of the *River Keziv,* surrounded by kermes oaks, terebinths, olive groves, and fruit orchards. On a high hill, 180 meters (590 feet) above the valley bottom, lie the ruins of ***Castle Montfort**. It was built by the Crusaders in the 12th century and then called Castellum Novum Regis (the King's New Castle). Saladin captured the castle in 1187, but it returned to Christian hands in 1192. The Courtenay family sold it to the Order of the Teutonic Knights of Saint Mary in 1228. They strengthened and enlarged the fortress, renaming it Starkenberg (a translation of the French Montfort). Because of its remote location, the stronghold provided a particularly safe place for storing the order's treasury and archives. In 1271, the castle was turned over to the Mameluke ruler Baibars, but the archives of the Crusaders miraculously survived intact.

Much of the castle is in ruins, but some parts remain—the large oval *keep* and the *Great Hall* (both with octagonal buttresses), an inner *courtyard,* living quarters and workshops, and the massive curtain walls. Stables and storage areas were located below ground level. A channel from the River Keziv supplied the castle with water.

On the far side of the gorge is the enchanting *Goren Park,* a fine restoration of a run-down woodland. The park includes kermes oaks, terebinths, laurels, Judas trees, and other species of flora, as well as facilities for picnickers and campers.

*

Back in Nahariya, continue on Route 4 through the northern districts of the town. You can see the kibbutz of *Sa'ar* on a hill to the right. A few kilometers farther, the road comes to **Akhziv** (36 km.; 22 miles from Haifa), situated on a hill at the mouth of the River Keziv with the Akhziv National Park. Once a Canaanite city, Akhziv was assigned by the Israelite leaders to the tribe of Asher, but its members were unable to gain control of it. Eventually, the town came into the hands of the Phoenicians, whose seafaring citizens found that the little inlets offered convenient shelter for their shallow-keeled vessels.

Excavations on the hill have unearthed interesting finds from the Bronze and Iron ages; these include a little pottery figure of a baker kneading dough in a long trough, and beautiful glass vessels of the Hellenistic period. In Byzantine times Akhziv, then called Ecdippa, was a populous little town. The Crusaders called the town Casal Imbert; the Arab fishermen who lived here until 1948 named it Az Zib. As part of a wider protest action against the British authorities in 1946, a Haganah unit blew up the bridge over the Keziv and cut the road to Beirut; all fourteen members of the unit were killed. The name of the *Yad Layad* youth hostel (to the right of the road) commemorates those who died.

The kibbutz *Gesher ha-Ziv,* established in 1949, has rich banana plantations and fruit orchards, as well as a large furniture factory and comfortable lodgings for visitors. A Club Méditerranée resort village spans part of the beautiful beach along the romantic harbor of ancient Akhziv.

Continuing north from Akhziv on Route 4, you will pass the moshav of *Liman* (38 km.; 24 miles from Haifa) and the road that turns west to Sasa (see page 149). The route ends at **Rosh ha-Niqra** (42 km.; 26 miles from Haifa), on the narrow summit ridge of the Hanita range. Just ahead lies the frontier with Lebanon.

The name Rosh ha-Niqra means the "Ladder of Tyre"—an evocative description of the sheer cliff that rises from the sea. A brief cablecar ride will take you down to the *grottoes*, carved over the centuries by the continuous action of the waves against the rock face. Walkways and boat rides provide unforgettable views of the deep blue waters contrasting with the milk-white rock. If you are feeling adventurous, the grottoes are particularly spectacular when the wind is high and the surf is up. A tunnel at the mouth of the caves once served the railroad that linked Haifa and Beirut.

Return to Akko

You may want to take in a few additional sights on the journey back to Akko from Rosh ha-Niqra. Return to the junction where the road (Route 899) to Sasa intersects Route 4, past the kibbutz of Kefar Rosh ha-Niqra on the left. Turn left on Route 899 and continue through the little development town of *Shelomi* to another junction where a steep road on the left runs up to *Hanita,* a kibbutz situated in wild hill country. It was founded in 1938 as one of the "tower and stockade" settlements whose task was to fend off hostile attacks as well as to cultivate the land. The kibbutz provides accommodations for visitors.

At this point, the magnificent

views extend as far as Haifa Bay and Mount Carmel and overlook large forested areas.

From Hanita, return to the intersection and continue south on Route 70 past the eastern outskirts of Shelomi (45 km.; 28 miles from the beginning of Travel Route 2 in Haifa). The road draws steadily closer to the hills that border the Akko Plain, and eventually skirts *Mazzuva,* a kibbutz founded in 1940, and runs to *Kabri* (see page 147). At this point, you cross the road that leads from Nahariya to Castle Montfort.

The road takes you past the moshav of *Netiv ha-Shayyara* (57 km.; 35 miles from the beginning of Travel Route 2 in Haifa) on the right, and the Arab village of *Shaykh Danun* and the moshav of *Amqa* on the left. The kibbutz of *Bet ha-Emeq,* founded in 1949 by immigrants from English-speaking countries, uses biogenetic methods to cultivate and improve seed strains. About three-quarters of the way to Akko, you will come to the village of *Kafr Yasif,* which is inhabited by Christian and Muslim Arabs and by Druzes. The Jews of Akko used to bury their dead here, although there are no longer any Jewish residents in the village. The next village, *Judayda,* is a Druze community. At *Yasif,* your road will link up with Route 85, the main road from Akko to Safed. Turn right on Route 85, which heads west between the Zevulun Valley and the Akko Plain, to return to ****Akko** (see page 141).

TRAVEL ROUTE 3: **Akko–*Safed–Rosh Pinna–Qiryat Shemona–Metulla (116 km.; 72 miles)

See map below and on page 156.

This route takes you through some of the most beautiful and dramatic scenery Israel has to offer. First you'll head east through Upper Galilee and then north through the majestic landscape of the Jordan Rift, which is part of the Great Rift that extends from Turkey all the way down into Kenya and Tanzania. As you travel along in the shadow of the imperious Golan Heights, you will encounter a fascinating blend of the old—Safed, Israel's highest city—and the new—Qiryat Shemona. The route also gives you a chance to visit the Dan Nature Reserve, a peaceful jungle with a plentiful water supply—so rare in Israel. The trip ends in Metulla, a tiny town that is Israel's most northerly settlement.

Leave **Akko* (see description beginning on page 141) on Route 85 heading east. At the end of the developed area, you will pass the site of Akko's earliest settlement (see page 141) on "Napoleon's Hill" to the right. The first section of road runs almost perfectly straight,

forming the boundary between Akko and the Zevulun Valley; fish ponds, cotton fields, and green fodder crops dominate the landscape. About 4 km. (2 miles) outside Akko, a road branches left to the Arab and Druze village of *Makr.* A few kilometers farther

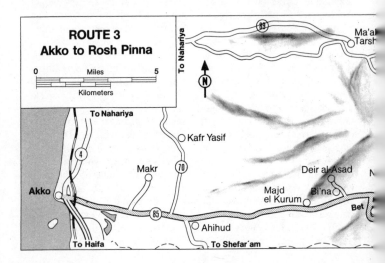

ROUTE 3
Akko to Rosh Pinna

0 Miles 5
Kilometers

To Naharija

To Naharija

Akko

To Haifa

Makr

Ahihud

To Shefar'am

Kafr Yasif

Majd el Kurum

Deir al-Asad

Bi'na

Bet

Ma'al
Tarsh

lies Route 70, which you can take north to *Kafr Yasif* and *Shelomi* (see page 149) or south to *Shefar'am* along the eastern edge of the Zevulun Plain. To the right of the road is the moshav of *Ahihud*, abundantly supplied with water from springs and wells.

Suddenly, almost without warning, the landscape grows hilly. From this point, Highway 85 runs through the *Bet ha-Kerem Valley*, forming the boundary between Upper Galilee, with mountains rising up to 1,200 meters (3,900 feet) high, and Lower Galilee, where the land elevations reach only about half that height. The gorge of the *River Hillazon* runs along to the right below the road; on the left, to the north, you will see the steep escarpments of *Mount Haluz*. On the nearer part of the hills, you can see large scale reforestation work in progress.

After passing the large Arab village of *Majd el-Kurum* (16 km./10 miles from Akko; population 5,600) and the smaller Arab villages of *Bi'na* and *Deir el-Asad*, you will come to the new town of **Karmi'el** (21 km./13 miles from Akko; population 9,000). Founded in 1964 and laid out in accordance with modern town-planning concepts, the town was established as part of a plan to increase the Jewish population in Galilee. Many of its residents are immigrants. Eight-to 12-story tower blocks alternate with four-story blocks, individual houses, and villas. Housing developments dot the sloping hills. The commercial center of the town is in the valley, and there is a separate industrial zone to the east.

Continuing east, you will pass the Arab villages of *Nahf* and *Sajur*, which climb the hillside on the

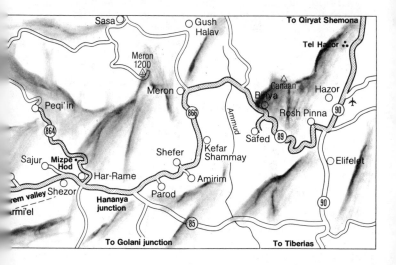

left, and the moshav of *Shezor* on the right. You'll notice that olives increasingly predominate the crops in the landscape, as they have for thousands of years.

At the large Arab Christian village of *Har Rame* (28 km.; 17 miles from Akko), with its ancient olive groves and abundantly flowing spring, a road to the left makes a steep ascent to *Peqi'in*. If you can spare the time, go up this road to *Mizpe Hod,* where you can take in the magnificent views of the successive ranges of hills of Lower Galilee, from the Sea of Galilee in the east to the Mediterranean in the west. Continue another 6 km. (4 miles) farther through wild mountain scenery to the romantic village of *Peqi'in* (*Buqeia*). Nestled at the foot of *Mount Ari,* Peqi'in is surrounded by gnarled olive trees, vineyards, tobacco fields, mulberry trees, and poplars. Druzes and Christian Arabs currently populate the town; but historically it was inhabited by Jews for at least 2,000 years (perhaps since Biblical times). Stones with Jewish emblems from a third-century synagogue have been incorporated into the 19th-century synagogue that now stands here. In the immediate surroundings of the village are the tombs of Talmudic scholars. It is said that the second-century mystic Shimeon Bar Yohay (also known as Rashbay) and his family hid here in a small cave for 13 years to escape Roman persecutors; they survived by eating the fruit of a carob tree and drinking water from a spring outside the cave.

Route 85 continues to the *Hananya Junction* (33 km.; 21 miles from Akko); a road cuts in here that runs south to the Golani Junction and then continues past Mount Tabor into the Yizre'el Valley. Stay on Route 85, which now swings north (left) and winds its way up the slopes of *Mount Meron* (1,208 meters; 3,963 feet)—the highest peak in Galilee. Below, to the right, is the kibbutz of *Parod,* lying on the boundary between Upper and Lower Galilee. Aptly named considering its location, Parod means "separation."

Beyond Parod to the right lies the moshav of *Amirim,* whose vegetarian inhabitants specialize in the growing of walnuts, almonds, and fruit trees. Some of the residents offer accommodations—in a magnificent setting—to travelers. To the left, surrounded by a forest, is the moshav of *Shefer,* whose families are mainly engaged in raising poultry. As you continue your tour, take some extra time to admire the landscape, because the route provides some of the finest panoramas in Israel. Far below on the right is the Sea of Galilee, and in the distance you can see the rounded peak of Mount Tabor.

At the moshav of *Kefar Shammay,* you get your first glimpse of the lofty town of *Safed* (Zefat) to the east, but the road curves in a wide arc to reach it. At 43 km. (27 miles from Akko) lies the moshav of *Meron,* which has ruins of a second-century synagogue. At this site, Joshua is believed to have won one of his greatest victories over the Canaanites (Joshua 11:1–9). During the Jewish War against the Romans (first century A.D.), the area was fortified by Flavius Josephus; however, it fell into the hands of the Romans, who made it one of their bases. Meron later became an important Jewish center where a large synagogue was built. Its stone architrave, believed to have been damaged in an earthquake, has been hanging loose for centuries: it is said that its fall will announce the coming of the Messiah.

At the time of the Bar-Kochba rebellion (A.D. 133–136), Meron was the home of Shimeon Bar Yohay (Rashbay), one of the spiritual leaders of the last desperate struggle against the Romans, and author of the *Zohar,* the principal work of the Cabala mystical tradition. For centuries, pious Jews have celebrated the festival of Lag Ba-Omer (33 days after the Passover) with a pilgrimage to Rashbay's tomb. Tens of thousands flock to Meron to pay homage to the holy man, and the hillsides are alight with their many small bonfires and religious dancing.

A good road reaches almost to the top of *Mount Meron*—a glorious picnicking spot. If you are feeling energetic, you will enjoy the nature trail that encircles the mountain. It runs through a dense scrub of kermes oaks, terebinths, laurels, and other trees; however, the summit is a military area—off-limits to visitors.

The road forks just beyond Meron. The branch to the left runs north to the Maronite Christian village of *Gush Halav* (Jish), the kibbutz of *Sasa,* and the Lebanese border. You should take the road (Route 89) that bears right toward Safed. Route 89 runs east over a kind of plateau, continuing toward *Mount Canaan* and the village of *Biriya* (now almost a suburb of Safed), and then begins a steep descent to Safed (52 km.; 32 miles from Akko).

*SAFED

Safed (population 15,000), Israel's highest town, lies at an altitude of 845 meters (2,772 feet) in a breathtaking location. To the northeast is Mount Canaan, Mount Meron lies to the west, and a spectacular view of the Sea of Galilee is seen to the southeast. Safed's refreshingly cool climate has made it a summer vacation center and health resort, and its winding lanes, ancient trees, and flower-filled courtyards add to its special charm.

History

Although Safed is not one of Israel's oldest cities, it has had an eventful history nonetheless. In *The Jewish War,* Flavius Josephus mentions a fortress called Sepph, which may be an early reference to Safed. In Talmudic times (16 centuries ago), bonfires were lit on Mount Canaan to announce the sighting of the new moon in Jerusalem and the beginning of a new month.

Safed rose to some consequence

in the time of the Crusades and changed hands a number of times. In the reign of Foulques of Anjou, king of Jerusalem from 1131–1143, a mighty stronghold was built on the summit of the hill—some remains still survive. The Knights Templar held the town, then lost it to Saladin in 1188; however, it was recaptured by Richard the Lion-Hearted in 1190. The Ayyubids destroyed Safed in 1220; although the Templars recovered it in 1248, the town was finally abandoned in 1266, when it was taken by the Mamelukes.

With the end of the Crusades in 1291, the Jewish city of Safed began to prosper. The influx of Spanish Jews expelled from their homeland in 1492 contributed greatly to the city's growth. In the 16th century, Safed became the largest Jewish community in the country and a spiritual center. Rabbi Joseph Karo, author of the *Shulan Arukh*, a meticulous compilation of all Jewish law, made his home here, as well as the poet Shelomo Alkabez, author of *Lecha Dodi*, a famous hymn. Perhaps the most celebrated resident of the time was Rabbi Isaac Luria, called Ari. As the leader of an important school of mysticism, he developed a cabalistic theory that examined earthly redemption and its relationship to heavenly matters. In 1563, the first Hebrew printing office was opened in Safed, and thereafter supplied the whole of the Diaspora with Jewish writings. The town competed with

Venice in the manufacture of textiles, and also exported olive oil, honey, silk, and spices.

Beset by earthquakes and local wars during the 17th century, Safed began to decline. Misfortune continued, capped by the worst disaster in 1837, when an earthquake cost 5,000 people their lives; epidemics also ravaged the population. The town began to recover toward the end of the 19th century, and by 1906 the population had increased to 13,000. But Safed was hard hit in World War I, and many perished from starvation and disease. By this time, Jews were in the minority, and the departing British authorities left control of the city in Arab hands. The Jews successfully resisted Arab attacks during the War of Independence; today, the town has a mixed population.

Attractions

The most picturesque part of Safed is the old *Jewish Quarter, with its many charming synagogues—among them the two *Ari synagogues,* Sephardi and Ashkenazi. Also worth seeing is the **Artists' Colony,** formerly the Arab quarter, whose winding lanes and charmingly restored houses retain the flavor of earlier times. Summer is the best and busiest season here, for many artists leave during the winter.

In addition to many private galleries, there are the *Artists' Club* (at the entrance to the colony) and the *Glicenstein Museum* (at the foot of the road up to the fortress of Mezuda).

The fortress of *Mezuda,* often called the Citadel, lies on the highest point of the hill. The road ascends the slope through a beautiful park planted with cedars, cypresses, and pines to the remains of Crusader and Mameluke fortifications and a monument to those who fell in the War of Independence in 1948.

There are a number of hotels on the slopes of *Mount Canaan,* which rises to over 1,100 meters (3,600 feet). Here, too, is one of the largest forests in Israel, with views of Mount Hermon, the Golan Heights, and the Sea of Galilee.

*

Return to the main road (Route 89) and continue east. Fresh vistas constantly open up as the road makes its steep, winding descent for 7 km. (4 miles) to Rosh Pinna. As the road twists and turns, you will see the Jordan Valley—from the Sea of Galilee to Mount Hermon—and, immediately to the east, the basalt wall of the Golan Plateau with its volcanic cones.

The road runs directly through the village of **Rosh Pinna** (58 km.; 36 miles from Akko), founded in 1878 by Jews from Safed who wanted to become farmers. Despite their good intentions, the settlers lacked the necessary farming skills and resources to successfully accomplish their goal. Plagued by hunger, disease, and exposure to frequent attacks by their Arab neighbors, they soon abandoned the little town. The settlement was reestablished in 1882 and given its present name, which means "foundation stone" (from Psalm 118, verse 22: "The stone which the builders rejected, the same is become the head of the corner.").

The new settlers were Rumanian immigrants who received generous help from Baron Edmond de Rothschild. Although they grew corn and tobacco, planted mulberry trees, and raised silkworms, their diligent efforts were only moderately successful, and the village did not grow significantly. As a result Rosh Pinna has preserved its old-world charm, and its practical, friendly, no-nonsense farmers are fourth and fifth generation descendants of the original Rumanian settlers.

At the other end of Rosh Pinna, you will join the road (Route 90) that runs almost due north from Tiberias to Metulla. You are now in the Jordan Rift, carved by the Jordan River and defined by steep hills.

To the left of the road is the little town of **Hazor** (61 km./38 miles from Akko; population 6,000), which was founded in 1953. Its main industry revolves around processing agricultural produce. Just beyond the village, Route 91 branches off to the right, running east via *Mishmar ha-Yarden* and *Gadot* to *Bnot Jakob* (Bridge of Jacob's Daughters), over the River

ROUTE 3
Rosh Pinna
to Metulla
0   Miles   5
Kilometers

potamia. Hazor's fame was widespread due to its location on the Via Maris, the main road between Egypt and Mesopotamia; it is mentioned several times, for example, in the "Execration Texts," Egyptian documents of the 19th century B.C. One century later, the Hyksos made Hazor one of their mightiest strongholds, after their conquest of Egypt.

The city was mentioned again in documents from the 14th century B.C., when Canaanite kings complained to the pharaoh about the aggressive behavior displayed by the warriors of Hazor.

Under Joshua's leadership, the tribes of Israel won their greatest victory over the Canaanites, who were led by Jabin, king of Hazor; later, in the battle of Megiddo, Deborah and her general, Barak, defeated a large Canaanite army under the command of Sisera of Hazor. The city did not fall to the Israelites, however, until the time of Solomon. By that time it had grown into a booming metropolis with a population of 40,000.

Thereafter, Hazor declined. In fact, after its conquest by the Assyrians in the eighth century B.C., it may have been completely abandoned—although excavation has revealed remains of a later, smaller city dating from the Hellenistic period.

Two of the ruins found on the site of Hazor are considered significant. The first is a large Canaanite *temple,* with stelae bearing representations of masks or hands raised in supplication. The temple also features two large figures of

Jordan, and then to the Golan Heights.

Stay on Route 90 north toward Metulla. On the left, you will come to the *site of ancient Hazor,* atop the imposing mass of ***Tel Hazor** (67 km.; 42 miles from Akko). Situated on the south edge of the Hula Basin, Hazor is an archaeological site of enormous importance. From at least the second millennium B.C., Hazor was one of the leading cities in the Fertile Crescent, an area extending from the borders of Sinai by way of Palestine and Syria into Meso-

lions at the entrance, sculptures, frescoes, and bas-reliefs, as well as ivory carvings of the Israelite period. The second major find is a deep shaft with steps that descend into a cistern supplied with water from a spring outside the town walls. Other remains at the site include massive casemate walls with weapons' placements, ruins of many public and private buildings, and numerous inscriptions. Many of the finds are displayed in the nearby *museum* at the entrance to the kibbutz of **Ayyelet ha-Shahar,** across the road from the ancient site.

The name "Ayyelet ha-Shahar" (Morning Star) was taken from the Arabic name of the site, which had been a wasteland before the kibbutz was established. The kibbutz was founded in 1917 at a time when food production was vitally important to settlers. The founders of the kibbutz were members of the Ha-Shomer (Guardians), the first Jewish defense organization. In time, they developed a prosperous farming community, with extensive apple orchards that flourished in the cooler air wafting down from Mount Hermon. Eventually, a limited amount of industry was developed as well.

Beyond Ayyelet ha-Shahar, the road descends into the Hula Basin. Once a wetlands area consisting of a shallow lake and expanses of marshland, it is now a cultivated region of great fields of cotton, alfalfa, and corn, as well as orchards and numerous fishponds. For most of the way, the road is lined by tall eucalyptus trees—whose thirsty specimens were originally planted here to help drain the marshes. The trees now provide welcome shade and necessary shelter from the wind.

After passing the moshav of *Sede Eli'ezer* (70 km.; 43 miles from Akko), you'll see a road that cuts in on the right leading to the *Hula Nature Reserve.* Within a limited area, the original marsh vegetation—consisting predominantly of papyrus reed and white and yellow water lilies—has been left untouched. The reserve is also the haunt of a variety of lovely water birds—herons, cormorants, storks, and, during certain seasons, pelicans—as well as many species of migratory birds. A few water buffalo have been reintroduced into this area, where they once thrived. You can rent a small boat to explore the ponds and waterways in the reserve.

To the left of the turn off for the reserve are the *Enan Springs* and their pumping station. Remains of a Neolithic settlement have been discovered here.

As you continue north, the natural walls surrounding you—the Galilean hills to the left and the Golan Heights to the right—rise progressively higher. Eventually, the northern frontier road veers off to the left and climbs into the hills, running past *Mezudat Koah, Sasa,* and *Elon* to *Rosh ha-Niqra* (see page 148). Continue on Route 90 alongside the western drainage canal from the former Lake Hula.

At the *Gome Junction* (82 km.; 51 miles from Akko), a road that turns off to the right leads to a series of kibbutzim (*Ne'ot Mordekhay, Lahavot ha-Bashan, Gonen*); the main road continues north for another 5 km. (3 miles) to the town of **Qiryat Shemona** (88 km./55 miles from Akko; population 20,000).

Founded in 1950, the town, whose name means "City of the Eight," was named for Joseph Trumpeldor and his seven companions, who were killed in 1920 in the defense of nearby Tel Hay (see page 160). The town lies in a lush green valley at the foot of *Mount Naftali* (almost 1,000 meters/3,300 feet high), opposite Mount Hermon and the Golan Heights. Along the valley runs a narrow line of hills—the "Snake Ridge"—formed of petrified lava.

Qiryat Shemona was originally a transit camp for new immigrants, who were employed as hired hands to work the fields. At a later stage, industry was developed here, and the town now has textile and metalworking plants as well as factories for processing fruit and vegetables. During the promotion of Jewish settlement on the Golan Heights, Qiryat Shemona became an important base and center of communications. Its location on the frontier of Lebanon has left it vulnerable to terrorist attacks.

Side trip to Dan

You can take a short excursion from Qiryat Shemona to Dan (8 km./5 miles)—especially recommended if you like picnics. From the north end of Qiryat Shemona, a side road runs northeast to Dan. After you cross the source streams of the Jordan—the *Nahal Iyyon* and the *Nahal Senir* (*Hazbani*)— you will come to the kibbutz of *Ha-Gosherim*. Founded in 1948, it's name means "Bridgebuilders." Soon after Ha-Gosherim, you come to the *Hurshat Valley Nature Reserve,* with ancient, spreading Tabor oaks, great tracts of grass, pools, ornamental ponds, streams, and small waterfalls. The park has facilities for picnicking, camping, and sports.

The road continues to the kibbutzim of *Dafna* and *Dan,* founded in 1939—the first "tower and stockade" settlements to be established in the northern Hula Valley. Malaria, once a fearsome enemy for settlers here, has been successfully eradicated.

Dafna takes its name from the Greek word for laurel (*daphne*): The name was often given to garden suburbs of Hellenistic cities in the first century B.C. This particular Dafna was once an outlying district of the city of Panaeas or Caesarea Philippi, located 3 km. (2 miles) northeast (see below). In addition to its agricultural production, the kibbutz has a factory that manufactures rubber and plastic shoes. Nearby is an amphitheater built to accommodate various cultural events for the surrounding area.

The kibbutz of Dan is named for the ancient site of Tel Dan (see below). It has a plastics factory and a natural history museum, the

Ussishkin House. A short distance away lies the moshav of *Sha'ar Yashuv*.

The *Dan Nature Reserve spreads north of Dan. The source of the River Dan—the principal tributary of the Jordan—is a spring here, fed by the ice-cold runoff from Mount Hermon.

Water flows almost constantly throughout the year from the pond formed by the spring. It tumbles over small waterfalls in streams that separate and then recombine; the water system supports a lush, dense growth of vegetation—a rare phenomenon in arid Israel. Tabor oaks and sycamores, Oriental planes, storax (the source of resin used in making incense), laurels, arbutus, Judas trees, and other species alternate with oleanders and various kinds of reeds. Narrow footpaths lead through the park to a water mill that was operating at the beginning of this century.

Adjoining the nature reserve is the ancient site of **Tel Dan**. On this hill, excavated in 1966, stood the Canaanite and Phoenician city of Layish (or Leshem), frequently cited in Egyptian documents from 2000 B.C. Layish lived in peace with its neighbors until the 12th or 11th century B.C., when it was conquered by the tribe of Dan, which had been driven out of its original settlement. Dan was the most northerly point in Israel during the time of the First and Second Temples. It was here that the notorious idolator Jeroboam, who led ten tribes of Israel in a revolt against his brother Rehoboam (Solomon's other son), built a pagan temple to worship a golden calf.

Excavations of the site have revealed the enormous earth ramparts around the town, a monumental entrance gate with a royal throne, and a paved street leading into the town center. There are also ruins of a temple and other structures.

The road runs east and northeast from Dan to the northern Golan Heights and Mount Hermon. *Banias (Panaeas), originally named for the Greek god Pan, lies at the source of the River Hermon (Banias). This Hellenistic city, once a center for the worship of Pan, was enlarged by one of Herod's sons. He renamed it Caesarea Philippi, and made it the capital of the territory assigned to him. According to Flavius Josephus, the river once had its source in the cave at the foot of the huge rock face; beside the cave are Greek inscriptions and niches for statues. The site, abandoned since 1967, is now a nature reserve.

Farther northeast, the road continues to the Crusader stronghold of *Qalaat Nimrud* (Subeibe), Nimrod's Castle, an impressive medieval fortress on a mountain spur with a commanding view of the countryside. Believed to have been built in the 12th century by Crusaders, control of the castle passed several times between Muslims and Christians. It is said that the fortress once served as the stronghold of the Assassins—a small, secret Muslim sect of murderers, whose infamous attacks terrorized Europe and the Middle East in the 13th century.

*

Return to Qiryat Shemona, and continue north on Route 90. In 2 km. (1.5 miles), you'll come to Tel Hay and the kibbutz of Kefar Gil'adi at the foot of the steep slopes of Mount Naftali, in Upper Galilee.

Tel Hay (108 km.; 67 miles from Akko, including side trips) and the kibbutz were founded in 1916 by members of Ha-Shomer (Guardian), the first Jewish defense organization, in order to produce food for the starving Jewish population during World War I. In 1920, when the area was incorporated into the French-mandated territory of Syria, Tel Hay was attacked by rebellious Arabs. Joseph Trumpeldor, founder of the Zionist movement in Russia and later one of the leaders of Palestine's Jews, was killed during the defense of the settlement along with seven companions. His last words, "It is good to die for our country," are inscribed on a memorial to the eight men in Lion Street. Tel Hay has a museum and a youth hostel.

Kefar Gil'adi is a large kibbutz, whose economy centers around agriculture and a quarry.

Side trip to Mount Naftali

At Tel Hay, a road branches off to the left; it runs southwest past a ruined Crusader fortress (the *Château Neuf*), and climbs up the steep summit ridge of Mount Naftali. The road then runs south along the frontier with Lebanon to the moshav of *Margaliyot,* the kibbutzim of *Menara* and *Yiftah,* and the fort of *Mezudat Koah.* The drive affords fine views of the Hula Valley to the east, and the hills of southern Lebanon to the west. You may wish to make the drive as a side trip, or to take it on your return journey from Metulla.

*

From Kefar Gil'adi, the road climbs the last 5 km. (3 miles) north to Metulla. To the right is the *River Iyyon,* which plunges down in four large waterfalls from Metulla to the valley. The nature reserve includes a beautiful hiking trail with splendid views.

The tiny town of **Metulla** (116 km./72 miles from Akko, including side trips; population 300), is Israel's most northerly settlement. Founded in 1896, this idyllic rural settlement has preserved its character as a moshav. Set in a beautiful location at an altitude of 525 meters (1,725 feet), it enjoys a pleasantly cool climate in summer.

TRAVEL ROUTE 4: Rosh Pinna–*Capernaum–Tabgha– *Tiberias–Karmi'el (77 km.; 48 miles)

See map below.

This route, from the hilly country of Upper Galilee to the low-lying land around the Sea of Galilee, takes in some of the most fascinating and significant sites in all of Israel. You will travel from the Mount of Beatitudes, where the spellbound multitudes listened to the parables of Jesus, to Tiberias, where Maimonides is buried, to the Horns of Hittim, where Saladin's warriors crushed the armies of the Crusades in 1187. The last part of the travel route takes you on a scenic drive through the Galilean countryside to Karmi'el, where you can rejoin the road to Akko.

From *Rosh Pinna* (see page 155), Route 90 runs due south through the hills toward the Sea of Galilee. You will pass the moshav of *Elifelet* to the left, whose settlers had to clear the land of huge basalt blocks before they could cultivate it. Beyond the settlement, you may be able to detect a number of dolmens made of similar blocks of basalt in the uncultivated land. These are megalithic tombs dating from around 5000 B.C.

The land slopes gradually downward toward the kibbutz of *Ammi'ad*. Just south of here, Route 85 (opened in 1980) slices west through Upper Galilee, pro-

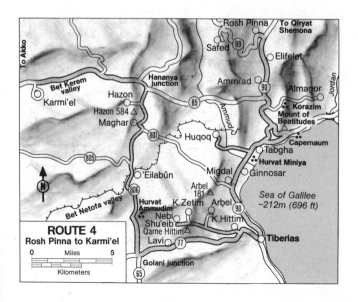

viding a shortcut to Akko. You continue on Route 90, which begins to run more steeply downhill. A few kilometers past the junction with Route 85, a road turns off eastward to the ruined synagogue of *Korazim* or *Chorazin* (Matthew 11:21), built of black basalt, and the moshav of *Almagor.* Next to the turn off stands the *Vered ha-Galil* restaurant (7 km.; 4.5 miles from Rosh Pinna), where you can hire an experienced guide to lead you on a trek on horseback through the surrounding area.

Route 90 begins a steep descent, punctuated by a series of sharp hairpin bends that afford breathtaking views of the Sea of Galilee, sandwiched between the Galilean hills and the Golan Heights. A side road branches off to the *Mount of the Beatitudes* (*Mons Beatitudinis*), the scene of Jesus Christ's Sermon on the Mount (Matthew 5–7, Luke 6:12–49). Today, the site is commemorated by a church, built in 1936–1938 and designed by Antonio Barluzzi, and a hospice—both are served by Italian Franciscan nuns. Route 90 continues its winding descent to the shores of the ***Sea of Galilee** (*Lake Gennesaret;* in Hebrew, *Yam Kinneret*).

Tabgha, or *En-Sheva,* as it is known in Hebrew, (12 km.; 7 miles from Rosh Pinna) was the scene of Jesus's miraculous multiplication of the loaves and fishes (Matthew 14:13–21; Luke 9:10–17; John 6:1–15). The Arab name derives from the Greek *Heptapegon* (Seven Springs); today there are still at least five springs,

Mosaic, Tabgha

some of which form small pools. The Byzantine-style *Church of the Multiplication,* consecrated in 1982, incorporates part of an old mosaic floor. The older mosaic depicts plants and birds, and the newer one shows a basket of bread between two fishes. A little way up the hill is the *Church of the Sermon on the Mount;* lower down, on the shores of the Sea of Galilee, is a Franciscan chapel, the *Church of the Primacy.* A carved rock, called the *Mensa Christi* (Christ's Table) is said to recall Christ's appearance there to His disciples after the Resurrection. If you wish to visit, remember to dress appropriately. Shorts and sleeveless blouses are not permitted in the Tabgha churches.

From Tabgha, drive 3 km. (2 miles) east along the north side of the Sea of Galilee to ***Capernaum,** which was Jesus's headquarters during the three years of His ministry in the area. Although excavation (and looting) took place at Capernaum intermittently throughout the centuries, systematic exploration did not begin until

1894, when the site was acquired by Franciscans. In 1905, the remains of a synagogue and an octagonal mosaic from a fifth-century chapel were discovered. The synagogue, roughly rectangular in plan and built of white limestone, dates from the second or third century A.D. Oriented toward Jerusalem—to the south—the synagogue has some outstanding stonework, with a richly decorated façade on the north entrance. The carved ornamentation includes Jewish motifs (pomegranates, grapes, olive branches, the six-pointed star of David, the five-pointed star of Solomon, the seven-branched menorah), as well as geometric designs. The synagogue was partly reconstructed in the 1920s. Visitors to the excavation site must be appropriately dressed; shorts are prohibited, even for men.

In the New Testament, Capernaum is referred to as Christ's place of residence after leaving Nazareth (Matthew 4:13). He taught in the synagogues here, and called His disciples together, saying, "Follow me, and I will make you fishers of men" (Matthew 4:19). Upon hearing these words, Peter and Andrew "left their nets and followed Him" (Matthew 4:20). But despite the many miracles performed here, the citizens of Capernaum and neighboring Korazim (Chorazin) and Bethsaida remained skeptical, so Christ departed with a fearsome curse, denigrating the cities and damning Capernaum to Hell (Matthew 11:20–24).

Capernaum: Ruins of the synagogue

Route 90 continues to the turn off for the youth hostel of *Kare De-she* (13 km.; 8 miles from Rosh Pinna) and runs southwest from there over a hill with the *Eshed Kinnarot* pumping station, part of Israel's National Water Carrier system. The Sea of Galilee is Israel's major freshwater reservoir.

The road now runs down into the Gennesaret Valley, a lush, green area of banana plantations, citrus fruit orchards, cotton, fodder crops, and vegetable fields. To the left is the site of *Hurvat Miniya,* on the shores of the lake. Here you can see a palace with beautiful mosaic floors, and a small port town of the Umayyad caliphs dating from the eighth century; the harbor is presumed to be older.

A road branches off on the right to the kibbutz of *Huqoq*. A city of the tribe of Naphtali once stood here. According to Biblical and Talmudic sources, this was also the location of the tomb of the prophet Habakkuk, a site venerated by Jewish pilgrims.

You now enter the gorge of the *River Ammud,* named for the tall columns (ammudim) of limestone that flank it. In this wildly beautiful setting, the remains of an early human, called *Palaeanthropus palaestinensis,* were discovered.

Continuing south on Route 90, you pass the kibbutz of *Ginnosar* (18 km.; 11 miles from Rosh Pinna). Founded in 1937, the kibbutz supports agriculture, industry, and lake fisheries. There are tourist accommodations and facilities, complete with a beach on the lakeshore. A pavilion on the grounds of the kibbutz contains an 8.5-meter- (28-foot-) long fishing boat that dates from the time of the Second Temple; it was found in 1986. Nearby is the regional museum of Bet Allon.

To the left of the road is **Migdal** (23 km.; 14 miles from Rosh Pinna), a moshav founded in 1910 that experienced considerable growth in the years following the arrival of the new immigrants in 1948. It occupies the site of the Migdal Nunia (Tower of the Fishermen), or Magdala, mentioned in the New Testament. This was the home of Mary Magdalene, who Luke called "a sinner" (7:37), and of whom Jesus said, "Her sins, which are many, are forgiven; for she loved much."

Flavius Josephus wrote of the stubborn resistance of the people of Migdal against Herod and the Romans. The Crusaders built a church here that the Mamelukes later used as a stable on the caravan route. Thereafter, both the church and the town fell into ruin. On the right of the road, near the lake, is a villa built by Lord Melchett (Sir Alfred Mond), who made a major contribution to settlement in this little valley.

Below Migdal, a road that branches off on the right runs northwest to the village of *Maghar* and up into central Lower Galilee (see page 167). To the south of this road, the mighty rock wall of *Arbel* rises above the gorge of the *Nahal ha-Yonim* (Stream of the Wild Pigeons); the cliffs are riddled with caves that were used as hiding places in the past. According to Flavius Josephus, the Maccabees fought the Romans at this spot. Above the cliffs, archaeologists found the remains of a synagogue built by Rabbi Nitai of Arbel; it is mentioned in the Talmud. The prophet Hosea also refers to Arbel (10:14).

Route 90 skirts the edge of the lake as it continues south; it passes a chapel and a small YMCA hostel, and soon reaches Tiberias. Beaches and restaurants line the shores of the lake to the left; houses and hotels dot the steep hillside to the right.

*TIBERIAS

Tiberias (*Teverya* in Hebrew; population 30,000), is an intriguing blend of antiquity and modernity—a place whose sacred areas seem unperturbed by the recreational pursuits of vacationers. One of the four holy cities of Judaism, Tiberias lies 210 meters (690 feet) below sea level on the Sea of Galilee, in a vacation land that extends from the shores of the lake to the slopes of the hills 400 meters (1,300 feet) above it. The climate is hot in summer but agreeably mild in winter, making Tiberias a favorite winter resort. Its hot springs have been frequented for their curative properties throughout the ages. In the surrounding area are many places sacred to Jews, Christians, Muslims, and Druzes.

History

The town was founded in the first century A.D. by Herod Antipas, son of Herod the Great, who named it for the Roman Emperor Tiberius. Roman generals came here to "take the cure" at the hot springs, which, at the time, were the most important in Galilee.

After Titus destroyed Jerusalem in A.D. 70, Tiberias became the spiritual and religious center of Judaism. (Coincidentally, the name works well in Hebrew— *tabur* is the Hebrew word for "navel" or "central point"). Between A.D. 200 and 500, Hebrew scholars here compiled the Gemara—the Aramaic commentary on the Mishnah (Oral Law); together, the two form the Talmud. The town eventually became the headquarters of the Sanhedrin (High Council).

The Crusaders held Tiberias for a short time, but it fell to Saladin after the battle at the Horns of Hittim in 1187. In the 16th century, Tiberias enjoyed a fresh period of prosperity, thanks to an influx of Jewish refugees from Spain— most notably Don Joseph Nasi, to whom Suleiman the Magnificent gave the city in 1562. In 1740, the city came under Bedouin control and prosperity continued; however, an earthquake in 1837 brought all activity to a temporary halt.

The War of Independence brought waves of violence to Tiberias, but since that time the town has stabilized and prospered.

Attractions

Behind the City Hall is the **Tomb of Maimonides** (1135–1204), who was a physician, philosopher, and the greatest Jewish scholar of the Middle Ages. A refugee from Spain, he became Rabbi of Cairo and personal physician to the Sultan of Egypt. The *Strong Hand* is his systematic explanation of the Mishnah, and his *Guide to the Perplexed* was an enduring and important contribution to all scholarship and thought in the Middle Ages. In his attempt to reconcile the writings of Aristotle (which were then known only in Arabic) with Jewish theology, Maimonides introduced the whole of Europe to Aristotle's thinking.

The restored ruins of an ancient synagogue known as **Hamat Tiberias** stand near the hot springs.

Its mosaic floor, featuring the twelve signs of the Zodiac, is one of the finest ever created. The Franciscan **Convent of Saint Peter** stands on the shores of the lake near the *Municipal Museum* (housed in a former mosque). It has a beautiful cloister and incorporates the apse of a Crusader church.

The **Tomb of Rabbi Meir Baal-Haness,** a second-century holy man who is revered as a miracle worker, lies 2.5 km. (1.5 miles) from the town center along the shady *Eliezer Kaplan Boulevard*. His tomb is one of the most sacred places in Israel.

*

There are two alternative routes from Tiberias to Karmi'el. If you are on a tight schedule, by all means take the shorter route. It backtracks on the lakeside road, then takes off northwest to Ammi'ad, and continues on Route 85 via Parod and Rama to Karmi'el (and on to Akko, if you wish).

If you have time, take the longer, scenic route. It follows Route 77 (the road to Nazareth) from Tiberias for 14 km. (9 miles) to the Golani Junction, winding its way up from the shores of the lake to the summit ridge. From here, there are stupendous views of the lake and surrounding area.

Soon after you leave Tiberias, you will see the moshav of *Mizpe,* founded in 1908, on the right. One of the smallest Jewish settlements

in the country, it still preserves the small farmsteads of its early years. Beyond this is the Arbe Valley, with the moshav shitufi of *Kefar Hittim,* founded in 1936. Two moshavs, *Arbel* and *Kefar Zitim,* are located farther down the valley. Soon a view opens up on the left into the larger and deeper *Yavne' el Valley,* now intensively cultivated and green almost all year round.

To the right is the extinct volcanic crater known as the **Horns of Hittim** (Qarne Hittim), the only clearly visible evidence of volcanic activity west of the Jordan. The crater contains the remains of the ancient Canaanite city of Madon, whose king, Jobab, fought against the Israelites in alliance with Jabin, king of Hazor (Joshua 11:1). There are also ruins of a synagogue of the late Roman period.

Saladin inflicted a decisive defeat on the Crusaders at this site in 1187. The Turkish leader is said to have won his victory by a cunning stratagem. The Crusaders had assembled an army to relieve the beleaguered town of Tiberias, and, clad in full armor, climbed the hill of Hittim en route to the Sea of Galilee. It was high summer, and Saladin ordered his troops to set fire to the bushes and scrub on the hill; the Crusaders, encased in their hot armor, could not repel the Muslim attack. Within a few months of the battle, Saladin wrested control of the whole country from the Christian forces.

On the northern slopes of the hill (which you can also reach on a

Fishermen on the Sea of Galilee

side road that branches off above Tiberias and runs via Kefar Hittim) is **Nebi Shu'eib,** the principal holy site in Israel for the Druzes. It is the location of the *tomb of Nabi Shueib*, the Druze name for the prophet Jethro, the father-in-law of Moses. Every spring, thousands of Druze pilgrims come here to celebrate their principal festival.

A short distance beyond the Horns of Hittim lies the religious kibbutz of *Lavi,* which, in addition to its agricultural work, runs a study center and a guesthouse. The kibbutz was founded in 1949 by immigrants from Britain, many of whom had come to Israel shortly before World War II.

The **Golani Junction** (40 km.; 25 miles from Rosh Pinna) was named for a military unit that played a major role in securing Galilee during the War of Independence in 1948. The forests in this area were planted by the Jewish National Fund; visitors are encouraged to join the reforestation effort by stopping to plant a tree. At the junction, turn right onto Route 806 running north to the Hananya Junction. It takes you over the Tur'an ridge, where the view suddenly opens up into the *Bet Netofa Valley,* whose bottom lies only about 50 meters (165 feet) above sea level. The valley is almost completely enclosed by hills. As a result, fertile alluvial soil carpets the valley, which is often flooded by the winter and spring rains. The road runs around the east side of the valley, passing the site of *Hurvat Ammudim*, with the ruins of a second-century A.D. synagogue.

After passing the Christian Arab village of *Eilabun* (50 km.; 31 miles from Rosh Pinna at the beginning of this travel route), the road cuts across the tunnel of the National Water Carrier. If you turn off the road about 100 meters farther on to the left, you can look down on the Bet Netofa Valley and the open channel of the National Water Carrier.

As you continue, you will notice an increasing number of olive plantations. Route 806 runs up to the large village of *Maghar* (62 km./39 miles from Rosh Pinna on this travel route; population 8,500), which is mostly occupied by Druzes, with some Arab Christians. The village is growing rapidly, and the many construction projects bear witness to its prosperity. Here the road is joined by the route that leads from Tiberias via Migdal (see page 164).

The road skirts *Mount Hazon* (584 meters; 1,916 feet), one of the highest peaks in Lower Galilee, and passes the moshav of *Hazon*. It then runs past the tomb of a medieval Jewish sage, shaded by a widely branching oak tree, and runs through olive groves. At the Hananya Junction, it joins the road from Safed to Akko. Turning left (west) here onto Route 85, you continue for 11 km. (7 miles) to *Karmi' el* (77 km.; 48 miles from Rosh Pinna at the beginning of this travel route). The journey from Karmi'el to Haifa via Akko is described (in the reverse direction) on pages 150–151 and 139–141.

TRAVEL ROUTE 5: *Haifa–Qiryat Tiv'on–**Nazareth (37 km.; 23 miles)

See map on pages 170–171.

This short route takes you through the hill country of Lower Galilee, steeped in Jewish and Christian history, to Nazareth, the scene of the Annunciation. Along the way, you can visit Bet Shearim, noted for its remarkably fine catacombs.

Leave *Haifa* (see page 120) and head southeast, skirting the high ridge of the Carmel range, which forms the southwestern boundary of the Zevulun Plain. At the *Mifraz Junction*, continue straight ahead on Route 75 through the outlying neighborhoods of *Tel Hanan* and *Nesher*, and past the large cement works.

The main road continues to the kibbutz of *Yagur* (11 km.; 7 miles from Haifa), which has a population of 1,240. Founded in 1922, Yagur soon became the largest communal settlement in the country; its members helped to develop Haifa's port and played a fundamental role in the creation of the industrial zones. The kibbutz now has a varied pattern of agricultural production as well as industrial enterprises, a metalworking and woodworking college, and various cultural institutions.

On the opposite side of the road is *Kefar Hassidim,* a village established in 1924 by a group of orthodox Jews from Poland, who dedicated themselves to upholding their traditional way of life. They drained the mosquito-infested marshland and reclaimed it for cultivation. After accepting many new immigrants, Kefar Hassidim split into two flourishing moshavs. Situated on the hills above them is the residential township of *Rekhasim*.

The road forks 2 km. (1 mile) beyond Yagur at the junction of *Ha-Amaqim*. The branch that bears to the right runs along the foot of the Carmel range and continues through the passage cut by the *River Kishon* between the Zevulun and Yizre'el valleys towards Megiddo. Take Route 75, which branches left, running up *Mount Tiv' on,* an outlying part of the Lower Galilean hills that separates the two valleys, and continues directly to Nazareth. To the left of the road is the kibbutz of *Sha' ar ha-Amaqim* (Gateway of the Valleys) established in 1935; to the right is *Oranim* (Pine Trees), the teachers' training college for the whole kibbutz movement.

A short distance beyond this is the garden city of **Qiryat Tiv'on,** situated amid kermes oaks on the low, chalk hills. A settlement named Qiryat Amal was established in 1937 as a garden suburb of Haifa; it was followed in 1945 by a similar settlement named Tiv'on. Both grew rapidly, and they were finally amalgamated under the name of Qiryat Tiv'on. In the years after the foundation of the state of Israel, large numbers of Bedouin, who had given up their nomadic lifestyle, built villas in the adjoining settlement of Basmat Tab'un. Tiv'on has many hotels and guesthouses, and is a good base for excursions in the surrounding area, with attractive hiking trails and footpaths.

On the outskirts of Qiryat Tiv'on, a short side road on the right leads to the site of **Bet Shearim.** Founded in the time of the Maccabees, the town was destroyed in A.D. 352 after an uprising against the Romans. Bet Shearim had its heyday in the second and third centuries, when it was the seat of the Sanhedrin. One of Judaism's preeminent figures, Rabbi Yehuda Hanassi, lived here around the year 200. He compiled the Mishnah, the first written record of the Oral Law, which, together with the Gemara, forms the Talmud.

Bet Shearim's main attractions—the *catacombs,* where members of the Sanhedrin were buried—cluster on a nearby hillside. Excavated between the 1930s and the 1950s, these 20 burial chambers revealed a wealth of stonework and carving. Even if your time is limited, don't miss the two most impressive sites. No. 20 contains around 200 sarcophagi and a great many bas-relief decorations and ancient inscriptions. Catacomb No. 14 houses the family tomb of Yehuda Hanassi. Of particular interest in the catacombs are the ancient stone doors with their stone hinges, which still work smoothly. The excavations also brought to light the remains of a fine second-century *synagogue,* several public buildings, and an oil press. A small museum contains a nine-ton slab of glass—the largest piece that dates from the ancient world.

In the nearby settlement of *Giv' at Zeid* stands an equestrian statue of Alexander Zeid, who was ambushed and shot here in 1939. Zeid lived in the area with his family as a watchman on land acquired by the Jewish National Fund in the 1920s.

A few kilometers farther to the left of the road is a turnoff to *Allonim* (Oak Trees). Founded in 1938, it was the first kibbutz established by members of the "Youth Aliyah" movement from Germany. Originally organized to bring children from Nazi Germany to Israel, the movement later

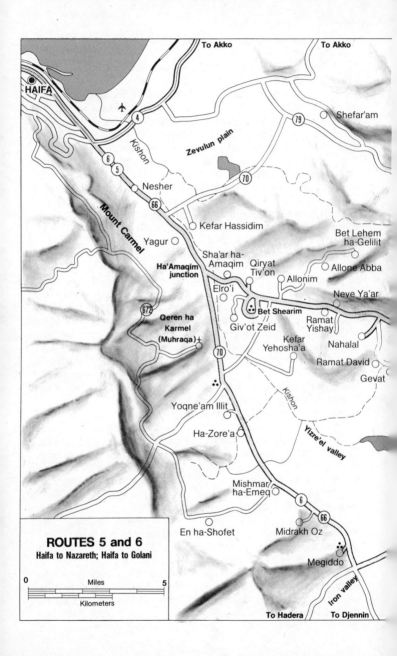

ROUTES 5 and 6
Haifa to Nazareth; Haifa to Golani

0   Miles   5

Kilometers

To Akko
To Akko

HAIFA

Shefar'am

Zevulun plain

Kishon

Nesher

Mount Carmel

Kefar Hassidim

Yagur

Bet Lehem
ha-Gelilit

Sha'ar ha-
Amaqim

Qiryat
Tiv'on

Allone Abba

Ha'Amaqim
junction

Elro'i

Allonim

Neve Ya'ar

Qeren ha
Karmel
(Muhraqa)

Bet Shearim

Giv'ot Zeid

Ramat
Yishay

Nahalal

Kefar
Yehosha'a

Ramat David

Gevat

Kishon

Yizre'el valley

Yoqne'am Illit

Ha-Zore'a

Mishmar
ha-Emeq

En ha-Shofet

Midrakh Oz

Megiddo

To Hadera

Iron valley

To Djennin

extended its efforts to include children from any persecuted Jewish community in the Diaspora. The kibbutz of Allonim engages in both agriculture and industry.

The side road leading to Allonim continues to the moshav shitufi of *Allone Abba*. The moshav began as a settlement founded by Germans belonging to the modern order of Templars, who declared their support for Hitler in the 1930s. They were interned by the British authorities during World War II, and finally deported. The kibbutz bears the name of a paratrooper who was killed during World War II while trying to save Jews in Nazi-occupied Europe. Nearby is the moshav of *Bet Lehem ha-Gelilit*.

Continuing along Route 75, you soon enter the northern Yizre'el Valley and the village of *Ramat Yishay* (23 km.; 14 miles from Haifa), which lies to the right. Another road that cuts in on the right leads to the moshav of *Bet Shearim*, founded in 1936. To the left is the agricultural experimental station of *Neve Ya'ar*, which was a German Templar village until World War II.

At a road junction near the ancient site of *Shimron*, Route 75 bears left directly to Nazareth, running up to the Nazareth Ridge in the hills of Lower Galilee. If you have time, you may want to take the road to the right (Route 73)—a longer route to Nazareth that runs beneath the ridge, along the north side of the Yizre'el Valley, to the kibbutzes of *Ramat David, Gevat, Sarid, Ginnegar*, and *Mizra*. If you take Route 73, you will come almost immediately to a sharp turn to the right; 1 km. (less than one mile) farther on is the moshav of **Nahalal.**

Founded in 1921, Nahalal (population 1,200) was the prototype for the moshav. Now the most common type of settlement in Israel, moshavim combine elements of private ownership with mutual aid and communal activities. When the first Jewish settlers arrived here, they labored to overcome an inhospitable area of marshland, whose hazards had defeated earlier efforts at settlement by Arabs and Germans.

The village, designed by the town planner Richard Kauffmann, is laid out in concentric circles. The communal institutions lie in the center, surrounded by residential and industrial buildings, which, in turn, are ringed by intensively cultivated areas, and then by extensively cultivated fields. Nahalal also boasts one of the country's first colleges of agriculture.

After returning to Route 75, continue to the kibbutz of *Yif'at*. Just beyond it lies the development town of *Migdal ha-Emeq* (population 13,000). Originally founded by Middle Eastern immigrants in 1952, the settlement struggled to maintain its existence during the early years. Happily, the establishment of a series of successful factories, including one that manufactures cosmetics, considerably improved the situation, and Migdal ha-Emeq has emerged as one of the country's rising towns.

Route 75 now runs along the upper edge of the *Balfour Forest*. Reforestation began here in the 1920s, making this one of Israel's oldest forests; it was also the largest until 1950. A center located here furthers the interests of reforestation by encouraging visitors to "Plant a Tree with Your Own Hands."

Route 75 next takes you to *Yafi' a* (Yafa). The town is mentioned in the Bible as Japhia, a city of the tribe of Zebulun. During the Jewish War, its citizens fought valiantly against the Romans. It is now a suburb of Nazareth, with a population of 6,500, mostly Christian Arabs.

The road now comes to Nazareth, 37 km. (23 miles) from Haifa.

**NAZARETH

To those who think of Nazareth as the pokey little village where Jesus spent his childhood, the modern bustling town will come as a complete surprise. With its population of 40,000, Nazareth nestles picturesquely amid the rolling hills of Lower Galilee. Despite the rigors of modern times, the centuries have scarcely changed the lifestyle of Nazareth, which is now the largest Arab town in Israel. The inhabitants are mostly Christians of various denominations; only a few are Muslims. Its Hebrew name is *Nazerat;* in Arabic it is *En Nasra*. Some distance outside the old town is *New Nazareth* (Nazerat Eylit), a Jewish development town with a modern industrial zone.

From here there is a fine view of the old city of Nazareth.

History

Because Nazareth is not mentioned in either the Bible or the Talmud, many scholars have concluded that no town of that name existed in the time of Jesus. Some suggest that Jesus's home town may have been Capernaum, and that the term Nazarene, as applied to Him, derived from the Syriac word *nesarya* (guardian). However, the clear references to Nazareth in the Gospels—on which the town's importance depends—directly challenges these theories.

Like so many other towns of the time, Nazareth was destroyed and abandoned during the Jewish War (66–67 A.D.), but it was later rebuilt by the joint efforts of Christians and Jews. A church was built here in 326 on the orders of Emperor Constantine, but the town decayed following its conquest by the Arabs. The Crusaders built a large basilica on the site of Constantine's Byzantine church, and Nazareth once again flourished, eventually becoming the see of a bishopric. In 1187, after the battle at the Horns of Hittim, Saladin captured Nazareth; 40 years later, it was rebuilt by Emperor Frederick II.

No Christians lived in Nazareth during the period of Turkish rule. However, the Franciscans were allowed to establish themselves in the town in 1620, under the protection of Fakhr ed Din, the Druze ruler of Lebanon. Napoleon held Nazareth in 1799, pitting his troops against a superior Turkish force; his army eventually withdrew. Under the mandate, Nazareth reached prominence again when it became the administrative center of Galilee for the British authorities. In 1948, during the War of Independence, the town served as the headquarters of the Arab forces.

Attractions

Nazareth's holy sights are dominated by the **Franciscan Convent** [1], which was completed in its present form in 1730. A small *museum* in the north wing displays objects dating from the Crusades that were recovered during excavation.

A flight of steps at the south wing of the convent leads up to the new Franciscan **Church of the Annunciation** [2], built in 1969 in an imitation of Italian Renaissance-style architecture. The church marks the spot where the angel is believed to have appeared to Mary to announce that she would give birth to Jesus (Luke 1:26). Tradition has it that this was the site of the Virgin's house; some say that after the Arabs conquered Nazareth, the house was carried over the sea by angels and set down in the Italian town of Loreto.

A dark, narrow staircase descends to the crypt of the church. Passing *"Mary's Kitchen"* [A], you enter *Saint Joseph's Chapel*

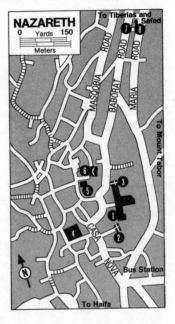

[B], with the *Altar of the Flight into Egypt* [a]. A narrow entrance leads into the *Chapel of the Annunciation* [C]; the *Altar of the Annunciation* [b] bears the inscription "Verbum caro hic factum est" (Here the Word was made flesh). *Gabriel's Column* [c] designates the spot where the angel stood, and *Mary's Column* [d], the stump of a red granite column hanging from the ceiling, marks Mary's place where she received the angel's message. The *Chapel of the Angel* [D], with the *Altar of Saint Gabriel* [e], the *Altar of Saint Joachim* [f], and a sixth-century Byzantine mosaic [g], have been closed to visitors.

To the north of the Church of the

Nazareth: Church of the Annunciation

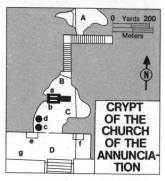

CRYPT OF THE CHURCH OF THE ANNUNCIATION

Annunciation stands **Saint Joseph's Church** [3], a modern building on the traditional site of Joseph's workshop. A dark cavern beneath the church is believed to have been the dwelling of the Holy Family. A circular projection in

"Joseph's workshop" in Nazareth

the middle of the floor has been identified as a table, and there are also a number of pits for food storage. Some authorities believe that the spot was a pagan tomb that was later converted into a dwelling.

The **Convent of the Sisters of Nazareth** [4] also contains a number of underground chambers, which some believe to be Joseph and Mary's house.

Nearby, *Bazaar Street* (Es Suq) leads to the **Old Synagogue** [5], where Jesus is believed to have taught (Luke 4:16). A small *mosque*, [6] dating from the Turkish period, lies to the northeast.

Women still come with earthenware vessels to draw water from **Mary's Well** [7], located on the town's main street, as they have since the time of Christ. The spring that supplies the water to the well is in the nearby Greek Orthodox **Church of Saint Gabriel** [8], which is well worth a visit to see its furnishings and decoration. The Greek Orthodox believe that this church rests on the true site of the Annunciation.

TRAVEL ROUTE 6: *Haifa–*Megiddo–Afula–Mount Tabor–Golani (77 km.; 48 miles)

See map on pages 170–171.

This route takes you through the Yizre'el Valley—the most fertile area in all of Israel—by way of settlements of compelling historical interest. Chief among these is Megiddo, which has known human habitation since the earliest times of prehistory, and which some believe will be the scene of mankind's last great battle between good and evil—Armageddon. You will also see Yizre'el, where Ahab's evil wife Jezebel met her fittingly gruesome death; and En Dor, where a medium (the "Witch of Endor") summoned the spirit of Samuel to advise King Saul on the eve of his battle against the Philistines. You can end this Travel Route 6 in Afula, where you can continue to Jerusalem following Travel Route 7, or you can follow Travel Route 6 on to Mount Tabor, the most imposing peak in Lower Galilee, and then to its end in Nazareth.

Head southeast from *Haifa* (see page 120), following the route outlined at the beginning of Travel Route 5 as far as the *Ha-Amaqim Junction* (12 km.; 7 miles from Haifa). At this point, bear right on Route 70 and follow the *River Kishon* through the narrow pass between the Tiv'on hills and the towering bulk of the Carmel range. You will pass the little Jewish village of *Elro'i;* in Roman times, the fort of Geva stood nearby. Beyond this point, a road to the left descends into the valley; it passes the moshav of *Kefar Yehoshua* (founded in 1927), which is laid out on a plan similar to that of Nahalal (page 172), before it joins Travel Route 5 near the kibbutz of *Allonim* (see page 169).

As you continue on Route 70, you will come to the *Yoqne'am Junction* (19 km.; 12 miles from Haifa). At this point, Route 70 branches off to the right, running between the Carmel range and the Menashe Hills to Zikhron Ya'aqov and the coastal plain.

Above the junction, you can see the southeastern tip of the Carmel range, *Qeren ha-Karmel* (in Arabic, *Muhraqa*), that rises an impressive 482 meters (1,581 feet). The *Monastery of Saint Elijah* sits on the site where, according to tradition, the prophet contended with the priests of Baal. At the junction, continue on Route 66 and you will pass a hill that was the site of the Canaanite city of *Yoqne'am* (Jokneam), one of the 31 cities captured by Joshua; it was assigned first to the tribe of Zebulun and later to the Levites.

You now come to the moshav of *Yoqne'am* (16 km.; 10 miles from Haifa), a farming village founded in 1935. On the hill to the right is the moshav of *Yoqne'am Illit* (population 4,580), founded in 1950, which is mainly industrial. Surrounded by forest on the left, lies the little valley of *Emeq ha-Shofet*. After you pass this forest, you will come to the kibbutz of **Ha-Zore'a** (23 km./14 miles from Haifa; population 850), founded in 1936 by members of a German youth movement. Although it is primarily an agricultural settlement, it also has a furniture factory and a plant that produces polythene sheeting for agricultural use. At the kibbutz, the *Wilfried Israel Museum* displays archaeological finds from the surrounding area, as well as a rich collection of Far Eastern art.

As you continue southeast, the broad expanse of the *Yizre'el Valley* stretches to the left. Beyond it you will see the Nazareth Ridge and Mount Tabor in Lower Galilee. Close to the road on the right are the *Menashe Hills*—the Menashe Forest represents one of the largest reforestation areas in Israel. The conduits of the National Water Carrier enter the Menashe Tunnel here.

The kibbutz of *Mishmar ha-Emeq* (25 km.; 15 miles from Haifa) lies off the road to the right. Founded in 1926, it was the first Jewish settlement on the southwest side of the valley, and one of the leading kibbutzes in the radical Ha-Shomer ha-Za'ir movement. The successful defense of this settlement in April 1948 proved to be a turning point in the War of Independence. In addition to its farming activity, Mishmar ha-Emeq has a plastics factory and an interesting local museum. If you wish,

you can take a scenic detour at this point up through the Menashe Forest to the kibbutz of *En ha-Shofet*.

Back on Route 66, you will pass the moshav of *Midrakh Oz* and enter ***Megiddo** (30 km.; 19 miles from Haifa). This ancient stronghold lies on an easily defensible hill at the point where the old Via Maris, which linked Egypt with Mesopotamia, emerges from the narrow Iron Gorge into the wide Yizre'el Valley.

Archaeological excavations have revealed an extraordinary wealth of historical information at Megiddo. Twenty-five levels of occupation have been identified at the site, ranging in time from the Early Bronze (or Copper) Age—the fourth millennium B.C.—to the Persian period of the fifth century B.C.

Megiddo's history is rife with warfare. Throughout the ages, it has been defended against enemy attack, taken by storm, burned down, and rebuilt. Great battles were fought here so often in the past that ancient tradition cites Armageddon (*Har Megiddo*—Mount Megiddo) as the scene of Man's final battle before the Messiah comes to redeem the world (Revelation 16:16: "And he gathered them together into a place called in the Hebrew tongue Armageddon").

A detailed hieroglyphic inscription found in Egypt described how Pharaoh Tuthmosis III (c. 1501–1447 B.C.) beseiged and captured Megiddo during his campaign to quell an uprising by his Canaanite subjects. The enemy had expected Tuthmosis to approach by one of two side roads through the valley; by choosing the main road instead, he successfully surprised his enemies and overcame them.

The Bible makes prominent note of Megiddo as the place where Deborah and Barak won their great battle against Jabin, King of Hazor (Judges 5:19: "by the waters of Megiddo"). Despite their victory, it was a long time before the Israelites were able to capture the Canaanite stronghold. Many believe David finally took Megiddo, and that Solomon rebuilt it. However, according to the Israeli archaeologist Yigael Yadin, the stables attributed to Solomon were more likely built by King Ahab around 850 B.C. to house the horses that powered his war chariots.

In 732 B.C., the Assyrian king Tiglath-Pileser III captured Megiddo. Josiah, King of Judah, lost his life in battle here in 609 B.C. as he attempted to halt the advance of Pharaoh Necho.

The Romans built a fort, Ferrata, near the town for their sixth Legion; their influence was preserved in the name of the Arab village of Lajun (from *legio*) which occupied the site until 1948. (Megiddo itself is known to the Arabs as *Tell el-Mutessilim,* the Hill of the Governor.) And the British general Allenby cleverly outmaneuvered the Turkish and German forces here in 1919, securing an important victory for his forces.

Restoration work has been done on some of the ruins of ancient Megiddo, and the site is well laid out with footpaths and signposts to direct visitors. Near the entrance is a *museum* that displays models of the stronghold during different periods, as well as items such as tools and seal rings.

After passing the *remains of walls* [1], you will come first to the *outer North Gate* [2] and then to the *inner North Gate* [3]—both date from the time of Solomon. Close by are a *town gate* [4] of the 15th century B.C. and a *gate* [5] of the Hyksos period (c. 1720–1570 B.C.). After you walk by an eighth-century B.C. *grain silo* [6], you will come to *"Solomon's Stables"* [7] and a *water tunnel* [8]. Opposite the stables are the remains of a Solomonic *palace* [9] and a nearby *scenic viewpoint* [10], beside a building that dates

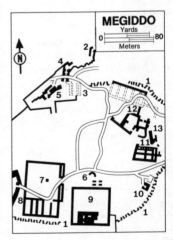

MEGIDDO

from the time of David. Near this is the *building* [11] where Solomon's war chariots were kept. The remains of a *Canaanite shrine* [12] dating from the 20th century B.C. and a *temple* [13] from the late fourth millennium B.C. are the most ancient finds on the site.

Return to Route 66 and head southeast for a brief drive to the *Megiddo Junction*. Route 66 continues straight ahead to Jenin where it meets other roads that will take you to Jerusalem via Nablus and Ramallah (see Travel Route 7). To continue on Travel Route 6, however, follow Route 65, which runs 10 km. (6 miles) due northeast to Afula (Route 65 to the right runs through the Iron Valley to Hadera). The road, which has since been widened, was hastily constructed by British forces for strategic purposes during World War II. Flanked by an avenue of eucalyptus trees, it runs through the flat southern section of the Yizre'el Valley—a region of fertile black earth whose main crops are wheat and cotton.

In 5 km. (3 miles), a road branches off on the right and runs past the nine moshavs of the *Ta'anakh Group*, established in 1955, to the kibbutz of *Yizre'el*. It occupies the site of the Biblical Jezreel, where the evil Jezebel was trampled by Jehu's horse (see page 182). Ta'anakh was planned as a type of regional settlement consisting of three or more villages grouped around a rural center; this center performs certain basic economic and social functions with

the support of an urban center—in this case, Afula.

Afula (43 km./27 miles from Haifa; population 25,000) is the largest settlement in the Yizre'el Valley. Scanty remains show evidence of human habitation here in prehistoric or Biblical times. The modern town was founded in 1925 by an American Zionist organization as a market center for the new settlements in the valley. Afula consists of a lower town in the valley and an upper town on the slopes of the hill of *Giv'at ha-Moreh*. Afula is an important center of communications and industry for the area. The town's industrial enterprises mainly involve the processing of agricultural products (sugar, textiles, flour).

The road now runs past the moshav of *Balfouriya* on the right, established in 1922. You will pass a number of factories and the regional hospital on the left before you come to the upper town of Afula on the slopes of Giv'at ha-Moreh to the right. At *Daverat* (50 km.; 31 miles from Haifa), a kibbutz founded in 1946, the rounded top of Mount Tabor can be seen a short distance ahead. The tip of the valley between Giv'at ha-Moreh and Mount Tabor is called Emeq Daverat—a name apparently derived from Deborah, who led the Israelites out from Mount Tabor to do battle with the Canaanites under Sisera (Judges 4). Travel 3 km. (2 miles) beyond the kibbutz and you will see a narrow road going off on the left: it runs up Mount Tabor, passing near the large Arab village of *Dabburiya* (population 4,000). The 4-km. (2.5-mile) stretch of road up Mount Tabor is narrow, steep, and winding, but it offers stunning views of the Yizre'el Valley and the successive ranges of hills in Lower Galilee, beyond which the snow-capped summit of Mount Hermon can sometimes be seen.

The large, squat form of **Mount Tabor** (in Hebrew, Har Tavor) rises to a height of 588 meters (1,929 feet) above sea level, topped by a broad, flat plateau. Although the surrounding area consists of black basalt, Mount Tabor itself is basically a huge block of limestone.

From time immemorial Mount Tabor has been regarded as sacred, and the lush, green vegetation of its slopes has undoubtedly contributed to the reverence accorded it. As early as the third century A.D., tradition claims Mount Tabor as the site of Christ's Transfiguration (Luke 9:28–36; Matthew 17:1–9)—although it is hardly the "high mountain apart"

of which Matthew speaks. In the time of Christ, it was covered with the remains of ruined houses.

A basilica was built on the mountain in the fourth century. In 1101, the Benedictines founded an abbey, which was richly endowed by the Crusader leader Tancred. The basilica, along with the other churches and religious houses on the hill, was destroyed by Saladin after his victory at the Horns of Hittim (1187). Saladin's successor, Malik el-Adil, built a fortress on Mount Tabor that withstood a long and unsuccessful siege by Christian forces during the fifth Crusade. It was finally destroyed by the Mameluke leader Baibars around 1263. Over 400 years passed before the Franciscans reestablished a Christian presence on Mount Tabor in 1631.

The best preserved ruins stand on the "Latin" part of the plateau (which is divided equally between the Roman Catholic and Greek Orthodox churches). Near the *Tower of the Winds* [1], an arched gateway built by the Arabs, lie the excavated remains of houses from

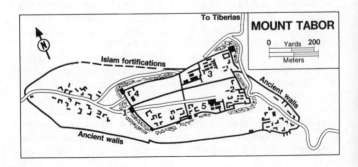

MOUNT TABOR

To Tiberias

0   Yards   200
Meters

Islam fortifications

Ancient walls

Ancient walls

Tabor: Franciscan church

the first century A.D. The Franciscan *Tabor Church* [2], consecrated in 1924, now stands on the site of the Crusaders' basilica. Beyond this is an old *bastion* which offers the best view of the site.

The Greek Orthodox *Church of Saint Elias* (Elijah) [3] retains two apses and the mosaic floor of an earlier Crusader church. To the west of this is the *Grotto of King Melchizedek* [4], where the ruler is said to have fed Abraham when he was fleeing from his foes. The *Franciscan convent* [5] can accommodate guests.

Return to Route 65 and continue east. A road that branches off to the right leads to the kibbutz of *En Dor,* established in 1948. If you follow the road 5 km. (3 miles) to the southwest, you will come to the historic site of Endor, where King Saul, deserted by the Lord on the eve of his battle with the Philistines on Mount Gilboa, per-

suaded a medium ("a woman that hath a familiar spirit") to summon up Samuel, from whom Saul sought advice (1 Samuel 28).

Continue on Route 65 to *Kefar Tavor,* a moshav founded in 1901, which has preserved its original character as a farming village. Here the road swings north, skirting the east side of Mount Tabor. To the left is the *Kadduri College of Agriculture.* Two km. (1.5 miles) farther, a road goes off to the left and leads to the kibbutz of *Bet Qeshet;* on the right, you can see the ruins of a late 16th-century Turkish caravanserai.

As you continue on the main road, you will come to the moshav of *Ilaniya* (Sejera) (66 km.; 41 miles from Haifa). It was founded in 1899 as a training farm by the Jewish Colonization Association, which had acquired land in this part of Lower Galilee for wheat growing. Its early settlers included Kurdish Jews and Russians who had been converted to the Jewish faith. David Ben-Gurion served here with a group of workers who formed the first self-defense organization to protect the settlement against attack. In 1907, they also founded the Ha-Horesh agricultural workers' organization, which undertook labor on a piecework basis. During the War of Independence, the defense of Ilaniya played a decisive part in achieving victory in Lower Galilee. A second moshav, *Sede Ilan,* was founded in 1949.

You now come to the **Golani Junction** (77 km.; 48 miles from

Haifa), one of Israel's most important crossroads. Here you join Travel Route 4, which comes from Tiberias (see page 167). Route 65 continues straight ahead through the *Bet Netofa Valley;* the road to the left (Route 77) leads toward Nazareth (92 km.; 57 miles from Haifa from the beginning of this travel route).

TRAVEL ROUTE 7: Afula–Jenin–*Samaria–Nablus–Ramallah–***Jerusalem (120 km.; 75 miles)

See map on page 188.

This route follows the course of the River Jordan as it flows south from Afula to Jerusalem through Judea and Samaria—areas now better known as the northern part of the Israeli-administered territories of the West Bank. Until the Six-Day War, this territory belonged to Jordan; however, for the last two decades the people here—Muslims and Jews alike—have been living under the auspices of the Israeli government.

Whatever the political climate, the landscape invariably appears dramatic and beautiful. South of Jenin, you can choose between two different routes to Nablus, which is the spiritual center of the world's few remaining Samaritans. One road takes you through the ancient site of Samaria; the other goes via Tubbas, site of the ancient Biblical town of Thevez.

Six km. (4 miles) from *Afula* (see page 179) on Route 60 lies the kibbutz of *Yizre'el,* situated in the western foothills of *Mount Gilboa.* It occupies the site of the Biblical Jezreel, where Naboth owned the vineyard coveted by Ahab and his evil wife Jezebel. It was here that Jezebel was trampled by Jehu's horse as punishment for her wickedness, and her body eaten by dogs (1 Kings 21; 2 Kings 9). The kibbutz was established toward the end of the War of Independence at this strategically important crossroads. To the right extends the southern Yizre'el Valley, with the Ta'anakh Group of moshavs (see page 179), four of which (*Avital, Metav, Perazon,* and *Ya'el*) lie near the road.

As you continue on Route 60, you will pass the Arab villages of *Sandala* (left) and *Muqeibila* (right)—which are still within Israel's pre-1967 boundaries—and then two West Bank villages, *Jalama* and *Arana.* Before long, you will come to **Jenin** (17 km.; 11 miles from Afula). Although somewhat isolated in the southern corner of the Yizre'el Valley between the Iron Hills of Samaria to the west and Mount Gilboa to the east, this little Muslim town of 13,500 has been occupied from time immemorial and enjoys good soil and an abundant supply of water from springs. In Egyptian inscriptions of the 20th and 19th centuries B.C., the town is called Kan or Bet ha-Gan (House of the Garden). In the Bible, it appears as En-gannim (Garden Spring), a city inhabited by the Levites in the territory of the tribe of Issachar. The remains of a Byzantine church lie near a modern Orthodox church. The Crusaders called Jenin "le Grand Guèrin."

From Jenin, Route 60 bends southwest, passing the pre-Biblical and Biblical site of *Yivle'am* (28 km.; 17 miles from Afula), and enters the fertile *Dotan Valley* (the Biblical Dothan; in Arabic, *Sahel Arraba*). This is the place where Joseph's brothers threw him into a pit and then sold him to a party of passing Midianite merchants (Genesis 27). Encircled by hills, the intensively cultivated valley is 10 km. (6 miles) long and up to 4 km. (2 miles) wide. Villages dot the hillsides around the valley.

The road forks 6 km. (4 miles) beyond Jenin, which gives you a choice of routes to Nablus: The westerly route (described below under option "A") takes in the ancient site of Samaria; the easterly route (described in "B" beginning on page 185) goes via Tubbas.

A: To Nablus via Samaria

Follow the route marked "A" on the map on page 188.

Follow Route 60 which cuts across the Dotan Valley as it heads first southwest and then south. In 1 km. (a half-mile), a side road branches off to the right toward Tulkarm; to the left is the ancient site of *Dotan*. Between the large villages of *Arraba* on the right and *Marka* (Merke), the road begins to wind its way out of the valley. To the right, you can see the embankment of the railroad that ran between Afula and Nablus until 1948. Soon after this, also on the right, is the new Jewish outpost settlement of *Dotan*.

The road continues south through beautiful and varied hill country, passing between the Arab villages of *Ajja* on the right and *Anza* on the left. Near the village of *Jaba,* a road branches off to the left into the *Sanur Valley,* one of the most fertile regions in northern Samaria. Beyond this lies the large village of *Silat edh Dhahr* to the right, and *El Fandaqumiya* to the left, which takes its name from the Greek *Pentekomias,* (Five Villages).

Between *Bazariya* on the right and *Burqa* on the left, the road winds its way downhill, and a side road veers off on the left to the site of ancient Samaria.

Samaria (45 km.; 28 miles from Afula) is known in Hebrew as *Shomeron;* the old Greek name for the city, Sebaste, is preserved in the name of the Arab village of *Sebastiye*, which adjoins the site. Samaria was originally founded around 880 B.C. by Omri, ruler of the northern kingdom of Israel. He bought the hill from a man named Shemer, and made the site his capital (1 Kings 16:24). Excavations made since 1908 have confirmed the Biblical account. The small capital of Omri's kingdom measured only 180 meters by 90 (200 yards by 100). Archaeologists have identified a number of structures within the town—parts of a carefully built wall with casemates built into it intermittently; the palace of Omri and Ahab; the ivory house that Ahab built for his wife Jezebel (whose delicate ivory carvings are now in the Rockefeller Museum in Jerusalem); and storehouses, in which potsherds with inscriptions—mostly receipts for wine and oil—were found.

In the eighth century B.C., Jeroboam II enlarged the city; but, it was destroyed by King Sargon of Assyria in 722, and most of its inhabitants were exiled. Settlers from Kutha and Babylon moved in and intermarried with the few remaining Israelites. Before long, the population developed a new identity as the Samaritans. In the fourth century B.C., the Samaritans vainly rose up against Alexander of Macedon, who punished the rebels and settled Macedonians in the town.

Samaria was taken by the Hasmonean king John Hyrcanus in 107 B.C. In the following century, it was enlarged and rebuilt on a magnificent scale by Herod the Great, who surrounded it with a wall 4 km. (2½ miles) long. He named the city Sebaste (the "august city") in honor of his patron, Caesar Augustus.

In Roman times, several hundred thousand Samaritans inhabited this region; today they number fewer than 1,000, most of whom live in Nablus (see page 186). Among other things, the parable of the Good Samaritan (Luke 10:25–37) illustrates the prejudice that the Jews of the time felt toward this group. Their enmity was largely based on religious differences, for the Samaritans recognize only the Pentateuch (Torah) and the book of Joshua as the word of God, and claim to be the true descendents of Abraham and Moses.

The remains of ancient Samaria are indeed impressive. Near a third-century Byzantine *basilica,* dedicated to John the Baptist and said to contain his tomb, are the remains of the Israelite *town walls.* A *tower* of the Macedonian period and a *theater* are well preserved. On the highest point of the hill are the excavated remains of *Omri's palace,* near which are fragments of the giant *Temple of Augustus.*

On the east side of the Arab village of Sebastiye are remains of the Crusader *Church of Saint John,* part of which is incorporated into the mosque.

Samaria is surrounded by pleasant green hill country. To the east are the villages of *Ijnisinya, Nisf Jubeil,* and *Beit Umrin.*

At the village of *Deir Sharaf* (48 km.; 30 miles from Afula), Route 57 goes off to the right (west) toward Tulkarm and Netanya. Continue east on the main road (Route 57/60). Signs of habitation in-

Mosque, Sebastiye

crease as you pass a number of oil mills by the roadside. Soon you come to **Nablus** (58 km./36 miles from Afula; see page 186).

B: To Nablus via Tubbas

Follow the route marked "B" on the map on page 188.

If you take the left-hand road (Route 588) at the fork in the Dotan Valley (see page 183), you will pass through gently rolling country to the villages of *Qabatiya* and *Az Zababida* (33 km.; 20.5 miles from Afula). The latter has a sizable Christian Arab community—a rarity in Samaria. At this point, a road on the right runs west into the *Sanur Valley,* and one to the left runs northeast and east to various villages, the largest of which is *Tilfit.* The main road continues through the vil-

lages of *Kufeir* and *Aqabe* to **Tubbas** (57 km./35 miles from Afula; population 20,000). This is the Biblical Thevez, where Gideon's son Abimelech was slain by a woman who "cast a piece of a millstone upon (his) head, and all to brake his skull" (Judges 9:53). In recent decades, Tubbas has grown from a village into a town. From here, a road runs down into the Jordan Valley.

Seven km. (4 miles) beyond Tubbas, you will come to the ancient site of *Tell al Far' a.* This site is usually identified with the Biblical Tirzah, capital of the northern kingdom of Israel after the abandonment of Shechem (Sichem) and before the foundation of the new capital of Samaria. Lying on a geological boundary line between hard limestone and soft chalk, the area is abundantly supplied with springs, whose water flows down in deep gorges into the lower Jordan Valley. Eight km. (5 miles) from Tubbas, a road goes off on the left and runs through the deeply slashed Far'a (Tirza) Valley into the Sukkot Valley (Jiftliq) and down to the Damiya Bridge over the Jordan (see page 196). Beyond this junction, you pass the springs of *Ein el-Beida* and *Ein el-Qudeirat,* which form little waterfalls. Here, too, are magnificent trees and a number of small restaurants—an ideal place to pause in your journey. Opposite is *Jebel Kabir,* at 767 meters (2,517 feet) one of the highest peaks in Samaria. Farther on, you will see some striking rock formations in the gorge on the west side of Jebel Kabir. On the hill is a Jewish outpost settlement.

The road now runs for 5 km. (3 miles) through the *Askar* (Sokher) *Valley* to **Nablus** (in Hebrew, *Shechem* or *Sichem*). The town lies in a narrow valley between *Mount Eval* or *Jebel Islamiye* to the north (940 meters; 3,084 feet) and *Mount Gerizim* to the south (881 meters; 2891 feet). Nablus is the largest town in the Israeli-administered territories of the West Bank; its official population is around 50,000, but if the refugee camps and the neighboring villages are included, this figure swells to nearly 100,000—almost all of whom are Arabs.

The town's good soil, abundant water supply, and excellent location have provided it with the wherewithal for a thriving economy since ancient times. Sichem (or Shechem) is first mentioned in the Egyptian "Amarna Letters" of the 14th century B.C., in which the local king is accused of collaboration with the invading Khabiru. Abraham first came here at the Lord's bidding (Genesis 12:6). Joshua, at age 110, spoke his last words to the Children of Israel at Shechem and was buried here (Joshua 24). At this site, Gideon's son Abimelech made the first attempt to establish a monarchy in Israel (his skull was crushed in Tubbas; see page 185). Solomon's son Rehoboam had himself anointed king in Shechem; it was here that his brother Jereboam's northern tribes started their rebellion against his rule.

After the destruction of the northern kingdom of Israel by the Assyrians in the eighth century B.C., the new rulers settled groups of foreigners in Shechem much as they had in Samaria (see page 183). These people, like their neighbors to the north, became known as Samaritans. Nablus is their spiritual center, and the summit of Mount Gerizim is their holiest site. The Samaritans meticulously follow the precepts of the five Books of Moses, and recognize none of the other Old Testament books save Joshua as holy scripture. The Samaritans were a powerful group in the time of the Second Temple and then again under the Romans, but their numbers steadily dwindled after the coming of Islam. There are now only around 600 of them, more than half of whom live in Nablus, and the rest in Holon, south of Tel Aviv. An impressive experience—for those who can see it—is the Samaritan celebration of the Passover on Mount Gerizim, during which lambs are sacrificed in strict accordance with the Biblical prescriptions.

The Hasmonean ruler John Hyrcanus destroyed the Samaritan temple on Mount Gerizim. During the Jewish War, the Roman Vespasian reduced Shechem to rubble. He then founded a new city, Flavia Neapolis, from which the Arabic form Nablus derives. This new city was established to the west of the old town, at the foot of Mount Eval, where the narrow Nablus Valley opens out into the broad Sokher Valley. Here you can see the impressive remains of the ancient city, including walls and temples.

Because Nablus has been continuously inhabited, comparatively few old buildings have been preserved; furthermore, large areas of the town were destroyed by earthquakes in 1838 and 1927. Reconstruction since the 1930s has created spacious markets and wide streets in the town's center and villa suburbs on the slopes of Mount Gerizim and Mount Eval. Many of its factories manufacture soap from the olive oil produced in the surrounding area. A small Jewish community survived in Nablus until the beginning of the 20th century. Since 1967, the town has been the focal point of Muslim Arab nationalism.

The summit of Mount Gerizim affords superb views of the area. On the eastern slopes stands *Jacob's Well,* one of the holy places of the Samaritans. The Crusaders built a church here on the ruins of an earlier fourth-century church, but it was destroyed soon afterwards. The site is now occupied by the Greek Orthodox *Saint Joseph's Church,* built in 1903.

The *Samaritan Quarter* (in Arabic, *Haret es Samira*) is on the west side of town; its population numbers around 250. The Torah housed here in the synagogue is reputed to be the oldest in Israel.

Burial caves containing interesting sarcophagi of the Hellenistic and Roman periods were discovered at *Balata.*

From Nablus, you continue south on the Ramallah road (Route 60), which runs around the east side of Mount Gerizim, passes the Balata refugee camp on the left, and enters the *Mikhmetat Valley* (Sahel Mukhna). Olive groves spread over the hillsides, and fields cover the valley. To the right is the village of *Huwwara,* where a small population of Samaritans once dwelled; the village has been wholly Muslim since the 19th century. It suffered devastating damage from an earthquake in 1927.

After you pass the village of *Einabus,* a side road branches off to the right to a number of other villages. Between the villages of *Yasuf* (69 km.; 43 miles from Afula) and *Yitma,* the road coils steeply downhill in a series of hairpin bends; as it then begins to climb again, the vistas become more varied. At the village of *As Sawiye,* the road enters the *Levona Valley;* totally enclosed by hills, it offers the finest scenery on the whole route. The Levona Valley was the scene of one of Judas Maccabeus's victories. The road climbs up the south side of the valley in a series of tight bends.

At the village of *Sinjil* (85 km.; 53 miles from Afula), said to have been known as Saint Gilles (Giles) during the Crusades, a road on the right veers off to a number of villages in southern Samaria; a road on the left runs down through the village of *Turmus Aiya* into the valley and comes to the historic site of *Shillo,* the Biblical *Shiloh.* The Ark of the Covenant was kept here before it was transferred to Jerusa-

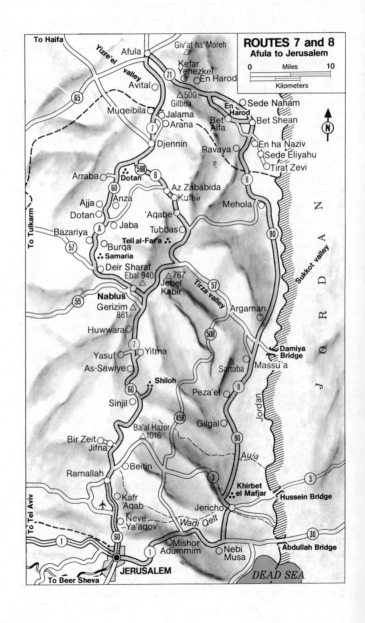

ROUTES 7 and 8
Afula to Jerusalem

0   Miles   10

Kilometers

N

To Haifa

Yizre'el valley

Afula

Giv'at ha'Moreh

Kefar Yehezkel

En Harod

Avital

71

65

Gilboa △500

Muqeibila

Jalama

Arana

En Harod

Sede Naham

Bet Alfa

Bet Shean

7

Djennin

Ravaya

En ha Naziv

Sede Eliyahu

Tirat Zevi

Arraba

Dotan

588

B

Az Zababida

Kufeir

Mehola

Ajja

Anza

Dotan

'Aqabe

Tubbas

8

Bazariya

A

Jaba

57

Burqa

Tell al-Far'a

Samaria

Deir Sharaf

Ebal 940

△767

Jebel Kabir

Tirza valley

57

90

55

Nablus

Gerizim △ 881

Argaman

Huwwara

508

J O R D A N

Yasuf

7

Yitma

As-Sawiye

Shiloh

Sartaba

Massu'a

Damiya Bridge

60

Peza'el

8

Sinjil

Ba'al Hazor △1016

458

Gilgal

Bir Zeit

Jifna

90

Auja

Ramallah

Beitin

Kafr 'Aqab

Khirbet el Mafjar

3

Hussein Bridge

Jericho

Neve Ya'aqov

Wadi Qelt

3

To Tel Aviv

1

60

Mishor Adummim

Nebi Musa

30

Abdullah Bridge

1

JERUSALEM

To Beer Sheva

DEAD SEA

Jordan

Sukkot valley

lem, and Joshua divided the land among the tribes of Israel here. Ruins discovered at the site include a rock-cut mausoleum, mosaic floors from Byzantine churches dedicated to Eli (the high priest of Shiloh) and Samuel, and wine cellars. Most of the items date from the post-Biblical period. Nearby is the Jewish outpost settlement of Shillo.

You leave Samaria at this point and enter northern Judea. Route 60 runs below *Mount Ba'al Hazor,* the highest peak in Judea (1,016 meters; 3,333 feet), and through the narrow *Wadi el-Haramiye* (Valley of Robbers). The picturesque village of *Silwad,* with its mosque, perches atop a crag high above the road.

Soon after *Ein Siniya,* a road branches off to the right to *Jifna* (ancient Gophna) and *Bir Zeit,* both mostly Christian Arab towns. The *Arab University,* formerly a teachers' training college, is in Bir Zeit.

Olive trees dominate the landscape. After you pass a large military camp, you will come to the historic village of *Beitin,* the Biblical *Bethel.* Here Abraham built an altar, Jacob had his dream, the Ark of the Covenant was set up, and Samuel was dedicated to God. Archaeological evidence has shown that the site was occupied until the end of the Second Temple period. The present Arab village has grown rapidly in recent years. Nearby is the new Jewish outpost settlement of *Bet El.*

Continue on Route 60 another 2 km. (1.5 miles) to reach the double town of **Ramallah-El Bira** (105 km., 65 miles from Afula). Situated at an altitude of 870 meters (2,850 feet), this is one of the prettiest urban areas in the West Bank. It has a total population of 25,000; but while Ramallah is mostly Christian, El Bira is wholly Muslim.

Ramallah is sometimes identified with the Biblical city of Ramah (Ramathaim-zophim), and El Bira is thought to be the Biblical Beeroth. During the Crusades, the town was inhabited by Christians who called it "La Grande Mahomerie."

The Bible makes many references to this area, which lies within the territory of the tribe of Benjamin. Samuel lived here as a seer, and King Saul performed many of his well-known deeds here.

Before the Israeli occupation of the West Bank, Ramallah was a popular resort, where cool breezes offered relief from the summer heat. The town was a favorite among wealthy Jordanians —even frequented by King Hussein. Because of its altitude, Ramallah was the site of the British radio transmitter during the Mandate. The town's economy is now closely tied to Jerusalem, barely 15 km. (9 miles) away. An attractive town with an Eastern flavor, its many small sidewalk restaurants offer a welcome respite for hungry travelers.

Route 60 runs through El Bira, with Ramallah lying just off it to the west (right). At the south end of town, the road runs close to the site of *Tell en Nasba* on the left; this is the Biblical *Mizpah,* where Samuel lived as a Judge and Saul was elected king.

Shortly after you leave the precincts of Ramallah-El Bira, you enter the city limits of Jerusalem. The road runs past *Atarot Airport* on the left; to the right is the village of *Kafr Aqab,* and *Qalandiya,* a refugee camp. You will soon come to the new industrial zone of *Atarot* on the left, from which a road runs west to *Latrun.* Beyond this, also to the left, is the large,

new suburb of *Neve Ya' aqov.* Until 1948, Atarot and Neve Ya-aqov were Jewish rural settlements that were abandoned during the War of Independence. After passing through the Arab suburbs of *Beit Hanina-East* and *Shu' afat* and between the new districts of *Giv' at Shapira* and *Ramat Eshkol,* you enter ***Jerusalem** proper (120 km.; 75 miles from Afula) by way of *Sheikh Jarrah* district, where a road runs up on the right onto Mount Scopus. See the description of Jerusalem beginning on page 31.

TRAVEL ROUTE 8: Afula–*Bet Shean–**Jericho–***Jerusalem (142 km.; 88 miles)

See map on page 188.

This route travels about as far back in history as you can go—all the way to Jericho, the oldest city in the world. Jericho is also the lowest town on earth, at nearly 300 meters (950 feet) below sea level. On the way to this venerable old city, you will visit Bet Shean—a comparative newcomer that has only been settled since about 4000 B.C.! The 18 different levels of occupation that archaeologists have uncovered at Bet Shean reveal a history of conquest upon conquest, and there are many fascinating ruins from all different periods of Israel's history. The trip terminates in Jerusalem.

Like Travel Route 7, this route from Afula to Jerusalem along the Jordan Rift runs through the Israeli-occupied West Bank for most of the way.

The first section of the route takes you southeast through the Yizre'el Valley from Afula to Bet Shean in the narrow side valley of Harod, between southeastern Lower Galilee and Mount Gilboa. The valley descends almost 200 meters (650 feet) to join the Rift Valley of the Jordan.

As you leave *Afula* (see page 179) on Route 71, you will pass the town's sugar factory. To the left rises the hill of *Giv' at ha-Moreh,*

with the kibbutz and the moshav of *Merhavya* at its foot. In 1908, Ha-Shomer (the "Guardian" organization that was the earliest forerunner of the Israeli Army) established a camp settlement on this site. Three years later, the Zionist Organization opened a training farm here. After World War I, the kibbutz of Merhavya (which eventually became the ideological center of the radical Ha-Shomer ha-Za'ir movement) was established in 1921, and was followed a year later by a moshav with the same name. In addition to agriculture, the kibbutz runs a printing works, a plastic tubing factory, and a regional secondary school. On the slopes of Giv'at ha-Moreh is the little Arab village of *Sulam,* the Biblical *Shunem,* home of the beautiful Abishag, who cared for David in his old age (1 Kings 1–5). Here, too, the prophet Elisha brought a great lady's son back to life (2 Kings 4:18–37).

The road continues past the moshav of *Kefar Yehezkel* (10 km.; 6 miles from Afula) and, just beyond this, the kibbutz of *Geva*—both established in 1921. Just off the road is the spring of **En Harod,** at the foot of the steep face of Mount Gilboa to the right. Jael, the wife of Heber the Kenite, deceived and killed the Canaanite general Sisera at this site after his defeat at the hands of Deborah in the battle of Megiddo (Judges 4:17–22). Gideon judged his warriors by the way they drank water from this spring (Judges 7:1–8).

The Crusaders fought three battles against Saladin at En Harod—in 1183, 1197, and 1217. In 1260, the Mameluke sultan Baibars inflicted a decisive defeat here on the invading Mongols. The area around the spring is now a nature reserve. The nearby moshav of *Gid'ona* is named after Gideon.

The road soon drops below sea level. When you have traveled 12 km. (7.5 miles) from Afula, a road branches off on the left to the imposing Crusader stronghold of **Belvoir Castle* (Kokhav ha-Yarden). The fortress, which commands a spectacular view, was built in 1173; just 15 years later, Saladin handed the Crusaders a massive defeat here at the Horns of Hittim. Belvoir was the last Crusader fortress to fall to the sultan's forces.

Just beyond Belvoir, to the left of the road, are the kibbutzes of *En Harod* and *Tel Yosef.* They were founded in 1921 on an area of marshy land that had been ac-

Belvoir Castle

quired by the Jewish National Fund. During the Arab revolt of 1936–1939, the British major Orde Wingate trained settlers in En Harod to function as shock troops of the Haganah self-defense organization. Vegetables and fruit are now grown here, carp are bred in ponds, and there are a number of industrial enterprises. Between En Harod and Tel Yosef are a large theater and the *Sturman House,* a musem that displays the local flora and fauna, archaeological finds, and documents illustrating the history of the area. En Harod also contains the *Mishkan ha-Omanut Art Gallery.* The *Trumpeldor House* in Tel Yosef boasts a rich collection of documents chronicling the early days of Jewish settlement of Israel in the 20th century.

Near *Shatta prison* (15 km.; 9 miles from Afula), you may choose between two parallel roads. Route 70 runs straight ahead through the *Bet Shean Valley* past the kibbutzes of *Bet ha-Shitta* (founded in 1935) and *Sede Nahum* (founded in 1937) to the town of Bet Shean (see below). To the right, under the steep face of Mount Gilboa, are fields of cotton and fodder plants, fruit orchards, and carp ponds; to the left are the gentle basalt hills of the Yissakhar range in southeastern Lower Galilee.

The road that branches off to the right at Shatta leads to *Hefzibah* and **Bet Alfa,** at the foot of Mount Gilboa. Since their establishment in 1922, these two kibbutzes have

successfully drained the marshland in the valley and developed the area for agriculture. Bet Alfa also boasts a precision engineering plant.

Bet Alfa's greatest attraction was discovered in 1928, when workers digging a trench to lay a water main exposed a well-preserved mosaic floor of a sixth-century synagogue. The mosaic pictures are somewhat naive and rudimentary, but strangely fascinating nonetheless. At the entrance to the prayer hall, the mosaic bears a dedicatory inscription in Greek and Aramaic. The lowest field [A] depicts Abraham's sacrifice of Isaac. The central roundel [B] shows the sun chariot of Helios surrounded by symbols of the months; in the corners, female figures symbolize the sea-

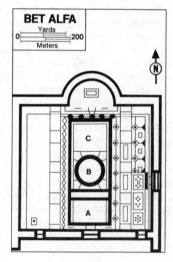

sons. In the upper field [C] are representations of a Torah ark, menorahs, animals, and incense ladles. The mosaic pavement in the right-hand aisle has abstract ornamentation.

From the little information available, it appears that the Jewish community in Bet Alfa ceased to exist soon after the completion of the synagogue.

Soon after passing Bet Alfa, you will come to the *En ha-Shelosha (Sakhna) Park*. You can swim in the crystal clear, slightly salty pond (formed by a spring), which can scarcely be called cold even in winter. An interesting feature is the kidney-shaped block of travertine formed from lime deposited by the water. The road that snakes up to the top of Mount Gilboa, with many hairpin bends, starts beside the park.

The next kibbutz, *Nir David,* was the first Jewish settlement in the Bet Shean Valley. This "tower and stockade" village was built in a single night in 1936. Two km. (1.5 miles) beyond it, a road branches off to the right to join the Jericho road and bypasses Bet Shean. As you continue on the road past the kibbutz of *Mesillot,* you come to Bet Shean (25 km.; 15 miles from Afula).

*Bet Shean

Lying on the old road (the Via Maris) between Egypt and Mesopotamia, Bet Shean (population 13,000)—the Biblical Bethshan—is one of the oldest towns in the world.

Named for a Canaanite divinity called Shan or Shoan, Bet Shean has been occupied since the Early Bronze Age (fourth millennium B.C.) at least. Excavations have exposed 18 separate occupation levels; it appears that each successive conqueror destroyed the existing town and built a new one on its ruins.

In the late second millennium B.C., Bet Shean came under Egyptian rule a number of times; the Pharaohs, such as Seti I, left stelae with decorative reliefs and hieroglyphic inscriptions as reminders of their authority.

Mosaic floor, Bet Alfa

The Philistines took Bet Shean from the Canaanites after they defeated the Israelites on nearby Mount Gilboa around 1100 B.C. In celebration of their triumph over the Israelites, the Philistines nailed the bodies of Saul and his son, Jonathan, to the town walls; the Israelites came from Yavesh Gilead on the opposite bank of the Jordan, recovered the bodies, and buried them (1 Samuel 31). David finally incorporated Beth-shan into his kingdom; but, even after 300 years of Israelite rule, the town still preserved much of its Canaanite and Philistine character.

After successive occupations by the Assyrians, the Babylonians, and the Persians, Bet Shean reached its maximum extent under Roman and Byzantine rule (first through sixth centuries A.D.). Then called Scythopolis, after a legendary Scythian invasion, the city spread around the whole hill; a large church was eventually built here over the ruins of pagan temples. The town featured large theaters, an amphitheater, and a hippodrome; wealthy citizens built themselves luxurious villas here.

From the third century onward, Christian influence in the town increased. At this time, agriculture still flourished; rice, cotton, and indigo were grown, and there were groves of palms. After the Arab conquest in the seventh century, however, the irrigation channels fell into disrepair, areas of marshland formed, and malaria became a scourge.

At the beginning of the twentieth century, Bet Shean (then called Beisan) was nothing more than a poverty-stricken village of mud huts. Although its Jewish inhabitants were forced to abandon the village during the Arab revolt of 1936–1939, new Jewish "tower and stockade" settlements were being established in the surrounding area at the same time. Following a brief attack by Jewish forces during the War of Independence, the Arab population left Bet Shean, and was replaced a short time later by new Jewish immigrants.

Located near Saul Street, the *Municipal Museum* [1] houses a large collection of archaeological finds from the surrounding area. Saul Street leads to the *Municipal Park* [2], which has an open-air museum. Facing this is the *Serai* [3], whose construction incorporates ancient stones and columns; it formerly housed Turkish gov-

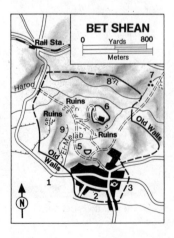

ernment offices. On the west side of the new part of the town are the remains of a *hippodrome* [4].

In the valley of the little *River Melab* is a third-century **Theater* [5]—the best-preserved Roman theater in Israel. Opposite it lies the hill of *Tell el-Husn* [6], the site of the Philistine city. It features the temple of the Canaanite fertility goddess Astarte on the south side, and the temple of Dagon, on which Saul's head was exposed, on the northern slopes.

Tell el-Mastaba [7] boasts many Byzantine remains. The ruins of a **monastery* [8], built in 567, contain a splendid Byzantine mosaic floor.

There are also fine mosaics in the *Baths* [9] at the foot of the hill. The *River Harod* is spanned by a *Roman bridge,* and remains of colonnades lie on the banks of the Melab.

*

From Bet Shean, continue south on the Jericho road (Route 90). You will soon come to a crossroads. The road that leads west to Nir David (see page 193) runs past a water mixing plant, where water with low salt content is mixed with water of medium to high salt content for agricultural use. Highly saline water is used for supplying the many carp-breeding ponds.

The road that goes off to the left (east) leads to a number of religious kibbutzes in the valley—*En ha-Naziv, Sede Eliyahu,* and *Tirat Zevi.* The valley's principal crops are dates and cotton.

As you continue on Route 90, you can see Mount Gilboa to the left. You now pass through the moshavs of *Rehov, Revaya,* and *Sede Terummot,* which were settled by Jews from Kurdistan in 1951 and 1952. About 12 km. (7 miles) from Bet Shean, you cross the pre-1967 frontier and enter the Israeli-administered territory of Judea and Samaria—better known as the West Bank. After passing the Arab villages of *Bardala* on the right and *Tell el-Beida* on the left, you will reach the south end of the Bet Shean Valley. At this point, a road branches off on the right to the hot springs of *Hamam el-Melih* and *Tayasir,* and from there to *Tubbas* in Samaria (see page 185).

You are now in the lower Jordan Valley. Route 90 bears southwest, for the hills of northeastern Samaria are closer to the Jordan, and then swings southeast alongside them, close to the Jordan frontier. You pass the moshav shitufi of *Mehola* (40 km.; 25 miles from Afula), the first settlement established in the lower Jordan Valley after the Six-Day War; it has an impressive new synagogue. There is little room for agriculture along the western bank of the river; however, on the eastern side—in Jordan—you can see large fields, intensively cultivated with the aid of polythene sheeting and spray irrigation. This region, supplied with water by the Yarmouk-Jordan Canal, has developed into one of the most productive agricultural areas in Jordan, and includes many new villages.

You can easily distinguish the two different levels of the Jordan Valley—the upper terrace and, 30 meters (100 feet) lower, the alluvial bed of the valley, caught between hills of whitish-gray marl. On this lower level, the River Jordan itself follows a winding course in innumerable tight meanders. Opposite are the hills of Gilead (in Arabic, *Ajlun*).

A short side road leads to the moshav shitufi of *Argaman*. Then, as you continue on Route 90, the valley suddenly opens out into the *Sukkot Valley* (Jiftlik). The *Tirza Valley* (Wadi Fari'a) opens out to the northwest, with the road leading to Nablus (Route 57). Since 1958, and particularly since 1967, the valley has been settled by both Jewish refugees and Bedouin who have adopted a more sedentary life. In recent years, farming methods have been modernized, and the farmers have brought every usable bit of ground under the plow.

A side road to the left leads to the *Damiya* or *Adam Bridge*, one of the two crossing points from Israel into Jordan. Crossing is permitted for non-Jews only.

To the west, you can see the cone-shaped summit of *Mount Sartaba* (Alexandrion), 377 meters (1,237 feet) above sea level; its white chalk cliffs rise 600 meters (2,000 feet) above the bottom of the valley. The hill, which was fortified by the Hasmoneans, probably takes the name of Alexandrion from the Hasmonean ruler Alexander Jannaeus, or Yan-

nai. In the time of the Mishnah and the Talmud, bonfires were lit on the hill to mark the new moon and the beginning of a new month in Jerusalem; a chain of similar beacons on hilltops throughout the country conveyed the news all the way to the exiled Jews in Babylon. At the foot of the hill is the moshav shitufi of *Massu'a* (Beacon), 69 km. (43 miles) from Afula.

South of Mount Sartaba, the land opens out into the stretch known as the *Peza'el Valley*, and the hills of southern Samaria now withdraw slightly to the west. As you move south, the climate becomes noticeably hotter and drier, and the soil generally becomes saltier and more desertlike; however, some areas of the Peza'el Valley have better earth and sufficient supplies of groundwater. These conditions have allowed the establishment of many new Jewish frontier settlements in this area, such as the moshav of *Peza'el* and the kibbutz of *Gilgal*.

Route 90 goes over a low range of hills and then descends into the *Jericho Valley*, the most southerly section of the Jordan Rift before the Dead Sea. You will pass through the Arab refugee and Bedouin settlement of *Auja el-Tahta* (88 km.; 55 miles from Afula), on the River Auja, which forms the boundary between Samaria and Judea.

The country becomes more desolate as you approach the *Jericho Oasis*. On its northern edge lie the ruins of ***Khirbet el-Mafjar,** where you can see *His-*

ham's Palace, a mosque, a bath-house, a columned courtyard, and an ornamental pond. The palace was formerly attributed to the Umayyad caliph Umar Hisham (724–743); it is now known to have been built between 743 and 744 by Hisham's successor, Al Walid ibn Yazid. It was destroyed by an earthquake only three years after its construction in 747. Byzantine artists decorated the palace with representations of plants, animals, and human figures, contravening the Islamic ban on human representation in art. One mosaic in the small bathhouse is particularly fine. It depicts gazelles grazing under orange trees; one of the gazelles is being attacked by a lion. Some of the buildings have been ravaged through the centuries, and their stones were used in the construction of other buildings. Some stucco figures and frescoes from Khirbet el-Mafjar

A figure from Khirbet el-Mafjar

are displayed in the Rockefeller Museum in Jerusalem.

From Hisham's Palace, it is a short distance to *Tel Jericho,* the site of the ancient city, and the modern town of Jericho (98 km.; 61 miles from Afula).

**Jericho

Jericho (in Arabic, *Ar Riha;* population 7,000), is the lowest town on earth, lying 250–280 meters (820–920 feet) below sea level in one of the most beautiful and fertile oases in the Near East. It is the most ancient town in the region and probably the oldest town in the world.

The site of Jericho was already occupied in the eighth millennium B.C., that is, during the Mesolithic period (Middle Stone Age); by the early Neolithic period (around 7000 B.C.), it was surrounded by a wall 2 meters (6 feet) thick and defended by a stone tower 9 meters (30 feet) high. Although the art of making pottery was still unknown here, crops were already being grown in the oasis with the aid of irrigation. The water came from the spring later known as Elisha's Spring (in Arabic, *Ein es Sultan*).

In the late Neolithic period (around 6000 B.C.), archaeological evidence shows that the town was destroyed and then rebuilt with a new wall surrounding it. Artifacts uncovered from this period include primitive pottery and human skulls covered with a clay mask and shells set in the eye sockets.

Neolithic tower, Jericho

During the Bronze Age (3200–1200 B.C.), Jericho was destroyed and rebuilt 17 times, but thereafter, signs of occupation cease. No trace has been found of the fabled walls that were shattered by the powerful blasts on the horns wielded by Joshua and the Israelites (Joshua 6), according to the Biblical account. These walls may have been built of clay bricks, which would have disappeared over time. Joshua's ban on the rebuilding of Jericho was broken in the time of King Ahab by Hiel the Bethelite (1 Kings 16:34).

Jericho was resettled by Jews returning from exile in Babylon. In Hellenistic times, it was moved southwest to the mouth of the Qelt gorge, where excavations begun in 1979 have revealed palaces that stood in the first century B.C. The palaces belonged to the sons of the Hasmonean queen Alexandra. Here, too, Herod built a splendid winter palace, in which he died.

Jericho was destroyed again in the time of the Jewish War. During Byzantine times, the town stood on its present location. Under the Arab caliphs, it was the chief town of a district whose main products were indigo and sugarcane. The Crusaders ran a sugar mill here.

After the time of the Crusades, Jericho remained a small village. The Egyptian governor, Ibrahim Pasha, destroyed the town when he was compelled to leave the country in 1840. In 1871, Jericho was burned down and did not grow again until the beginning of the 20th century. After 1948, its population increased enormously with the influx of Arab refugees; at the same time, it gained in popularity as a winter resort for the Jordanian upper crust. Then in 1967 Israeli troops occupied the town; the refugee camps emptied, and the population fell to its present level of 7,000.

Jericho is a fine town for strolling and browsing. Busy cafés line its many shady streets, and there is an interesting *market* where you can buy dates, bananas, mangoes, oranges, and other produce fresh from the surrounding plantations. A number of excellent Arab garden restaurants surround the market square.

The steep hill on the west side of the town is *Mount Dok*, where Jesus is believed to have been tempted by the Devil and to have fasted for 40 days (Matthew 4:1–11). The *Monastery of the Temptation* stands here. In the Middle Ages, the hill was known as Mons

Quarantana (Hill of the Forty); the present-day Arabic name of the monastery is *Deir Qarantal.*

The remains of a sixth-century *synagogue* with a mosaic floor can be found in a building on the northeast side of town.

A road (Route 3) runs 8 km. (5 miles) east from Jericho past the farm of *Musa el-Alami* to the *Jordan River.* The *King Hussein Bridge,* formerly the Allenby Bridge, is a crossing point into Jordan (for non-Jews only). A secondary road running farther south leads to the spot where Jesus is believed to have been baptized by John the Baptist. Four monasteries stand nearby: Greek Orthodox, Syrian, Ethiopian, and Roman Catholic.

From Tel Jericho, a road runs northwest to *Tayyibe, Ofra, Beitin* (Bethel), and *Ramallah* (see page 189).

*

When you leave Jericho, continue south on Route 90 for 7 km. (4 miles) to a junction. From here, the road to the left runs east to the Abdullah Bridge (a crossing point into Jordan), and meets the continuation of Route 90, which runs south along the west side of the Dead Sea to *En Gedi* and *Sedom* (see page 231). However, turn right at the junction on Route 1, and begin the climb through the Judean Desert to Jerusalem.

Before the road enters the hills, take a look behind you at the northern tip of the Dead Sea and,

beyond this, the steep face of the Moab Plateau in Jordan. The slopes of the hills, which are mostly chalk with intervening layers of dark-colored quartz, are completely bare; many show sharp folds—the signs of the violent tectonic processes that accompanied the formation of the Rift Valley. There is some vegetation here, particularly in the springtime, but ground cover remains fairly sparse until shortly before you reach Jerusalem.

A short side road on the left leads to *Nebi Musa,* the burial place of Moses according to Muslim tradition. Religious ceremonies are held here in spring.

About 12 km. (7 miles) from Jericho, you will see a sign that marks the sea level: It indicates that you have climbed more than 250 meters (820 feet) in this short distance.

Soon after this sign, a road branches off to the right and runs back to Jericho along the south side of the *Wadi Qelt* (Nahal Kerit)—10 km.(6 miles) of difficult driving. In this deep gorge, there are two perennial and abundantly flowing springs, whose water is carried to Jericho in open channels; an aqueduct stood here in Roman times. Hermit monks occupied the caves in the steep rock faces in the fifth century, and in the sixth century large religious buildings stood here. The Greek Orthodox *Saint George's,* or Kouzibas Monastery, now occupies the sites of these buildings and others of the Crusades.

Continuing toward Jerusalem on Route 1, you come to the *Inn of the Good Samaritan,* where the Turks once maintained a police post. The road runs through a defile flanked by reddish cliffs bearing the Biblical name of *Ma'ale ha-Adummim.* Ma'ale means "ascent," and Adummim derives either from adom (red) or from the Edomites, whose territory beyond the Jordan is reached from this road. At this point, the road climbs to *Mishor Adummim* (on the left), a recently established satellite town of Jerusalem with an industrial zone. A new road runs north from here along the eastern slopes of the hills of Judea and Samaria and into the Far'a and Buqei'a valleys.

From Mishor Adummim the road turns southwest, and you will soon see Mount Scopus and the Mount of Olives on the horizon. The road continues past cultivated fields and hillsides planted with pines. In this part of the country, which receives five to seven times more rainfall than the Dead Sea area, the scanty vegetation of the desert gives way to lush Mediterranean flora.

*El Azariya (136 km./85 miles from Afula; population 2,000), the *Bethany* of the New Testament, has an almost entirely Arab population. In recent years, thanks to their nearness to Jerusalem, El Azariya and *Abu Dis,* its neighbor to the south, have grown considerably in size and now merge with the city limits of Jerusalem. For a detailed description of El Azariya (Bethany), see Walk 11 in Jerusalem (page 93).

The road now turns into the *Valley of Jehoshaphat,* as the upper Kidron Valley is called. Passing between the Temple Mount and the Mount of Olives, it continues as the Jericho Road (Derekh Yeriho) into *****Jerusalem** (142 km.; 88 miles from Afula; see page 31).

TRAVEL ROUTE 9: ***Jerusalem–Ben Gurion Airport (–*Ramla)–*Tel Aviv (61/71 km.; 38/44 miles)

See map on page 202.

This travel route takes you through the Jerusalem Corridor, the route from the capital to Tel Aviv that crosses the ancient strongholds of the Israelites and the Philistines. Many important scenes from the Old Testament were played out at this point in this region: Joshua made the sun stand still here; Samson was born in this area; and the legendary battle between David and Goliath took place here as well.

Nor did the fighting end with the dawn of the modern era. Because of its strategic location, this route was critical during World War I and the War of Independence. During the Six-Day War, the corridor provided the only access for Jews into Jordanian-controlled Jerusalem.

Head northwest from ***Jerusa-lem* (see page 31) on the continu-ation of the Jaffa (Yafo) Road (Route 1). The modern express-way runs down the western slopes of the Judean Hills, offering a brief glimpse of Ramallah, with its radio towers on the horizon. Between recently planted areas of forest, you'll be able to see the new Jerusalem suburb of *Ramot;* the minaret atop the summit of *Nabi Zamwil* marks this spot where Samuel is buried, according to Jewish and Muslim tradition. Dur-ing the wars of 1948 and 1967, this summit was an important strategic point.

On the hillside to the left of the road, you will pass Jerusalem's largest cemetery. The picturesque Arab village of *Beit Iksa* soon comes into sight on the right; the road now enters the valley in which *Moza* lies. Founded in 1894 as the first Jewish rural settlement in the neighborhood of Jerusalem, Moza bears a Biblical name— "Exodus." To the left, you'll see a brickworks established before World War I, as well as a number of modern villas; above them, the Jerusalem Forest forms a crescent around the city.

The road soon begins its ascent up the west side of the valley, pass-ing *Moza Illit* on the left, a moshav established in 1933. If you take the road on the left, which soon runs into the highway, you will pass Moza Illit on the right and then the *Arza* sanatorium. (The name is taken from a cypress tree that The-odor Herzl planted here in 1898; it

was later felled by Arabs.) Water fills the reservoir in the valley to the left only in winter; during the rest of the year, it serves to main-tain the water table. The reservoir curves around the hill, on which sits *Bet Zayit* (House of the Olive Tree), a moshav established in 1949. Beyond the moshav, you can see the *Hadassah University Hos-pital.*

The road climbs in a series of sharp hairpin curves, known as the "Seven Sisters," to the *Har'el Junction* in the little town of **Mevasseret Zion** (25 km.; 15 miles from Jerusalem). Two dis-tricts comprise the town: the settlement of *Ma'oz Zion,* estab-lished in 1951 by Jewish stone-masons from Iraqi Kurdistan who found work in the nearby quarries; and the newer garden suburb of *Mevasseret Yerusha-layim* (Herald of Jerusalem). Above it rises *Qastel,* a hill named after a fort (in Latin, *castellum*) built by the Roman legions that be-sieged Jerusalem during the Jew-ish War. During the War of Independence in 1948, this road served as a vital link between Tel Aviv and Jerusalem; the Arabs cut the road here but were eventually driven back.

From the *Har'el Pass* (30 km.; 19 miles from Jerusalem), the road descends into a pleasant valley. In about 2 km. (1.5 miles), a road branches off on the left to the *Aqua Bella (En Hemed) Nature Reserve.* The ruins of a Crusader convent stand here on the banks of a stream, set amid large kermes oaks, terebinths, and pomegranate trees.

Soon after you pass the convent, another road goes off on the right to *Qiryat Anavim, Abu Ghosh,* and *Ma' ale ha-Hamisha.* **Qiryat Anavim** is a thriving kibbutz set amid green forests and orchards; its members run a hotel and raise dairy cattle and poultry. In its present state, it's hard to imagine that the settlers who established it in 1921 found the barren hillside and poor soil inhospitable to farming in the early years. The name of the kibbutz, in the form "Qart Anab" (City of Vines), appears in Egyptian inscriptions of the second millennium B.C. Later, the town lay on the boundary between the tribes of Judah and Benjamin; it was known at that time as Qiryat Ye'arim (Kirjath-jearim), the "City of Forests." The Ark of the Convenant was kept here for 20 years after its recovery from the Philistines, until David carried it in triumph to Jerusalem (1 Chronicles 13:5).

The village of ***Abu Ghosh** lies in the valley. It was named for a 19th-century Arab who lived here and levied a toll on pilgrims traveling to Jerusalem. Many of the present residents are his descendants. Abu Ghosh occupies the site where a Roman fort once stood; later, it was the location of an Arab caravanserai. During the Crusades, a monastery called Castellum Fontenoide was built here. The Crusaders mistook this site for Emmaus, where Christ ate a meal with two of his disciples (see page 204). In the 19th century, the locale was bought by the French government, and Benedictine monks carefully restored the

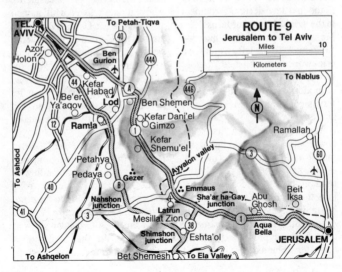

Crusader church, which is built over a spring. The church is now cared for by Lazarists. An inscription in the wall of the church bears the name of Legio X Fretensis, the Roman legion that besieged Jerusalem in A.D. 70.

On the hill to the north (which is probably the site of ancient Qiryat Ye'arim), a number of artifacts have been unearthed that date from the Early Bronze Age to Byzantine times. A convent now occupies the site, dedicated to Nôtre-Dame de l'Arche de l'Alliance (Our Lady of the Ark of the Covenant), which has a towerlike statue of the Virgin and Child.

From Abu Ghosh, a short side road on the right climbs past the children's village of *Qiryat Ye'arim* to the kibbutz of **Ma'ale ha-Hamisha,** founded in 1938 during the Arab revolt. The name means "Ascent of the Five," commemorating five members of the kibbutz who were shot here. Apart from farming and fruit-growing, the kibbutz maintains a candy factory and a guesthouse in the forest. At the entrance to the guesthouse stands a monument to the defenders of the settlement by the sculptor Nathan Rapaport, who also created the memorial called "Defenders of the Warsaw Ghetto" in Poland. From Ma'ale ha-Hamisha, a road takes you back through beautiful scenery to Qiryat Anavim.

Continue past the police station in Abu Ghosh to the western access road to the Tel Aviv highway (Route 1); you will soon pass the moshavs of *Neve Ilan* and *Yad ha-Shemona*. The latter was established by Finnish Christians and named in memory of eight Finnish Jews killed in the Holocaust.

The highway runs past the moshav of *Sho'eva* (to the left). A road on the left leads 4 km. (2 miles) to *Shoresh,* a moshav shitufi with a large vacation hotel, and the religious moshav of *Bet Me'ir.*

The highway descends through the *Sha'ar ha-Gay Gorge* and the *Martyrs' Forest* (Ya'ar Hakedoshim), whose trees were planted in memory of the six million European Jews exterminated by the Nazis. Various sections of the forest are named after European towns and villages destroyed by the Nazis.

At the end of the gorge, the hills of dolomitic limestone give way to the white chalk formations of the Judean Foothills, which rise to a height of 450 meters (1,475 feet). At this point, you can choose between two alternative routes to Tel Aviv. The direct route, described below under "A," takes you along the highway (Route 1) via Ben Gurion Airport; the other option goes by way of Ramla (see the description under "B" beginning on page 205).

A: Via Ben Gurion Airport

Follow the route marked "A" on the map on page 202.

Route 1 runs through rolling country, with exits to *Ramallah* on the right and *Ashqelon* to the left. The fertile **Ayyalon Valley,** where many a battle was fought throughout history, stretches to the left. Here Joshua, coming down from Gibeon, won his great victory over the Canaanites, calling out "Sun, stand thou still upon Gibeon; and thou, Moon, in the valley of Aijalon" (Joshua 10:12). In 165 B.C., Judas Maccabeus inflicted a decisive defeat on the Seleucid army in this valley. The armies of the Crusades marched through it on their way to Jerusalem; nine centuries later, General Allenby's British troops followed the same route. During the War of Independence in 1948, Jewish forces attempted unsuccessfully to capture a police post held here by the Arab Legion, under British command; 20 years later, in the Six-Day War, the stronghold fell with little resistance. The village of *Imwas,* site of ancient Emmaus, stood here until 1967; renamed Nicopolis by the Romans, this was the site where the risen Christ ate with two of his disciples (Luke 24). (Another legend locates Emmaus in the village of El-Qubeiba, on the road to Ramallah.) Excavation of the site brought to light the remains of a Roman villa, over which were built a third-century basilica and a Crusader baptistery from the 12th century.

The Trappist abbey of *Latrun* perches on the edge of the Ayyalon Valley. It occupies the site of a 12th-century castle built by the Knights Templar, which they called Toron des Chevaliers; its Arabic name was later misinterpreted as *Castrum Boni La-*

tronis (House of the Good Thief). The present abbey, founded in 1937, is famous for the excellent wine that the monks make from the grapes they grow (visitors may also purchase the wine).

The highway cuts across the Ayyalon Valley, most of which was a no man's land between 1948 and 1967. On its western edge, to the left, is a reservoir in which floodwater is stored in winter. Above it are the moshavs of *Mishmar Ayyalon* and *Kefar Bin-Nun.* The road continues through flatter country, passing the moshavs of *Kefar Shemu'el, Kefar Dani'el,* and *Gimzo.* The highway then crosses a road leading to the town of *Lod.*

Nearby stands *Ben Shemen* (Son of Oil), a moshav founded in 1908. The first settlement established by the Zionist Organization, it was originally a training center for agricultural workers; a "Herzl forest" was planted here later, and a small moshav was established in 1921. In 1927, a youth village was opened; children came here with the "Youth Aliyah" immigration movement, at first from Germany and later from other countries. During the 1948 war, the school withstood an eight-month siege, and the moshav was rebuilt on a larger scale in 1952.

The highway comes to a crossroads with Route 40. To the left, Route 40 leads to the town of Lod; to the right, it goes to *Ben Gurion Airport* and *Petah Tiqva,* where it joins the road to Haifa (see page 134). You can see part of the airport from the highway.

Side trip to Lod

Taking Route 40 to the left, you travel for 3 km. (2 miles) to ***Lod** (population 38,000), known in antiquity as *Lydda*. The town's celebrated Jewish scholars earned it the title of a "second Jerusalem," and it was also an important trading center. In Roman times, it became the chief town of a district under the name of *Diospolis*.

Lod is the location of the once-famous double shrine of *Saint George and El Khadr*. Saint George, venerated by both Christians and Muslims (although he was recently stripped of his sainthood by the Catholic Church), is said to have been born here, and was buried here after his martyrdom. In the southern part of town, a new white mosque acts as a signpost to the El Khadr Mosque and its neighbor, the Greek church of Saint George. The present **Saint George's Church** [1]

ST. GEORGE'S/EL KHADR

was built in 1870 on the ruins of a cathedral built by Richard the Lion-Hearted, which in turn occupied the site of a sixth-century Byzantine basilica. Over the entrance is a figure depicting Saint George in his familiar role of dragon-slayer. Within the church, two apses and the first two piers in the nave survive from the Crusader building. Steps lead down into the crypt, which contains an empty sarcophagus; the lid (renewed in 1871) bears a figure of Saint George. The western aisles of the Crusader church form the **El Khadr Mosque** [2], which incorporates columns and an apse from the Byzantine basilica. One column bears a Byzantine dedicatory inscription.

*

When you return to Route 1 after leaving Lod, the highway enters an increasingly developed area, although plantations of citrus fruits still flank the road. After you pass the outskirts of townships like *Bet Dagan* and *Azor* on the left and *Kefar Shalem* on the right, you will come into the fringes of **Tel Aviv** (61 km./38 miles from Jerusalem; see page 106).

B: Via Ramla

Follow the route marked "B" on the map on page 202.

At the end of the *Sha'ar ha-Gay Gorge* (see page 203), take the road to the left (Route 38). This road runs between pine-covered slopes along the boundary between the chalk formations of the Judean foothills and the limestone of the gorge.

You will pass *Mesillat Zion* (28 km.; 17 miles from Jerusalem), a moshav established in 1950 by Jews from southern India. Its main sources of income are poultry and fruit; flowers and certain varieties of fruit are grown in greenhouses. In 3 km. (2 miles) you come to the moshav of *Eshta'ol*, established in 1949 by immigrants from Yemen. Here a road branches left to the *Martyrs' Forest* (Ya'ar Hakedoshim; see page 203). A monumental gateway leads into a memorial chamber in a cave, which lists the names of the Jewish communities wiped out by the Nazis in the Holocaust.

Optional return to Jerusalem

If you don't want to drive all the way to Tel Aviv, you can easily head back to Jerusalem from this point. A second road to the left runs up through the hills amid forests that are occasionally interrupted by peach orchards. After passing a pumping station just before the moshav of *Ramat Razi' el*, you come to a side road on the left. It leads to the moshav of *Kesalon;* turning left again, you will reach the **Fire Scroll Monument.** In the form of a Torah scroll, this sculpture depicts scenes from Jewish history—the Children of Israel entering the Promised Land,

David with his lyre, Jews suffering in concentration camps, the pioneers returning to Israel, and the building up of the new state. An inscription on the inside of the scroll depicts Ezekiel's vision of the resurrection of the dead and the Israelites' return to their own land. The monument stands on a projecting spur of the Judean hills, from which the view extends over Bet Shemesh, the foothills, and the coastal plain to the Mediterranean.

The road continues east from *Ramat Razi' el.* As you pass below the sanitarium and radio station of *Etanim,* there is a panoramic view over the hills to the Hebron ridge. The road runs below the kibbutz of *Zova* and a distant hill on which the Crusaders built their castle of *Belmont* on the remains of Byzantine structures. It then descends through forested country to the gorge on the upper course of the *River Soreq,* with the Hadassah Hospital on the opposite slope, and enters the city limits of Jerusalem at the village of *En Kerem.* Designated a national monument, it is traditionally believed to have been the birthplace of John the Baptist.

*

If you are continuing on to Tel Aviv, the road continues along Route 38 from Esta'ol to the *Shimshon Junction* (28 km.; 17 miles from Jerusalem). The junction is named for the Israelite hero Samson, who is believed to have been born in the nearby village of *Zor'a:* "And the woman bore a son, and called his name Samson. . . And the Spirit of the Lord began to move him at times in the camp of Dan between Zorah and Eshtaol" (Judges 13:24–25). This was the place where Samson performed his first heroic deeds, and from here he set out against the Philistines.

The development town of **Bet Shemesh** (population 12,000) lies 2 km. (1 ½ miles) south of the junction on Route 38. The Biblical town of Beth-shemesh, whose name means "House of the Sun," stood on a strategically important hill above the *Soreq Valley.* By the second millennium B.C., it had already become a place of some consequence, and in the time of the Judges and the early Kings, the town's inhabitants prevented the Philistines from advancing through the valley into the territory of the tribe of Judah. Bet Shemesh is also the place where the Ark of the Covenant entered Israelite territory after the Philistines surrendered it (1 Samuel 6:12). Excavations have brought to light many traces of human settlement on the hill, mainly dating from the Bronze Age (second century B.C.).

The modern town of Bet Shemesh was founded in 1895, when Bulgarian Jews bought land from a British missionary society and established the little village of Hartuv. In 1949, many new immigrants came to a *ma'bara*

(transit camp) here; from these modest beginnings, the town has grown to its present size. It now has a large cement works and factories that manufacture aircraft engines, electronic apparatus, bicycles, and instant coffee.

From Bet Shemesh, a road runs south into the *Ela Valley* (Terebinth Valley)—where David faced Goliath—and on to *Bet Guvrin* and the Lakhish district.

Return to the Shimshon Junction. When the direct road to Jerusalem via Latrun was cut off during the War of Independence, Jewish forces needed another route to the capital; the new route—much of it constructed under enemy fire—is known as the "Heroes' Road," which starts at the Shimson Junction. It turns sharply to the right, heading northwest past the Eshta'ol tree nursery, and through the "President's Forest" and other forested areas. After passing the moshavs of *Tarum, Kefar Uriya,* and *Ta'oz,* and the kibbutz of *Har'el,* the road enters flatter country, with plantations of conifers and carob trees.

About 12 km. (7.5 miles) from the Shimshon Junction, you come to the Nahshon Junction (38 km.; 24 miles from Jerusalem). To the left is the road to Ashqelon (Route 3); the road to the right runs into the Ayyalon Valley. Straight ahead lies Route 44 to Ramla, which is the road you follow through vineyard-covered land. About 5 km. (3 miles) beyond the kibbutz of *Mishmar David* lies the site of **Gezer.** Although not particularly rewarding for non-archaeologists, the site is more easily accessible from the Mishmar Ayyalon-Ramla Road (Route 424).

Commanding the western approaches to Judea, Gezer lay on the Via Maris, the ancient route from Egypt to Mesopotamia, and it was a place of importance as early as the 15th century B.C. We know from the Amarna Letters that the neighbors of King Malki'el had written from Gezer to the Pharaoh, complaining bitterly of the Egyptian's aggressive activities. The Pharaoh's reply was brief, but perhaps not to the point: "Send me forty fair concubines."

A king of Gezer was among the Canaanite kings defeated by Joshua, but the town did not come under Israelite rule until Solomon received it as a dowry upon his marriage to an Egyptian princess. Dating from this period, the "Gezer Calendar" found here designated each month by its corresponding farming activity. Archaeologists discovered a stone bearing a Hebrew inscription that read, "The boundary of Gezer," thus confirming the identity of the site.

Although Gezer had been destroyed on several occasions, it was still habitable in Roman times, when it was a battleground during the Maccabean Revolt. The Crusaders, who called the hill Mont Gisart, also fought here. At the beginning of the 20th century, a British Zionist organization called the Old Maccabees bought

the site; however, the first Jewish settlement (a kibbutz) was not established until 1945. During the War of Independence, Gezer was the scene of bitter fighting, but it remained in Jewish hands. The pumping station near the site is part of the National Water Carrier system.

It is 10 km. (6 miles) from Gezer to Ramla. The main crops in this area are cotton and wheat; plantations of citrus fruits can be seen just before you reach Ramla. To the left of the road are the moshavs of *Pedaya* and *Petahya;* to the right are *Bet Uzzi' el, Azarya,* and *Yad Rambam.* Lying farther off the road is the moshav of *Mazli' ah,* one of the few settlements of the schismatic Karaite sect in Israel. (The sect, founded in the eighth century by a Persian Jew, stresses the right of the individual to interpret scripture according to his own conscience. The sect has been in decline since the 12th century; the largest population of Karaites today live in Crimea.)

By the standards of other sites in Israel, ***Ramla** (54 km.; 34 miles from Jerusalem; population 39,000) is a relatively young town, having been founded in 716 by the Ummayad caliph Suleiman the Magnificent. The name means "sand," reflecting the nature of the soil in the surrounding area. In the 11th century, Ramla was an important trading town. It became the see of a bishop during the Crusades, and later it was a staging point for pilgrims on the way to

Mecca. In 1799, Napoleon set up his headquarters in Ramla, and it was from here that he conquered the neighboring town of Jaffa on his way to attack Akko.

When Ramla surrendered to the Israeli army in July 1948, it was inhabited mostly by Arabs. They departed in large numbers and new Jewish immigrants moved in. Ramla is now an industrial town with a large cement works. The town is part of the Tel Aviv sprawl, although plantations of citrus fruits and cultivated fields break up the urban landscape here.

The *Franciscan church* in Herzl Street is dedicated to Saint Joseph of Arimathea, who took Christ's body from the cross for burial (John 19:38). This dedication reflects the Crusaders' belief that Ramla was ancient Arimathea. The *Great Mosque* was originally built in the 12th century as a Crusader church.

Ramla's principal sight and landmark is the tower [1] of the *White Mosque,* standing 30 meters (100 feet) high. According to an inscription over the doorway, the tower was built in 1318 by the Egyptian sultan Mohammed en Nasir, who incorporated the minaret of an eighth-century mosque [2] in its construction. Practically nothing remains of this earlier mosque. Vaulted underground chambers [3] surround the fountain [4] in the center of the courtyard. Although both Christian and Muslim tradition claim that these are the tombs of saints of holy men, they are, in fact, the cellars

Tower of the White Mosque

of a caravanserai that once stood here. There are magnificent views from the top of the tower.

Some distance off the main road lies a massive *cistern,* at which 24 camels could be watered at the same time. Christians believe that Saint Helen ordered

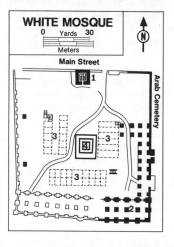

its construction, while Muslims claim it was built by Harun el-Rashid. The underground chamber housing the cistern, 30 meters (100 feet) square, has a rib-vaulted roof whose image is reflected in the water.

From Ramla, Route 40 cuts northeast to *Lod (see page 205) and Ben Gurion Airport.

Continuing to Tel Aviv on Route 44, you will see *Nir Zevi* on the right, a moshav founded in 1954 by Argentinian Jews. Farther on to the left of the road are the large military camps of *Zerifin* and beyond them, to the south, the little town of *Beer Ya'aqov*.

About 2 km. (1.5 miles) beyond Beer Ya'aqov, a road branches off to the right to *Kefar Habad* (population 2,500), a village established in 1949 by strictly religious Hasidic immigrants from Russia.

At the *Bet Dagan Junction* (64 km.; 40 miles from Jerusalem), the road to the left runs south via *Rehovot* to *Beer Sheva* (see page 261); the road to the right runs northeast to *Yehud* and *Ben Gurion Airport*. To the left of the junction is the *Vulcani Institute of Agricultural Research;* beyond it lies the *Meteorological Institute of Israel*. To the right, beyond the junction, is the moshav of *Mishmar ha-Shiv'a*.

Continuing on Route 44, you'll soon reach the *Shiv'a Junction*, where the Geha Expressway (Route 4) runs south to Ashdod and Ashqelon and northeast to Bene Beraq. At this point, you have entered the districts of Tel Aviv, with the large industrial zone of *Holon* to the left.

Route 44 runs through **Azor** (68 km./42 miles from Jerusalem; population 5,700), which was established in 1948. A burial site excavated here dates to the Early Bronze Age (fourth millennium B.C.) and is probably one of the earliest traces of human settlement in Israel. The Crusaders built a small castle here, the Château de la Plaine. There is an unusual little nine-domed mosque dating from the early days of Turkish rule (16th century).

Next, you come to what seems like a large, green island floating in a sea of houses—these are the fields and gardens of the oldest college of agriculture in the country, *Miqve Yisra'el*. The foundations of the college were laid by the Alliance Israélite Universelle in 1870, eight years before the first attempt to establish Jewish villages. Miqve Yisra'el features an avenue of tall palms and a beautiful botanical garden.

A short distance away, you'll come to a junction. The road to the left leads to the towns of *Holon* and *Bat Yam;* the one straight ahead goes on to Jaffa (Yafo); the road to the right takes you to the southern districts of ***Tel Aviv** (71 km.; 44 miles from Jerusalem; see the description beginning on page 106).

TRAVEL ROUTE 10: ***Jerusalem–***Bethlehem– *Hebron–Arad–**Masada–*En Gedi– ***Jerusalem (239 km.; 149 miles)

See map on page 212.

Travel Route 10 takes you in a wide loop south and east of Jerusalem. The first stop is Bethlehem, the birthplace of Christ and a very important attraction for many visitors to Israel. The route continues through Hebron, where Abraham and Sarah settled upon their arrival from Ur, to the ancient hilltop fortress of Masada on the coast of the Dead Sea. Along the way you will find yourself immersed in the increasingly desertlike landscape in which hundreds of generations of Israelites, Bedouin, and other hardy peoples have found purchase and made a life in the inhospitable terrain.

Leave ***Jerusalem* (see description beginning on page 31) from the southern district of the city, and pick up the Hebron Road (Route 60). After you pass the railroad station, you will run through the Talpiyot district; its large industrial zone to the right of the road extends into the *Refa'im Valley.* Below the kibbutz of *Ramat Rahel,* situated to the left of the road, you cross the pre-1967 frontier into the Israeli-occupied West Bank, now the administrative district of Judea and Samaria. A few hundred meters beyond this you come to a pass (elevation 817 meters; 2681 feet) where the fortified Greek Orthodox monastery of **Mar Elias** is located. Founded in the sixth century, the monastery suffered severe damage in an earthquake and was rebuilt in 1160 by the Byzantine Emperor Manuel I (Comnenus). The monastery is dedicated to the prophet Elijah or Elias—an important figure in all three of the region's chief religions—who is said to have stayed here during his flight from Queen Jezebel (1 Kings 19). On the opposite side of the road, to the left, is a monument to the Pre-Raphaelite painter William Holman Hunt, who visited Palestine in 1854 to obtain authentic material for his religious paintings.

The pass affords splendid panoramic views: Jerusalem spreads to the north; the Refa'im Valley stretches westward; the Judean desert lies to the east, extending down to the Dead Sea and over to the Moab plateau; and the valley opens out in front of the hills around Bethlehem to the south. To the southeast you can see the hill topped by the Herodion (see page 218), which looks like a volcanic crater from this distance. The green expanse of cultivated land to the west side contrasts sharply with the increasingly desertlike terrain to the east.

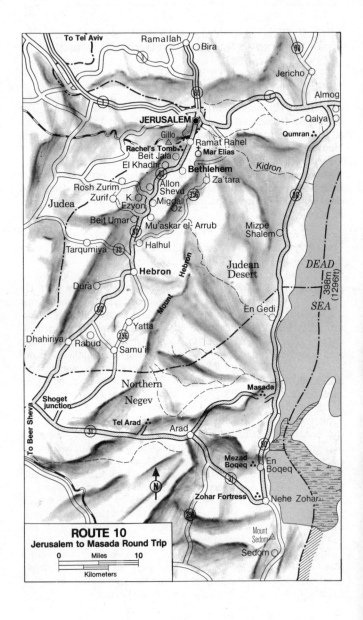

To Tel Aviv
Ramallah
Bira
94
Jericho
Almog
JERUSALEM
Qalya
Gillo
Qumran
Rachel's Tomb
Ramat Rahel
Beit Jala
Mar Elias
El Khadhr
Bethlehem
Kidron
Rosh Zurim
Allon
Za'tara
Zurif
Shevu
356
K.
Ezyon
Migdal
Oz
Judea
Beit Umar
Mu'askar el- Arrub
Mizpe
Shalem
35
Halhul
DEAD
Tarqumiya
Judean
398m
(1296ft)
Hebron
Desert
SEA
Hebron
Mount
Dura
En Gedi
60
Yatta
356
Dhahiriya
Rabud
Samu'i
Northern
Masada
Negev
Shoget
junction
Tel Arad
Arad
To Beer Sheva
60
Mezad
En
Boqeq
Boqeq
Zohar Fortress
Nehe Zohar
N
258
Mount
Sedom
ROUTE 10
Jerusalem to Masada Round Trip
Sedom
0   Miles   10
Kilometers

You soon reach a junction where a road branches off to the right to *Gillo,* a large new suburb of Jerusalem. The Tantur inter-denominational Christian study center, built on land belonging to the Knights of Saint John, stands at the junction. The developed outer districts of Jerusalem and Bethlehem have gradually begun to merge in this area.

To the left of the road are re-mains of the "upper aqueduct." Partially constructed in Hasmo-nean and Herodian times—and completed sometime later—the aqueduct carried water to Jerusa-lem from Solomon's Pools.

Soon after you pass the aque-duct, you enter the city limits of Bethlehem. You will come to a small, domed building that is tra-ditionally believed to contain the *Tomb of Rachel,* Jacob's wife, who died here after giving birth to Benjamin. Sir Moses Montefiore gained possession of the building in 1841, and since that time—apart from the years between 1948 and 1967—it has been a Jewish place of prayer, particularly fre-quented by women who wish to pray for a child. The site is also sa-cred to Muslims and Christians, and there is a Muslim cemetery nearby.

Bear left where the road forks, and after you pass *David's Well* (from which three of David's war-riors fetched water in the face of the Philistine occupation), you will enter Bethlehem by Manger Road (10 km.; 6 miles from Jeru-salem).

***BETHLEHEM

Bethlehem is best known, espe-cially to Christians, as the birth-place of Jesus Christ. The town, whose name means "House of Bread" (or, in the Arabic *Beit Lahem,* "House of Food") was also King David's birthplace. Situ-ated in a very fertile area, Bethle-hem today has a population of around 15,000, mainly Arab Christians; if the neighboring towns of *Beit Sahur* to the east and *Beit Jala* to the west are included, the total population swells to 32,000.

History

After the Israelites, led by Joshua, took possession of the Promised Land, Bethlehem lay within the territory of the tribe of Judah. The area was the scene of the idyllic tale of Ruth and Boaz, the great-grandparents of David. It was in Bethlehem that Samuel anointed David king. After the Israelites re-turned from the Babylonian cap-tivity, the people of Bethlehem became the subjects of the Edomites (descendants of Esau). It was only in the first century B.C. that the Hasmonean ruler John Hyrcanus incorporated Bethle-hem and the Edomites into his kingdom. It then remained under Jewish control until the fail-ure of the Bar-Kochba rebellion (A.D. 135).

The early Christians recog-nized Bethlehem as the birthplace of Christ, and the Evangelists refer to Micah's prophecy (Micah 5:2) that the Messiah would come from Bethlehem (Matthew 2:6; Luke 2:11; John 7:42). In the fourth century, the Empress Helena (Saint Helen), mother of Constantine the Great, built a church over the Grotto of the Nativity. In the sixth century, Saint Jerome settled in Bethlehem; under the patronage of Saint Paula (347–404), a patrician Roman matron who established two monasteries here, he produced much of the Latin version of the Bible—the Vulgate—which is still used by the Roman Catholic Church.

Under the Arab caliphs (7th–11th centuries), Bethlehem drew many Christian pilgrims, some of whom came from as far afield as Europe. In the first Crusade, the town fell to Tancred's forces without resistance, and the first Crusader kings, Baldwin I and II, were crowned here. Although Bethlehem held no position of consequence in later centuries, it remained the focal point of many pilgrims. In the mid-19th century, when the Ottoman Empire was forced to make concessions to the European powers, construction began on new churches and monasteries, religious institutions, and schools for Christians.

Attractions

For many visitors, Bethlehem's chief attraction is **Manger Square** [1], which stands in front of the Church of the Nativity. A bustling place at all times, it truly comes into its own in late December and early January, when all the major Christian denominations put on enthusiastic displays. On its south side is the *Mosque of Omar,* and from its west side a narrow market lane, *Najajreh Street,* runs up to the market square (see page 218).

On the east side of Manger Square stands the ***Church of the Nativity** [2], one of the great

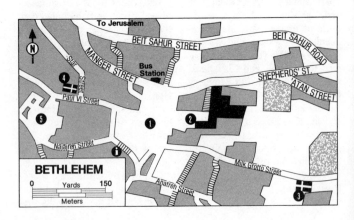

BETHLEHEM

0 Yards 150

Meters

pilgrimage sites for all Christians. Fortresslike monasteries surround it on three sides: a Roman Catholic one to the north; a Greek Orthodox one to the southeast; and an Armenian one to the south.

Empress Helena built the first church (a basilica) on this site over the Grotto of the Nativity, after earlier Roman temples had been cleared from the spot. Despite many changes through the centuries—this church was destroyed by fire, rebuilt by Emperor Justinian in 531, and subsequently altered many times—the ground plan of the original church is still recognizable.

Legend has it that in 614 the conquering Persians did not destroy the church because they wanted to spare the mosaic of the Three Kings on the façade.

After the Crusaders took Bethlehem in 1099, the Church of the Nativity was rebuilt (1161–1169).

Church of the Nativity, Bethlehem

It rapidly fell into decay under Mameluke rule: an expressive 15th-century German pilgrim likened it to "a barn without hay, a pharmacy without medicine pots, a library without books." It suffered further indignity in 1646 when the Turks removed the lead roof and melted it down to make bullets.

An extensive restoration program began in 1670 under Greek Orthodox direction. But the rivalry among the various Christian denominations led to clashes, and eventually the structure of the Church of the Nativity was damaged. The theft of the silver star over the Grotto of the Nativity in 1847, illustrative of the disagreements between Russia and Europe over custody of important sites in the Holy Land, was one of the causes of the Crimean War.

Around the mid-19th century, sections of the complex of buildings were assigned to the various Christian denominations. In 1835, an earthquake caused great damage, and in 1869, a fire destroyed the medieval decoration of the Grotto of the Nativity.

From the *forecourt* [A], which was once the atrium of the Constantinian basilica, you enter Justinian's *narthex* [B] through a tiny doorway measuring only 1.2 meters by 0.8 meters (4 feet by 3 feet). Higher up on the façade you can see the pediment of a pointed-arch doorway from the Crusades; the present doorway dates from around 1500. This "needle's eye" still preserves the remains of a

CHURCH OF THE NATIVITY

0   Yards   30

Meters

N

wooden door from 1227, with carvings by Armenian artists. In spite of all the different restorations and alterations throughout the ages, the *interior* [C] of the church is still highly impressive. Its four rows of 11 monolithic columns of red limestone topped by marble capitals were once thought to date from the time of Constantine; but they are now believed to have been part of Justinian's rebuilding.

Traces of gold mosaic decoration from 1169 remain above the columns, including representations of the ancestors of Christ and the seven Ecumenical Councils. Frescoes of various saints, proba-

bly dating from around 1130, adorn the upper parts of many of the columns; the saints' names appear in Greek and Latin.

Of particular interest are the remains of a *mosaic floor* that date to the time of Constantine. Wooden covers protect these sections, which you can ask the custodian to raise so that you can view them. Also not to be missed is a stone *font* [D] from the time of Justinian (c. 527– 565).

The *choir* [E], which was raised during the Crusades, stands exactly over the Grotto of the Nativity. The *high altar* [F] and the *Altar of the Circumcision* [G] both belong to the Greek Orthodox

Church; the *Altar of the Virgin* [H] and the *Altar of the Three Kings* [I] belong to the Armenian Orthodox.

Two flights of *stairs* descend into the Grotto of the Nativity. The semicircular steps of red limestone probably date from the time of Justinian; the bronze doors and marble door frames are from the Crusades.

The *Grotto of the Nativity* is a low, irregularly shaped marble chamber, partly faced with marble. At its eastern end lies the supposed *birthplace of Christ* [L]. An altar stands in a small niche, above which can be seen scanty remains of a 12th-century mosaic depicting the Nativity.

Below the altar, a silver star bears the inscription "Hic de Virgine Maria Jesus Christus natus

GROTTO OF THE NATIVITY

est" (Here Jesus Christ was born of the Virgin Mary). The star is a replica of the one that mysteriously disappeared in 1847.

On the south side of the grotto, three steps lead down to the *Altar of the Manger* [M], which belongs to the Roman Catholic Church. Saint Helena discovered the original clay manger here, which she replaced with a silver one. The *Altar of the Three Kings* [N] stands opposite it, where the three kings are believed to have worshiped the Christ Child.

The other grottoes beneath the church are generally accessible only from the Roman Catholic *Saint Catherine's Church* [O], which was built by Franciscans in 1881. From the south side of the church, a passage leads to the *Chapel of the Holy Innocents* [P]—which commemorates the massacre of the children of Bethlehem—*Saint Joseph's Chapel* [Q], the *tombs of Saint Paula and her daughter* [R], the *tomb of Saint Eusebius* [S], and the *tomb of Saint Jerome* [T], who is said to have written his translation of the Bible in the adjoining *Saint Jerome's Chapel* [U].

On the north side of the Church of the Nativity stands the *cloister* [V], which is full of atmosphere; it probably dates from the Crusades. At the southeast corner of the church is the Greek Orthodox *Saint George's Chapel* [W], built in the 12th century as the sacristy.

About 400 meters (440 yards) southeast of the Church of the Nativity lies the **Milk Grotto** [3], where Mary is believed to have hidden with her Child before the flight into Egypt.

From Manger Square, *Paul VI Street* (named to commemorate a visit by the Pope) runs west, passing the magnificent *Syrian Orthodox Church* [4]. Off the street to the left is *Market Square* [5], where you can buy a variety of handcrafted articles, such as olive wood carvings and mother-of-pearl work—mostly decorated with Christian themes—in addition to other local products.

Side trip to the *Herodion

Take the road from Bethlehem that runs east past the *Field of the Shepherds*—traditionally the spot where the angel announced the birth of Christ to the shepherds. Continue through the little town of *Beit Sahur,* past *Ruth's Field,* and through the village of *Za'atra,* occupied by Bedouin who have adopted a settled life. You will soon come to the ***Herodion** (11 km.; 7 miles from Jerusalem).

This mountain stronghold stands at the summit of a hill, *Jebel Fureidis,* 758 meters (2,487 feet) high. Because of the hill's truncated conical shape, it was long thought to be of volcanic origin; but, in fact, it was deliberately given this form when the Herodion was built.

Herod the Great, who had been made king of Judea by the Romans in 37 B.C., built this massive structure both as a place of refuge and as a mausoleum. Following his death in Jericho, his body was brought here for burial. During the Jewish War, the fortress was occupied by the Zealots, a faction of Jews who violently opposed idolatrous worship. The Herodion was destroyed by Hadrian during the Bar-Kochba rebellion. Later the site was occupied by hermits, who have left inscriptions in Greek.

Excavations conducted by an Italian priest, V. Corbo, have established that the Herodion was surrounded by two circular walls with four round towers. Herod is believed to have been buried in one of the towers. The results of the excavations confirmed Flavius Josephus's detailed description of the magnificence of this fortress. There is a superb view over the Judean Desert from the summit of the hill.

Side trip to Mount Gillo

Leave Bethlehem on the Hebron Road (Route 60) and turn right into a road that runs west amid peach orchards to *Beit Jala.* Continuing up through the little town, which is built on a steep hillside, you climb through olive groves to the summit of *Mount Gillo,* the Biblical *Giloh.* A field school was founded here for the study of the varied flora and fauna of the region. From the summit, views extend to the north of Jerusalem and to the east over the Judean Desert to the Dead Sea. Just before you reach the summit, a narrow but perfectly negotiable road goes off on the right to the Salesian monastery of *Cremisan,* whose monks make excellent wine.

*

The main road (Route 60) to Hebron runs past large quarries that supply building stone for Jerusalem and the surrounding area and provide employment for the residents of the neighboring refugee camp of *Dahisha.* About 12 km. (7.5 miles) from Jerusalem, a road turns off on the right to the Muslim village of *El Khadr.* The village's arched gateway has a figure of Saint George, who, in popular Muslim belief, is identified with the prophet Elijah; his Arabic name, El Khadr (the Green One), also refers to Elijah. To the left of the road are the three pools known as **Solomon's Pools,** which were probably formed in Hasmonean times and later developed by Herod to supply water to the Herodion. In Roman times, two aqueducts also conveyed water from the springs to Jerusalem. The water supply system was restored and further improved in the time of the Turkish sultan Suleiman the Magnificent and under British mandate.

Beside the pools stands the dilapidated 16th-century Turkish fortress of *Qal' at el-Burak* (Castle of the Pools). A narrow road runs down past the pools to the village of *Artas,* from which there is a view of the convent and orphanage of *Santa Maria dell'Orto,* built in 1901. The gorge in which Artas lies is traditionally believed to be the site of the "garden enclosed" (*hortus conclusus*) of the Song of Solomon, and the name of the village may be derived from the Latin *hortus.*

After passing El Khadr and Artas, Route 60 runs up into the Hebron hills. Grapes, the predominant crops of this area, are mainly used for making raisins.

Past *El'azar,* a moshav shitufi established in 1975, you come to the kibbutz of **Kefar Ezyon** (20 km.; 12 miles from Jerusalem), where a road to the right goes to the other settlements in the *"Ezyon group."* Kefar Ezyon was established in 1943, and, until the outbreak of the War of Independence, there were three other villages (Massu'ot, Yizhaq, Revadim, and En Zurim) nearby. In December 1947, these settlements were raided by Arabs from the surrounding villages. Worse trouble followed in May 1948, when a superior number of troops of the British-led Arab Legion attacked the beleaguered Jewish settlements, killing 240 of the defenders and taking 260 prisoners.

After the Six-Day War, Kefar Ezyon was rebuilt by the descendants of the original settlers. The kibbutzim of *Rosh Zurim* and *Migdal Oz,* the township of *Allon Shevut,* and the moshav shitufi of *El'azar* were established later. All of these religious settlements have limited farmland and are seeking to develop industry.

Almost all the larger Arab villages lie several kilometers from the Hebron Road—*Nahalin* and *Jaba* to the west, and *Beit Fajjar* to the east. The road runs down into a valley with the Biblical name *Emeq ha-Berakha* (Valley of Blessing), where the college of agriculture established by Jordan and the experimental farm of *Ein Arrub* are located. To the right of the road lies the former refugee camp of *Mu'askar el-Arrub*, which is now a village. After passing a side road that runs west to the villages of *Beit Umar* and *Zurif*, you enter a stretch of country where many of the hillsides have been reforested. The road continues to climb, and reaches its highest point in the Hebron hills, 1,020 meters (3347 feet), at the large village of *Halhul* (30 km.; 19 miles from Jerusalem). The center of Halhul still contains the traditional local type of construction —small houses packed closely together, with walls of massive ashlar blocks and domed roofs. Nowadays, however, Halhul has begun to adopt the more urban aspects of a town and is starting to merge into Hebron.

Route 60 now brings you to Hebron, 32 km. (20 miles) from Jerusalem.

HEBRON

The town, known in Hebrew as *Hevron* and in Arabic as *El Khalil*, is known as the city of the patriarch of Abraham, who was buried here. It is situated at an altitude of 930 meters (3,050 feet), sur-rounded by vine-covered hills, some of which rise to over 1,000 meters (3,300 feet). It has a population of 40,000, almost all of whom are Arabs.

History

Sacred to both Muslims and Jews, Hebron is one of the oldest towns in Israel and has been jealously fought over throughout its long history. Implements dating from the middle Bronze Age have been found here, indicating that the city may have been founded in the 18th century B.C.

Hebron plays a central role in the Old Testament story of the Patriarchs. Upon his arrival from his native Ur in Mesopotamia, Abraham purchased the cave of Machpelah as a family tomb, together with the adjoining field. This action constituted a decisive step in his transition from a nomadic existence to settled life. Abraham, his wife Sarah, Isaac, Jacob, Rebecca, and Leah are all said to be buried here.

After Saul's death, David ruled Israel from Hebron for seven years before transferring his capital to Jerusalem. Solomon's son, Rehoboam, fortified the town. After the destruction of the First Temple, the Edomites became masters of Hebron, until they were conquered and converted by the Hasmonean ruler John Hyrcanus. Shortly thereafter, the Romans burned down the town during the Jewish War. Hebron was an insignificant village under Byzantine rule, but it was during this period that a church was added to the Haram el-Khalil, the massive structure built by Herod over the cave of Machpelah. The Arabs, who arrived in the seventh century, called the place El Khalil (The Friend)— for the patriarch Abraham who was a friend of God—and added a mosque to the church structure. During the Crusades, most of the few Jews who remained in the town were expelled. From the 12th century until 1967, non-Muslims were forbidden to enter the mosque.

In the violent riots and fighting between Muslims and Jews in 1929, 67 of the 200 Jews living in Hebron were killed. During the Six-Day War, the town surrendered to Israeli forces without resistance. The Jewish settlement of Qiryat Arba was established on a hill northeast of the town.

Attractions

Hebron is a town rich in Eastern character. Its narrow lanes and busy bazaars teem with innumerable little shops, booths, and the workshops of craftsmen (particularly pottery, glass-blowing, and tanning shops).

The main feature of interest in the town is the ***Haram el-Khalil,** an enormous structure topped by two minarets that stands over the *cave of Machpelah*. The exterior walls date from the time of Herod the Great (39–4 B.C.), but it has been greatly enlarged; its present form reflects contribu-

Approach to the Haram el-Khalil

tions of the Byzantines, the Crusaders, and the Arabs.

From the *principal entrance* [A], a right-angled flight of steps leads to the *Forecourt* [B], which contains mausoleums with cenotaphs for *Abraham* [C] and his wife *Sarah* [D], as well as for *Jacob* [E] and his wife *Leah* [F]. From here, a small *porch* [G] leads into the *Mosque* [H], which is divided into three aisles by four piers and contains cenotaphs for *Isaac* [I] and his wife *Rebecca* [J]. All the cenotaphs date from the 14th century and stand on the exact spots where, according to an ancient tradition, the patriarchs and their wives were buried in the cave of Machpelah. The cave below is no longer accessible.

In the mosque, note the very fine carved wooden *pulpit* [K] that Saladin brought here from Ashqelon in 1191, and the ancient

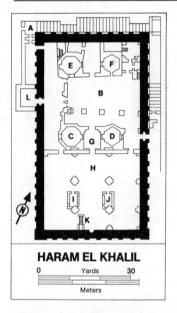

HARAM EL KHALIL

0   Yards   30

Meters

stained-glass windows. One final feature of interest is the site that Muslims revere as the *Tomb of Joseph* [L] (although Jews claim that he is buried at Neblus).

*

Hebron stands at a crossroads for a number of interesting routes. If you wish, you can take Route 35 west via *Tarqumiya* and *Bet Guvrin* to *Qiryat Gat* (see page 252), and continue from there to *Ashqelon* (see page 259). Another road runs southeast of Hebron to the large village of *Yatta,* on the edge of the desert, the ruined synagogue of *Susiya* with its interesting mosaic floor, and on to *Samu' i* (the Biblical Eshtemoa), with im-

pressive remains of a synagogue of the Talmudic period.

To continue Travel Route 10, follow Route 60 south from Hebron. It begins a gradual descent into the Beer Sheva depression in the northern Negev, about 200 meters (650 feet) above sea level. The country is intensively cultivated at the beginning of the route, but the productivity of the soil declines as you continue south, reflecting the decreased annual rainfall of the region. About 7 kilometers (4 miles) south of Hebron, the road passes through a number of small Arab villages, some of which were established fairly recently. A side road on the right leads to the large village of *Dura,* the Biblical Adoraim.

You will pass a number of reforestation projects and then the village of *Rabud* (perhaps the Biblical Debir or Kirjath-sepher), where there is a Roman mausoleum. About 20 km. (12 miles) from Hebron lies the large Muslim village of *Dhahiriya.* Its center, characterized by closely packed houses of stone or sun-dried brick, reflects Palestinian village design and architecture in ancient times.

The landscape becomes increasingly desertlike as you head farther south and the road twists more steeply downhill. Some 10 km. (6 miles) from Dhahiriya you will cross Israel's pre-1967 frontier again and leave Judea-Samaria. At the *Shoqet Junction* (68 km.; 42 miles from Jerusalem), Route 60 continues for another 13 km. (8 miles) through flat

A Bedouin girl of the Negev

As you continue east on Route 31, the loess soil gradually gives way to the chalk hills of *Qiryatayim,* only to reappear near an abandoned sisal plantation 21 km. (13 miles) from *Shoqet.* At this point, a road goes off to the left to **Tel Arad,** the site of ancient Arad.

When the Israelites came to this area from Sinai seeking a direct route to the Promised Land, the king of the Canaanite city of Arad drove them back into the wilderness (Numbers 21:1), condemning them to years of wandering on the meandering route over the plateau beyond the Jordan. Excavations (1962–1967) by Israeli archaeologists on Tel Arad brought to light the remains of a great city of the Early Bronze Age (2900–2700 B.C.), built on the ruins of even earlier settlements. Over these, a later city was constructed which appeared to be Israelite (probably built by Solomon) and included a temple and Hebrew inscriptions on potsherds. Despite these discoveries, no trace has been found of the Late Bronze Age city mentioned in the Bible, whose king fought with the Israelites; it is assumed that this Arad existed elsewhere in the Negev. (Egyptian inscriptions refer to several places of the same name in the Negev, thus supporting this assumption.)

country to *Beer Sheva* (see page 232); however, you turn left (east) at the junction on Route 31 toward Arad.

Route 31 runs through a rolling landscape of yellowish-brown loess, gullied by flash floods. The inhabitants are mostly Bedouin, who are gradually turning from their traditional nomadic customs to a settled life. Black goatskin tents rub shoulders with crude huts and houses. Barley or wheat is sown in the cultivated fields in winter. When rain has been plentiful, a lush green carpet of seedlings covers the fields in spring; but in the frequent drought years, the grain does not ripen.

About 5 km. (3 miles) from the Shoqet Junction, a road branches off to the left and runs northeast for 13 km. (8 miles) to *Yatir,* one of the largest reforestation areas in the country, located on the very edge of the desert.

About 10 km. (6 miles) farther east along Route 31 lies the modern town of **Arad** (99 km./62 miles from Jerusalem; population 10,000). It was founded in 1961 on a site conveniently located near the

Dead Sea Works (see page 237) and the Negev phosphate mines. Favored with a cool and agreeable climate, the town lies 610 meters (2,000 feet) above sea level and almost 1,000 meters (3,300 feet) above the Dead Sea.

The layout of this desert city reflects careful planning. It is divided into a series of neighborhoods linked by roads. The blocks of houses are built around courtyards that contain shops and gardens, which are sheltered from the fierce desert winds. On the east side of the town are a number of hotels with views ranging over the Judean Desert to the Dead Sea. Its dry climate has made Arad a popular retreat among those who suffer from asthma.

The town grew rapidly as a result of the discovery of oil in the vicinity, but the nearly exhausted reserves now only provide enough oil to meet local needs. However, an industrial zone centered around the manufacture of building materials and textiles on the southern outskirts of town, as well as large chemical plants established near the phosphorus mines of *Zefa-Ef'e,* southeast of *Dimona* (30 km.; 19 miles from Arad) ensure Arad's future.

From Arad, you can take a road that runs for 21 km. (13 miles) northeast and then ends at the west side of the fortress of *Masada* (see page 225), where you can climb on foot to the summit. You must return to Arad to continue your journey on Route 31 to the *Zohar Junction,* at the southwest corner

of the Dead Sea. Here the landscape changes suddenly as the road descends steeply through the desert, with its barren chalk and limestone hills.

As you continue southeast from Arad on Route 31, you will see the fortress of ***Zohar** (Mezad Zohar) on the left, shortly before you reach the Dead Sea. This guard post, built by the Nabateans in the first century B.C., later commanded a Roman road that ran down through the narrow gorge. There is a breathtaking view of the ********Dead Sea* from here, which appears as a blue expanse between the white chalk hills.

Not far away, another viewpoint offers a vista that includes the fence surrounding the large salt pans and part of the Dead Sea Works themselves. At the road junction near the shores of the Dead Sea lies the little town of *Neve Zohar* (130 km.; 81 miles from Jerusalem), with a number of restaurants and small hotels. On a low hill in front of the sheer wall of the Judean Desert to the left stands the fortress of *Haya,* another Roman guard post from which a watch could be kept on the desert tribes. To the right (south) can be seen the northern peak of Mount Sedom. A road runs south between the hill and the Dead Sea to *Sedom* (see page 237).

Turn left onto Route 90 at the Zohar Junction. To the right (east) you can see the evaporation basin in the Dead Sea, with white lumps of salt floating in the water. To the left is the nearly vertical face of the Rift Valley below the Judean Desert, whose steepest escarpments rise to a height of several hundred meters. Past the *Zohar Hot Springs,* where there is a kiosk and swimming facilities, you come to **En Boqeq** (138 km.; 86 miles from Jerusalem). Many visitors come here to "take the cure" at its hot springs, which are said to be particularly effective for psoriasis, and to enjoy its beaches. A Roman guard post, *Mezad Boqeq,* stands in front of the rock face on a hill to the left.

Just beyond En Boqeq stretches the *Lashon* (Lisan) peninsula, formed of soft saline marl (crumbly earth rich in lime). It reaches across from the east side of the Dead Sea, separating the large northern basin from the smaller, much shallower, southern basin. Because much of the southern basin has dried up, water is brought to the large evaporation basin of the Dead Sea Works through a canal from the northern half.

A number of dry valleys slash the rock face on the west side of the valley: the *Nahal Ye'elim, Nahal Rahaf,* and *Nahal Qanna'im.* These valleys form small peninsulas of stones and gravel at the shores of the Dead Sea.

Continuing north on Route 90, you will note that the flat terrace bordering the Dead Sea becomes wider and the rock face withdraws westward. You come to the *Masada Junction* (150 km.; 93 miles from Jerusalem following Travel Route 10). From here, a road runs through bizarre rock formations

of soft local marls that have been so eroded by flash floods that they look like an enchanted city—complete with streets, statues, and palaces. The road finally arrives at the foot of the hill of Masada.

Masada

The scene of one of the most celebrated struggles in Jewish history, Masada towers as both an imposing mountaintop fortress and an important symbol for the Jewish people. Before you make your way to the top, you may want to visit the restaurant, museum, and other facilities for travelers at the foot of the hill. Then, if you are feeling energetic, you can make the 45-minute walk up the winding path to the fortress; if not, a cable car takes visitors to the top.

The rocky hill of Masada (in Hebrew, *Mezada*) has almost vertical walls on all sides. Although it

The rock fortress of Masada

is only 49 meters (161 feet) above sea level, the hill towers almost 450 meters (1475 feet) above the Dead Sea. Deep gorges surround it on all sides: the *Ben Ya'ir Gorge* (north), and the *Mezada Gorge* (west and south). The top, which is almost completely flat, measures 600 meters (660 yards) from north to south and 300 meters (330 yards) from east to west at its narrowest point (in the middle). It is an ideal defensive position.

The best source of information on the history of Masada and the events for which it is celebrated is that reliable historian Flavius Josephus (37–c. 95), whose *Antiquities of the Jews* and *The Jewish War* provide a rich, contemporary account of the events he describes. The hill was first fortified either by Jonathan, brother of Judas Maccabeus, in the second century B.C., or by the Hasmonean king Alexander Jannaeus in the early first century B.C. The principal structures on the hill, including a sumptuous three-level palace, were built by Herod the Great, who recognized the natural defensive properties of the site. He surrounded the perimeter of the hill with strong walls. He then built a palace on the west side, and a splendid residential palace on three natural terraces at the northern tip of the hill (the uppermost terrace rose 20 meters/65 feet above the middle one, which was 15 meters/50 feet above the lower terrace). Other construction included a small palace, large storerooms, offices, and much else

besides. The most important feature of all was the provision of large cisterns, in which rainwater was collected and stored.

After Herod's death, a Roman garrison was stationed on Masada (A.D. 6–66). Following the repression of the Jewish rebellion in A.D. 70, the Jewish Zealots fled into the desert rather than abandon their struggle. Menahem Ben Yehuda gained control of the fortress by a stratagem; for three years, the Jews, commanded by El'azar Ben Ya'ir, withstood a siege by Roman forces.

General Flavius Silva commanded the Romans' Tenth Legion, with its numerous auxiliaries. His troops (about 15,000 strong) built a wall encircling the whole hill and set up eight camps around it in order to prevent any possibility of the Zealots' escape. On the west side, where the hill is lower and less steep, the Romans built up a great earthen ramp, along which they ascended and tried to break down the walls of the fortress with battering rams. At first, these attempts were unsuccessful, but they finally managed to create a breach, through which they threw lighted torches and set the wooden supporting beams on fire.

The defenders of the fortress—numbering 960 men, women, and children in all—showed the Romans that they were not short of water by hanging wet cloths over the walls and letting the water drip down. When at last they saw that further resistance was hopeless,

Ben Ya'ir delivered a fiery address to the Zealots, after which they killed each other rather than allowing themselves to be taken prisoner by the Romans. When the Romans entered the fortress they found only dead bodies, together with great stores of food. In Herod's palaces, the Zealots had installed storehouses for weapons and other supplies, living quarters for families, ritual baths (*miqva'ot*), a synagogue, and a treasury containing a large hoard of silver shekels.

After the fall of Masada, a Roman garrison probably occupied the fortress for a time. There was still a settlement here in Byzantine times, and excavations have unearthed remains of a church dating from that period.

In 1838, two Americans, Edwin Robinson and Edward Smith, identified the hill as the site of the fortress described by Flavius Josephus; however, Masada was not thoroughly excavated and restored until 1963–1965. The team of archaeologists from the Hebrew University was led by Yigael Yadin, who was assisted by thousands of volunteers from Israel and other countries.

The most impressive structure on Masada is Herod's *palace,* built on three levels at the northern tip of the hill. In the residential apartments on the uppermost level, the walls and ceilings were decorated with frescoes, while the floors were adorned with black-and-white mosaics—the oldest yet found in Israel. A fabulous view of

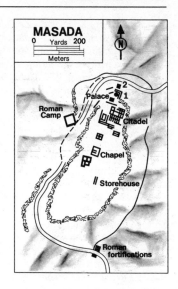

the area as far as En Gedi extends from the semicircular *middle terrace* [1]. On the *lower terrace* [2] you can still see sandstone columns and painted stucco walls.

Among the articles found in the *synagogue* were Torah scrolls from the time of the Zealots, scrolls of the original text of the "Book of the Wisdom of Ben Sira," and scrolls with texts identical to those discovered at Qumran (see page 229).

*

Return to Route 90 from Masada and continue north to En Gedi, 26 km. (16 miles) away, along the narrow strip of land between the rock walls on the west and the shores of the Dead Sea on the east. You will pass the mouths of three more dry watercourses (*Nahal Ze'-elim, Nahal Mishmar,* and *Nahal Hever*), and from time to time you will catch a whiff of the sulfurous hot springs on the shores of the lake. There is a beach at *Hamme Mazor,* maintained by the kibbutz of En Gedi, which boasts medicinal black mud and a large self-service restaurant.

*En Gedi (176 km.; 109 miles from Jerusalem) is an extraordinary oasis lying 395 meters (1,295 feet) below sea level. En Gedi (whose name means "Goat's Spring") has an abundant supply of fresh water, which seeps down through the rocks from the western slopes of the Hebron hills and surfaces in a series of springs. Although the oasis lies in one of the driest and hottest regions in the world, it is one of the most northerly enclaves of the moist tropical Sudanese vegetation zone.

The ancients who settled here knew the value of this oasis, and used the land to grow spices, particularly balsam. En Gedi is mentioned in the Old Testament as one of the cities of the tribe of Judah (Joshua 15:62), and it was here that the young David sought refuge from Saul's wrath (1 Samuel 24). The Song of Solomon refers to the "vineyards of En-gedi" (no doubt meaning gardens of sweet-smelling herbs and spices). The Romans left the Jewish inhabitants of En Gedi undisturbed—despite the fact that they had given refuge to the last of Bar-Kochba's rebel forces, according to letters of Bar-Kochba found in caves in the nearby Hever Gorge.

Excavations at various points have revealed five different occupation levels at En Gedi. The most interesting features discovered include the beautiful mosaic floor in a synagogue of the Byzantine period, with representations of peacocks eating grapes and the inscription "Peace over Israel," and a Hebrew inscription threatening punishment for those who "create discord in the community, revile friends in the presence of non-Jews, steal the property of friends, or betray the secrets of the city" (perhaps referring to the method of growing balsam). The site was abandoned in later periods.

The present kibbutz of En Gedi was established in 1953, when the site could be reached by boat from the Dead Sea. The settlers planted large groves of date palms, mainly in the valley of the *Nahal Arugot,* to the west of the hill on which the settlement was built. Dams were

Ibex in the En Gedi nature reserve

constructed to store the water that rushed down after the rare rain falls, bringing with it rich, alluvial soil. Bananas and other fruits for export, as well as flowers, are now also grown here.

Near the wadi of the *Nahal David* lies the entrance to the *nature reserve* north of En Gedi. Here you will see rare trees and shrubs, among them the "apple of Sodom" with its thin-skinned, completely hollow fruits, and rare animals such as the ibex, a wild goat with huge, curving horns.

A steep path leads up to a large waterfall, 200 meters (650 feet) above the Dead Sea, that plunges year-round from a high cliff into a small pool. Lush evergreen hanging and climbing plants surround the falls, while a few meters away stand totally bare rock faces in sharp contrast.

Until 1967, the armistice line ran north of En Gedi, so that as you continue on north you reenter the administrative district of Judea-Samaria, the territory known as the West Bank. The rock walls, rising to 500 meters (1,650 feet) and sometimes higher, draw close to the shores of the Dead Sea. The road (Route 90) to Qalya and Jericho, which you are now following, was forged through this difficult terrain in the early 1970s. It frequently rises high above the Dead Sea, offering tremendous views of the wild surrounding country.

At the kibbutz of *Mizpe Shalem* near the Dead Sea (190 km.; 118 miles from Jerusalem following Travel Route 10), there are springs

that have given rise to brackish reed marshes. The kibbutz, established in 1971, originally stood high up on the rim of the rock wall; a viewpoint there can be reached on a steep, winding road running past the deep gorge of the *Nahal Darga*.

About 12 km. (7.5 miles) farther on, you cross the *River Kidron*, which flows through the Judean Desert from Jerusalem to the Dead Sea. On the banks of the river are remains of a small fortress, probably built by the Hasmonean kings, which continued in use into Byzantine times. Another 5 km. (3 miles) farther north is the spring of *En Zugim* (Ein Fashka), surrounded by a growth of reeds and tamarisks; the area is now a nature reserve. You can swim out into the Dead Sea from the slightly saline pools.

Some distance away from the Dead Sea is the hill of **Qumran** (209 km.; 130 miles from Jerusalem following Travel Route 10). It was occupied in the second and first centuries B.C. by a settlement of Essenes; members of this ascetic Jewish sect produced the famous Dead Sea scrolls, which are now in Jerusalem. The site had been inhabited even before the establishment of the Essenian settlement, which was destroyed in 31 B.C. and then rebuilt. There are remains of assembly and dining rooms, a flour mill, a dyer's workshop, a pottery workshop, and other workshops. Most interesting of all is a room believed to be the scriptorium in which the scrolls were written.

Qumran, where the Dead Sea Scrolls were found

One striking feature at Qumran is its great number of water channels, pipes, collecting basins, and baths; they no doubt served ritual purposes, for the Essenes had strict standards of purity and cleanliness. No living quarters have been found: It is assumed that the members of the community lived in tents or in nearby caves.

From the south end of the site you can see the cave where the first scrolls were found to the west. To the east is a cemetery; excavations carried out in 1953–1956 by the Jordanian Department of Antiquities, the Palestine Archaeological Museum, and the Dominican-run École Biblique have revealed that there were 1,200 graves here.

To the north of the hill of Qumran is the kibbutz of *Qalya*, established in 1968 as an outpost settlement at the northwest corner of the Dead Sea. The settlement took its name from a lakeside hotel and the first potash factory; these structures stood here until the War of Independence but were destroyed by the Jordanians. "Qalya" is an acronym formed from the initial letters of the Hebrew phrase "The Dead Sea has come to life again." The kibbutzim of Qalya and of *Almog* (founded in 1977), to the north, grow their crops on soil that was once highly saline but from which the salt has been removed.

After you pass a number of old Jordanian military camps and the sites of the hotel and potash works destroyed in 1948, you will come to a stone marking the lowest point on the surface of the earth: 396 meters (1,299 feet) below sea level. Here the route turns west and, passing between banks of Lisan marl, joins the road coming from the Abdullah Bridge over the Jordan. It is also joined by the road from Jericho to Jerusalem. The route from here to Jerusalem is described in Travel Route 8 (pages 199–200). After a total journey of 239 km. (149 miles) you return to ***Jerusalem* (see description beginning on page 31).

TRAVEL ROUTE 11: ***Jerusalem–*Beer Sheva– Dimona (–Sedom)– *Elat (332 km.; 206 miles)

See map on page 238.

This route takes you down through lands bordering the desert to the heart of the Negev, the spectacular wasteland that makes up much of the Sinai Peninsula. Along the way you will stop in Beer Sheva—the ancient Beersheba of the Bible—where a blend of antiquity and modern living make for a dynamic environment. There are side trips to a large desert erosion crater (the Makhtesh Gadol) and to Sedom, the modern town that marks the site of the wicked city of Sodom. On the way to Elat, at the tip of the Red Sea, you will also see the Timna Gorges, where King Solomon is said to have operated his famous copper mines. The last stop is the seaside town of Elat, where plenty of diversions await those who enjoy swimming, sunbathing, and what some aficionados consider the best snorkeling in the Middle East.

Travel Route 11 follows the more easterly of two possible routes from Beer Sheva, running south along the Jordanian frontier and through the Arava Valley. The westerly route via Qiryat Gat, Beer Sheva, and Mizpe Ramon is described in Travel Route 12 in the reverse direction. You can combine travel routes 11 and 12 for a site-filled round trip tour starting from Beer Sheva to Elat (Travel Route 11) and returning from Elat to Beer Sheva (Travel Route 12).

See Travel Route 10 (pages 211–222) for a description of the road from Jerusalem to the *Shoqet Junction.* Between the Shoqet Junction and Beer Sheva, Route 60 runs for 13 km. (8 miles) through gently rolling country characterized by the yellowish soil found in desert border lands. This is a region of dry farming (mainly wheat), practiced by kibbutzniks and, to an even greater extent, by Bedouin who have chosen a settled way of life. Their huts and black goatskin tents dot the roadside.

About 7 km. (4 miles) before you arrive in Beer Sheva's town center, you come to *Omer* (population 2,800). Although founded in 1949 as a moshav shitufi, it has become a suburb of Beer Sheva.

Some of the residents still do a little farming. Two km. (1.5 miles) beyond Omer, a road branches left to the site of ancient Beer Sheva and on to *Tel Shiva,* one of five Bedouin villages established in the Negev. At about this point, you can spot a monument off in the distance that is dedicated to the Jewish fighters for the Negev. To the left of the road spans the industrial zone of Beer Sheva; to the right are the newer residential districts and the University campus.

*Beer Sheva

The capital of the Negev, Beer Sheva (population 120,000) has a pleasant climate that is not unduly hot even in summer.

The history of Beer Sheva—the Biblical Beersheba—goes back at least 6,000 years, although the town has moved some distance away from its original site during the course of time.

In the Early Bronze Age (fourth millennium B.C.), there was a thriving farming settlement on the edge of the broad wadi (dry river bed) of the Nahal Beer Sheva. It had round or rectangular houses, with the lower half set deep into the yellowish-brown soil. The town's inhabitants grew wheat and herded sheep, goats, and cattle. There were also craftsmen in the village who smelted copper from the land of Edom or the Elat area, carved cult vessels out of basalt (which was also imported), and fashioned figurines and jewelry from bone, shells, semiprecious stones, and ivory.

The Bible contains frequent references to the little town. Abraham set up his tents, planted a tamarisk, and had visions of the one God in Beersheba. Isaac came here with his flocks and negotiated a settlement with the Philistine king Abimelech of Gerar, thus ending the disputes between their herdsmen over possession of the precious wells.

Toward the end of the second millennium B.C., the area was occupied by the seminomadic Israelite tribe of Simeon (Shime'on), whose members were eventually absorbed into the tribe of Judah. Beer Sheva then declined in importance for a time, but it took on a fresh, renewed significance under the kings of Judah. The town marked the southern boundary of the permanently settled part of their kingdom—hence the expression "from Dan to Beersheba." The city was rebuilt in the 6th and 5th centuries B.C. by Jews returning from the Babylonian captivity, but it soon fell under the domination of the Edomites. In the 2nd century B.C., the Edomites were forcibly converted to the Jewish faith by the Hasmonean king John Hyrcanus.

After the Roman occupation of the country in 63 B.C., Beer Sheva became a frontier town. During the Byzantine period, from the fourth century A.D. to the Arab invasion in the seventh century, the town enjoyed great prosperity; however, its fortunes began to decline when the Arab conquest opened the door to the nomadic Bedouin. The last remains of Roman and Byzantine buildings disappeared in the 19th century, when the people of Gaza carried off columns, dressed stone blocks, and other building materials.

Turkish authorities made Beer Sheva the new capital of the Negev in 1900, the better to control the Bedouin who roamed the wide surrounding area. Swiss and German architects prepared a town plan that included wide streets intersecting at right angles, square blocks of buildings, and public buildings designed in the German colonial style of the period. Within this grand framework, the Bedouin and other Arabs who settled in the town built their customary mud dwellings, which did not harmonize with the European design scheme. A town council and a district council were established, and Bedouin sheikhs were appointed to positions of authority. However, the town had made little progress by 1914, when a census counted around 800 Muslim residents and a few Jewish families.

During World War I, Beer Sheva was the headquarters of the Turkish and German army that fought on the Suez and Sinai fronts. Many people were brought in to work on the fortifications and provide other services for the army; a branch line of the Jerusalem-Jaffa railway was also built to connect Jaffa and southwestern Palestine. On October 31, 1917, allied troops commanded by General Allenby captured the town from the German and Turkish forces.

Having lost its status as a strategically vital point, Beer Sheva stagnated after the war. In 1920, a number of Jewish workers planted a tree nursery here (from which a few eucalyptus trees survive today) and experimented with growing vegetables and other crops. By 1922, Beer Sheva's population had grown to 2,356, of whom only 38 were Jews. Thereafter, the number of inhabitants swelled in "good" years—those with plenty of rain —and declined during periods of drought. The last Jewish residents left the town during the disturbances of 1936–1939, but increased efforts were made to acquire land in the Negev.

During the War of Independence, the Egyptian army set up its headquarters in Beer Sheva, but when the town fell to the Israeli army on October 21, 1948, it was totally uninhabited. The first Jewish settlers—new immigrants —came to Beer Sheva at the beginning of 1949, and by the end of the year the population had risen to 1,800.

Modern Beer Sheva is a dynamic town of wide, tree-lined avenues where you can easily forget that you are in the midst of the desert. The main feature of interest in the *old town* (built by the Turks) is the *Municipal Museum* [1], housed in a former mosque. Its collections document the history of the town and the Negev. Opposite the museum is a *police post* [2]

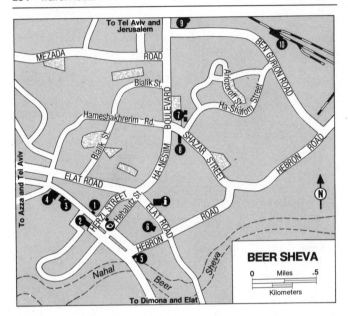

that dates from the time of the British mandate. To the northwest is the *Biological Institute* [3], whose research mainly revolves around desert vegetation; the *British Military Cemetery* [4] of World War I adjoins the institute grounds. *Abraham's Well* [5] is ascribed to Abraham because of its great antiquity. A modern building houses the *Bedouin Market* [6]; until a few years ago, it was the scene of a busy eastern market on Thursday mornings.

In the center of the town are the *Negev Institute* [7] for the study of arid zones and the *Community Center* [8], which runs various cultural programs.

Farther north is *Ben Gurion* *University* [9], whose ultra-modern buildings lie just west of the *railroad station* [10].

Beer Sheva's industrial area, which produces textiles, electronics, chemicals, and ceramics, is mainly concentrated in the northeastern part of the town.

*

Continue your journey on Route 25, the main road to Dimona (35 km./22 miles from Beer Sheva), which crosses the broad *Wadi (Nahal) Beer Sheva*—usually dry —and turns northeast at the *Nevatim Junction*. To the right, you'll pass a plant where research is conducted on the use of waste mate-

Bedouin market, Beer Sheva

rials in the improvement of soils. Also to the right are the typical desert farm buildings of *Bet Eshel* (House of the Tamarisk). The small moshav, founded in 1943 as one of the first experimental settlements in the Negev, now serves as a museum. Completely isolated and located near Egyptian headquarters during the War of Independence, the little moshav held out against attacks until Beer Sheva was taken by Israeli forces in October 1948 in an operation code named "The Ten Plagues." The members of the moshav later moved to the Yizre'el Valley.

As you continue on Route 25, the landscape becomes increasingly desolate. Soon you come to the moshav of *Nevatim,* a patch of vivid green in the midst of barren surroundings. Nevatim and ten other settlements in the Negev were built in a single night in Octo-

ber 1946. After the 1948 war, immigrants from Cochin in southern India settled here. Flowers, early vegetables, and other crops are grown in greenhouses to conserve water.

The hilly terrain becomes increasingly desertlike. Frequently you will see small groves of eucalyptus or tamarisk trees growing in depressions, irrigated with water stored after the rare rain falls. The road runs past an ancient site on a hill; this is probably the desert city of *Aro'er,* which belonged to the tribe of Judah. Just before you reach Dimona, a road branches to the right to the little development town of *Yeroham* (see page 250), with its surrounding experimental plantations of olives, almonds, and other fruits. To the left of the junction is a filtration plant for silica sand, one of the minerals found in the nearby erosion craters (*makhteshim;* see pages 236 and 245). Other industrial installations adjoin this plant, including a large textile factory. A eucalyptus grove spreads to the right of the road.

Despite its location in the midst of the desert, **Dimona** (117 km./73 miles from Jerusalem; population 28,000) boasts tree-lined avenues, green lawns, and a busy shopping center. It was founded in 1955 to provide better living conditions for employees of the Dead Sea Works. Most of the town's residents come from eastern countries and work in local industry, the Dead Sea Works, the phosphate mines of Oron, Zin, and Zefa Ef'e, or in chemical plants.

On the slopes of the hill north of town stretches a forest of pine and eucalyptus trees, which manage to thrive in spite of the desert climate. Farther along the road you will pass the restricted area that surrounds an experimental nuclear reactor.

About 9 km. (6 miles) southeast of Dimona lies the ancient site of ***Mamshit** (in Arabic, *Kurnub*). The town, which was probably founded by the Nabateans, served as a staging point for the caravans that brought incense, myrrh, and other precious wares from southern Arabia to the West. In Roman times, a wall surrounded the caravanserais, stables, warehouses, and houses. Churches were added to the town in Byzantine times, and it has been known by the Greek name Mampsis or Mamphis. The excavated buildings are well preserved, and some of them have been restored. Three dams created reservoirs of the water that surged down the Wadi Kurnub after the winter rains and supplied the town's water.

Side trip to the *Makhtesh Gadol crater

Route 25 from Dimona has been running southeast alongside the railroad line. You will reach an underpass leading to a junction where you turn off on the road (Route 206) that branches south (right) toward the phosphate mines of *Oron* and *Zin*. Take Route 206 for 12 km. (7.5 miles) and then turn right into the narrow *Yorhe'am Gorge,* which leads to the large erosion crater called ***Makhtesh Gadol,** a cirque surrounded by rock walls rising vertically for hundreds of meters.

*

About 22 km. (14 miles) from Dimona on Route 25, you will come to a junction where, if you wish, you can turn north on Route 258 to *Arad* (see page 223). Soon after the junction, Route 25 begins a winding course between steeply scarped hills and dry river gorges (wadis) toward the Jordan Valley. From the *Mizpe ha-Kikkar overlook, there is a tremendous view over the hills, the Jordan Rift, and the Edom plateau beyond it. Then, descending into the Rift Valley, you come to the *Arava Junction* (150 km.; 93 miles from Jerusalem). The road continues east then abruptly turns north (as Route 90) toward Sedom and the Dead Sea;

MAMSHIT

0   Yards   300

Meters

North Gate

West Gate

Headquarters

Houses

Serai

Tower
West Church

East Church

British police post

Route 90 to the right runs south down the Arava Valley to Elat.

Side trip to Sedom (Sodom)

According to Genesis, Sodom and Gomorrah were the two Cities of the Plain that God destroyed because of the wicked carnal practices of their inhabitants. Sedom marks the traditional site of Sodom.

Route 90 begins its run north to Sedom (17 km.; 11 miles from the Arava Junction) between bizarrely shaped banks of white, lime-rich earth. Thorny acacias thrive in the landscape, and there are occasional date palm trees. After you pass the new settlement of *En Tamar* (Spring of the Palm Trees) on the left, you'll see a narrow road that turns off on the right to the moshav of *Ne' ot ha-Kikkar,* on the edge of the Sedom salt marshes. In spite of the harsh climate, these settlements—with the help of spray irrigation—grow early vegetables and flowers for export.

The road runs northwest alongside the Sedom salt marsh (on the right), where the predominant plants are reeds and tamarisks. In recent decades, the level of the Dead Sea has fallen and the marsh has been drying up, with consequent changes in the vegetation. You soon come to the *Dead Sea Works,* where factories produce potash and bromine. Beyond the factories are the salt pans where table salt is recovered by water evaporation.

Beyond the salt pans to the left of the road spans *Mount Sedom,* an enormous bank of salt 10 km. (6 miles) long and 2 km. (1.5 miles) wide, with layers of chalk crossed by layers of salt that has been thrust up to the surface. As rain dissolved the salt over time, it created bizarrely shaped columnar formations on the hillsides; periodically, some of these break off and tumble down the steep slope. The strange salt columns may have inspired the Biblical story of Lot's wife who, in defiance of the angel's command, looked back on the burning cities of Sodom and Gomorrah and was transformed into a pillar of salt (Genesis 19:17–26).

Running between Mount Sedom and the large evaporation basin of the Dead Sea Works, Route 90 continues for another 9 km. (6 miles) to the Zohar Junction (see page 224), where you can take Route 31 to Arad or continue north to Masada and En Gedi (see Travel Route 10).

*

From the *Arava Junction* (see page 236), Route 90 runs south down the whole length of the Rift Valley in the Wadi el Arafa, heading almost due south along the frontier with Jordan to Elat.

Soon after the junction, you will come in sight of dazzlingly white formations of chalk marl, through which the *Nahal Zin* has cut its broad wadi. A side road cuts left (east) to *Iddan,* a moshav es-

**ROUTES
11 AND 12**
Jerusalem to Elat;
Elat to Beer Sheva
0   Miles   25
Kilometers

JERUSALEM
Bethlehem
Hebron
En Gedi
Shoqet junction
Arad
Beer Sheva
Tel Sheva
Neve Zohar
Mash'abbim junction
Haluza
Dimona
Arava junction
Mamshit
Yeroham
En Tamar
Shivta
Oron
Sede Boqer
Nahal Zin
Iddan
Avedat
Hazeva
Merkaz Sapir
En Yahav
Mizpe Ramon
Zofar
Paran
Zihor junction
Yahel
Qetura
Gerofit
Yotvata
Hay Bar
Samar
Timna gorges
Be'er Ora
Amram's Pillars
Elot
Elat
RED SEA

tablished in 1979. After leveling the barren hills of sand, its settlers began the intensive cultivation of early vegetables and other crops.

The landscape becomes increasingly monotonous as the road continues south. About 25 km. (15 miles) from the junction lies *En Hazeva,* the most abundantly flowing spring on the west side of the Arava Valley. In spite of the military post here, visitors are welcome at the spring. Nearby is a huge and ancient lotus tree (*Zizyphus spina-Christi*) and other desert trees. The small communal settlement of *Ovot,* which is unusual in both social composition and religious views, is located here. Just 3 km. (2 miles) beyond Ovot, a road branches left to the *Hazeva Field School,* which conducts studies of the flora and fauna of the Arava Valley, and *Hazeva,* a moshav established in 1965, which grows dates, early vegetables, and flowers. The development of an increasing number of such "artificial oases" has been made possible by the discovery of large reserves of slightly saline groundwater in the Arava Valley—a surprising find in a region with an annual rainfall of only 30–50 millimeters (1–2 inches).

The road climbs almost imperceptibly, and at the turn off for *En Yahav*—the oldest (founded 1951) as well as the most populous moshav settlement in the Arava Valley—you are almost at sea level. The moshav grows early vegetables, flowers, and dates.

Merkaz Sapir (198 km.; 123

miles from Jerusalem following Travel Route 11) is a new rural service center for the settlements in the Arava Valley. At this point, the Rift Valley steadily narrows, and the granite and sandstone walls of the Edom plateau to the east draw closer. You'll notice that the umbrella thorn, whose home is in the African savanna, becomes more profuse as you continue south.

Route 90 heads past the kibbutz of *Zohar*, established in 1968, and it eventually comes to the mouth of the broad wadi of the *Nahal Paran*, which runs down from eastern Sinai by way of the Paran plateau. Here is the moshav of *Paran*, established in 1972. Another 28 km. (17 miles) farther south, the valley bottom reaches its highest point—230 meters (755 feet) above sea level—and then begins its gradual descent toward the sea. As you continue, you will pass *Yahel*, a kibbutz established in 1976.

Near the kibbutz of *Qetura* (273 km.; 170 miles from Jerusalem following Travel Route 11), the westerly route from Beer Sheva via Mizpe Ramon (see Travel Route 12) meets Route 90. About 4 km. (2 miles) beyond this junction, a road cuts to the left and runs up a steep hill to the kibbutz of *Gerofit*. It offers a fine view of the lush green fields and orchards of the two kibbutzim, extending eastward to the Jordanian frontier, flanked by the grayish yellow desert.

As you continue on Route 90, you'll come to **Yotvata,** a kibbutz established in 1951 as one of the first Jewish outpost settlements in the desert. Although the Biblical Jotbathah, which the Children of Israel passed on their long wanderings in the wilderness (Numbers 33:34), is believed to have been located farther south on the Gulf of Elat, there is no doubt that Yotvata was the site of a Roman frontier fort designed to repel the nomadic Bedouin from the settled land.

The Arabic name of the site, *Ein Ghadyan,* may have derived from the Latin "ad Dianam," which suggests that a temple to Diana, the goddess of hunting, once stood here; the presence of deer and gazelles in this area support this theory. The animals are attracted by the small springs located in the area that not only serve Yotvata's agricultural endeavors but also supply water to Elat.

The kibbutz grows dates, early vegetables, and flowers, and also raises cattle that supply dairy products to Elat. Travelers can enjoy fresh milk, cocoa, ices, and other refreshments served at the *restaurant* on the left side of the road.

Beyond the restaurant lies a picnic site, nicely shaded by date palms, and the entrance to the large **Hay Bar Safari Park,** where ostriches, wild oxen, wild asses, and many other creatures roam freely. Within the park is a *playa* (salt pan). Its brackish water supports a dense growth of umbrella thorns, tamarisks, and other plants that provide grazing and shade for the animals. The nature reserve is visible to the left (east) as you continue south of Yatvata, and you can observe the animals from your car, particularly near watering holes.

The Arava Valley narrows, and the imposing walls of granite, porphyry, and other ancient rocks flank it on both the western and eastern sides. Jagged peaks, intricately eroded rock faces, and a varied pattern of land formations provide interesting vistas as you head south on Route 90.

After passing *Samar* (289 km.; 180 miles from Jerusalem following Travel Route 11), a kibbutz founded in 1976, a side road cuts to the right. It leads to the Timna gorges, the supposed site of the copper mines of Solomon.

Side trip to the *Timna gorges

The road to the Timna gorges runs through a wild and barren landscape of red, dark purple, and blackish, rocky hills. A side track leads to the *"Mushroom,"* a wind-sculpted rock formation. From the turnoff from Route 90, a drive of 9 km. (6 miles) brings you to *"Solomon's Pillars"*—sandstone pinnacles soaring 50 meters (165 feet) high, and ranging in color from ocher to red. Opposite is *Mount Timna,* where the ruins of an Egyptian slave-labor camp that dates from the second millennium B.C. were found. The ruins indicate that copper was already being worked here at the time. The ruins

of an Egyptian temple dedicated to the goddess Hathor, who was often represented as a cow or with cow's horns, were discovered at the foot of Solomon's Columns; however, they have been reburied to preserve them. The copper mines ("King Solomon's Mines") were probably worked, not in the time of Solomon, but during the time of king Uzziah of Judah. The present copper mines are not open to visitors, and you must return from here to the main road near the kibbutz of Samar.

*

As you continue on the main road (Route 90), you can see the *Timna copper mine* to the right. When world copper prices fell, the mine was closed for several years; in 1980, however, operations were begun again on a smaller scale. The expanses of greenish mud left by the washing of the ore can be seen in the Arava Valley.

After you pass the entrance to the *Beer Ora* youth camp to the right (304 km.; 189 miles from Jerusalem following Travel Route 11), you come to a side road that leads to *Amram's Pillars.* The road is difficult, but the extraordinary scenery makes the trip well worth your while. Passing between ancient rocks like porphyry and banded gneiss, you come to a row of gigantic pillars of bright purple and rose pink sandstone, set against a backdrop of massive, white limestone hills.

Through the Negev by jeep

As you approach the town of Elat on Route 90, you will be treated to occasional glimpses of the blue waters of the Gulf of Aqaba, located at the tip of the Red Sea. To the right of the road lies the kibbutz of *Elot*. Established in 1962, it maintained a temporary camp on the coast at Elat and prepared the way for the foundation of the town. Like Yotvata, Elot raises a dairy herd and poultry as well as farms banana plantations, groves of date palms, and fields of fodder crops. It also boasts a few doum palms, an unusual species that splits into two or three branches— Elot is the most northerly point at which this picturesque tropical tree is found.

After a journey of 332 km. (206 miles from Jerusalem following Travel Route 11), Route 90 runs into Elat.

*Elat

The town of Elat (population 21,000) lies at the north end of the Gulf of Elat (the Gulf of Aqaba), an offshoot of the Red Sea. It nestles into a primeval landscape that displays almost every shade of red against a background of rugged mountains. Although the temperature hovers around 35°C (95°F) in summer, and it rarely falls below 20°C (68°F) in winter, Elat's dry air keeps the heat perfectly tolerable. The annual rainfall is only 80–100 millimeters (3–4 inches), all of which seem to fall in the course of a few days in winter.

There has been a port at the tip of the Gulf of Elat for at least 3,000 years, although its location has changed several times over the centuries. Elat's most frequent site seems to have been the east coast of the gulf, a little to the south of present-day Aqaba in Jordan. The port is first mentioned in the Bible in Deuteronomy (2:8) as a staging point for the wanderings of the Children of Israel through the wilderness. King David took Elat from the Edomites, and in the neighboring town of Ezion Geber Solomon—with the help of King Hiram of Tyre—he built a fleet for trade with the distant land of Ophir (2 Chronicles 8:18). In the eighth century B.C., King Uzziah (Azariah) of Judah rebuilt the port of Elat, but after his time, it was lost to the Syrians.

During the Hellenistic period, the port was called Berenice; under the Nabateans, it was known as

Aila. A port also stood here in Roman and Byzantine times.

The Jewish population of the town increased in the seventh century A.D. when Mohammed drove the Jews out of Arabia but allowed them to live here under his protection. The name Aqaba appeared at this time. The Crusaders, under Baldwin I, captured the Elat coast in 1116, and erected a castle on Pharaoh's Island (which belongs to Egypt) in the Gulf of Aqaba; from here, Raynaud de Châtillon set out to wreak havoc on Arab shipping, and perhaps to capture Mecca and Medina as well. The town was recaptured in 1167 by Saladin, who attacked both by land and by sea, and then disassembled his ships to transport them overland.

From the 14th century on, the coast was abandoned. The town of Aqaba appeared in the news during World War I when it was captured from the Turks by T.E. Lawrence (Lawrence of Arabia) and Emir Feisal. After the war, western Palestine retained only a short strip of coast; the Israelis gained possession of this strip on March 13, 1949 in a bloodless operation, code named "Uvda" (Fact).

The first step towards the foundation of the modern town was the establishment of a temporary kibbutz camp on the shore. Shortly thereafter, Egypt closed the Strait of Tiran at the southern end of the gulf, hindering the development of the town until the Sinai campaign of 1956. Soon afterwards, construction began on the harbor,

the road from Elat to Beer Sheva via Mizpe Ramon, and the first pipeline from Elat to the north. In 1959, Elat received municipal status, although it had only 3,500 inhabitants at the time—well below the usual minimum population of 20,000 required for such recognition. The renewal of the Egyptian blockade in 1967 endangered Elat's existence and was one of the causes that prompted the Six-Day War. After Israel's victory, the town developed rapidly: The road from Elat to Sedom opened in 1967, the new harbor and the oil harbor to the southwest were improved, and a new pipeline was laid in 1968. Elat now operates three plants that desalinate seawater.

When the Timna copper mines closed in the early 1980s, endangering Elat's economy, development of the town's vacation and tourist trade became a priority in order to protect it. Elat now has about 30 hotels, two campgrounds, a youth hostel, and a

The "fjord" of Elat

resort village with nearly 170 Moorish-style villas. The 12-km.- (7.5-mile-) long beach offers magnificent facilities for swimming, sunbathing, diving, sailing, waterskiing, and surfing.

As you enter the town, you will see the industrial zone on a hill to the left. This area consists mainly of small factories, particularly jewelry works that use malachite and azurite from the Timna mines. To the right is the *municipal airport,* which offers domestic flights to Lod and Jerusalem. The road approaches the coast, with the *hotel zone* and *beach* to the left, and passes near the (closed) frontier with Jordan and an ancient Israelite fortress.

The boating marina, Elat

The road to the right runs up to the shopping and commercial district and to the residential areas beyond. In this hot climate, all the buildings are constructed in an open architectural style—and almost all have air-conditioning. Before the founding of Elat, not a blade of grass grew here, but now the town's tree-lined avenues and small areas of grass belie the painstaking labor that has gone into creating and maintaining its beauty.

The road that runs straight ahead (south-southwest) leads past the *Old Harbor* to the *New Harbor.*

Beyond the harbors stretches the *Coral Beach Nature Reserve,* a protected area that offers extraordinary snorkeling. A road to the right leads into the *Nahal Shelomo Gorge.* After passing a number of hotels and another beach, you come to Elat's principal tourist attraction since it opened in 1975 —the ***Underwater Observatory.** A bridge leads to a shaft, where you descend by a staircase to a depth of 4.5 meters (15 feet) below the water's surface and observe the rainbow-colored world of corals, exotic tropical fishes, and much else besides. On land, there is an *Aquarium* that displays tanks of phosphorescent fishes, stone fishes, and other forms of brillantly colored marine life from the Red Sea.

A short distance from the Observatory, the road from the international airport enters from the hills to the northwest; a little beyond this is the road into *Solomon's Gorge,* the starting point for excursions into Elat's granite hills.

Just 8 km. (5 miles) south of Elat's town center lies the current Egyptian frontier.

TRAVEL ROUTE 12: *Elat–Mizpe Ramon–*Avedat (–*Shivta)–Yeroham–*Beer Sheva (239 km.; 149 miles)

See map on page 238.

This route can be combined with Route 11 as the return segment of a round trip, as it takes you back to Beer Sheva from Elat. The scenery along this route is even more spectacular than that of Travel Route 11. One of the high points—literally and figuratively—is the Makhtesh Ramon, a gigantic erosion crater bigger than New York's isle of Manhattan. You can pause at the visitors' center for a short lesson in geology before you try to take in the fantastic sprawling rock formations, some of which are hundreds of millions of years old. The route continues through the ancient town of Avedat, with an optional side trip—actually a shortcut—through Shivta, the "Pompeii of Israel."

The sights in the southern Arava Valley that lie within the first 51 km. (32 miles) as you travel north along Route 90 from *Elat* (see page 241) to the *Qetura Junction* are described in Travel Route 11 (pages 239–241) in the reverse direction. At the junction, bear left on Route 40. The road climbs steeply to the northwest for the first 10 km. (6 miles), running up from the Arava Rift Valley through the gorge of a wadi to a height of around 450 meters (1475 feet) above sea level. It then follows a more level course to the *Zihor Junction* (91 km.; 57 miles from Elat), with views to the right (east) of the wide valley of the *Nahal Hiyon* and its tributaries, the Arava Valley beyond, and the rock wall of the Edom plateau on the horizon. The chalk and limestone hills give the landscape a yellowish white to pale gray coloring, relieved sporadically by flora. A growth of dull green vegetation covers the hills for a short period after the heavy winter rains.

The road becomes more winding and the scenery more varied as you near the southern edge of the *Paran Valley,* the largest wadi in the Negev. Route 40 descends between bright red rocks to the bed of the wadi in a series of hairpin curves. (The color of the rocks comes from limonite, an iron ore.)

The road then crosses the bed of the wadi. Few visitors have the chance of seeing the wadi during the winter rains, but after a heavy downpour, the muddy yellow water surges dangerously, sweeping along everything in its path—even endangering heavy vehicles. These flash floods may gush through the wadi on sunny, cloudless days as the result of rainfall higher up the wadi, many miles away.

After climbing the north side of the gorge, the road runs in an almost straight line through a wide

TEL AVIV-YAFO

0 Yards 500

Meters

To Haifa

Jabotinsky Street

Havarkon Street

Ibn Gvirol Street

Arlozorov

Ben - Gurion Boulevard

Bloch Street

King David Boulevard

Ben - Jehuda Street

Frishman- Street

Disengoff

Reines

Solomon

Street

Dizengoff Street

Ben - Bograshov

Street

King

George Street

Kaplan Street

Ibn Gvirol Street

Allenby Street

Samuel

Herbert - Quay

Hakovshin Street

Hacarmel

Street

Street

Street

Street

Allenby

Street

King

George

Street

Sheinkin St.

Petah Tikva Road

Yafo Road

Eylat Street

Levinsky Street

Levanda Street

Hamasger St.

Hakovshin

Street

Jerusalem Boulevard

Shalma

Road

Shalma

Hai

Zion

Road

YAFO

Yehuda Hayamit St.

Shevtey Israel Street

Yephet

Street

Ben Zvi Street

Ben Zvi Street

Kibbuz

Galuyot

Street

Rail S°a.

To Jerusalem

To Jerusalem

The remains of a synagogue at Capernaum, where Jesus often preached, overlook the Sea of Galilee.

Archaeologists discovered a complex irrigation system in the remains of Avedat, a third-century B.C. Nabataean city situated on a hill in the Negev Desert.

The Church of the Annunciation was constructed on the site where the Archangel Gabriel is believed to have appeared to the Virgin Mary to foretell the birth of Jesus.

Hebron's ancient, narrow lanes and bazaars house the shops and workplaces of Arab traders and craftsmen.

Beer Sheva's Bedouin market has sold camels, goats, and sheep for centuries; it now offers hand-woven goods and embroidery, as well as manufactured housewares.

Irrigation transforms the desert with palm groves, vegetable fields, and fruit orchards.

The lunar landscape of central Negev, features oddly-shaped rock formations that jut between high plateaus and deep craters.

The famous Dead Sea Scrolls were found near the ruins of an Essene settlement at Qumran.

The gorges and dry valleys of the Negev desert create a beautiful yet eerie land-scape.

Elat's Coral World Underwater Observatory offers a glimpse of the vibrant and beautiful marine life beneath the Red Sea.

Surrounded by sandy beaches and azure water, Elat has become one of the top resorts on the Red Sea coast.

valley with the Hebrew name of *Ha-Meshar* (the Plain). It then ascends its northwestern side in a series of hairpin bends to a height of around 600 meters (2,000 feet) above sea level. The scenery becomes more varied, with rock formations characteristic of the stony desert—white chalk slopes covered with angular pieces of black flint, sharply pointed peaks, and broad tabular hills, with dark-colored bands of gravel running from one hill to another, interrupted by the erosion of the land between them.

After a journey of 137 km. (85 miles) from Elat, you will come to the gigantic crater of ***Makhtesh Ramon.** It is the largest erosion crater in the Negev, 35 km. (22 miles) long and 12 km. (7.5 miles) across at its widest point. Passing between the jagged, dark-colored pinnacles on the south face, many

The road to Mizpe Ramon

of which date from the Pre-Cambrian Era (3,800 million to 7000 million years ago), you enter the undulating terrain of the crater floor. After passing a gypsum mine on the left and a clay pit on the right, the road climbs up the steep north wall of the crater in a series of hairpin curves known as the *Ma'ale ha-Azma'ut* (Independence Staircase). When you reach the top (800 meters; 2,600 feet above sea level), stop a moment to view the whole crater, whose north wall falls off almost vertically to its bottom. The black patches there indicate the presence of basalt and reddish patches bear evidence of Nubian sandstone laid down during dry periods in the early Mesozoic Era (230 million–195 million years ago). The crater widens from its high western tip to the east and northeast, where two projecting arms enclose the hill of *Har Ardon.* Umbrella thorns and small shrubs grow along the small rivulets that thread through the floor of the crater.

Immediately beyond the rim of the crater lies the little development town of **Mizpe Ramon** (153 km./95 miles from Elat; population 3,000). Founded in 1954, it is the most daring enterprise of its kind, housing laborers involved in the phosphate, gypsum, clay, and glass sand works. The town developed slowly and crept to a complete standstill when the road from Sedom to Elat opened, thus diverting traffic from the area. However, since the Israeli evacuation of Sinai, which has led to the establishment of new military camps and some industry in this area, Mizpe Ramon has been given a new lease on life.

A visitors' center in the town provides programs and displays on the fascinating geology of the area. An interesting park near the road has statues carved from the rock. Beyond the town, you can see the three domes of a large astronomical observatory off in the distance.

From Mizpe Ramon, Route 40 makes a gentle descent as it continues northwest through an expanse of barren, stony desert to Avedat.

*Avedat

Avedat was founded in the fourth or third century B.C. on the high hill that dominates this expanse of sandy soil to the east. It was presumably named to honor the Nabatean king Avedat II (Oboda), who was worshiped as a god here. The town was established at a fork in the ancient caravan route from the Mediterranean coast; one branch headed east to Petra, in the land of the Edomites, and the other led south toward Elat. Travelers to ancient Avedat treated themselves to its local specialty— a wine made in the heart of the desert—although the labor involved in making it was reflected in correspondingly high prices.

After the Romans annexed the Nabatean kingdom in A.D. 106, Avedat seems to have been aban-

doned for a time; however, the site was reoccupied in the third century by a people who had assimilated Roman civilization. During this period, massive dwellings were built on the east side of the acropolis. Avedat apparently remained a pagan town for quite some time: A third-century inscription here refers to the god Zeus-Avedat. The first Christian text dates from the year 541, when Avedat was at the height of its prosperity.

The road then branches off Route 40 to a *parking area* [1]. Near this is a Byzantine *bath house* [2], probably intended for the use of travelers, that offered cold, hot, and steam baths. On the slope of the hill stands a *Byzantine house* [3], and beyond this a Nabatean *cave dwelling* [4] that contains an inscription from a later period.

Avedat: Byzantine chapel

A steep path winds uphill, passing the scanty remains of the Byzantine town walls and more *cave dwellings* [5]. On the terrace lie the remains of a *market* [6]. On the summit of the hill where a Nabatean temple once stood are the ruins of a *monastery* [7], with the *North Church* [8] and the *Basilica of Saint Theodore* (or South Church) [9], which has a well-preserved font. Northeast of the church stands the Byzantine *fortress* [10], built of large ashlar blocks, with a tall watchtower at the east corner and a large cistern. The remains of a *wine press* [11] and some *houses* [12] of the Roman period can be seen on the south side of the site. To the northeast lie a *cistern* [13] and the vestiges of a *Roman camp*.

Excavations uncovered the ruins of an extensive water supply system that included channels for collecting rainwater, which was then conveyed to the terraces in the valley bottom. Scientists from the Hebrew University have reconstructed part of the system and are studying possible methods of using stored rainwater to grow olives, vegetables, and corn without another main water source.

*

About 3 km. (2 miles) northwest of Avedat, a short side road cuts off from Route 40 and leads to an overlook that offers a view of a narrow gorge below, where the springs of *En Avedat* and *En Mor* have formed a little island of green, enclosed by vertical rock walls.

Continuing on Route 40, the road skirts the western end of the gorge of *Zin* and comes to the **Midreshet Sede Boqer,** on the north rim of the gorge. This institute opened in 1965 on the initiative of David Ben Gurion, the first president of Israel, who took part

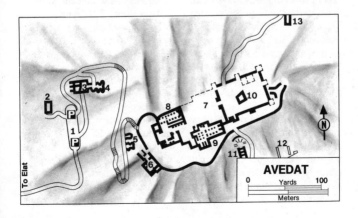

AVEDAT

in its planning. The center includes a boarding school for young people from the Negev, a teachers' college, and a prestigious research institute that specializes in the enhancement of living conditions in the desert while preserving the integrity of its ecology.

From the entrance to the center you can walk to the tombs of Ben Gurion and his wife Pola; there is a fabulous view over the Zin Gorge, which divides the Negev into north and south. The white, yellow, and reddish hills that flank the broad wadi in its zigzag course are characteristic of a wild desert landscape.

From the Sede Boqer institute, a road descends into the Zin Gorge—the wilderness of Zin through which the Israelites passed in their wanderings.

The main road continues to the kibbutz of **Sede Boqer** (190 km.; 118 miles from Elat). When this lonely outpost was established in 1952, it faced the improbable task of inventing new ways to use the waterless land of the plateau. The earliest settlers attempted to rear beef cattle: hence the name of the settlement, which means "Field of the Cattle Herds." The kibbutz members now grow peaches, olives, wheat, cotton, and poultry.

To set a personal example of pioneering spirit in the distant Negev, David Ben Gurion made his home in Sede Boquer. (He was particularly keen to develop this region of Israel.) Since his death in 1973, the modest, green wooden cabin where he and his wife lived has been open to visitors.

Continuing from Sede Boqer, you will see an irrigation dam on the right. At this point, Route 40 branches off to the left and runs about 12 km. (7 miles) northwest to *Mash' abbe Sade* in the southern Beer Sheva plain. En route, it passes a road that gives access to the ancient site of Shivta, one of the most extraordinary surviving vestiges of an ancient culture in existence.

Side trip to *Shivta

Route 40 provides a shortcut to Beer Sheva as well as interesting side trips. The alternate route to Beer Sheva on Route 204 via Yeroham is described on page 250.

To see Shivta, bear left on Route 40 where the road branches just beyond Sede Boqer. Route 40 runs northeast toward Mash'abbe Sade; about 6 km. (4 miles) before it reaches that settlement, you turn left on Route 211, which shoots off to the west and leads to Nizzan on the borders of Sinai. A short distance past the moshav shitufi of *Ashalim,* turn left on the side road that leads to Shivta.

*Shivta (in Arabic, *Subeita*) has been called the Israeli Pompeii, for the streets, churches, and buildings of this 1,500-year-old city have been preserved almost perfectly. The town flourished from the fourth to the 12th or 14th centuries, but then faded out of memory, only to be rediscovered in 1839 by the American archaeologist, Edwin Robinson (who also identified Masada). The dry climate has kept the buildings in excellent form, and the remoteness of the site made the demolition of buildings and the removal of building materials extremely difficult until very recently. The archaeologists, therefore, were left with little to do in the way of restoration, and occupied themselves mainly by labeling and marking the site.

It is astonishing that a sizable town like this (with a population estimated between 6,000–10,000) could exist in such a desolate area, where the annual rainfall is only 50–100 millimeters (2–4 inches). The methods of irrigation and cultivation adopted by the inhabitants were similar to those of Avedat (see page 247).

Shivta was founded by Nabateans in the second or first century B.C. After the annexation of the Nabatean kingdom by Rome in A.D. 106, Shivta, like Avedat, began to decline. Between the fourth and seventh centuries, however, it enjoyed a fresh period of prosperity, during which its three churches—the *North Church* [1], the *Central Church* [2], and the *South Church* [3]—were built. Among the other structures that date from the same period are the craftsmen's shops around the market square, the *wine presses* [4], a large *oven* [5], the *town hall* [6], and most of the other buildings. Cisterns were constructed, faced with small stone blocks and water-

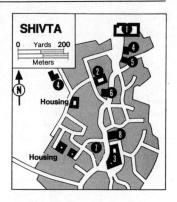

resistant mortar. Every resident was required to have cisterns of this kind adjoining his house, with pipes leading into them, so that not a drop of rain would be wasted; in addition, every citizen had to take a turn in maintaining the large public *cistern* [7].

Toward the end of the Byzantine period, Bedouin raids became more frequent, and Shivta was fortified with dry-stone walls that linked the outermost houses in the town. After its capture by the Muslims, who built a *mosque* [8] in the center of town in 634, Shivta seems to have existed for several more centuries, until the 12th and perhaps even the 14th century.

From Shivta, backtrack to Route 40 and continue to the *Mash'abbim Junction,* where there is a well, known as *Bir Asluj* during the British mandate. A British police post stood here during that time.

From Mash'abbim, a side road (Route 222) cuts northwest for 5 km. (3 miles) to the kibbutz of

Revivim (Dewdrop), the most southerly of three experimental settlements established in the Negev in 1943. Here 15 young people coped with unfamiliar soil and climatic conditions, channeling water from the flash floods in the nearby wadi into their fields, and trying to establish friendly relations with the Bedouin of the surrounding area. During the War of Independence, this completely isolated settlement held out against attacks by superior local forces and then against the Egyptian army. The original desert farmstead and the wartime dugouts have been reconstructed as a museum. Revivim is now a flourishing community of farmers, fruit-growers, and cattlemen.

The road continues northwest from Revivim for 40 km. (25 miles) through the *Haluza dunes* and past the scanty remains of the Nabatean town of Haluza to the *Urim Junction* in the northwestern Negev.

Backtracking again to Route 40 at Mash'abbim Junction, you continue northeast, passing the kibbutz of *Mash'abbe Sade* (founded in 1949), which has a plant for desalinating brackish spring water by the process known as "reverse osmosis." Continue to the *Negev Junction* (Zomet ha-Negev), where the road from Yeroham joins Route 40 from the southeast.

*

If you do not take the shortcut on Route 40 or the side trip to Shivta, bear right at the junction north of Sede Boqer and follow the road (Route 204) straight to **Yeroham** (208 km./129 miles from Elat; population 7,000). The town was founded in 1951 with the goal of developing agriculture in this area, but when this plan faltered, Yeroham became a *ma'bara* (transit camp for new immigrants) and then a "development town," whose residents found jobs (though not enough of them) building roads and in the glass, sand, and ceramic clay workings in the nearby craters, *Makhtesh Gadol* and the *Makhtesh Ramon*. The recent opening of a factory for bottling mineral drinks has not improved the situation much. Yeroham's water comes from a dammed-up wadi to the west of the town, near the site of a similar dam built by the Romans.

If you wish, you can take Route 225 southeast from Yeroham, which runs through the Makhtesh Gadol to *Oron* (see page 236).

From Yeroham you can continue northeast on Route 204 for 14 km. (9 miles) to Dimona (see page 235), and from there continue to Beer Sheva on Route 25, as in Travel Route 11. Travel Route 12, however, continues northwest on Route 224 to the *Negev Junction* (Zomet ha-Negev), joining Route 40 (see above). From the junction, it is 19 km. (12 miles) through the northeastern fringes of the Haluza dunes—now mostly planted with eucalyptus trees and blue acacias—to **Beer Sheva** (239 km.; 149 miles from Elat): see the description beginning on page 232.

TRAVEL ROUTE 13: *Beer Sheva–Qiryat Gat–Rehovot–*Tel Aviv (112 km.; 70 miles)

See map on page 254.

If you've made the round trip circuit on travel routes 11 and 12, you'll find that this route sharply contrasts with the desert you have left behind. On the way from Beer Sheva to Tel Aviv, you will traverse some of the richest and most productive land in Israel—the result of years of intensive work and planning by the many dedicated members of kibbutzim and moshavim who established their settlements here. Along the way you'll see the Chaim Weizmann Institute, one of the world's leading scientific centers and the site of the Rehovot Conferences, where important global issues are regularly debated. Weizmann and his wife are buried here at the Yag Chaim Weizmann.

Leave *Beer Sheva* (see page 232) on Route 25, the old road to Tel Aviv, and head northwest past the Desert Inn. (The more direct route on the new road—Route 40—runs almost due north, but it is less scenic.) The first part of the road runs through a fairly desolate region of undulating loess soil, traversed here and there by zig-zagging wadis, the most important of which is *Nahal Pattish.* After 14 km. (9 miles) of driving, you come into a densely settled and intensively cultivated area known as the *Merhavim* district. The road forks and Route 25 branches to the left to Gaza (see page 257), passing the *Eshel ha-Nasi* (Tamarisks of the President) college of agriculture (named after President Chaim Weizmann) where students train for farming in the Negev. Follow the road that branches right, Route 264, to Qiryat Gat.

Eucalyptus trees line the road for most of the way. To the right lies the kibbutz of *Mishmar ha-Negev,* one of the 11 settlements established during the night of October 6, 1946. Their establishment transformed the pattern of settlement in southern Israel and the northern Negev. Wheat and cotton are grown here, and there are also fruit orchards and a factory. A small archaeological museum on the kibbutz displays finds from an ancient site in the region, perhaps the Biblical Gerar.

Farther along the road to the right, you will see the houses, huts, and goatskin tents of a large Bedouin tribe—an encampment that has evolved into a permanent settlement called *Rahat.* A nearby dam stores up water from the winter rains.

To the left of the road lies the kibbutz of *Shoval* (25 km.; 15 miles from Beer Sheva), founded in 1946 on the "night of the eleven settlements." The name of the kibbutz probably dates from Biblical times: It appears in the form "Sobila" on the Madaba mosaic map. From Shoval, it is 4 km. (2

A Bedouin in the Negev

miles) to *Bet Qama,* where the northern Negev ends and the southern coastal plain begins. Established in 1949, the kibbutz runs a factory that produces office equipment, in addition to its varied agricultural activities. A road runs west from Bet Qama to a group of eight moshavim founded in 1953, and another road runs east to the kibbutzim of *Devira* and *Lahav.*

Route 264 terminates in Bet Qama, where you join the new road (Route 40) from Beer Sheva to Qiryat Gat and continue north through undulating country, flanked by fertile fields. Shortly before you reach Qiryat Gat, you will pass through the most southerly settlements in the *Lakhish*

district—*Ahuzazam, Shalva, No'am, Uzza,* and others. Since its development in 1954, this district has become the model for other settlements grouped around a "village center."

Qiryat Gat (48 km./30 miles from Beer Sheva; population 23,500), founded in 1954 as the urban center of the Lakhish district, lies near an ancient site thought to be the Philistine city of *Gath.* Qiryat Gat was planned as a regional center and lies at an important junction on the Lod-Beer Sheva railroad. Its first industrial establishments were cotton ginning mills and factories for spinning and weaving; a clothing factory, a sugar mill, and other industries followed later.

The east-west road intersects Route 40 at the *Pelugat Junction* northwest of Qiryat Gat: Route 35 (to the right) runs southeast to Bet Guvrin and Hebron, where you can pick up Route 60 to Jerusalem; Route 35, to the left, runs northwest to Ashqelon. A number of large eucalyptus groves grow near the junction. In the 1948 war, this area was the scene of decisive battles with the Egyptian army, in which Gamal Abdel Nasser—who eventually became President of Egypt—was an officer. At the request of the United Nations, the Israeli forces allowed the encircled Egyptians to withdraw.

Farther along Route 40 you will pass more groups of villages belonging to the Lakhish district: to the left are a number of moshavim, including *Zavdi'el* and *Nir Banim;*

to the right, the kibbutzim of *Gat, Galon,* and *Bet Nir,* followed by *Sequlla, Menuha,* and others. To the left of the road, you will see a large plantation of tall pecan trees that belong to the moshav of *Avigedor.* Just beyond the development town of *Qiryat Mal'akhi* (population 10,500) lies the busy *Zomet Ahim Junction* (64 km.; 40 miles from Beer Sheva), where Route 40 merges briefly with Route 3 heading northeast; running southwest from the junction, Route 3 will take you to Ashqelon (see page 259).

You are now in one of the most intensively cultivated regions in Israel. The number of citrus plantations increases, but fields of flowers, vegetables, cotton, fodder plants, and wheat also thrive. You will pass a succession of villages (mostly moshavim). About 5 km. (3 miles) from the merge with Route 3 lies the *Re'em Junction,* from which you can travel northeast on Route 3 toward Jerusalem. Continue on Route 40 for 8 km. (5 miles), at which point you will come to *Gedera* (77 km./48 miles from Beer Sheva; population 6,000), founded in 1884 by young Russian Zionist members of the Bilu movement. Having spent most of their limited resources purchasing the land, they lacked proper equipment for plowing the barren soil. Vineyards originally established by Baron Edmond de Rothschild have now given way to plantations of citrus fruits and other intensive crops. Gedera has a number of rest homes, including some that cater to people with lung diseases.

Near Gedera are *Kannot,* a children's village run by the Youth Aliyah immigration movement, and *Uri'el,* a home for the blind. About 9 km. (5.5 miles) north of Gedera, to the left of the road, lies the kibbutz of *Giv'at Brenner* (population 1,500), Israel's largest collective village. It was founded in 1928 by young immigrants from Lithuania and Italy, who were later joined by German settlers. The kibbutz now has a number of plants that manufacture a variety of goods from sprinkling equipment and textiles to furniture and baby foods. The village's Enzo Sereni Cultural Center bears the name of one of the leaders of the kibbutz movement; during World War II, this aged hero was dropped behind the enemy lines to rescue Jews in Nazi-occupied Europe. He was taken prisoner in Italy and later killed in the Dachau concentration camp. The kibbutz itself is named for Y.H. Brenner, the Hebrew writer and socialist thinker.

From the *Bilu Junction,* take the road that goes off on the left to the town of **Rehovot** (90 km./56 miles from Beer Sheva; population 61,000), which lies within the Tel Aviv sprawl. The town was originally a traditional moshav founded in 1890 by a group of Polish Jews. Although they planted vines and grew wheat, citrus fruits eventually became the basis of the town's economy. The original settlers were joined by immigrants

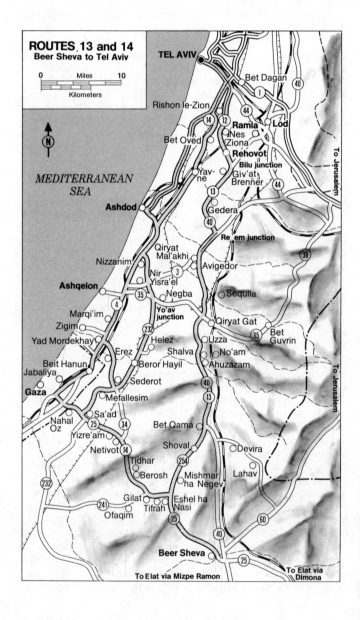

ROUTES 13 and 14
Beer Sheva to Tel Aviv

0   Miles   10
Kilometers

N

TEL AVIV

Bet Dagan

40

Rishon le-Zion

14 12

44

Ramla   Lod

Bet Oved

Nes
Ziona

Rehovot

Bilu junction

MEDITERRANEAN
SEA

Yav-
ne

Giv'at
Brenner

44

13

Ashdod

Gedera

40

Re'em junction

38

Qiryat
Mal'akhi

Nizzanim

Nir

3

Avigedor

Ashqelon

Yisra'el

Negba

Sequla

Yo'av
junction

Qiryat Gat

Marqi'im

4

35

35

Bet
Guvrin

Zigim

232

Helez

Uzza

Yad Mordekhay

Erez

Shalva

No'am

Beit Hanun

Beror Hayil

Ahuzazam

Jabaliya

Sederot

40

Gaza

Mefallesim

13

Nahal
Oz

Sa'ad

25

34

Bet Qama

Yizre'am

Netivot

14

Shoval

Devira

Tidhar

254

Berosh

Mishmar
ha Negev

Lahav

232

241

Gilat

Eshel ha
Nasi

Ofaqim

Tifrah

25

60

40

Beer Sheva

25

To Elat via Mizpe Ramon

To Elat via
Dimona

To Jerusalem

To Jerusalem

from Yemen, and the first factories were built in the 1930s. With the opening of the Sieff Research Institute in 1934, headed by Professor Chaim Weizmann, Rehovot became one of Israel's leading scientific centers; it was renamed the *Weizmann Institute* in 1949. It consists of 19 research departments grouped in five disciplines —biology, biophysics and biochemistry, chemistry, mathematics, and physics. It is particularly active in the fields of biodynamics, plant genetics, isotope research, cancer research, and nuclear research.

The whole area that encompasses the institute, including Weizmann's villa, his grave, and the grave of his wife Vera, forms the Yag Chaim Weizmann (Chaim Weizmann Memorial). The Weizmann Foundation fosters international scientific collaboration to aid humanitarian causes, and the international Rehovot Conferences held here focus on global concerns such as the role of science in the developing countries, world health, and the problems of urbanization.

Opposite the Weizmann Institute is the *Faculty of Agriculture* of the Hebrew University, which also acts as a research station of the Ministry of Agriculture.

About 4 km. (2 miles) beyond Rehovot lies *Nes Ziona* (population 13,500), founded in 1883 on the initiative of a single immigrant from Russia. Until 1948, it was the only farming village that had both Jewish and Arab inhabitants; however, the Arabs left during the War of Independence, acting on the instructions of their leaders. Plantations of citrus fruits continue to play an important role in the town's economy, although industry and Tel Aviv's urban sprawl are beginning to encroach. Nes Ziona also boasts a biological research center.

Nes Ziona merges imperceptibly into **Rishon le-Zion** (98 km./61 miles from Beer Sheva; population 84,000). The town, whose name means "First in Zion," was indeed the first Jewish settlement in Palestine. Established as a moshav in 1882 by ten pioneers from Russia, the enterprise nearly collapsed before Baron Edmond de Rothschild came to its aid. He introduced viticulture in place of wheat, and built a large winery in 1889, which still operates. The economic situation of the village continued to improve in the early 20th century with the introduction of citrus plantations. During World War I, the Turkish governor assigned Rishon le-Zion 2,000 hectares (5,000 acres) of sand dunes, extending it westward to the coast. Industry began to develop here in the 1930s.

Among the interesting sights that remain in "old" Rishon le-Zion are the winery, the palm garden in the town center, and the parts of the original town—such as Nahlat Yehuda—occupied by Yemeni Jews.

It is 4 km. (2 miles) from the center of Rishon le-Zion to the *Bet*

Dagan Junction (see page 210); from there, continue for 7 km. (4 miles) on the road described in Travel Route 9 (see page 210) to

*Tel Aviv (112 km.; 70 miles from Beer Sheva): see the description beginning on page 106).

TRAVEL ROUTE 14: *Beer Sheva–*Gaza–*Ashqelon–*Ashdod–*Tel Aviv (122 km.; 76 miles)

See map on page 254.

This route takes you from Beer Sheva to Tel Aviv by way of Gaza and Ashqelon, two of the most ancient towns on the western coast of Israel. The road passes through the hotly contested Gaza Strip—an area often in the news, for possession of this sliver of land is as critical now as it was in the time of Samson. (An alternate route that bypasses the Gaza Strip is also described.)

Leave *Beer Sheva* (see page 232) on Route 25, the old road to Qiryat Gat, and follow it as described in Travel Route 13 (see page 251) to the college of agriculture at *Eshel ha-Nasi*. From here, bear left on Route 25, which runs northwest. You will pass an agricultural research institute and fruit-tree nursery, a forest-tree nursery (on the right), and the moshavim of *Tifrah* and *Gilat* (on the left), which are part of the Merhavim regional settlement scheme. Although this land now blossoms under intensive cultivation, it was a barren desert just a few decades ago. The "Hunger Road" (Route 241)—built by the British authorities to provide employment for starving Bedouin during a period of drought—cuts off to the left and stretches into the western Negev. About 4 km. (2 miles) along this road lies the development town of *Ofaqim* (population 11,200).

Continuing toward Gaza on Route 25, you will come to a group of moshavim—*Tidhar, Berosh,* and *Te'ashur*—named for the three trees (cypress, box, and pine) that the prophet Isaiah predicted would flourish in the wilderness (Isaiah 41:19). To the left of the road beyond the moshavim lies the development town of *Netivot* (15 km./9 miles from Beer Sheva; population 7,500). Nearby stands a pumping station of the National Water Carrier, from which conduits reach out to different parts of the Negev.

After you pass the seed-producing farm of *Yizre'am* and a number of moshavim on the left, you will come to the religious kibbutz of *Sa'ad* (23 km.; 14 miles from Beer Sheva), established in 1947 by young people from Germany and Austria. During the War of Independence, Egyptian artillery fire demolished the fledgling settlement, but the pioneers held out in dugouts. They rebuilt the kibbutz on a site located slightly farther to the east after the war. The National Water Carrier supplies water for the kibbutz's agricultural activities, which include farming, fruit growing, and raising dairy cattle. The kibbutz also operates a metal goods factory and has a fine modern synagogue.

Bypassing the Gaza Strip

If you want to avoid the Gaza Strip, turn right onto Route 232 at Sa'ad, which turns sharply to the right again in 5 km. (3 miles) at the kibbutz of *Mefallesim,* founded in 1949 by immigrants from South America. Before you reach the development town of *Sederot* (population 8,300), you can either turn left onto Route 34, which joins the coast road to Ashqelon via *Yad Mordekhay* (see page 258), or you can continue straight ahead on Route 232 via *Beror Hayil* to the *Yo'av Junction,* near the kibbutz of *Negba,* thus bypassing Ashqelon as well as the Gaza Strip.

*

If you wish to continue to the Gaza Strip, Route 25 from *Sa'ad* to Gaza runs past a beautiful forest park of eucalyptus trees on the right. You will often see parallel rows of eucalyptus or tamarisk trees growing in the fields of the northwestern Negev. They act as windbreaks to prevent the fine loess soil from blowing away. In 2 km. (1.5 miles)

you will come to *Nahal Oz,* a kibbutz established in 1951 as an outpost facing Gaza. Until 1967, it served as a base from which to prevent infiltration by members of the Palestine Liberation Organization into Israel. After another kilometer (about a half-mile), you will enter the Gaza Strip and the eastern suburbs of ***Gaza** (in Hebrew, *Azza;* 33 km./21 miles from Beer Sheva). This ancient city serves as the chief town (population 130,000) of the Gaza Strip, which has been occupied by Israel since 1967.

Gaza has been the most important city in the southern coastal plain from time immemorial. Ancient Egypt continually tried to gain control of this outpost in Asia. When the Israelites won possession of the Promised Land toward the end of the 13th century B.C., Joshua assigned Gaza to the tribe of Judah. It remained in the hands of the Canaanites, however, until the Philistines made it one of their five city-states. According to the Bible, it was here that Samson performed his heroic deeds, was blinded, and pulled down the pillars of the temple.

Beseiged by Alexander the Great, the city's residents refused to surrender; when Gaza finally fell, the Macedonians sold its recalcitrant inhabitants into slavery. The important harbor, which was used by the Nabatean caravan traders, became a bone of contention between the Ptolemies and the Seleucids after Alexander's death. In Roman and Byzantine times,

Gaza continued as a flourishing and vital city.

The Arabs defeated the Byzantines here in 635; under its new Arab rulers—and later under the Crusaders—Gaza retained its importance. After a brief period of decline, it enjoyed a rebirth in the 15th century as a trading town. In World War I, General Allenby's British forces overran Gaza despite fierce resistance by the Turks and Germans. After the last Jews left Gaza during the disturbances of 1929, it became a purely Arab town.

During the War of Independence in 1948, the Egyptian army occupied Gaza, and the armistice agreement left the town and the 60-km.- (37-mile-) long Gaza Strip under Egyptian administration. Large numbers of Arab refugees flocked into the territory, which was occupied by Israel in the Six-Day War of 1967.

Gaza's main tourist attraction is the *Great Mosque,* originally a 12th-century Crusader church that was converted into a mosque in the time of the Mamelukes. Visitors are shown the tombs of Mohammed's great-grandfather and uncle, who are said to have been caravaneers who died in Gaza. According to Arab tradition, Samson's tomb also lies in Gaza— although according to the Bible, he was buried in his hometown of Zorah.

The hill of *Ali Muntar,* southwest of the town, offers very fine views of the area.

From Gaza, continue 8 km. (5 miles) to the north end of the Gaza Strip, by way of the suburb of *Jablya* and the village of *Beit Hanun.* The densely populated land is also intensively cultivated—including the sand dunes that reach right up to the road on the left. A new industrial complex run jointly by Israelis and Arabs stands on the strip's frontier. A straight road runs from here to the beach, 5 km. (3 miles) away.

Continue north across the wadi of the *Nahal Shiqma.* To the right lies *Erez,* a kibbutz established in 1949 as an outpost facing the Gaza Strip. To the left of the road is the kibbutz of *Yad Mordekhay,* founded in 1943 by young Jews from Poland. During the 1948 war, the kibbutzniks held out for six days against Egyptian attacks, until the settlement was completely destroyed. The survivors —along with the wounded—managed to fight their way through to the Israeli lines. In October 1948, Israeli forces recovered the site. The kibbutz is named after Mordecai Anilewicz, who fought in the Warsaw ghetto uprising against the Germans in World War II. A bronze statue to commemorate the heroes of the ghetto stands beside the ruins of the water tower (destroyed in 1948), and there is also a museum documenting the Holocaust and the resistance in the Polish ghettoes. A model illustrates the fighting in 1948.

West of Yad Mordekhay lie the kibbutzim of *Karmiya*—founded in 1950 by young immigrants from France—and *Ziqim.* The nearby *Shiqma Dam* channels the winter rains first to a settling basin, where they deposit the silt they brought with them, and then to the coarse sand of the dunes, where the influx of water raises the water table in the area.

About 4 km. (2.5 miles) off the road to the right is *Gevar' am,* a kibbutz founded in 1942, where rich reserves of groundwater were found deep below the surface of the land. Some of this water is now channeled to the Negev. Near the kibbutz stand the oil wells of Helez and Beror Hayil.

Route 34, the direct road from Netivot via Sederot bypassing the Gaza Strip (see page 257), now runs into Route 4 on the left.

Route 4 continues through country that becomes steadily greener with plantations of citrus fruits. After you pass the kibbutz of *Mavqi' im,* you will come to the turnoff for ***Ashqelon** (61 km./38 miles from Beer Sheva; population 51,000). From the earliest times, this ancient city's harbor has been coveted by neighboring states. In the 12th century B.C., Ashqelon was one of the five city-states of the Philistines, who established a temple here to their god of agriculture, Dagon. It was in Ashqelon that Samson slew 30 men and took their garments so that he could pay the forfeit for a wager he had lost. The city held out against the Israelites and the Assyrians, but fell to the Babylonians in the time of Nebuchadnezzar; its king was then carried off into captivity.

Herod was born here, and embellished the city with fine buildings, although it did not lie within his kingdom. In the time of the Ummayad caliphs, Ashqelon enjoyed a period of greater prosperity. It withstood the Crusaders longer than other towns, and was not taken until Baldwin II made a successful attempt in 1153. Saladin destroyed the city 34 years later, and it never recovered. On a site to the east of ancient Ashqelon, the Egyptian governor founded the little town of Majdal around 1839, in which he settled weavers from Egypt. Most of the remains of the old city of Ashqelon were carried away for use in the building of the new town.

The Israelis captured Majdal in 1948, which was then occupied by Jewish immigrants. In 1952, it became the new town of Ashqelon.

The civic center in the *Afridar* district includes the town hall, the municipal museum, and a clock tower. The seafront caters to the town's tourist trade, with its beach and hotels.

To the south of this area lies the site of ancient Ashqelon—now a *National Park*—with columns and remains of walls that bear witness to its one-time splendor.

To the north, in the *Barne' a* district, is a Roman tomb with interesting frescoes: one portrays two nymphs cavorting by a stream; another (on the ceiling) depicts themes connected with vine-growing and wine.

Route 4 north from Ashqelon skirts along the edge of the indus-

Archaeological Park, Ashqelon

trial zone. A road (Route 35) that branches to the right runs east via Bet Guvrin to Hebron; 2 km. (1.5 miles) farther on, another road (Route 3) runs northeast via Qiryat Mal'akhi toward Jerusalem. As you continue toward Ashdod on Route 4, you will pass large expanses of sand dunes on the left; to the right are many moshavim, among them *Nir Yisra'el, Bet Ezra,* and *Sede Uzziyahu.*

You will pass the kibbutz of *Nizzanim* (founded in 1943), which fell to the Egyptians in 1948 after a desperate resistance and was rebuilt after the territory was recovered by Israel. You now come to the southern access road into ***Ashdod** (85 km./53 miles from Beer Sheva; population 58,700). According to the Book of Joshua (11:22), this ancient coastal city was inhabited by giants ("Anakim"). Later it was one of the five Philistine city-states. When the Philistines captured the

Ark of the Covenant from the Israelites, they kept it here in the temple of Dagon before sending it back to Israelite territory. In Hellenistic times, there were two Ashdods; one lay inland, east of the belt of the dunes, and the other, called "Ashdod on Sea," was then the country's largest port. The town was destroyed by the Hasmoneans, and later passed into the hands of Herod. After its destruction by the Mamelukes in the 13th century, Ashdod degenerated into a village of mud huts, and its inhabitants abandoned it completely during the 1948 war.

Construction of a new harbor at the mouth of the River Lakhish began in 1956, and a new town was built beside it. Laid out on an area of dunes 10 km. (6 miles) long by 4 km. (2.5 miles) across, the town was given a regular plan consisting of 16 neighborhood units surrounding a central main shopping and commercial district. A zone of light industry spreads along the River Lakhish, while to the north lies an area of heavy industry, including a power station that serves the southern part of the country and Israel's second largest oil refinery (the largest is located in Haifa). Ashdod has become a growing, vital city once again.

From Ashdod, you can continue toward Tel Aviv on the expressway, which mostly runs through empty dune country for 17 km. (11 miles) to the west side of Rishon le-Zion (see page 255). Or you can take the old road, which runs slightly to the east of the expressway and takes you through the little town of **Yavne** (102 km.; 63 miles from Beer Sheva).

Yavne has had an eventful history. In the eighth century B.C., King Uzziah of Judah captured it from the Philistines. After the Babylonian exile it became a Hellenistic town, with the Greek name of Iamnia. After the destruction of the Second Temple, Rabbi Yohanan Ben Zakkay was granted permission by Emperor Vespasian to transfer his religious college from Jerusalem to Yavne, thus ensuring the preservation of the Jewish faith. At the time, Jews all over the world considered Yavne the center for learning, and the Sanhedrin—the highest Jewish judicial and legislative body— sat here.

In the 12th century, the Crusaders built a large church here, which was later converted into a mosque and now lies in ruins.

During the 1948 war, the Egyptian advance on Tel Aviv was halted at Yavne. The town now lies within Tel Aviv's urban sprawl.

From Yavne, continue for 18 km. (11 miles) to the junction with the road from Jerusalem to Tel Aviv. You will pass the outer districts of *Rehovot* (Kefar Geviral, Tirat Shalom), the youth village of *Ayanot,* and the moshavim of *Bet Oved, Bet Hanan,* and *Neta' im,* west of *Nes Ziona,* and finally run through the western districts of *Rishon le-Zion* (see page 255). The route then continues to the *Shiv' a Junction,* from which you drive 6 km. (4 miles) to ***Tel Aviv** (122 km.; 76 miles from Beer Sheva), as described in Travel Route 9 (page 210). The description of Tel Aviv begins on page 106.

Practical Information

This chapter is divided into two sections. The first, **General Trip Planning**, offers information you'll need for planning and researching your trip, as well as tips on transportation to and around Israel and other items of interest. (See listing in *Contents* for the full range of subjects covered.)

The second section, **Town-by-Town**, is organized alphabetically by town and provides information that will be helpful on site, such as local tourist offices, transportation, hotels, and restaurants.

GENERAL TRIP PLANNING

Choosing When to Go. Depending upon where you wish to visit and what activities you intend to pursue, Israel offers you many choices in any season. Among the events in spring are the *En Gev Music Festival* held during Passover and the *Spring in Tel Aviv Festival,* which features international art, music, and dance. Winter, too, is alive with cultural activities; the *Israel Philharmonic* begins its annual season, and theaters all over the country offer traditional and avant-garde plays.

The best times to visit Israel are during the spring and autumn, when the weather is pleasant and sunny. However, the winters are rarely harsh, and snow only falls in the more hilly regions. Summers are very hot and dry in the areas around the deserts. If you prefer a seaside vacation, Israel has near-idyllic weather conditions on the Mediterranean and Red Sea coasts in both summer and winter.

During the summer months, the most pleasant areas to seek out include Jerusalem, Galilee, the Carmel Mountains, and the Mediterranean coast. Winters tend to be more comfortable in Elat, the Dead Sea area, and along the Red Sea coast.

Be sure to pack light, comfortable clothing, and include an item or two—such as a sweater or blazer—for chilly evenings. Although dress is usually informal in most places in Israel, you may want to bring something more fancy for evening wear. Also pack comfortable, low-heeled shoes or sneakers for extensive city walks and clambering around archaeological sites. Remember: Wearing shorts, sleeveless tops that leave shoulders bare, and similar forms of casual attire is considered disrespectful when visiting synagogues, mosques, or other religious sites.

Average Temperatures and Climate. Israel has two main seasons, summer and winter, with a brief spring and autumn. Summer weather lasts from April through October, with very hot temperatures, reasonable humidity, and very little rain.

Below is a listing of average daily temperatures by month in centigrade and Fahrenheit in Israel:

Average Daily Temperatures

	Jan.		Feb.		Mar.		Apr.		May		June	
	C°	F°	C°	F°	C°	F°	C°	F°	C°	F°	C°	F°
Elat	15	60	17	62	20	68	24	75	28	82	31	87
Haifa	13	55	13	56	25	59	19	66	20	67	23	73
Jerusalem	9	48	10	51	12	54	16	61	20	68	22	72
Sedom	16	61	16	64	21	69	27	81	28	83	33	92
Tel Aviv	14	57	14	57	15	60	18	63	21	70	24	75
Tiberias	14	56	14	58	17	62	20	68	24	76	28	82
Zefat	7	43	8	46	9	49	14	57	20	68	22	72

	July		Aug.		Sept.		Oct.		Nov.		Dec.	
	C°	F°	C°	F°	C°	F°	C°	F°	C°	F°	C°	F°
Elat	32	90	33	91	30	86	27	80	22	72	17	63
Haifa	25	77	26	78	25	76	21	71	18	65	14	56
Jerusalem	24	75	24	75	23	73	21	69	16	60	11	52
Sedom	34	93	34	93	32	89	28	82	23	73	18	64
Tel Aviv	26	78	26	79	26	79	22	76	18	65	14	57
Tiberias	30	85	30	87	28	83	25	77	20	68	16	61
Zefat	24	75	24	75	22	72	19	67	15	60	9	49

Calendar and National Holidays. There are three principal religions in Israel, and each has its specific calendar year with separate celebrations. It is also important to note that the Jewish and Muslim calendars are only used for calculating religious holidays and holy days, and are not the standard reference for dates in day-to-day life.

The *Gregorian calendar* (also known as the Christian or western calendar), universally used throughout the world, is also the standard reference for time in Israel. It is based on a solar year of 365 days and is divided into 12 months with an extra day added every four years (leap year).

The *Jewish calendar* is based on a lunar year consisting of 354 days—11 days shorter than a solar year. Thus, national holidays and high holy days fall on different days of the Gregorian calendar every year. It creates an additional problem in that the Passover ritual must be celebrated in the spring. To compensate for this gap between the two calendars—which widens every year—seven leap years are calculated into the Jewish calendar for every nineteen-year period. These leap years result in the addition of an extra month to the calendar every four or five years, thus bringing the Jewish calendar in line with the solar year. This month follows Adar, and is called "Adar 2."

Hebrew Months (Gregorian Calendar Approximation)

Thisri (September/October)	*Nissan* (March/April)
Heshvan (October/November)	*Iyar* (April/May)
Kislev (November/December)	*Sivan* (May/June)
Tevet (December/January)	*Tamuz* (June/July)
Shevat (January/February)	*Av* (July/August)
Adar (February/March)	*Elul* (August/September)

The *Muslim calendar,* also based on the lunar year, consists of 12 months but does not include any leap years in its calculation.

Muslim Months

Moharem	*Rajab*
Safar	*Shaaban*
Rabie el-Awal	*Ramadan*
Rabie el-Thanie	*Shawal*
Gomadui el-Awal	*Zo el-Ke' da*
Gomadui el-Thanie	*Zo el-Hega*

Listed below are the major holy days and holidays observed in Israel, an explanation of each, and the approximate dates on which they fall.

Jewish Holiday	*Hebrew Date (Approx. Gregorian Month)*
Rosh Hashanah (New Year)	Thisri 1–2 (Sept./Oct.)
Yom Kippur (Day of Atonement); highest holy day period of fasting and atonement for sins committed during the past year	Thisri 10 (Sept./Oct.)
Sukkoth (Tabernacles); commemorates the exodus from Egypt	Thisri 15–21 (Sept./Oct.)
Simchat Torah; celebrates the law of the Torah	Thisri 22 (Sept./Oct.)

Jewish Holiday (cont.)	*Hebrew Date* (cont.) (*Approx. Gregorian Month*)
Hannukah (Festival of Lights); celebrates the victory of Judas Maccabeus and the rededication of the Temple when one day's supply of oil miraculously lasted eight days	Kislev 25–Tevet 3/4 (Dec.)
Tu B' Shevat (New Year of Trees); traditional tree-planting festivities	Shevat 15 (Jan./Feb.)
Purim (Festival of Esther); commemorates the Jews' emancipation from the tyranny of the Persians	Adar 14 (Feb./March)
Passach (Passover); commemorates the Jews' exodus from Egypt to Jerusalem; marks the end of slavery for Jews in Egypt	Nissan 15–21 (March/April)
Holocaust Day; commemorates those who perished in the holocaust during World War II	Nissan 27 (April)
Independence Day; declaration of the founding of the state of Israel in 1948	Iyar 5 (April/May)
Lag Ba'Omer; originally a period of respite from a series of political and natural disasters	Iyar 18 (April/May)
Jerusalem Liberation Day; commemorates the 1967 liberation of the city	Iyar 28 (May/June)
Shavuot (Feast of Weeks, Pentecost); recalls God's gift of the Ten Commandments to Moses and the Israelites	Sivan 6 (May/June)
Tisha B'av; remembers the decimation of the First and Second Temples in Jerusalem	Av 9 (July/Aug.)

Listed below are major Muslim holy days and holidays, with an explanation of each. Muslim holy days correspond to the emergence of the new moon each month; thus, holy days fall on different days and months every year. Because the Muslim calendar is ll days shorter than the solar calendar and does not use leap years to bring it in line, it is difficult to offer equivalent Gregorian calendar months.

Muslim Holiday	*Muslim Month*
Ras el-Sana el-Hegira (New Year)	Moharem
Moulid el-Nabi (Mohammed's birthday)	Rabie el-Thanie
Elisa We' al Me' araj; Ascension of Mohammed	Gomadui el-Thanie/Rajab
Fast of Ramadan; month of fasting that lasts each day from dawn to sunset	Ramadan
Id el-Fitr; a three-day feast that marks the conclusion of Ramadan	Ramadan/Shawal
Id el-Adha; sacrificial festival commemorating Abraham's act of faith to God	Zo el-Hega/Moharem

Listed below are the major holy days observed by the Druze, a small sect that broke off from Islam in the 11th century. The Druze worship the prophet Jethro, the father-in-law of Moses. While most Druze currently reside in Lebanon, there are also small groups living in parts of Galilee and along the Carmel mountain range. Although subject to Israeli law, Druze have specific governing power within their community. The Druze usually adopt the names of the months used by Muslims to define their holy days.

Druze Holiday	*Muslim Month*
Nabi Sablan; pilgrimage to tomb of the prophet Nabi Sablan in Kfar Hurfesh	Moharem/Safar
Nabi Shu' eb; four-day worship of the prophet Jethro	Ramadan
Nabi Eliahu; day of rest and visiting the prophet's tomb	Rabie el-Thanie/Gomadui el-Awal

The Christian holy days and holidays follow the traditional western calendar.

Weight, Measure, and Temperature Equivalents. Throughout the text, metric weights and measures are followed by U.S. equivalents in parentheses; likewise, centigrade degrees are translated into Fahrenheit temperatures. The following table is a quick reference for U.S. and metric equivalents.

Metric Unit	U.S. Equivalent	U.S. Unit	Metric Equivalent
Length		**Length**	
1 kilometer	0.6 miles	1 mile	1.6 kilometers
1 meter	1.09 yards	1 yard	0.9 meters
1 decimeter	0.3 feet	1 foot	3.04 decimeters
1 centimeter	0.39 inches	1 inch	2.5 centimeters
Weight		**Weight**	
1 kilogram	2.2 pounds	1 pound	0.45 kilograms
1 gram	0.03 ounces	1 ounce	28.3 grams
Liquid Capacity		**Liquid Capacity**	
1 dekaliter	2.64 gallons	1 gallon	0.37 dekaliters
1 liter	1.05 quarts	1 quart	0.9 liters
1 liter	2.1 pints	1 pint	0.47 liters

(*Note: there are 5 British Imperial gallons to 6 U.S. gallons.*)

Dry Measure		Dry Measure	
1 liter	0.9 quarts	1 quart	1.1 liters
1 liter	1.8 pints	1 pint	0.55 liters

To convert centigrade (C°) to Fahrenheit (F°):
$C° \times 9 \div 5 + 32 = F°$.
To convert Fahrenheit to centigrade:
$F° - 32 \times 5 \div 9 = C°$.

Time Zones. Israel operates on East European Time (two hours ahead of Greenwich Mean Time; seven hours ahead of Eastern Standard Time). Therefore, if it is noon EST in New York and Toronto, it is 7:00 P.M. in Tel Aviv; when it is noon GMT in London, it is 2:00 P.M. in Tel Aviv. There is an 8-hour time difference between Sydney, Australia and Tel Aviv. Therefore, when it is noon in Sydney, it is 4:00 A.M. in Tel Aviv.

Israel observes Daylight Savings Time (Central European Time plus one hour) from early April to September.

Israelis use either a 12-hour or a 24-hour clock to express time; the 24-hour (military) clock is used to differentiate between the morning and evening hours. Therefore, midnight is expressed as 2400 hours; 1:00 A.M. is 0100 hours; noon is 1200 hours; 1:00 P.M. is 1300 hours, etc.

Passport and Visa Requirements. All visitors to Israel must carry a valid passport to enter the country, and may stay for up to three months. Citizens of the United States, Australia, and Canada must obtain a visa, which is issued when you arrive. British subjects may enter Israel without a visa.

If you intend to travel on to an Arab country after visiting Israel, you must follow certain procedures beforehand to avoid problems crossing borders. Most Arab nations will deny entry to anyone holding a passport with an Israeli stamp. As all visitors must fill out an entrance form called the AL 17 before arriving in Israel, you can solve this dilemma by asking to have your entrance form stamped, and not your passport. Another solution is to obtain a transit visa at the Israeli border, which permits you to visit Israel for five days before continuing on to other destinations. The visa can be lengthened for an additional ten days once you are inside Israel.

Customs Entering Israel. The following items may be imported duty-free for personal or professional use: personal property (jewelry, watches, furs, etc.), one still camera and one movie camera with 10 rolls of film each, one portable typewriter, one tape recorder, 250 cigarettes or 250 grams of tobacco, two liters of wine or one liter of alcohol, and one-quarter liter of perfume. For reasons of security, you must remove all film from inside your cameras before entering the customs area.

Customs Returning Home from Israel. Be sure to arrive a few hours before your flight departure and be prepared for a lengthy inquiry at customs when leaving Israel; this is a normal procedure in keeping with Israel's rigid security standards. In addition, there is a $10 airport tax required per person.

To simplify passage through customs, travelers who have nothing to declare are now commonly given a green card to fill out on the return trip. Travelers with goods to declare must follow the red signs as indicated in the airport.

If you travel with items from home that were manufactured abroad (e.g., cameras), carry all receipts with you so that you will not have to pay duty.

It is forbidden to export antiquities (defined as man-made objects dated before A.D. 700) without a permit obtained from the Department of Antiquities and Museums in Jerusalem. You must also pay an export fee of 10 percent of the purchase price. For more information, contact the Department of Antiquities and Museums, P.O. Box 586, Jerusalem.

U.S. citizens returning from Israel may declare $400 worth of purchases duty-free; for the next $1,000, there is a 10% duty tax. For goods exceeding $1,400, the duty rates vary. Specific arrangements can be made to combine individual exports. You may also return with 200 cigarettes, 100 non-Cuban cigars, and one liter of alcohol. Another option is to mail packages under $50 duty-free, as long as they're not mailed to your own address. You can send only one package marked UNSOLICITED GIFT—VALUE UNDER $50 to each address during a 24-hour period. The U.S. has recently established the GSP, or Generalized System of Preferences, which allows a U.S. citizen to export particular items that exceed the $400 limit duty-free. A list can be obtained at a customs office.

Many items are prohibited in the U.S. (e.g., certain species of plants, items made from tortoise shell, products made from endangered species, etc.). If you attempt to bring in such items, they will be confiscated at customs. The U.S. Customs Service publishes a pamphlet called "Know Before You Go" that details prohibited products. To receive it, write to: U.S. Customs Service, 6 World Trade Center, Customs Information, Room 201, New York, N.Y. 10048; tel. (212) 466-5550.

British subjects are permitted £32 of duty-free purchases, plus 200 cigarettes, 100 cigarillos, or 50 cigars (any equivalent of 250 grams of tobacco), one liter of alcohol over 22% proof, two liters under 22% proof, or two liters of table wine, and 50 grams of perfume.

Canadians may bring back duty-free purchases of $100, or $300 if you've been away seven days or more. This includes 200 cigarettes, 50 cigars, two pounds of tobacco, and 40 oz. of liquor. Packages marked UNSOLICITED GIFT—VALUE UNDER $40 may be mailed to Canada duty-free (one package during a 24-hour period).

Australian residents may return with $400 worth of duty-free purchases, 250 grams of tobacco, and one liter of alcohol.

Embassies and Consulates in Israel. General information and assistance can be obtained at the following offices:

American Embassy
71 Hayarkon Street
Tel Aviv 63903
tel. (03) 654-338

Australian Embassy
185 Hayarkon Street
Tel Aviv 63405
tel. (03) 243-152

British Embassy
192 Hayarkon Street
Tel Aviv 63405
tel. (03) 249-171

Canadian Embassy
220 Rehov Hayarkon Street
Tel Aviv 63405
tel. (03) 228-122-6

Israeli Embassies and Consulates. Listed below are a few offices of the Israeli embassy or consulate:

In the U.S.:	3514 International Drive Washington, D.C. 20008 tel. (202) 364-5500
In the U.K.:	2 Palace Green London W8 tel. (01) 937-8050
In Australia:	6 Turrana Street Yarralumla Canberra ACT 2600 tel. (061) 62 73-1309
In Canada:	410 Laurier Avenue Suite 601 Ottawa, Ontario K1R 713 tel. (613) 237-6450

Getting to Israel by Air. *From the U.S.:* The major air carriers that fly directly from New York to Tel Aviv include El Al Israel Airlines, Tower Air, and Trans World Airlines. Other airlines that fly to Tel Aviv with a stopover in Europe include Air France, Alitalia, British Airways, Iberia, KLM Royal Dutch Airlines, Lufthansa German Airlines, Olympic Airways, Sabena Belgian World Airlines, and Scandinavian Airlines System.

From the U.K.: The major air carriers that fly directly from London to Tel Aviv include El Al Israel Airlines and British Airways. Other airlines that fly to Tel Aviv with a stopover in Europe include Air France, KLM Royal Dutch Airlines, Olympic Airways, and SwissAir.

From Canada: The major air carrier that flies directly from Montreal to Tel Aviv is El Al Israel Airlines. Other airlines that fly to Tel Aviv with a stopover in Europe include Air France, Alitalia, British Airways, Iberia, KLM-Royal Dutch Airlines, Olympic Airways, and SwissAir.

From Australia: The major air carrier that flies from Sydney to Tel Aviv with a stopover in Europe is Olympic Airways.

There is a bewildering variety of ever-changing special fares, hotel packages, fly-drive, and other deals that depend upon the travel season, the amount of time you can spend, the number of places you wish to visit, etc. Keep an eye on the advertisements in your newspaper's travel section and make your travel arrangements through a reliable agent or tour operator to get the best fares and packages possible.

Note: Always confirm both your departing and return flights at least 72 hours before your scheduled departure. Many airlines tend to overbook flights, and it is always wise to double-check.

Getting to Israel by Boat. Ocean cruises have long been considered a luxurious, albeit costly, way to travel and explore new countries. Among the cruise lines sailing from various international ports to Israel are Chandris, Costa, Cunard, Epirotiki, Exprinter, Royal Cruise Lines, and Princess. For detailed information, contact these companies or your travel agent.

Hotels and Other Accommodations. Where you decide to lodge in Israel depends upon your taste; you can rely on the elegant surroundings of a luxury hotel to cater to your every need, or you can have the unique experience of communal living while staying on a kibbutz. You can camp, or you can enjoy a visit at a resort village.

Free information concerning accommodations can be obtained before leaving home from any Israeli Government Tourism office, or from any local tourism office in Israel. The Israeli Government Tourist Office rates hotels according to five categories: Luxury; First Class; Second Class; Third Class; and Fourth Class. Our rating system is based on the Israeli categories and you will find hotels classified in the Town-by-Town section as follows:

> 🏨🏨🏨 Luxury and First Class hotels
> 🏨🏨 Second and Third Class hotels
> 🏨 Fourth Class hotels

Luxury and First Class designators indicate the quality of service, accommodations, and amenities offered, with prices rising accordingly.

It is always advisable to book rooms in advance—especially during the high seasons, which extend from March through May, and September through October. Hotels are also crowded during Easter, Christmas, and Passover. During these peak periods, the rates are at their highest.

In most hotels, the rate for children under 6 is set at one-half the regular price, and children from ages 6 to 12 receive a 30 percent reduction.

Kibbutz Inns. The approximately 250 kibbutzim located in Israel are agricultural communes in which all property is owned collectively by the individuals living in and contributing to it. Although no one receives a salary, most expenses, including general housing, medical care, and education, are absorbed by the community. In addition to their agricultural work, some kibbutzim have added informal guesthouses that are serviced by its members. The standards of comfort are roughly equivalent to third class hotels—but with lower prices. Kibbutz inns are known for their delightful rural surroundings and their fresh farm repasts; as a guest, you can relax in the beautiful countryside and have the opportunity to see how a kibbutz operates. For more information, write to Kibbutz Inns, 90 Rehov Ben Yehuda, Tel Aviv 63437.

Holiday Villages. If you are seeking a relaxed atmosphere in which to sun and swim, you might consider a stay in a holiday village. Open only during the summer, these facilities attract younger travelers because of their informality. Located on the shore, these villages provide facilities for water sports enthusiasts. They also offer nightclub entertainment and dancing during the evenings.

Currency Regulations and Credit Cards. Since its introduction in 1985, the Israeli unit of currency is the New Israeli Shekel (NIS), which is composed of 100 agorot. The government issues bank notes for 1, 5, 10, 50, 100, and 500 IS, and coins in denominations of 1, 5, and 10 agorot, and a half-shekel.

There are no limits on the amount of currency that you can bring into or take out of the country. Regulations, however, are subject to sudden change; we recommend that you check with your bank before leaving. Your national currency may be exchanged at most banks or at the airport. To obtain the best rate of exchange before leaving home, first track currency fluctuations in the newspaper and then change your money at a bank.

Many stores and restaurants will accept foreign currency, including U.S. dollars, British pounds sterling, Canadian dollars, and Australian dollars. However, you can expect to receive your change in Israeli Shekelim.

Business Hours and Closings. The Jewish Sabbath (Shabbat) begins on Friday with the setting of the sun and ends Saturday evening at nightfall; thus, Saturday is the official day of worship and rest throughout Israel. On most high holy days, too, official observance begins at sundown and ends at nightfall the following day. During this time, all Jewish businesses and stores close, as well as most restaurants. Public transportation also ceases, with the exception of occasional taxicabs. In larger cities, such as Tel Aviv, some restaurants and public transportation continue to operate.

For Muslims, mid-day collective prayers are conducted on Fridays; therefore, all Muslim-run businesses and (most) restaurants remain closed.

Banks are usually open Sunday through Friday; on Sunday, Tuesday, and Thursday, banking hours are from 8:30 A.M.–12:30 P.M., and from 4:00–5:30 P.M.; on Monday and Wednesday, hours are from 8:30 A.M.–

12:30 P.M.; on Fridays and the eve of holy days, banks remain open from 8:30 A.M. to noon. Many hotels offer banking services with additional hours.

Government offices and businesses are open from 9:00 A.M.–5:00 P.M. Sunday through Friday; they close at noon on Fridays and the eve of high holy days. Stores are generally open from 8:00 A.M.–1:00 P.M., and from 4:00–7:00 P.M. Jewish shops are open Sunday through Friday; they close at 2:00 P.M. on Friday afternoons and on the eve of high holy days. Christian stores usually close on Sunday, and Muslim shops close on Friday. Hotel shops customarily remain open in the evenings.

Museum hours vary greatly in Israel; in larger cities, many museums now include additional hours on the weekend. Always check the hours before embarking on a long day's journey to a particular museum. Hotels will usually have listings of local museums and their respective hours. Synagogues, churches, and mosques also have variable hours—so, once again, check ahead before including them in your schedule.

Postage. Post offices are open Sunday, Monday, Tuesday, and Thursday from 8:00 A.M.–12:30 P.M. and from 3:30–6:30 P.M.; Wednesday from 8:00 A.M.–2:00 P.M.; and Friday and the eve of holy days from 8:00 A.M. to noon. Like other government offices, they are closed on high holy days and the Sabbath.

Air mail not exceeding 10 grams going to the United States and Canada costs 70 agorot, 60 agorot to Great Britain, and 90 agorot to Australia. Aerograms and postcards to the United States, Great Britain, Australia, and Canada cost 40 agorot. The mail circulation tends to be slow from Israel, so don't be surprised if you arrive home before your postcards and letters do.

Telephones. There are two different types of public telephones. Those located in drug stores, large shops, and restaurants only accept coins and are used for local calls. Other public phones accept both coins and *assimon* (tokens that you can purchase at the post office), which are used for long distance and international calls. Also, you can make long distance calls from any telegraph office. Telephone books are printed in Hebrew and English.

Help and Emergency Numbers

14	General Directory Information	101	Ambulance
15	Time	102	Fire Department
18	International Operator	171	International telegrams
100	Police assistance		

Traveling in Israel. Whether you travel by bus or train, drive a car, or walk, Israel is relatively easy to explore. With the country's pervasive archaeological sites that recall its extraordinary past, even the most mundane bus ride is transformed into a cultural smorgasbord of Biblical, architectural, and social history.

Taxis. There are two types of taxi service: standard and *sherut*. Sherut service is a shared cab system. You ride with other travelers but you pay an individual seat price, depending upon the distance you are traveling. The sherut travel between major cities or along the main bus routes in some towns. Regular taxis operate by fixed prices (you can ask to see their standard price list). Keep in mind that after 9:00 P.M. and on the Sabbath, rates usually increase by 25 percent.

Buses. The bus system in Israel is extensive and relatively inexpensive. Aside from their regular urban routes, city buses also stop at major tourist sites. Buses run from 5:00 A.M.–10:00 P.M.; in Tel Aviv, Jerusalem, and Haifa, some buses run until midnight. Some bus lines, such as Israelbus, distribute free vouchers that entitle you to discounts at specific restaurants and museums throughout Israel.

Egged Tours feature Round-About-Tickets, which are good for unlimited travel around Israel for periods of 7, 14, 21, or 30 days. Egged Tours also offer a series of private bus tours that travel to specific cities and sites, lasting from one day to a few days or a week. Prices include sleeping accommodations at three, four, or five-star hotels if your tour extends two days or more. Although children under five years of age are not permitted on Egged Tours, you can get a 20 percent discount for children of twelve and under traveling on a day tour, or a 10 percent reduction for children on overnight tours. Tickets may be purchased in advance at El Al offices worldwide.

Bus trips can be booked in advance, or through your hotel. You can also arrange ahead of time to be picked up by the bus on the day of your trip. For further information and reservations, contact Egged Tours at their main offices, or check your local Israel Government Tourist Office.

Egged has offices at the following locations: In Tel Aviv: 15 Frishman Street, tel. (03) 24 22 71-6; 59 Ben Yehuda Street, tel. (03) 24 22 71-6; Kikar Namir (Atarim Square), tel. (03) 28 31 91. In Jerusalem: Central Bus Station, 224 Yafo Road, tel. (02) 30 48 68; 44A Yafo Road (Zion Square), tel. (02) 22 34 54; Beit Tannous, tel. (02) 24 81 44.

Trains. There are over 550 km. (340 miles) of track crisscrossing Israel. The three main railway lines extend from Tel Aviv to Nahariya via Haifa, Tel Aviv to Jerusalem, and Tel Aviv to Beer Sheva via Dimona.

Surprisingly, rail fares are as cheap as bus fares—and frequently even lower. It is always advisable to book your seat in advance. Train service is suspended on the Sabbath and on holy days. To obtain information concerning timetables, fares, and general inquiries, contact Israel Railways, P.O. Box 44, Haifa, tel. (04) 64 17 61.

Subway. Israel's lone subway system is located in Haifa, and shuttles between the Mount Carmel area and central Haifa. Hours are from 5:30 A.M. to noon Sunday through Thursday, 5:30 A.M.–4:00 or 5:00 P.M. on Fridays, and 5:00 P.M. to midnight on Saturdays.

Airport Transportation. A number of bus companies offer shuttle service from the airports to Tel Aviv, Jerusalem, and Haifa. Sherut and standard taxi service is also available from Ben Gurion Airport to various destinations. (See Town-by-Town listings for more information.)

Air Travel. Arkia (Israel Inland Airlines) offers frequent service linking Israel's main cities, such as Tel Aviv, Jerusalem, Rosh Pinna, Elat, and Haifa. Small charter flights accommodating up to ten people, such as those run by Air Sinai, Shahaf Aviation, and Nesher Airlines, also provide domestic service.

Driving in Israel. The country's highway system extends over 4,000 km. (2,500 miles), with most of its expressways concentrated in northern Israel. Roads are generally well maintained.

Documentation. All drivers must carry an international driver's license, or their own national driver's license (check with the nearest Israeli consulate or tourism office to find out if you need an international license). You can apply for an international license at your local Automobile Association of America or its equivalent in Britain, Canada, and Australia. National driver's licenses must be accompanied by a translation and confirmation in Hebrew, which can be processed at your local AAA.

You must purchase temporary insurance through an Israeli company in case of an accident; an International Insurance Certificate (called a green card) can be used if it is validated for Israel (this can also be processed via your local AAA).

Car Rentals. Car rental agencies can be found in the major cities and at the airports. Companies such as Avis, AI (Ansa International), Budget, Hertz, and Inter Rent have offices throughout Israel.

Note: Car-rental agencies close on the Sabbath from Friday afternoon through Saturday evening.

Driving Regulations. In Israel, driving is on the right-hand side of the road. The general rule at an intersection is that the car to your right has the right of way. Drivers are fairly aggressive in Israel, so be prepared—especially in crowded areas.

Seat belts are required on major roads and highways.

Speed Limits. On expressways and major highways the speed limit is 90 km. (55 mph) or 80 km. (50 mph) on larger roads. The speed limit is 50 km. (30 mph) in cities, although in larger cities it may be as high as 60 km. (35 mph) or 70 km. (45 mph).

Gas. The network of service stations is not particularly dense, and it is advisable to keep your tank full and, if possible, carry a spare can. Many service stations are closed in the evening, on the Sabbath, and on holy days.

Assistance. In case of a breakdown, you can contact the Israel Automobile and Touring Club (MEMSI), tel. (03) 62 29 61. There are no charges for assistance until after 5:00 P.M., and you do not need to be a member of MEMSI to get help.

Food and Restaurants. The influx of emigrés from disparate cultures greatly contribute to the variety of cuisines available in Israel. Thus, you can dine on traditional Jewish cooking, or sample Arab, German, Turkish, or Asian cuisine, to name a few.

Lunch is considered the main meal of the day, although breakfast is also a hearty affair. Most hotel dining rooms offer an overwhelming array of breakfast items, from baked goods to fruits. Dinner is invariably the lightest meal of the day.

Meals are generally served during the following hours: breakfast from 7:00–10:00 A.M., lunch from noon to 3:00 P.M., and dinner from 7:00–9:00 P.M.

Jewish dietary law revolves around the practice of preparing kosher food. Most restaurants in Israel are kosher, and while Arab restaurants are not kosher, they also do not offer pork dishes.

Electricity. Voltage in cities and towns is 220, and units require a three-pronged plug. Don't forget to bring an adapter for your electrical appliances.

Sports. From scuba diving to windsurfing, horseback riding to bicycling, you'll never be at a loss for physical activity in Israel. While floating on the Dead Sea might not be considered a sport, it is assuredly a novel activity that you won't forget.

A number of marathons and competitions in Israel will coax you into becoming an avid spectator—if not participant. Events include the International Tiberias Marathon and the Kinnereth Cross Country, in which runners come from all over the world to compete. Another event of mass participation is the Jerusalem March; thousands of Israelis and non-Israelis walk together to Jerusalem as a festive show of national unity.

If you fancy water sports, Israel offers wonderful opportunities—especially on the Mediterranean coast and the Sea of Galilee. Temperate water conditions make diving possible year-round. The Red Sea surf boasts an extraordinary underworld seascape for scuba divers; you can get marvelous views of the brightly colored corals and tropical fish of this subterranean paradise. To further enhance your diving experience, Haifa offers archaeological diving tours. Full information can be obtained from the Israel Diving Federation, 16 Hamatsiv Street, Tel Aviv, tel. (03) 3 08 41. If you prefer to stay dry, Elat's Coral World Underwater Observatory provides an unusual opportunity to descend into an underwater glass tower where you can marvel at the intriguing configurations of the reef and the creatures that inhabit it.

Among the best areas for horseback riding are Netanya and Elat, where you can travel on the backs of "Arabian steeds" through the Arava—the wilderness of Israel. If you prefer more mechanized travel, the Jerusalem Cyclists' Club (POB 7281; tel (02) 82 38) leads small groups of bicyclists on tours through Israel for periods of one or two weeks.

Areas along the Red Sea and the Mediterranean, as well as the Gulf of Elat and the Sea of Galilee, provide good fishing. For more information on restrictions and regulations, contact the Elat New Commercial Center, tel. (059) 22 68; the Andromeda Yachting Club (Tel Aviv), tel. (03) 82 47 25; and Blue Beach (Sea of Galilee), tel. (067) 2 01 05.

There are a number of good golf courses, including one located among the Roman ruins of Caesarea.

Other interesting activities include rock climbing in Jericho, tree planting, working on a kibbutz, and participating in an archaeological dig.

Spas. Israel has long been renowned for its health-inducing spas. The tradition of the spas began over 2,000 years ago during the heady days of the Roman Empire. Thousands of visitors still gravitate to these centers annually to bask in the mineral-laden waters that are reputed to ease the symptoms of arthritis, rheumatism, respiratory conditions, and to speed the healing of post-operative conditions. New technological advances include underwater massage, ultraviolet treatments for the skin, and electro-hydrotherapeutic baths. More traditional care includes mud packs and seaweed wraps.

Primary health resorts include the Yesha Hot Springs, the Zohar Hot Springs, En Boqeq, and Arad, located in the Dead Sea region, and the Tiberias Hot Springs that lie near the Sea of Galilee. The Dead Sea area has the additional advantages of a dry climate and a 10 percent higher oxygen content in its air. Surprisingly, there is less danger of sunburn here because the higher atmospheric pressure at this low level admits fewer ultraviolet rays.

For complete listings and more information on each spa's area of specialization, contact your nearest Israeli Government Tourist Office, or the Health Resorts Authority, Rehov Hamelekh George 24, Jerusalem 94262.

Shopping. If you are looking for fine handcrafted jewelry, by all means, shop in Israel. The many bazaars, markets, and workshops will entice you with their distinctive designs and their use of unusual fabrics, woods, and other materials. To help you locate reliable merchandise, the Ministry of Tourism awards a seal of recommendation to deserving shops, which they proudly display. This seal indicates that the shop has met the high standards of the Ministry of Tourism, thereby assuring customers of quality goods and responsive service.

If you're shopping for diamonds, Netanya is the center of the diamond-cutting business. Israel specializes in fine jewelry and meticulous craftsmanship in precious and semi-precious jewels and metals. The oriental markets promise intricate and beautiful handwoven rugs, the artists' colonies in Akko, Bethlehem, Hebron, Jaffa, Jerusalem, and Nazareth are well known for their lovely blown glass, ceramics, embroidery, and antiques. Carvings made from olive wood are popular souvenirs. Major cities also offer fine-quality leather goods, art, and furs for sale.

VAT Refund. In stores recommended by the Ministry of Tourism, you should be able to apply for the VAT Refund (Value Added Tax), which will reimburse you approximately 20 percent of the purchase price (the 20 percent combines a 5 percent discount given by the store with the 15 percent tax). In order to be eligible to receive the VAT refund, your purchase must exceed $125, and it must be made in foreign currency or with a credit card. Certain products are not eligible, such as photographic products, electrical products (e.g., stereo equipment), or any form of tobacco. The procedure for the VAT refund is slightly complicated: The goods purchased and a receipt are sealed in a bag and stamped by the store. The sealed bag must remain intact (unopened) until you deliver it to Israeli customs on your way home. There, a customs officer will open and inspect the bag, and then you will receive your refund before your departure. In unusual cases where you cannot receive your refund in Israel, you may apply for it when you reach home.

The good news is that the customary 15% VAT is not applicable to visitors on charges for accommodations, car rentals, hotel restaurants, or domestic airline travel.

Clothing Sizes. Listed below are standard clothing size equivalents for the United States, Great Britain, and Europe. Clothing sizes in Israel correspond to European sizes.

		U.S.	U.K.	Europe
Chest	*Small*	34	34	87
	Medium	36	36	91
		38	38	97
	Large	40	40	102
		42	42	107
	Extra Large	44	44	112
		46	46	117
Collar		14	14	36
		14$\frac{1}{2}$	14$\frac{1}{2}$	37
		15	15	38
		15$\frac{1}{2}$	15$\frac{1}{2}$	39
		16	16	41
		16$\frac{1}{2}$	16$\frac{1}{2}$	42
		17	17	43
Waist		24	24	61
		26	26	66
		28	28	71
		30	30	76
		32	32	80
		34	34	87
		36	36	91
		38	38	97
Men's Suits		34	34	44
		35	35	46
		36	36	48
		37	37	49$\frac{1}{2}$
		38	38	51
		39	39	52$\frac{1}{2}$
		40	40	54
		41	41	55$\frac{1}{2}$
		42	42	57
Men's Shoes		7	6	39$\frac{1}{2}$
		8	7	41
		9	8	42
		10	9	43
		11	10	44$\frac{1}{2}$
		12	11	46
		13	12	47

	U.S.	U.K.	Europe
Men's Hats	6¾	6⅝	54
	6⅞	6¾	55
	7	6⅞	56
	7⅛	7	57
	7¼	7⅛	58
	7½	7⅜	60
Women's Dresses	6	8	36
	8	10	38
	10	12	40
	12	14	42
	14	16	44
	16	18	46
	18	20	48
Women's Blouses and Sweaters	8	10	38
	10	12	40
	12	14	42
	14	16	44
	16	18	46
	18	20	48
Women's Shoes	4½	3	35½
	5	3½	36
	5½	4	36½
	6	4½	37
	6½	5	37½
	7	5½	38
	7½	6	38½
	8	6½	39
	8½	7	39½
	9	7½	40
Children's Clothing	2	16	92
(*One size larger for knitwear*)	3	18	98
	4	20	104
	5	22	110
	6	24	116
	6X	26	122
Children's Shoes	8	7	24
	9	8	25
	10	9	27
	11	10	28
	12	11	29
	13	12	30
	1	13	32
	2	1	33

	U.S.	U.K.	Europe
Children's Shoes	3	2	34
	4$\frac{1}{2}$	3	36
	5$\frac{1}{2}$	4	37
	6$\frac{1}{2}$	5$\frac{1}{2}$	38$\frac{1}{2}$

Tourism Offices. Branches of the Israeli Government Tourism Office can assist with general inquiries, and provide useful sources of information. These offices carry regional and city maps, provide extensive hotel listings, and also offer literature on special sights.

In Israel:

Rehov Hamelekh George 24
Jerusalem
tel. (02) 23 73 11

Rehov Mendele 7
Tel Aviv
tel. (02) 22 32 66/7

Rehov Herzl 18
Haifa
tel. (04) 66 65 21

Municipality Building
Akko
tel. (04) 91 02 51

Magen David Adom Building
Arad
tel. (0 57) 9 79 11

Commerical Centre, Afridar
Ashqelon
tel. (0 51) 2 74 12

Derekh Ben Gurion 43
Ecke Rothschild
Bat Yam
tel. (03) 88 97 66

Bet Tenu'at Hamoshavim
Beer Sheva
tel. (0 57) 3 60 02

Ben Gurion Airport
Lod
tel. (03) 97 14 85

Manger Square
Bethlehem
tel. (02) 94 25 91

New Commercial Centre
Elat
tel. (0 59) 22 68

Egged Bus Station
Sederot Hagaaton
Nahariya
tel. (04) 92 21 26

Rehov Casanova
Nazareth
tel. (0 65) 5 41 44

Kikar Haatzmaat
Netanya
tel. (0 53) 2 72 86

In Israel

Al Mightaribin Square
Ramalah
tel. 93 35 55

Municipality Building
Safed
tel. 3 06 33

Rehov Nazareth 8
Tiberias
tel. (0 67) 2 09 92

In the U.S.:

350 Fifth Avenue
New York, N.Y. 10118
tel. (212) 560-0650

5 South Wabash Avenue
Chicago, IL 60603
tel. (312) 782-4306

6380 Wilshire Blvd., Suite 1700
Los Angeles, CA 90048
tel. (213) 658-7462

In the U.K.:

18 Great Marlborough Street
London W1V 1AF
tel. (01) 434-3651

In Canada:

180 Bloor Street West, Suite 700
Toronto, Ontario M5S 2V6
tel. (416) 964-3784

The Israeli Government Tourism Office does not maintain a branch in Australia.

The Voluntary Tourist Service (VTS), which is run by Israeli volunteers, also supplies information about Israel, including important festivities, religious ceremonies, or even ways in which to casually make Israeli acquaintances. VTS offices are open daily (not including the Sabbath and high holy days) from 8:30 A.M.–1:30 P.M. Information centers are located at 28 Bialik Street, Tel Aviv, tel. (03) 5 09 19; Jaffa Gate (Old City), tel. (02) 28 81 40; and 7 Keller Street, Mount Carmel, Haifa, tel. (04) 8 51 95. The VTS is also represented at Ben Gurion Airport and in all the larger hotels in Jerusalem, Tel Aviv, and Haifa.

TOWN-BY-TOWN

This section is organized alphabetically by town. To help you locate each town, we've indicated the part of Israel in which it is situated, and also have shown the local telephone dialing code. Each listing provides information on tourist offices, air and ground transportation—including connections to other towns—accommodations, and restaurants.

Hotels are classified according to our own rating system, which is based on the one used by Israel's Ministry of Tourism (see page 271 for a more complete explanation).

Afula (Yizre'el Valley; telephone dialing code 065)
Transportation: *Bus:* Nazareth, Bet Shean, Hadera, Tiberias.

Akhziv (Mediterranean coast; telephone dialing code 04)
Transportation: *Bus:* Akko, Haifa, Rosh ha-Niqra. **Accommodations:** *Kibbutz inn:* Gesher Haziv, on sea, tel. 92 77 11 (48 rooms with air conditioning, swimming pool). *Resort village:* Club Méditerranée, on sea, tel. 92 32 91 (250 rooms); Akhziv Land, with museum; Akhziv Diving Club. **Restaurant:** Wimpy.

Akko (Mediterranean coast; telephone dialing code 04)
Information: Tourist Information Office in Municipality Building, near town walls, tel. 91 02 51. **Transportation:** *Bus:* Haifa, Nahariya, Safed. **Accommodations:** 🏨🏨🏨 Palm Beach Club Hotel, on beach, tel. 91 28 91, telex 46 340 (bar, night club, swimming pool, tennis). 🏨🏨 Argaman Motel, tel. 91 66 91, telex 46 866. Nes Ammim Guesthouse, Old City, tel. 92 25 66. **Restaurants:** Abu Cristo (fish), Old City; Ptolemeus, on harbor; Zor, to north.

Arad (Negev; telephone dialing code 057)
Information: Tourist Information Office in shopping center, Magen David Adom Building, tel. 9 81 44. **Transportation:** *Bus:* Beer Sheva, Hebron, Masada. **Accommodations:** 🏨🏨🏨 Masada, P.O. Box 62, tel. 95 71 40 and 95 72 60, telex 5 212 (bar, restaurant, night club, swimming pool). 🏨🏨 Margoa, Mo'av Street, P.O. Box 20, tel. 95 70 14/15, telex 5 308 (air conditioning, bar, restaurant, night club, clinic for asthma sufferers); Nof Arad, Mo'av Street, tel. 95 70 56/57 (air conditioning, bar, restaurant, night club, swimming pool. 🏨 Arad, 6 Hapalmach Street, tel. 95 70 40 (air conditioning, bar). **Restaurants:** Rachel, Wimpy, both in shopping center; Hatzav Hamahir, 2 Hen Street; Chevrat Ezrat Cholim, 15 Hen Street.

Ashdod (Mediterranean coast; telephone dialing code 055)
Transportation: *Train:* Tel Aviv, Haifa, Jerusalem, Ashqelon. *Bus:* Tel Aviv, Jerusalem, Beer Sheva, Ashqelon. *Car rental:* Avis, Rogozin Street, tel. 2 22 98. **Accommodations:** 🏨🏨 Miami, 12 Nordau Street, on beach, tel. 2 20 85/86 (bar, restaurant, night club). 🏨 Orly, Norden Street, tel. 3 45 50 and 3 15 49. **Restaurants:** Pagoda (Chinese), 11 Ha-Eshel Street, tel. 2 19 14; Pizza Don Pedro, Commercial Center A.

Ashqelon (Mediterranean coast; telephone dialing code 051)
Information: Municipal Tourist Office, Afridar, tel. 3 24 12. **Transportation:** *Train:* Tel Aviv, Gaza. *Bus:* Tel Aviv, Gaza, Beer Sheva; bus station at corner of Bialik and Hanitzachon streets. *Sherut taxis:* Zahal

Street, Migdal; Merkaz Michari, Afridar. **Accommodations:** 🏨🏨🏨
Dagon, Ashqelon Beach, 2 Moshe Dorot Street, tel. 3 61 11 (bar, swimming pool, restaurant); Shulamit Gardens, 11 Hatayassim Street, tel. 3 62 22, telex 26 398 (bar, restaurant, swimming pool). 🏨 Samson's Gardens, 38 Hatamar Street, tel. 3 46 66. *Resort village:* Ashqelon, next to National Park, tel. 3 67 33, telex 5 414 (200 rooms, miniature golf, riding). **Restaurants:** Ma'adan Café, town center; Hanitzhon (Mideastern), 149 Herzl Street; Puerta del Sol (fish), Barnea.

Ayyelet ha-Shahar (kibbutz in Upper Galilee; telephone dialing code 067)
   Transportation: *Air:* from Rosh Pinna airfield to Tel Aviv and Jerusalem. *Bus:* Haifa–Akko–Safed–Ayyelet ha-Shahar; Haifa–Nazareth–Tiberias–Ayyelet ha-Shahar. **Accommodations:** *Kibbutz inn:* Ayyelet ha-Shahar, tel. 3 53 64 (restaurant, bar, swimming pool).

Bat Yam (Mediterranean coast; telephone dialing code 03)
   Information: Municipal Tourist Office, 43 Ben Gurion Road, at corner of Rothschild Street, tel. 58 97 76. **Transportation:** *Bus:* Tel Aviv. **Accommodations:** 🏨🏨 Armon Yam, 95 Ben Gurion Road, tel. 58 24 24, telex 35 414 (bar, restaurant). 🏨 Bat Yam, 53 Ben Gurion Road, tel. 86 43 73 (bar); Bosforus, 2 Jerusalem Street, tel. 87 52 31; Sarita, 127 Ben Gurion Road, tel. 58 91 83. **Restaurants:** Armon Yam, 95 Ben Gurion Road; Pundak Hanessim, 93 Ben Gurion Road; Turkish Restaurant, 61 Ben Gurion Road.

Beer Sheva (Negev; telephone dialing code 057)
   Information: Nordau Street, tel. 3 60 01/03; Ministry of Tourism, 118 Herzl Street. **Transportation:** *Air:* Elat, Haifa. *Train:* Tel Aviv, Dimona; station in Ben Gurion Street, near University. *Bus:* Tel Aviv, Jerusalem, Elat; Bus station at junction of Herzl and Haatzmaut streets. *Sherut taxis:* Keren Kayemet Street, tel. 3 91 44. *Car rental:* Avis, Hevron Street, tel. 7 17 77 and 3 33 45; Hertz, tel. 7 38 78; Kopel Tours, tel. 7 88 60. **Accommodations:** 🏨🏨🏨 Desert Inn, tel. 7 49 31/34, telex 5 266 (bar, restaurant, night club, tennis, swimming pool). 🏨🏨 Zohar, 3 Shadar Boulevard, tel. 7 73 35/36 (bar, restaurant). 🏨 Arava, 37 Histadrut Street, tel. 7 87 92; Aviv, 48 Mordei Hagataot Street, tel. 7 80 59; Hanegev, 26 Haatzmaut Street, tel. 7 70 26. **Restaurants:** El Patio de Santos (fish, Mideastern), 41 Hadassah Street; Morris (European and Mideastern), 40 Trumpeldor Street; Pizzeria Papi, 37 Histadrut Street; Pundak Hatzot, 131 Keren Kayemet Street.

Bethlehem (West Bank; telephone dialing code 02)
   Information: Manger Square, tel. 74 25 91. **Transportation:** *Bus:*

Jerusalem (No. 21), Hebron; bus and *sherut taxi* station in Manger Square. **Accommodations:** 🏨 Bethlehem Star, Al Baten Street, tel. 74 32 49, telex 34 167 (bar, restaurant); Handel, Dehaishe Street, tel. 74 24 94 (bar, restaurant). **Restaurants:** Vienna, Milk Grotto Street; Horse Shoe, Paul VI Street.

Bet Shean (Yizre'el Valley; telephone dialing code 065)
Transportation: *Bus:* Afula, Tiberias, Jericho.

Bet Shearim (National Park in Yizre'el Valley; telephone dialing code 04)
Transportation: *Bus:* Haifa, Nazareth.

Caesarea (Qesarya) (Mediterranean coast; telephone dialing code 063)
Transportation: *Train:* Tel Aviv, Hadera. *Bus:* Netanya, Hadera. **Accommodations:** 🏨🏨🏨 Dan Caesarea, tel. 6 22 66, telex 46 216 (bar, restaurant, swimming pool, tennis, riding, Israel's only 18-hole golf course). 🏨 Mediterranean Nubeiba, Michmoret Beach, tel. 9 31 13 (restaurant). *Kibbutz inn:* Nachsholim, on beach, tel. 39 09 24 (55 rooms with air conditioning). **Restaurants:** Chez Charly (Mideastern, fish); Harbour Citadel (fish), Mitzudat; Herod's Palace (night club).

Capernaum (Kefar Nahum) (Sea of Galilee; telephone dialing code 067)
Transportation: *Bus:* Tiberias, Safed. **Accommodations:** 🏨 Ramat Holiday Village, tel. 6 36 36, telex 6 786 (restaurant, beach); Kinar Holiday Village, tel. 6 36 70, telex 3 61 343 (restaurant, bar, swimming pool, tennis). *Hospice:* Ospizio Monte de Beatitudine, P.O. Box 87, Tiberias, tel. 2 08 79.

Elat (Eilat) (Gulf of Aqaba; telephone dialing code 059)
Information: Government Tourist Center, Hatmarim Boulevard, tel. 7 22 68 and 7 67 37. **Transportation:** *Air:* Tel Aviv, Jerusalem, Haifa, Beer Sheva; airport on Hatmarim Boulevard. *Bus:* Tel Aviv (Jerusalem)–Beer Sheva–Dimona–Elat; bus station for long-distance buses on Hatmarim Boulevard, for local city buses opposite Egged bus station. *Car rental:* Avis, at Airport, tel. 25 50 and 40 16/17; Hertz, Tourist Center, tel. 66 87; Avigdar, Hatmarim Boulevard, tel. 7 33 36 (cars and jeeps); Gindi, New Tourist Center, tel. 7 35 49 (cars and jeeps); Zohar, Bel Hotel, tel. 01 24. **Accommodations:** 🏨🏨🏨 Aviya-Sonesta Beach Hotel, Taba Beach, tel. 7 92 22, telex 77 64 (bar, restaurant, night club, swimming pool, surfing); Caesar, North Beach, tel. 7 61 61, telex 7 732 (bar, restaurant, night club, swimming pool, tennis); Club In (holiday villas),

on Coral Beach, tel. 7 51 22, telex 7 730; King Solomon's Palace, North Beach, tel. 7 91 11, telex 7 765 (bar, restaurant, swimming pool); Moriah Eilat, North Beach, tel. 7 21 51, telex 7 775 (bar, restaurant, swimming pool); Neptune, North Beach, tel. 7 31 31, telex 7 711 (bar, restaurant, swimming pool); Queen of Sheba, North Beach, tel. 7 21 21/26, telex 7 776 (bar, restaurant, swimming pool, tennis); Lagoona, North Beach, tel. 7 94 44, telex 7 775 (bar, restaurant, swimming pool); Red Rock, North Beach, tel. 7 31 71, telex 7 717 (bar, restaurant, swimming pool); Shulamit Gardens, North Beach, tel. 7 51 51, telex 7 738 (bar, restaurant, swimming pool). *Kibbutz inn:* Ye'elim, 40 km. (25 miles) north of Elat in the kibbutz of Yotvata, tel. 74 33 62 (holiday villas, air conditioning, swimming pool). 🏨 Americana, North Beach, P.O. Box 72, tel. 7 51 76/79, telex 7 749 (bar, restaurant, swimming pool); Etzion, Hatmarim Boulevard, tel. 7 41 31/32, telex 7 747 (bar, restaurant); Moon Valley, tel. 7 51 11, telex 7 770 (bar, restaurant, swimming pool). 🏨 Melony Club Aparthotel, 6 Los Angeles Street, tel. 7 31 81/85 (bar, restaurant, swimming pool); Melony Tower Aparthotel, Zolit Elite Center, tel. 7 51 35/36 (bar, restaurant); Adi, New Commercial Center, tel. 7 61 51/55, telex 7 759 (bar, restaurant); Caravan Sun Club, Coral Beach, tel. 7 13 45/47, telex 7 753 (bar, restaurant, swimming pool, tennis); Dalia, North Beach, tel. 7 51 27/28 (bar, restaurant); Dekel, Hativat Hanegev Street, tel. 7 31 91; Blue Sky Caravan, North Beach, tel. 7 39 53/54 (bar). **Restaurants:** Eddie's Hide-A-Way (steaks); La Coquille (fish); Mi Tsu Yan (Chinese); Shrimp House (fish).

En Boqeq (Dead Sea; telephone dialing code 057)
   Transportation: *Bus:* Arad, Neve Zohar. **Accommodations:** 🏨🏨🏨 Ein Bokek, tel. 9 09 31/34 (restaurant, swimming pool, tennis); Galei Zohar, tel. 9 08 51/54 and 9 78 48, telex 52 94 (restaurant); Lot, tel. 8 43 21, telex 52 18 (bar, restaurant); Moriah Dead Sea Spa Hotel, tel. 8 42 21, telex 52 84 (restaurant, swimming pool, private beach, tennis); Shulamit Gardens, tel. 8 43 51, telex 52 03 (restaurant, swimming pool); Tsell Harim, tel. 9 69 91, telex 53 96 (bar, restaurant, swimming pool).

En Gedi (Ein Gedi) (Dead Sea; telephone dialing code 057)
   Transportation: *Bus:* Jericho, Neve Zohar, Jerusalem, Beer Sheva. **Accommodations:** 🏨 En Gedi Beach Holiday Village, tel. 8 43 03 (bungalows, swimming pool). *Kibbutz inn:* Guest House, tel. 8 47 57, telex 53 64 (101 rooms, air conditioning, swimming pool, tennis, self-service restaurant, sulfur baths).

En Gev (Ein Gev) (kibbutz on Sea of Galilee; telephone dialing code 06)
   Transportation: *Boat:* Tiberias (8 km.; 5 miles), three times daily.

Bus: hourly service from Tiberias (25 km.; 15 miles). **Accommodations:** *Kibbutz inn:* Holiday Village, Sea of Galilee, tel. 75 80 27, telex 6 682.

En Hod (Ein Hod) (Mediterranean coast; telephone dialing code 04)
Transportation: *Train:* Tel Aviv–Haifa. *Bus:* Haifa, several times daily. **Accommodations:** *Kibbutz inn:* Nir Etzion, 1 km. (about a half-mile) south, tel. 84 25 41 (74 rooms). **Restaurants:** specialty restaurant.

Haifa (Mediterranean coast; telephone dialing code 04)
Information: Municipal information offices: City Hall, tel. 64 53 69; Hanevim Street, Hadar, tel. 66 30 56; 119 Hanassi Boulevard, Carmel, tel. 8 36 83; Central Bus Station, 170 Yafo Street, tel. 51 22 08. Government information offices: 18 Herzl Street, tel. 66 65 21/23 (open 8:00 A.M.–6:00 P.M.); Shed 12, Harbor, tel. 66 39 88. For information on events in Haifa dial 64 08 40 (24 hour service).
Transportation: *Air:* TWA, 120 Haatzmaut Road, tel. 53 56 10; Arkia, 4 Ibn Seinah Street, tel. 66 77 22/23; British Airways, 3 Habankim Street, tel. 53 53 60; El Al, 80 Haatzamaut Road, tel. 64 09 66. *Train:* Tel Aviv, Jerusalem, Nahariya. Station: Plumer Square, Haatzmaut Road, tel. 64 17 61. Timetable information: dial 64 17 61. *Bus:* Central Bus Station on Jaffa Road, at corner of Hey Hayam Street (reached on city buses 10, 12, 22, 26, 40, 42): buses to Tel Aviv, Jerusalem, and Galilee. Bus station for buses to Akko and Nahariya: opposite train station. *Tours:* Egged Tours, 4 Nordau Street, tel. 64 31 31; United Tours, 5 Nordau Street, tel. 66 56 56. *Sherut taxis:* Arie (to Tel Aviv, Jerusalem, Nahariya, and Safed), 72 Haatzmaut Road, tel. 66 35 95; Aviv (to Tel Aviv, Jerusalem, and Tiberias), 6 Nordau Street and 39 Haatzmaut Road, tel. 66 63 33; Kavei Hagahl (to Akko and Nahariya), 7 Hanevim Street, tel. 66 64 50; Mahir (to Hadera and Afula), 1 Aharon Street, tel. 66 46 46. *Car rental:* Avis, 28 Nathon Street, tel. 67 46 88; 3 Levontin Street, Hadar, tel. 66 09 98; Dan Carmel Hotel, tel. 8 49 59; InterRent, Ratzel Street, tel. 64 54 81/84; Hertz, 8 Shabtai Levi Street, tel. 66 66 55; Europcar, Egged Tours, Central Bus Station, tel. 52 95 04; Kopel Tours, 4 Manachyim Street, tel. 8 80 11/12.
Accommodations: *Hotel reservations:* 5 Nordau Street, tel. 64 54 04. ▦▦▦ Beth-Shalom Carmel, Hanassi Boulevard, tel. 38 62 11, telex 46 606 (bar, restaurant, swimming pool); Nof, 101 Hanassi Boulevard, tel. 38 87 31, telex 46 532 (bar, restaurant); Shulamit, 15 Kiryat Sefer Street, tel. 24 28 11, telex 46 724 (bar, restaurant); Zion, 5 Baerwald Street, tel. 66 43 11/15, telex 46 602 (bar, restaurant). ▦▦ Beth-Shalom Carmel, 110 Hanassi Boulevard, tel. 8 04 81 (bar, restaurant); Carmelia, 35 Herzl Street, tel. 52 12 78/79 (bar, restaurant); Dvir, 124 Yafe Nof Street, tel. 8 91 31 (bar, restaurant); Lev Hacarmel, 23 Heine Square, tel. 8 14 06/07;

Nesher, 53 Herzl Street, tel. 64 06 44; Talpiot, 61 Herzl Street, tel. 67 37 53/54; Yaarot Hacarmel, Mount Carmel, tel. 22 91 44/49 (bar, restaurant). *Outside Haifa:* Young Judaea, 17 km. (10 miles) east, tel. 44 29 76 (130 beds); Kyriat Tivon, 18 km. (11 miles) southeast, tel. 93 14 82 (100 beds). *Kibbutz inns:* Beit Oren, Mount Carmel, 17 km. (10 miles) from Haifa, tel. 22 21 11 (76 rooms); Nir Etzion, on slopes of Carmel range, tel. 84 25 41 (74 rooms). *Hospice* of the Order of St. Charles Borromaeus (German nuns), 105 Jaffa Road, tel. 52 37 05; Beth-El, 40 Hagefen Street, tel. 52 11 10.

Restaurants: Balfour Cellar (international cuisine), 3 Balfour Street, tel. 66 22 99; Banker's Tavern (international), 2 Hanbankim Street, tel. 52 84 39; Rondo (grills), in Dan Carmel Hotel; Pagoda (Chinese), 1 Bat Galim Avenue, tel. 52 45 85; Chin Lung (Chinese), 126 Hanassi Boulevard, tel. 8 13 08; Taiwan (Chinese), 59 Ben Gurion Avenue; Finyan (Mideastern), Mahanyim Street; Pininat Ha-Mizrach (Mideastern), 35 Ben Gurion Road; Benny Orin (Mideastern), 23 Halutz Street, Hadar; Rimini (Italian), 119 Hanassi Boulevard; Popolo (Italian), 17 Ben Gurion Road; Neptune (fish), 10 Margolin Street; Misadag (fish), Bat Galim.

Museums: Admission to museums is free on Saturdays; visitors can get a three-day free pass to all museums from the tourist office. *National Maritime Museum,* 198 Allenby Road (10:00 A.M.–5:00 P.M.); *Illegal Immigration and Naval Museum,* 204 Allenby Road (9:00 A.M.–3:00 P.M.); *Haifa Museum,* 26 Shabtai Levi Street (ancient and modern art, including Jewish art of the Mediterranean region, and ethnology); *Music Museum and Amli Library,* 23 Arlosorov Street (musical instruments, book exhibitions); *Gan Ha'em Museum Complex,* 124 Hatishbi Street (prehistoric artifacts, natural history; 8:00 A.M.–2:00 P.M.); *Museum of Japanese Art,* 89 Hanassi Boulevard (10:00 A.M.–1:00 P.M. and 4:00–7:00 P.M.); *Mane Katz Museum,* 89 Yafe Nof Street (Jewish painting; 10:00 A.M.–1 P.M.); *Chagall House,* 24 Zionut Avenue (contemporary Israeli artists; 10:00 A.M.– 1:00 P.M. and 4:00–7:00 P.M.); *Dagon Museum,* Harbor (history of grain handling in Israel; conducted tour daily at 10:30 A.M.).

Hazor (Tel Hazor) (archaeological site in Upper Galilee; telephone dialing code 067)

Transportation: *Air:* Tel Aviv to Rosh Pinna by Arkia, and from there 6 km. (4 miles) by taxi or bus. *Bus:* Rosh Pinna, Tiberias. **Accommodations:** *Kibbutz inn:* Ayyelet ha-Shahar, tel. 3 73 64, telex 6 646 (124 rooms).

Hebron (Hevron) (West Bank; telephone dialing code 02)

Transportation: *Bus:* Jerusalem, Bethlehem, Beer Sheva. **Accommodations:** ⌂ Al Naher El Khalid, at entrance to town.

Herzliya (Mediterranean coast; telephone dialing code 052)
Transportation: *Train:* Tel Aviv. *Bus:* Tel Aviv. **Accommodations:**
⌂⌂⌂ Dan Accadia, on beach, tel. 55 66 77, telex 341 811 (bar, restaurant,
night club, swimming pool, tennis); Daniel Hotel and Spa, on beach, tel.
54 44 44, telex 341 812 (bar, restaurant, swimming pool, tennis); Sharon
and Sharon Towers, on beach, tel. 7 87 77, telex 341 810 (bar, restaurant,
night club, swimming, tennis). ⌂⌂ Tadmor, 38 Basel Street, tel. 7 83 21,
telex 33 598 (bar, restaurant); Cymberg, 29 Hamaapilim Street, tel. 7 21
79; Eshel, on beach, tel. 7 02 08, telex 35 562. *Kibbutz inn:* Shefaim, 10
km. (6 miles) north, tel. 7 01 71 (115 rooms; swimming pool). **Restaurants:** Henry VIII (international cuisine), opposite Sharon Hotel, tel. 93
85 85; Osteria d'Antonio (Italian), opposite Sharon Hotel, tel.93 28 80;
Safari (South African), Hanassi Street, at corner of Keren Hayesod
Street, tel. 93 74 04; Zevulum, beach restaurants at Sharon Hotel, tel. 93
00 46; Chez Roger, Hasharon Square.

Jericho (West Bank; telephone dialing code 02)
Transportation: *Bus:* Jerusalem, En Gedi, Bet Shean. **Restaurants:**
Al Khayyam, Al Gandoul, and Green Valley Park (garden restaurants
around the market square on Ein al Sultan Street).

Jerusalem (Telephone dialing code 02)
Information: Municipal Tourist Office, 34 Jaffa Road, tel. 22 88 44
(Sunday through Thursday 8:00 A.M.– 6:00 P.M., Friday and day before
public holidays 8:00 A.M.–2:00 P.M.); Government Tourist Office, 24
King George Street, tel. 24 12 81/82, and Jaffa Gate, tel. 28 22 95/96.
Information about day-to-day events in Jerusalem, tel. 24 11 97 (daily
until 6:00 P.M., Fridays until 2:00 P.M.; closed Saturday).
Transportation: *Air:* Arkia office, Klal Center, tel. 22 58 88 and 23
48 55. Atarot airport, on Ramallah road. Services to and from Tel Aviv,
Haifa, Elat, and Rosh Pinna. *Train:* Station: Remez Square, Abu Tor.
Services to Tel Aviv. Timetable information: tel. 71 77 64. *Bus:* Munici-
pal buses run from 6:00 A.M. to midnight; Central Bus Station at 224
Jaffa Road. Bus routes: No. 1, Central Bus Station to Old City; No. 4,
Station to Givat Shapira; No. 6, Station to Bet Hakerem; No. 7, Qiryat
Zans to Ramat Rachel; No. 9, Central Bus Station to Mount Scopus; No.
11, Kfar Shaul to Mea Shearim and Central Bus Station; No. 12, Damas-
cus Gate to Mount Herzl; No. 15, Binyane Ha Umma to Koveshe Ka-
tamon; No. 18, Gonen to Central Bus Station; No. 19, Jaffa Gate to Qiryat
Hadassa; No. 20, Jaffa Gate to Ha Nurit. *Sherut taxis:* Most of the out-of-
town sherut taxis have stands on Jaffa Road, Zion Square. Offices and
directions: Arjek (Tel Aviv, Haifa), 41 Jaffa Road, tel. 22 47 45; Aviv (Tel
Aviv, Haifa), 4 Dorot Rishonim, tel. 22 73 66; Atid (Tel Aviv), 4 Ben
Yehuda Street, tel. 22 45 68; Kesher (Tel Aviv), 6 Lunz Street, tel. 22 23
50; Ha Umma (Mediterranean coast), 226 Jaffa Road, tel. 53 33 33; Yael

Darma (Ashqelon, Beer Sheva, Elat), 2 Lunz Street, tel. 22 69 85; Markaz Habira (Tel Aviv), 3 Lunz Street, tel. 22 22 45 45; Nesher (Ben Gurion airport), 21 King George Street, tel. 22 30 00. Sherut taxis also ply the bus routes. *Car rental:* Europcar, Egged Tours, 42A Jaffa Road, tel. 23 16 04, 22 41 98, and 22 34 54; InterRent, tel. 23 27 85; Hertz, 18 King David Street, tel. 23 13 51; Zohar, 174 Jaffa Road, tel. 24 33 07/08, and 22 King David Street, tel. 23 44 05; Avis, 210 Jaffa Road, tel. 53 44 64 and 52 50 30, in the King David Hotel, tel. 22 22 50, the Hilton Hotel, tel. 53 31 22, and the Plaza Hotel, tel. 28 81 33; Kopel Tours, 8 Hillel Street, tel. 22 26 22; Yehuda Tours, 23 Hillel Street, tel. 22 77 40 and 23 31 47.

Accommodations: *Hotel reservations:* 8 Shamai Street, tel. 22 46 24. 🏨🏨🏨 Hyatt Regency, 32 Lehi Street, tel. 82 13 33, telex 26 174; Intercontinental, Mount of Olives, tel. 28 25 51, telex 25 285 (bar, restaurant, tennis); Jerusalem Hilton, Givat Ram, tel. 53 61 51, telex 26 155 (bar, restaurant, tennis); Jerusalem Plaza Sheraton, 47 King George Street, tel. 22 81 33, telex 26 160 (bar, restaurant, swimming pool); King David, 23 King David Street, tel. 22 11 11, telex 25 228 (bar, restaurant, swimming pool, tennis); King Solomon, 222 King David Street, tel. 24 14 33, telex 26 424 (bar, restaurant, swimming pool); Mount Scopus, Sheikh Jarrah, tel. 28 48 91/92 (bar, restaurant); St. George International, Saladin Street, tel. 28 25 71/75, telex 26 425 (bar, restaurant, swimming pool).

🏨🏨 Ambassador, Sheikh Jarrah, tel. 28 25 15, telex 26 466 (bar, restaurant); American Colony, Nablus Road, tel. 28 24 21/23, telex 25 362 (bar, restaurant); Ariel, 31 Hebron Road, tel. 71 92 22, telex 26 243 (bar, restaurant); Capitol, 17 Saladin Street, tel. 28 25 61/62, telex 25 399 (bar, restaurant); Central, 6 Pines Street, tel. 22 31 11, telex 26 157 (restaurant); Jerusalem Moriah, 39 Keren Hayessod Street, tel. 23 22 32, tel. 25 383 (bar, restaurant); Jerusalem Tadmor, 1 Hagai Street, Beit Hakerem, tel. 51 31 21, telex 26 302 (restaurant); King's, 60 King George Street, tel. 63 52 32, telex 25 227 (restaurant); National Palace, 4 Az Zahra Street, tel. 28 22 46/48, telex 25 381 (bar, restaurant); Panorama, Hill of Gethsemane, tel. 28 48 86/87 (bar, restaurant); Ritz, 8 Ibn Khaldoun Street, tel. 28 48 53/54 (bar, restaurant); Ramada Shalom, Beit Vegan, tel. 42 31 11, telex 25 341 (bar, restaurant, swimming pool); Tirat Bat Sheva, 42 King George Street, tel. 23 21 21 (restaurant).

🏨 Alcazar, 6 Almutanbi Street, tel. 28 11 11, 28 86 28, and 28 88 00 (bar, restaurant); Christmas, Saladin Street, tel. 28 25 88 (bar, restaurant); Commodore, Mount of Olives, tel. 28 48 45 (bar, restaurant); Eilon Tower, 34 Ben Yehuda Street, tel. 23 32 81 (bar, restaurant); Gloria, Jaffa Gate, tel. 28 24 31/32 (bar, restaurant); Holyland East, 6 Rashid Street, tel. 28 48 41/42, telex 25 428 (bar, restaurant); Jerusalem Tower, 23 Hillel Street, tel. 22 21 61, telex 25 345 (bar); Jordan House, Nur ed Din

Street, tel. 28 34 30; Lawrence, 18 Saladin Street, tel. 28 25 85, telex 25 379 (restaurant); Metropole, 6 Saladin Street, tel. 28 25 07 (restaurant); Mount of Olives, Mount of Olives Road, tel. 28 48 77 (restaurant); Neveh Shoshana, 5 Beit Hakerem Street, tel. 52 17 40 and 52 42 94 (restaurant); New Metropole, 8 Saladin Street, tel. 28 38 46 (bar, restaurant); New Orient House, 10 Abu Obideah El Jarrah Street, tel. 28 24 37; New Regent, 20 Az Zahara Street, tel. 28 45 40 (restaurant); Palace, P.O. Box 19143, tel. 28 49 81 (bar, restaurant); Palatin, 4 Agrippa Street, tel. 23 11 41 (restaurant); Park Lane, Mount Scopus, tel. 28 22 08, telex 25 377 (bar, restaurant); Pilgrims' Inn, Rashida Street, tel. 28 48 83 (restaurant); Pilgrims' Palace, King Suleiman Street, tel. 28 48 31 and 28 33 54 (bar, restaurant); Ram, 234 Jaffa Road, tel. 53 52 31/34, telex 26 161 (bar, restaurant); Rama Gidron, 15 Ein Zurim Boulevard, tel. 71 77 22, telex 46 596 (restaurant); Rivoli, 3 Saladin Street, tel. 28 48 71 (bar, restaurant); Shepherd, Mount Scopus, tel. 28 22 71/72, telex 25 377 (bar, restaurant); Strand, Ibn Jubeir Street, tel. 28 02 79 and 28 49 98 (bar, restaurant); Windmill, 3 Mendeli Street, tel. 66 31 11 (bar, restaurant); Y.M.C.A., 26 King David Street, tel. 22 71 11 (bar, restaurant); Y.M.C.A. Aelia Capitolina, 29 Nablus Road, tel. 28 23 75/76 (bar, restaurant).

Hospices: Advance booking in hospices is necessary. Hospice of St. Charles Borromaeus (German), P.O. Box 28020, tel. 63 77 37; Sisters of Nôtre-Dame de Sion, En Kerem, P.O. Box 17015, tel. 41 57 38; Casa Nova (Franciscans), 10 Casa Nova Street, P.O. Box 1321, tel. Christ Church Hospice (Anglican), Jaffa Gate, P.O. Box 14037, tel. 28 20 82; St. Andrew's Hospice (Church of Scotland), P.O. Box 14216, tel. 71 77 01; Lutheran Hospice, St. Mark's Road, P.O. Box 14051, tel. 28 21 50.

Kibbutz inns: Kiryat Anavim, 11 km. (7 miles) west of Jerusalem, tel. 34 89 99 (93 rooms; garden, swimming pool); Ma'ale Hahamisha, 12 km. (7 miles) west of Jerusalem, tel. 34 25 91 (146 rooms; air conditioning, swimming pool); Mitzveh Rachel, tel. 72 12 17 (86 rooms; swimming pool); Shoresh, 17 km. (11 miles) west of Jerusalem, tel. 34 11 71 (94 rooms; air conditioning, swimming pool).

Restaurants: Abu Tor (continental), 5 En Gogel Street, tel. 71 88 42 and 71 86 68; Alpin (vegetarian), 25 King George Street, tel. 22 66 26; Ashafit (continental, kosher), 20 Marcus Street, tel. 63 00 78; Au Sahara (Moroccan), 16 Jaffa Road, tel. 23 32 39; Balalaika (Russian, kosher), 234 Jaffa Road, tel. 53 54 87; Chez Mati (French), 29 King David Street, tel. 22 37 79; Chez Simon (French), 15 Shamai Street, tel. 22 56 02; Chung Hwa (Chinese), 1 Zangwill Street, tel. 42 27 46; Dagim Beni (fish, kosher), 1 Mesilat Yesharim Street, tel. 22 24 03; Europa (Hungarian, kosher), 42 Jaffa Road, tel. 22 89 53; Fish Shlomo (fish, kosher), 27 Salmon Street, tel. 23 36 31; Formosa (Chinese), 36 Ben Yehuda Street, tel. 22 53 73; Georgia (Russian, kosher), 4 King George Street, tel. 22 75 77; Goliath, 28 King David Street; Goulash Inn (Hungarian), En Kerem, tel. 41 92 14; Hassan Afendi (Mideastern), 3 Rashid Street, tel. 28 35 99; Heppner's (American), 4 Lunz Street; Hesse (French), 5 Ben Shetah Street, tel. 22 68 93; Kfir (Mideastern), 25 Saladin Street, tel. 28 05 55; Leah (Hungarian, kosher), 15 Kerem Kayemet Street, tel. 66 21 66; L'Entrecôte (French), 6 Hillel Street, tel. 24 55 15; Lev (international), 31 Hillel Street, tel. 22 59 11; Leviathan (seafood), 11 Rashid Street, tel. 28 36 55; Mandarin (Chinese), 2 Shlomzion Hamalka Street, tel. 22 28 90; Marina (Chinese), 3 Ahad Ha'am Street, tel. 3 12 73; Merkaz (international), 26 Bezalel Street, tel. 22 68 35 and 28 62 79; Mishkanot Haroim, East Talpiot, near Government House, tel. 71 76 60; Mishkenot Shaananim (French, kosher), Yemin Moshe Street, tel. 22 51 10 and 23 34 24; Oftagun (American, strictly kosher), 36 Jaffa Road, tel. 2 22 17; Palmachi (Mideastern, kosher), 13 Shamai Street, tel. 23 47 84; Pizzeria Papi (Italian, kosher), 9 Ben Hillel Street, tel. 22 39 14, and 234 Jaffa Road, Central Bus Station; Pizzeria Rimini (Italian), 43 Jaffa Road, tel. 22 65 05, and 15 King George Street, tel. 22 55 34; Ramah (Mideastern, kosher), 34 Agripas Street, tel. 22 56 65; Rimon (Mideastern, kosher), 4 Lunz Street, tel. 22 27 72; Rondo (continental), 41 King George Street, tel. 23 22 23; Sea Dolphin (fish), Al Rashid Street, tel. 28 27 88; Shemesh (Mideastern, kosher), 21 Ben Yehuda Street, tel. 22 24 18; Sindbad (Mideastern), 23 Suleiman Street, tel. 27 20 52; Stark (Hungarian, kosher), 21 King George Street, tel. 22 67 57; Venezia (Italian), Ben Shetah Street, tel. 23 47 93; Citadel (Chinese), 14 Hativat Yerushalayim Street, tel. 28 88 87.

Masada (Mezada) (Dead Sea; telephone dialing code 057)
  Transportation: *Bus:* Jerusalem–Hebron–Masada; Jerusalem–Jericho–Masada; Beer Sheva–Masada. **Accommodations:** ฿ Masada Guesthouse (30 beds).

Metulla (Upper Galilee; telephone dialing code 067)
  Transportation: *Air:* Tel Aviv–Rosh Pinna. *Bus:* Akko–Safed–Qiryat Shemona–Metulla; Tiberias–Qiryat Shemona–Metulla. **Accommodations:** ฿ Arazim, tel. 4 41 43 (bar, restaurant, swimming pool, tennis); Hamavri, tel. 4 01 50 (bar, restaurant); Sheleg Halevanon, tel. 4 46 15.

Mizpe Ramon (Negev; telephone dialing code 057)
  Transportation: *Air:* Tel Aviv–Mizpe Ramon. *Bus:* Beer Sheva, Elat.

Nablus (Shechem) (West Bank; telephone dialing code 065)
  Transportation: *Bus:* Jerusalem, Tel Aviv. **Restaurants:** Jacob's Well, in town center; Jerusalem, on hill.

Nahariya (Mediterranean coast; telephone dialing code 04)
   Information: Municipal Building, Ha-Ga'aton Boulevard, tel. 92 21 21. **Transportation:** *Train:* Tel Aviv; station on Ha-Ga'aton Boulevard. *Bus:* Egged bus station on Ha-Ga'aton Boulevard, tel. 92 34 44; Haifa–Akko–Nahariya (every 15 minutes), Nahariya–Rosh ha-Niqra. *Car rental:* Taxi Galil, 71 Herzl Street, tel. 92 55 55. **Accommodations:** 🏨🏨🏨 Carlton, 23 Ha-Ga'aton Boulevard, tel. 92 22 11/16 (bar, restaurant, night club, tennis). 🏨🏨 Astar, Ha-Ga'aton Boulevard, tel. 92 34 31; Eden, Meyasdim Street, tel. 92 32 16/17 (bar, restaurant); Frank, 4 Haaliya Street, tel. 92 02 78/79, telex 35 562 and 35 654 (bar, restaurant); Pallas Athene, 28 Hamaapilim Street, tel. 92 23 81/82 (bar); Panorama, 6 Hamaapilim Street, tel. 92 05 55 (restaurant). 🏨 Kalman, 27 Jabotinsky Street, tel. 92 03 55 (bar, restaurant); Karl Laufer, 31 Hameyasdim Street, tel. 92 01 30; Rosenblatt, 59 Weizmann Street, tel. 92 34 69 and 92 00 69 (restaurant). *Kibbutz inns:* Gesher Haziv, 5 km. (3 miles) east, tel. 82 57 15 (48 rooms; air conditioning); Beit Hava, 5 km. (3 miles south in moshav of Shave Zion, tel. 92 23 91 (85 rooms; swimming pool). **Restaurants:** Penguin (international), Ha-Ga'aton Boulevard; Florida (Mideastern), on beach; Hazafon (Hungarian and Mideastern, Ha-Ga'aton Boulevard. **Museum:** Municipal Museum (archaeology, modern painting) in Town Hall.

Nazareth (Lower Galilee; telephone dialing code 065)
   Information: Government Tourist Office, Casanova Street, tel. 7 05 55 and 7 30 03. **Transportation:** *Bus:* Haifa, Tiberias, Tel Aviv; bus station on Maria Road. *Sherut taxis:* tel. 5 44 12 and 5 50 40. **Accommodations:** 🏨🏨 Grand New Hotel, St. Joseph Street, tel. 7 30 20/21 (bar, restaurant); Hagalil, Paul VI Street, tel. 7 13 11 (bar, restaurant); Nazareth, tel. 7 20 45 and 5 45 02 (bar, restaurant). *Hospices:* Casa Nova (Franciscans), near Church of the Annunciation, tel. 5 43 55; Sisters of Nazareth (Roman Catholic), tel. 5 43 04; St. Charles Borromaeus (German), 316 Street 12, tel. 5 44 35; St. Joseph's (Greek Catholic), tel. 7 05 40. **Restaurants:** Abu Nassar (Mideastern), Casanova Street; Astoria (Lebanese), Casanova Street; Israel (Mideastern), Casanova Street.

Netanya (Natanya) (Mediterranean coast; telephone dialing code 053)
   Information: Haatzmaut Square, tel. 2 72 86. **Transportation:** *Train:* Tel Aviv, Jerusalem; station in Harakevet Road, tel. 2 34 70. *Bus:* Central Bus Station at junction of Herzl and Benyamin streets; departures for Tel Aviv every 10 minutes. *Tours:* Egged Tours, 28 Herzl Street, tel. 2 87 03, and 7 Haatzmaut Square, tel. 2 87 02. *Sherut taxis:* Sharon Taxi, 1 Shmuel Hanatziv Street, tel. 2 23 23. *Car rental:* Avis, 1

Ussishkin Street, tel. 3 16 19; Hertz, 8 Haatzmaut Square, tel. 2 88 90; Europcar, Haatzmaut Square, tel. 2 83 33.

Accommodations: 🏨 Dan Netanya, Nice Boulevard, tel. 3 00 44, telex 341 998 (bar, restaurant, tennis). 🏨 Beit Ami, 41 King Solomon Street, tel. 9 12 22, telex 35 484 (bar, restaurant); Blue Bay, 37 Hamelachim Street, tel. 3 71 31, telex 341 819 (bar, restaurant); Feldman, 9 Hashiva Street, tel. 2 21 93 and 3 72 45 (restaurant); Galei Zans, 6 Melahim Street, tel. 3 92 41/42 (bar, restaurant); Galil, Nice Boulevard, tel. 9 20 96 and 9 12 06, telex 341 920 (bar, restaurant); Gan Hamelech, 10 King David Street, tel. 3 93 41 (bar, restaurant); Goldar, 1 Ussishkin Street, tel. 3 81 88, telex 341 894 (bar, restaurant); Grand Yahalom, 13 Gad Makhnes Street, tel. 3 53 45, telex 341 917 (bar, restaurant); Hof, 9 Haatzmaut Square, tel. 3 13 04 and 2 28 25 (bar, restaurant); King Solomon, 18 Hamaapilim Street, tel. 3 84 44, telex 0341 867 (bar, restaurant); Metropol Grand, 17 Gad Makhnes Street, tel. 3 80 38, telex 35 487 (bar, restaurant); Park, 7 King David Street, tel. 3 33 47, telex 341 835 (bar, restaurant); Maxim, 8 King David Street, tel. 3 93 41 (bar, restaurant); King David Palace, 4 King David Street, tel. 2 28 30 (bar, restaurant); Orly, 20 Hamaapilim Street, tel. 3 30 91/92 (bar, restaurant); Palace, 33 Gad Makhnes Street, tel. 3 76 31 (bar, restaurant); Princess, 33 Gad Makhnes Street, tel. 3 60 61 (bar, restaurant); Residence, 18 Gad Makhnes Street, tel. 3 37 77/78, telex 341 933 (bar, restaurant); Sironit, 19 Gad Makhnes Street, tel. 4 06 88 (bar, restaurant); Topaz, 25 King David Street, tel. 3 60 52, telex 341 667 (bar, restaurant); Yahalom, 11 Gad Makhnes Street, tel. 3 53 45, telex 341 917 (bar). 🏨 Atzmauth, 2 Ussishkin Street, tel. 2 25 62 (bar, restaurant); Daphna, 29 Rishon le-Zion Street (bar); Gal Yam, 46 Dizengoff Street, tel. 2 26 03 (restaurant); Ginot Yam, 9 King David Street, tel. 2 30 07 (bar, restaurant); Galei Hasharon, 42 Ussishkin Street, tel. 2 51 25, telex 41 946 (bar, restaurant); Grinstein, 47 Dizengoff Street, tel. 2 20 46 (bar, restaurant); Margoa, 9 Gad Makhnes Street, tel. 3 44 34/35 (bar, restaurant); Metropol, 18 Rishon le-Zion Street, tel. 3 80 38, telex 35 487 (bar, restaurant); Mizpe Yam, 4 Karlebach Street, tel. 2 37 30 (bar, restaurant); Reuben, 25 Ussishkin Street, tel. 2 31 07 (bar).

Restaurants: Capris, 27 Herzl Street, tel. 2 35 69; Golden Fish, 10 Haatzmaut Square; Los Troncos (South American), on the Tel Aviv-Haifa Road, tel. 9 11 82; Renaissance (French), 9 Haatzmaut Square, tel. 2 86 53; Taipeh (Chinese), 7 Haatzmaut Square.

Neve Zohar (Dead Sea; telephone dialing code 057)

Transportation: *Air:* Tel Aviv–Sedom, Haifa–Sedom. *Train:* Tel Aviv–Dimona. *Bus:* Tel Aviv–Beer Sheva–Arad–Neve Zohar, Jerusalem–Hebron–Arad–Neve Zohar. **Accommodations:** 🏨 Moriah Dead Sea, in En Boqeq, Sedom, tel. 8 42 21, telex 5 284 (air conditioning, heated indoor pool with sea water, open-air pool, private beach). 🏠 Shefach Zohar Guest House, tel. 9 09 04.

Petah Tiqva (Judean plain; telephone dialing code 03)
Transportation: *Bus:* Tel Aviv–Petah Tiqva. *Car rental:* Run-Car, 1 Shpigel Street, tel. 90 52 92 and 90 50 87.

Qiryat Shemona (Upper Galilee; telephone dialing code 06)
Transportation: *Air:* Tel Aviv–Rosh Pinna, Jerusalem–Rosh Pinna. *Bus:* Tiberias–Rosh Pinna–Qiryat Shemona, Akko–Safed–Rosh Pinna–Qiryat Shemona. **Accommodations:** 🏨 North, tel. 4 17 05/07 (bar, night club). *Kibbutz inns:* Kefar Giladi, tel. 94 14 14 (150 rooms; restaurant, swimming pool); Hagoshrim, tel. 94 52 31 (120 rooms; restaurant, tennis); Kefar Blum, tel. 9 43 66 (46 rooms; swimming pool).

Ramallah (West Bank; telephone dialing code 02)
Information: Al Mughtaribin Square, tel. 95 35 55/56. **Transportation:** *Bus:* Jerusalem–Ramallah. **Accommodations:** 🏨 Miami, Jaffa Street, tel. 95 28 08 (bar, restaurant).

Ramat Gan (Judean plain; telephone dialing code 03)
Transportation: *Bus:* Tel Aviv (Nos. 33 and 35). **Accommodations:** 🏨 Kefar Hamakkabia, Ramat Hen, tel. 74 97 22 (resort village hotel). **Restaurant:** Bob's Pizzeria, opposite Bar Ilan University, tel. 75 92 47.

Rehovot (Judean plain; telephone dialing code 054)
Transportation: *Bus:* Tel Aviv. **Accommodations:** 🏠 Margoa, 11 Moskovitz Street, tel. 5 13 03. *Kibbutz inn:* Hafetz Haim, 8 km. (5 miles) south, tel. 59 38 88 (57 rooms; swimming pool).

Rosh ha-Niqra (Mediterranean coast; telephone dialing code 04)
Transportation: *Train:* Tel Aviv–Nahariya. *Bus:* Tel Aviv–Haifa–Akko–Nahariya–Rosh ha-Niqra. **Restaurant:** Inn, on cliffs.

Rosh Pinna (Upper Galilee; telephone dialing code 067)
Transportation: *Air:* Tel Aviv, Jerusalem. *Bus:* Haifa–Akko–Safed–Rosh Pinna, Tiberias– Rosh Pinna.

Safed (Zefat) (Upper Galilee; telephone dialing code 067)
Information: Municipality Building, 7 Jerusalem Street, tel. 3 06 33. **Transportation:** *Air:* Tel Aviv–Rosh Pinna; Arkia office in Rosh Pinna, tel. 3 73 01/02. *Bus:* Tiberias–Rosh Pinna–Safed; Haifa–Akko–Safed. *Tours:* Egged buses: Haatzmaut Square, tel. 3 11 22. **Accommodations:** 🏨 Rimon Inn, Artists' Colony, tel. 3 06 65/66, telex 6 611 (bar, restau-

rant, swimming pool); Ron, Hativat Yiftah Street, tel. 7 25 90, telex 6 742 (bar, restaurant); Zefat, Mount Canaan, tel. 3 09 14, telex 72 579 (bar, restaurant). ▣ Berinson House, tel. 7 25 55 (bar, restaurant); Central, 37 Jerusalem Street, tel. 7 26 66/67 (bar, restaurant); David, Mount Canaan, tel. 3 00 62 (bar, restaurant); Hof Hagalil, Mount Canaan, tel. 3 15 95 and 7 08 80 (bar, restaurant); Pisgah, Mount Canaan, tel. 3 01 05 and 7 00 44 (bar, restaurant); Ruckenstein, Mount Canaan, tel. 3 00 60 (bar, restaurant). ▣ Beit Yair, 59 Jerusalem Street, tel. 3 02 45 (bar, restaurant); Motel Canaan, Mount Canaan, tel. 7 09 29; Friedman, 2 Bak Street, tel. 3 00 36; Hadar, tel. 3 00 68 (restaurant). **Restaurants:** Pinati (Mideastern), 82 Jerusalem Street; Hamifgash (international), 75 Jerusalem Street; Azmon and Batia (Mideastern), Jerusalem Street. **Museums:** permanent exhibitions in Artists' Colony; Glicenstein Museum (sculpture, pictures).

Sedom (Sodom) (Dead Sea; telephone dialing code 057)

Transportation: *Air:* Tel Aviv, Haifa. *Bus:* Tel Aviv–Beer Sheva–Dimona–Sedom, Jerusalem–Hebron–Beer Sheva–Dimona–Sedom.

Tel Aviv (Telephone dialing code 03)

Information: municipal tourist offices at 42 Frishman Street/corner of Dizengoff Street, tel. 22 36 92, 45 Jerusalem Boulevard (Jaffa), tel. 83 46 31, and Atarim Square, tel. 27 86 68. Government Tourist Office, 7 Mendele Street, tel. 22 32 66/67.

Transportation: *Air:* Ben Gurion Airport, tel. 97 14 85; flight information, tel. 97 14 61. El Al, 32 Ben Yehuda Street, tel. 29 93 33; confirmation of El Al flights, tel. 62 52 52; Arkia (Israel Inland Airlines), tel. 21 81 81 and 22 66 40; British Airways, 59 Ben Yehuda Street, tel. 22 92 51l; TWA, 74–76 Hayarkon Street, tel. 65 12 12.

Ben Gurion Airport (formerly Lod), Israel's largest and most important airport, lies 18 km. (11 miles) east of Tel Aviv and 50 km. (31 miles) west of Jerusalem. Airport buses run between the airport and the city terminal (at the Central Bus Station) every half-hour from 4:30–11:00 A.M., and every hour from 11:00 A.M.–10:00 P.M. (until 5:00 P.M. on Fridays); on Saturdays and public holidays, they run hourly from 5:00–10:00 A.M. and thereafter according to flights in and out. Egged buses also run every 15 minutes from 5:00 A.M.–10:00 P.M. There are also bus services to Jerusalem and Haifa.

There are flights from Ben Gurion to Europe, the U.S., South America, and South Africa, and to the following cities within Israel: Jerusalem, Elat, Haifa, Rosh Pinna, Beer Sheva, Sedom, and Mizpe Ramon. Domestic flights are operated by the Arkia airline, which flies both from Ben Gurion and from the smaller airfield at Sede Dov, north of Tel Aviv. Arkia offices: 88 Hahasmonaim Street, tel. 3 07 72, and 11 Frishmann Street, tel. 23 73 35.

Train: Services to Haifa and Nahariya; Jerusalem; and Beer Sheva and Dimona. Information about departures, tel. 25 42 71. Trains to Haifa leave from Merkaz Station, at the junction of Arlosoroff and Petah Tiqva streets; trains to Beer Sheva and Jerusalem leave from Darom Station, in Kibbutz Galuyot Street, near the junction of Holon and Lod streets.

Bus: Coach service to points outside the city starts from the Central Bus Station on Hagalil Street, at the junction of Yafo and Har Zion streets. Reservations: Egged Tours, 59 Ben Yehuda Street, tel. 24 22 71 and 24 21 35/36; Atarim Square, tel. 28 31 91/93 and 28 44 91; 8 Mendele Street, tel. 24 21 34 and 24 22 71.

Sherut taxis for out-of-town journeys start from Hamoshawot Square (at junction of Lilienblum and Herzl streets, in the south of the city). Offices: Atid (to Jerusalem), 46 Lilienblum Street, tel. 61 50 11; Arje (Haifa, Nahariya, Jerusalem), 4 Mikveh Israel Street, tel. 61 38 36; Aviv (Haifa, Tiberias, Jerusalem), 32 Rothschild Boulevard, tel. 62 28 88; Borclay (Hadera, Afula), 23 Ahad Ha'am Street, tel. 61 10 55; Hasharon (Netanya), Mikveh Israel Street, tel. 61 21 32; Kesher (Jerusalem), 33 Rothschild Boulevard, tel. 61 14 88; Ron (Ashdod), 1 Perez Street, tel. 61 14 88; Yael Daroma (Ashqelon, Beer Sheva, Elat), 44 Yafne Street, tel. 62 25 55.

Tours: Bus tours of Israel are run by the following companies (among others): Egged Tours, Ben Yehuda Street, tel. 24 22 71 and 24 21 35/36; Atarim Square, tel. 28 31 91/93 and 28 44 91; 8 Mendele Street, tel. 24 21 34 and 24 22 71. United Tours, 113 Hayarkon Street, tel. 29 81 81/85 and 29 10 26; 4 Bograshov Street, tel. 5 91 06. Ista (student tours), 2 Pinsker Street, tel. 5 96 13.

City transportation: Sherut taxis run along the bus routes (bearing the same numbers as the buses) and operate on the Sabbath, when the buses do not run. You can stop them by holding out your hand. Routes in direction of Jaffa: Nos. 10, 18, 25, 41, and 46. Routes in direction of Shalom Mayer Tower: Nos. 1, 4, 18, 25, and 41. Routes in direction of Main Synagogue: Nos. 4, 5, 12, and 18. Routes in direction of University: Nos. 25, 26, 27, 45, and 79. Routes in direction of Central Bus Station: Nos. 4 and 5.

Car rental: Hertz, 10 Karlebach Street, tel. 26 41 41; Avis, 80 Hamasger Street, tel. 33 63 63/68, and 75 Hayarkon Street, tel. 5 10 93 and 5 37 42; InterRent, 160 Hayarkon Street, tel. 24 04 89 and 24 95 91; Zohar, 112 Hayarkon Street, tel. 28 72 53/54; Adi, 106 Hayarkon Street, tel. 22 34 96 and 22 85 11; Sun Tours, 6 Bograshov Street, tel. 65 99 05 and 65 86 02; Europcar, 5 Shalom Street, tel. 65 11 81/83; Ramtour, 134 Hayarkon Street, tel. 22 66 23; Eldan, Shalom Department Store Parking Area, tel. 5 47 96; Run-Car, 124 Hayarkon Street, tel. 23 21 60; Kopel Tours, 252 Hayarkon Street, tel. 45 21 11; Run, 107 Hayarkon Street, tel. 22 38 52.

Accommodations: *Hotel reservations:* 111 Allenby Road, tel. 61 25

67; 4 Reiness Street, tel. 24 83 06. 🏨🏨🏨 Astoria, 10 Kaufmann Street, tel. 66 33 11 (bar, restaurant); Carlton, Hayarkon Street, tel. 29 12 91, telex 342 690 (bar, restaurant); Dan Tel Aviv, 99 Hayarkon Street, tel. 24 11 11, telex 33 705 (bar, restaurant); Plaza Tel Aviv, 155 Hayarkon Street, tel. 29 95 55, telex 35 847 (bar, restaurant); Ramada Continental, 121 Hayarkon Street, tel. 29 64 44, telex 341 367 (bar, restaurant); Tel Aviv Hilton, Independence Park, tel. 24 42 22, telex 33 556 (bar, restaurant); Tel Aviv Sheraton, 115 Hayarkon Street, tel. 28 62 22, telex 342 268 (bar, restaurant, night club).

🏨🏨 Astor, 105 Hayarkon Street, tel. 22 31 41 (bar, restaurant); Avia, Savion B.G. Airport Area, tel. 75 22 21, telex 33 817 (bar, restaurant, tennis); Basel, 156 Hayarkon Street, tel. 24 41 61, telex 33 828 (bar, restaurant); Concorde, 1 Trumpeldor Street, tel. 65 92 41 (bar, restaurant); Country Club, Gelilot Junction, tel. 41 52 61, telex 32 376 (bar, restaurant, tennis); Habakkuk, 7 Habakkuk Street, tel. 44 00 11 and 44 31 10; Marina, 167 Hayarkon Street, tel. 28 22 44, telex 341 696 (bar, restaurant); Moriah Tel Aviv, 250 Hayarkon Street, tel. 24 12 52, telex 33 649, (bar, restaurant); Park, 75 Hayarkon Street, tel. 65 15 51, telex 33 474 (bar, restaurant); Ramat Aviv, 151 Haifa Road, tel. 41 31 81, telex 033 745 (bar, restaurant, tennis); Sinai, 11–15 Trumpeldor Street, tel. 65 26 21, telex 341 144 (bar, restaurant); Tal, 287 Hayarkon Street, tel. 45 52 81, telex 341 163 (bar, restaurant).

🏨 Adiv, 5 Mendele Street, tel. 22 91 41, telex 341 338; Ambassador, 2 Allenby Road, tel. 65 51 18/19; City, 9 Mapu Street, tel. 24 62 53, telex 34 12 20 (bar, restaurant); Armon Hayarkon, 268 Hayarkon Street, tel. 45 52 71/73, telex 341 730 (restaurant); Commodore, Dizengoff Circle, tel. 29 61 81, telex 342 232; Excelsior, 88A Hayarkon Street, tel. 65 54 86 (bar, restaurant); Florida, 164 Hayarkon Street, tel. 24 2184 (bar, restaurant); Maxim, 86 Hayarkon Street, tel. 65 37 21; Imperial, 66 Hayarkon Street, tel. 65 70 02; Kfar Hamaccabiah, Ramat Gan, Bernstein Street, tel. 94 77 11, telex 33 319 (bar, restaurant); Moss, 6 Nes Ziona Street, tel. 65 16 55 (bar, restaurant); Ora, 35 Ben Yehuda Street, tel. 65 09 41 (bar); Shalom, 216 Hayarkon Road, tel. 24 32 77 and 24 94 44; Star, 9 Trumpeldor Street, tel. 65 21 27/28 (bar); Wagshal, Bnei Brak, tel. 78 45 36; Wishnitz, 16 Damasek Street, Bnei Brak, tel. 77 71 41/43 (restaurant).

Restaurants: America House (kosher; roof restaurant), 35 King Saul Boulevard, tel. 26 89 33; Acropolis (Greek), Caliph Building, Jaffa, tel. 33 21 20; Ankara (Balkan), 192 Ben Yehuda Street, tel. 23 77 84; Baiuca (Brazilian), 103 Yehuda Hamamit, Jaffa, tel. 82 72 89; Balkan Corner, Rokah Boulevard, Ramat Aviv, tel. 41 74 40; Batia (kosher), 197 Dizengoff Street, tel. 2 13 35; Cartier of China, 2 King Saul Street, tel. 25 98 43; Casba (continental), 32 Yirmiyahu Street, tel. 44 91 01; Casa Mia (Italian), 38 King Solomon Street, tel. 23 98 56; Café de Paris (French), 17 Trumpeldor Street, tel. 25 88 03; Dolphin (fish), 16 Shalom Aleichem

Street, tel. 20 89 73 and 28 26 00; Gondola (Italian), 57 Pinsker Street, tel. 28 37 88; Happy Casserole, 342 Dizengoff Street, tel. 44 23 60; Holyland (kosher), 49 Bagrashov Street, tel. 28 73 82; Ha-Nemala (Mideastern), 44 Hatekuma Street, Jaffa, tel. 82 91 75; Hong Kong House (Chinese), 6 Mendele Street, tel. 24 73 00; Iran Food, 2 Zamenhoff Street, tel. 29 61 81; Jeannette, 4 Rezif Aliya Sheniya, tel. 82 55 75; Keton (kosher), 145 Dizengoff Street, tel. 23 36 79; Kum Kum (kosher), Sheraton Hotel, 115 Hayarkon Street, tel. 28 62 22; La Couronne (French), 22 Pinsker Street, tel. 25 99 66; Le Beaujolais (French), 33 Yirmiyahu Street, tel. 44 97 22; Le Versailles (French), 37 Geulah Street, tel. 5 55 52; Lipsky M.K. (continental), 45 Yefet Street, Jaffa, tel. 82 84 56; Little Old Tel Aviv (American), 300 Hayarkon Street, tel. 45 01 09; Golden Orange, in Shalom Drugstore, Atarim Square; My Zedeh's Place (kosher), Atarim Square, tel. 28 79 33; Mandy's Drugstore (American), 206 Dizengoff Street, tel. 23 43 04; Marina (Chinese, kosher), Marina Hotel, Atarim Square, tel. 28 22 44; Me and My Pizzeria, 293 Dizengoff Street, tel. 44 34 27; Non-Stop, 315 Dizengoff Street, tel. 45 71 15; Pizzeria Rimini, Malkhey Yisrael Square, tel. 26 39 87, 24 Ibn Gavirol Street, tel. 26 61 77, 93 Dizengoff Street, tel. 22 16 31, and 3 Ahusat Bait Street, Atarim Square, tel. 5 32 87; Plintzi (blintzes), 17 Yirmiyahu Street and 320 Dizengoff Street, tel. 44 36 17 and 44 62 94; Pundag (fish), 8 Frishman Street, tel. 22 29 48; Poseidon (fish), 14 Kedumim Square, Old Jaffa, tel. 82 90 18; Rishon Cellar (continental), 11 Allenby Road; Rasputin (Russian), 227 Hayarkon Street, tel. 44 51 11; Russalka (Russian), Hilton Beach, tel. 24 21 39; Safari (South African), Atarim Square, tel. 28 31 25; Selina (Vietnamese), 52 Hen Boulevard, tel. 45 12 82/83; Shaul's Inn (Mideastern, kosher), 11 Elyashiv Street, tel. Kerem Hatemanim, tel. 5 33 03; Singing Bamboo, 317 Hayarkon Street, tel. 44 34 00 and 45 87 85; Saigon House (Vietnamese), 17 Yehuda Hayamit Street, Jaffa, tel. 82 46 06; Taj Mahal (Indian), 12 Kedumim Square, Jaffa, tel. 82 10 02; Triana (Greek), 12 Karlebach Street, tel. 26 49 49; Via Maris (French), 6 Kedumim Square, Jaffa, tel. 82 84 51 and 86 84 07; Yamit (French), 16 Kedumim Square, Jaffa, tel. 82 53 53; Zion Exclusive (Mideastern, kosher), 28 Peduyim Street, Kerem Hatemanim, tel. 5 73 23.

Night life: Most of the hotels on the main beach have night clubs with dance shows. In addition, there are Peacock's Disco, Atarim Complex, Hayarkon Street; Rafi's Piano Bar, Yordai Hasira Street; Beit Hoven, Dizengoff Street; and the Jet Club, in the Avia Hotel. In Jaffa there are Omar Khayyam, The Cave, Khalif, Caravan, Peacock, and Sound and Light.

Tiberias (Teverya) (Lower Galilee; telephone dialing code 06)
   Information: Government Tourist Office. 8 Elkadeff Street, tel. 2 09 92. **Transportation:** *Bus:* Egged Tours, Hayarden Street, tel. 2 10 82.

Sherut taxis: tel. 2 00 98. *Boat trips* on Sea of Galilee: Kinneret Sailing Co., tel. 2 02 27. *Car rental:* Avis, Nazareth Street, Sonol Station, tel. 2 27 66. **Accommodations:** 🏨🏨🏨 Galei Kinnereth, Kaplan Avenue, tel. 9 23 31, telex 6 655 (bar, restaurant, swimming pool); Tiberias Plaza, P.O. Box 375, tel. 9 22 33, telex 6 663 (bar, restaurant, swimming pool); Ganei Hammat, Habanim Street, tel. 9 28 90, telex 6 674 (bar, restaurant, tennis); Golan, 14 Achad Ha'am Street, tel. 9 19 01/03 (bar, restaurant, night club); Hartman, 3 Achad Ha'am Street, tel. 9 15 55/56 (bar, restaurant, swimming pool); Washington, 13 Zeidel Street, tel. 9 18 61, telex 6 602 (bar, restaurant). 🏨🏨 Ariston, 19 Herzl Boulevard, tel. 9 02 44/46 (bar, restaurant); Astoria, 13 Ohel Yaacov Street, tel. 2 23 51/53 (restaurant); Tiberias, 19 Ohel Yaacov Street, tel. 9 22 70 (bar, restaurant); Daphne, Kiriyat Shaul, tel. 9 22 61/65 (bar, restaurant); Eden, Kiriyat Shmuel, tel. 9 00 70/72 (bar, restaurant); Peer, 2 Ohel Yaacov Street, tel. 9 16 41/42 (bar, restaurant, night club); Yaalon, Plus 200, tel. 9 19 51/53 (bar, restaurant). 🏨 Arnon, 28 Hashomer Street, tel. 2 01 81 (bar, restaurant); Continental, 2 Nazareth Street, tel. 2 08 26 (restaurant); Grand Romano, Gdud Barak Street, tel. 2 19 01/04 (bar, restaurant); Heller, 10 Yehuda Street, tel. 2 25 77 (bar, restaurant); Menora Gardens, tel. 9 27 70 (bar, restaurant); Polonia, Hagalil Street, tel. 2 00 07 (restaurant); Ron, 12 Achad Ha'am Street, tel. 2 02 59 (restaurant). *Kibbutz inns:* Hammat Gader, 20 km. (12 miles) from Tiberias, southeast of Sea of Galilee, tel. 75 10 39; Lavi, 5 km. (3 miles) west of lake, tel. 79 94 50 (54 rooms; swimming pool); Ma'agan, at southern tip of lake, tel. 75 37 53 (65 rooms; air conditioning); Nof Ginosar, on shores of lake, tel. 79 21 61 beach). *Hospices:* Terra Sancta (Franciscans), Old City, tel. 2 05 16 (30 beds); Monte di Beatitudine (Italian Franciscans), tel. 2 08 78 (50 beds); Church of Scotland Centre, tel. 9 01 44 (80 beds); Y.M.C.A., tel. 2 06 85 (30 beds). **Restaurants:** Hayan, Nof Kinneret, Galilei Gil, all on the main beach; Quiet Beach (fish); The House (Chinese); Donna Grazia (international); Pizzeria Rimini (Italian), Nazareth Street; Shell Beach (fish), Zefat Street, on shores of lake.

Index

If more than one page number appears next to the name of the town or attraction, the bold face number indicates the page where the detailed description can be found in the text.

308 Index